The
Harder Path

JOHN BIRT

The
Harder Path

THE AUTOBIOGRAPHY

timewarner
books

A *Time Warner* Book

First published in Great Britain in 2002 by Time Warner Books

Copyright © John Birt 2002

The moral right of the author has been asserted.

Unless otherwise stated, all photographs are from
the author's private collection.

A CIP catalogue record for this book
is available from the British Library.

ISBN 0 316 86019 0

Typeset in Baskerville by M Rules
Printed and bound in Great Britain by Clays Ltd, St Ives plc

Time Warner Books UK
Brettenham House
Lancaster Place
London WC2E 7EN

www.TimeWarnerBooks.co.uk

For Mum, Dad, Jane, JJ and Eliza

Contents

When the road through the mountains
forks, take the harder path.

Himalayan saying

Preface

The story of my life demonstrates how individuals are affected by the great forces of our times – by revolutionary cultural, social, economic and political shifts; by war, migration, slump, sectarianism and class division. It is a story which illuminates how some individuals fall tragic victim to such forces, and yet others can harness or rise above them. My own journey from poor circumstances to the top of the greatest cultural institution in the world offers a superb, close-up view of some of the extraordinary people and events that most shaped our era. And, in wrestling myself with some of the great seismic movements of the period, I enjoyed a white-water ride of tumbles and excitements, a great twentieth-century adventure, which these pages attempt to capture and to chronicle.

I

THE LIVERPOOL
YEARS

I

My Family

I was born in Liverpool in 1944 during an air-raid warning. I was a big baby, weighing in at ten pounds. My mother, Ida, took me home to Bootle, in the north of the city, where both my mother's and my father's families had lived for nearly a hundred years.

The first consequence of my birth was to reunite my mother with her family. When my mum – a Protestant – declared she wanted to marry my Catholic dad, her parents threatened to throw her out of their house, and out of her job – she worked in the dockland canteen managed by her father, my grandad Joe. When she married none the less, for she was determined by nature, her parents carried out their threat. We were a family where grudges could be held for years, where quarrels were not quickly forgotten, and where forgiveness did not come easily; but, when I was born, all was forgiven and forgotten. Moreover, my grandparents were soon reconciled to their first grandchild being baptised a Catholic.

The roots of my nanna's sectarianism didn't emerge for another half-century. Just before she died, aged ninety, she revealed to me that her own grandfather, Anthony Wilson, had been a Protestant baker and confectioner in the predominantly Catholic town of Baltinglass in County Wicklow, Ireland. One Sunday around 1860, the Catholic priest told his congregation that henceforth they should buy bread only from shops with the sign of the cross over the door. The Catholics duly boycotted Anthony Wilson's bakery, and within a week it had to be closed. The Wilsons sailed to Liverpool to start a new life with their nine children in a city itself racked by sectarianism. One hundred and thirty years later, my nanna shook with bitterness when she finally told me this long-suppressed story.

My great-great-grandfather had opened a canteen for dockers – then called a cocoa-room – by the Canada Dock in Bootle. Liverpool in 1860 was booming. It was one of the world's great cities, bigger than Manchester or Birmingham. Half the nation's exports passed through its docks. Cotton cloth was exported from Lancashire; wool from Yorkshire; machinery from the Midlands. Raw materials, tea and spices flowed in from every continent. The population of the city had doubled in thirty years. Liverpool was cosmopolitan and self-confident. Some of the most innovative architects of the age were creating one of Britain's most handsome cities. At the same time, Liverpool also experienced the worst poverty in the UK. Large numbers of people lived in cellars. Typhus, cholera and dysentery were rampant.

Liverpool continued to be a magnet: towards the end of the century, my American wife Jane's maternal grandfather William Townsend, an engineer, travelled to Liverpool from Chicago to install a pneumatic-tube system in a department store.

In 1900 when my nanna – the short, trim, busy, adventurous, strong-willed Anna Victoria – was born, her family still ran the same canteen. As a child, she often went on holiday to Northern Ireland, visiting relations. When she was sixteen, she met a young soldier, on leave from the trenches, under the clock at Bangor, a seaside town just outside Belfast. He was twenty-three, tall and slim, with watery blue eyes, a bony, angular, Celtic face and big hands. They went for a walk together in the woods and picked bluebells. When the war was over, she married the young soldier – my grandad Joe.

The story of how they met emerged only when my grandad died. At the funeral, my nanna insisted, without explanation, that there should be no flowers. Just before the coffin disappeared behind the curtains and into the furnace, she walked without warning to the altar and placed a previously hidden bunch of bluebells on the lid of the coffin.

We were moved and surprised by her gesture, for there had never seemed to be any sentiment at all in her relationship with Joe. They were an unequal match: Nanna was strong, driven and smart, while Grandad had always appeared weak, lackadaisical and slow thinking. He had been born in Belfast in 1895 into a staunch Loyalist family. As a boy, Joe would travel to farms with his father – a butcher – and watch him slaughter animals and chop them into meat. Joe lived in the Protestant heartland, half a mile from the Shankhill Road. To the pride of his family, young Joe played and marched in a fife-band. At an early age, he was taught, when thrown the challenge 'Friend or foe?' in the streets around him, always to answer 'Friend!' – for the threat could come from either side of the sectarian divide.

In 1912 Joe became a Covenanter, signing with other Loyalists the solemn declaration that he would fight for an independent Ulster if the London government conceded home rule for all Ireland. Carson, the fiercely populist Loyalist leader, preached that Ulster's Protestants faced the dread prospect of an authoritarian Roman Catholic state, leading to loss of individual liberty and the destruction of Ulster's fast-growing industries. By 1913, sectarian tensions had reached breaking point. Carson formed the UVF – the Ulster Volunteer Force – and my grandad signed up. Arms were smuggled in from Germany, and my grandad trained to use them. But the

Great War intervened and the impending civil strife in Ireland was averted.

Grandad volunteered for the 15th Battalion of the Royal Irish Rifles, a Protestant force and part of the 36th Ulster Division, which was based on the order of battle of the UVF. His battalion marched with marigolds in their caps to the tune of King William's march. In July 1916, Joe's regiment fought at the Battle of the Somme, where on the first day 150,000 men would go over the top. Of these over a third would be killed or wounded. The 15th Rifles were part of an advance of eight successive waves, at fifty-yard intervals, attacking strongly defended German positions at Thiepval. They marched steadily, weighed down by ammunition and equipment. Men fell every yard of the way. The loss of life was horrendous. In two days, the 36th Division lost 5,500 men. Whole areas of Belfast, and many towns and villages across Ulster, were plunged into grief. Joe was one of the survivors. He went on to fight on the Messines Ridge. On a well-fortified German salient, the Division lost seven hundred men. At Cambrai they were engaged in hand-to-hand fighting.

By the end of 1917 there had been many defeats and few victories. So many soldiers from the Division had been killed that Catholics were eventually drafted in to make up the numbers. At first, the UVF men objected but within a year the camaraderie of battle changed attitudes – so much so that on St Patrick's Day in 1918 the shamrock was distributed throughout the Division, and Mass was celebrated. In heavy fighting at St Quentin that winter, the Rifles were the last to pull out. Joe was captured and remained a prisoner of war till peace was declared.

Against the odds, my grandad had lived through the grimmest, most horrible and most costly war yet fought by mankind. I spent a lot of time with him when I was growing up. Grandad did not appear to have been traumatised by the war, but it was for ever on his mind; he couldn't reach out to people or take on the world; and he was occasionally cruel and always callous about suffering. He regaled me with stories that shocked me as a boy. He often told me about a

German soldier that he and his comrades had captured. They had joked with their prisoner, and had then indicated – to the German's surprise – that he could run back to his own lines. As the soldier set off, my grandad and his companions placed a grenade – unnoticed – in the German's pocket, and pulled the pin. It greatly amused my grandad that the German exploded into pieces twenty yards away.

Joe was cynical about his officers. One of his favourite stories was of a general coming to visit the front-line troops and inspecting them on parade a little way back from the lines. As the officer started his inspection, a distant shot rang out and kicked up the dirt twenty feet away. The general jumped in surprise and angrily demanded an explanation. 'It's a sniper, sir, over there on that hill!' The exact position – on the German side of the lines – was pointed out. The general was belligerent. 'How dare you expose me to a known enemy sniper? How long has he been there?'

'Three months, sir.'

'Why have you not taken him out?'

'Sir, he's a terrible shot! He always uses the same position. He always misses. We could take him out in an hour; but the Germans might put someone in his place who could really shoot!' (I often recounted Grandad's tale in the workplace when a colleague complained of an incompetent manager in a rival organisation.)

The Great War moderated Joe's view of Catholics. He resented the Protestant leaders who had stirred Loyalist hatred before the war but had remained behind at headquarters while he and his fellow soldiers advanced into enemy fire. When he found himself fighting alongside young Catholics, they became his comrades in arms and in misery, and he had felt a solidarity with them. So, two decades later, when my mother asked permission to marry my father, a Catholic, my grandad was noticeably less opposed to the idea than my nanna.

When the war ended, Anna and Joe were married. Three daughters were born – my mother Ida in 1922, followed by Muriel and Joan. A fourth, Jane, died aged five. The three sisters shared a bedroom together above the canteen in Strand Road, Bootle, which the capable Anna now ran. The family kept chickens in the garden and had two Jack Russells that would compete in the dockers' favourite bloodsport – chasing and killing captured rats released from a cage. One of Grandad's terriers was bought by the singer Gracie Fields.

In the 1930s, eleven people crammed into the three bedrooms above the canteen. As well as the immediate family, there were Nanna's mother and several of her brothers and sisters sheltering from the Depression. Overcrowding in Liverpool in the 1930s was the highest in the country. The Depression hit them hard: Anna and Joe were relieved if they could earn enough from their docker customers to pay their rent, wages and suppliers. If, in addition, they could all live and eat for free, they were thankful. Joe's mother – a cleaner in a motor showroom in Belfast – kept hounds. Occasionally, to supplement their diet, she would send to Liverpool by post a hare that the dogs had caught. However close to the edge of solvency her parents were, though, my mother – unlike my father – never lacked food, warmth, education or access to a doctor. On occasions, she even escaped to Northern Ireland to stay with relations in the country in a small cottage which had no conveniences, but which offered the prospect of carefree days playing in the hills and fields around. My mum and her two sisters did live, however, under the shadow of a dogmatic, strong-willed mother and in fear of a feckless and occasionally cruel father. When he thought they had misbehaved, Joe would beat them harshly with his belt. They cried for one another. My auntie Muriel hit her father back when she was nineteen and he never struck her again.

My mother left Bootle Grammar School when she was sixteen, in 1938, to become a pools clerk at Vernons. Just before her seventeenth birthday, she stopped on Coffee House Bridge in Bootle to watch some boys swimming and larking about in the dirty waters of the Leeds–Liverpool canal below. Leo Birt, a year older, stopped to look too, and then walked her home. They started going out together, though my mother kept her Catholic beau a secret from her family.

Leo's family had been brought to the brink of despair by division and drink. The Birts arrived in Liverpool in 1855, just a few years before my mother's family, from Newnham in Northamptonshire rather than Ireland. My great-great-grandfather William Birt – born in 1832 – was from a family of farm labourers dating back to the sixteenth century. William Birt was orphaned at eight, but learnt to make shoes in Northampton. In his early twenties, he moved north to Liverpool to set up a boot and shoe business right in the city centre, in Tithebarn Street. He married a dressmaker called Mary and started a family, who were brought up in their mother's Catholic faith. Until his death in 1895, aged sixty-three, he and his wife were running a small pork and cooked-meat butcher's in a narrow street of humble houses in Anfield, just a few hundred yards from Liverpool Football Club.

William's son – my great-grandfather James Frederick Birt – helped to set my father's family on the path to destitution. The heavily built James Frederick was first a salesman, then a bookmaker. When his wife – like his mother, also a Mary – became an alcoholic, he deserted her for a glamorous stage dancer and farmed his children out to relatives. At the age of eleven, his eldest son – my grandfather Bill – was placed in his grandmother's care at the pork butcher's shop in Anfield. When his grandmother died, he was sent to live with an aunt. Bill, the agent of so much misery, has always been considered a villain in my family for his selfishness and unreliability; but we gave no thought to the impact on him of his own traumatic childhood. Years later, as a young man of twenty-five, my grandfather passed a woman in a street in Liverpool, raised his hat to her, and walked on without speaking. 'Who was that?' his companion asked. 'That was my mother,' he replied. It had been the alcoholic Mary.

Bill went to St Edward's College and was a classmate of Richard –
later Archbishop – Downey. Bill was an excellent footballer, playing as
a schoolboy for the North of England; and he was a good enough
boxer to have been a sparring partner for Bombardier Billy Wells,
who later became the muscled striker of the Rank gong at the cinema.
He also had a fine baritone voice. But he was a person of poor character. The young Downey once rebuked him: 'You are an excellent
footballer, Birt, but an impudent huzzy!' After school, Bill studied to
be a priest; but, after two years, he got into a fight on the football field
and was advised he was unsuitable for the priesthood. For a while he
did no work but drank away a modest inheritance from his grandmother. When that money ran out, he became a bookmaker's clerk.
Just before the Great War he married my grandmother – another
Mary – the soft, gentle daughter of a coal-heaver famed for his
strength, who could lift a man standing on his shovel. The family were
devout and went to Mass every day. Mary was advised by Bill's
family – the Birts – not to marry him, but she persevered.

My grandfather started the war a sergeant in the Royal Horse
Artillery, but ended it a private. Nothing is known about what happened in between, except that he had a toe amputated, and that he
was involved in an incident when home on leave from the front. He
was walking up the steps of a urinal in Liverpool when he encountered a man in uniform struggling to tie his puttees. Bill stopped to
help someone he took to be a fellow solider, but, suddenly noticing
a flash on the man's uniform signifying that he was a 'Khaki
Docker' – who performed civilian not military duties – Bill leapt to
the conclusion that the man was a 'conshie', or conscientious objec-
tor. He boiled over and knocked the man down the steps. His
offence was reported to his Regiment. My grandfather's fierce commitment was tested when his own brother – himself the victim of a
rootless childhood – deserted the front line, and escaped to Ireland.
Bill's brother, my great-uncle, turned up on their doorstep one day
in 1926 in his bedroom slippers and in the throes of a nervous
breakdown. He ended his days as a nightwatchman.

When the war ended, Bill became the manager of a warehouse, but he lost his job through drink and became a docker. My father was born in 1921, the third child and only boy. He would have three sisters – Vera, Eileen and Pattie. Life in Liverpool in the 1920s and 1930s was hard. The number of registered dockers halved, and trade union militancy grew. By the end of the 1930s, Liverpool would have eighty thousand unemployed, double the national rate. Each day in the period, my grandfather presented himself for work with the mass of other dockers, and only occasionally would he succeed. As a boy, my dad would wait at the docks on Saturday – payday – for his father to receive his meagre wages or dole. He would then return home to his mother and three sisters with whatever share he was given for the household expenses. My grandfather would retire to the pub with the remainder. Normally the family's share would buy food for Saturday, but there was little left – and sometimes nothing – for the rest of the week. For most of the next seven days the family would go hungry. On Saturday night, Bill would return home blind drunk, often with no money for drink or for anything else till the following Saturday. He would sit at home in the week, sombre and taciturn, playing hands of cards by himself, or doing a crossword. Brushing his hair in the mirror, he would say: 'You're a good-looking man, Billy Birt!' Occasionally he sang. An unemployed uncle who lodged with the family was given a whippet by a bargee on the Leeds–Liverpool canal, and sometimes they raced that.

As the only boy in the family, my dad was expected to do the difficult jobs. He had to wait up on Saturday nights to help his near-senseless father to bed when he returned home. My grandfather couldn't make his daily bid for work without a union button from the TGWU; and there was no button unless you were up to date with your union subs. So my dad was sent to the union to plead with them to let him pay only one week's subs rather than the many weeks of arrears that were due, and to be allowed to take a new button home.

There was a special dread of sickness in the household, for there was little money for a doctor. My father had pneumonia in 1923 when he was two, and nearly died. When they went to Mass, Mary made her children stand at the back because their clothes were so shabby. A new baby came and died. They kept her body in a drawer for days, and lied about the exact day she passed away so that the insurance policy would apply and they would have the money to bury her. In 1928, despairing of their position and unable to deal with Bill, Mary called in the NSPCC and they quizzed my dad and his sisters about their father. It was a call for help the NSPCC ignored. They just wanted to know if Bill was cruel and beat the children; he did not, and they said so. They had a terrible sense afterwards that they had betrayed their mother. A chastened Bill tried to go teetotal, but his resolve lasted just two weeks.

Mary was a pious and selfless woman who gave her children enduring support and comfort, kneeling with them each night in prayer. But the NSPCC episode was an isolated one. She was too humble by nature to handle her husband's alcoholism and the dreadful price she and her family paid for it. Another relative describes her as 'destitute and careworn'. My father had a deep affection for his mother, and found her misery unbearable. It prompted in him a duty to protect and to provide which would never leave him.

Life got a little better when two unemployed uncles lodged with the family and brought parish relief into the household, and when my dad's two elder sisters began work – Eileen at Aintree Silk Works and Vera as an apprentice hairdresser. Eight people were crammed into their three-bedroom house, but they were no longer starving. They could afford to rent a wireless for one shilling a week. My grandfather listened to the serious talks on the BBC; the rest of the family enjoyed the entertainment.

Still, there was no money for a coat for my dad for rainy days, or to replace his boots when they became too small or were holed. As a result, he would often miss school in the winter. Despite this, he did well. His teachers pressed him to sit for a free scholarship to a Catholic secondary school newly opened in Bootle, which he passed. Mary was deeply worried about finding two pounds for the school uniform; but she scraped together the money over the summer, and Dad started at his new school, smart and polished. But old problems remained. He still had no coat and his mother kept him off school when the weather was bad. In 1933 – the worst year of the slump – he suffered a disaster. My father is naturally practical. That year, he resolved to repair his own holed boots with tools and a shoemaker's last bequeathed by his mother Mary's father, the coal-heaver. But Dad's boots were wet, so first he dried them in the oven. They emerged shrivelled, many sizes too small, and unwearable. He was off school for weeks before his boots could be replaced. There was another difficulty: he couldn't afford the books he needed for study. He fell behind. My grandmother suggested my father should return to his old school – which he did, briefly, before abandoning study altogether when he was thirteen. There was no great drive on my grandparents' part to get my dad to school at whatever cost. Rather, there was relief in 1935 that he was out working and bringing some extra money to the hard-pressed family. And my dad shared that feeling.

This bright boy's first job was as a window cleaner's assistant. He went through a succession of trades, moving on quickly to any job that would pay him more. He was an apprentice moulder, skimming impurities off molten metal; a delivery boy to a series of retailers; an oven boy; a stacker; and a labourer in a cooperage, making tea for the workers on a wood fire. In 1938, aged seventeen, and four years out of school, my dad had the first lucky break of his life. The agent from the Prudential insurance company called one day, accompanied by his superintendent Peter Mahon. The Mahons were Bootle's foremost Catholic family, with a strong sense of civic duty, and dominated its politics for generations. Peter Mahon was a councillor and would become a Labour MP. (In 1971, he was expelled from the party for standing in Liverpool as an anti-abortion candidate.) Mahon questioned my father and discovered he had been in the same form at school as Mahon's brother Eric. Mahon asked my father if he would be interested in a job with the Pru, and supplied an introduction. Thus my dad – no doubt, from Mahon's perspective, a bright Catholic lad in need of a leg-up – got his first white-collar job and became the Man from the Pru.

My dad found it easy to understand insurance policies, to do the figurework and to manage the money. He worked in the office or pounded the beat all day on foot, collecting premiums in cash. He became involved in the day-to-day dramas that families were insuring against. A girl in Seaforth was raped and murdered. Her tearful mother came in to collect the money to bury her. My dad paid out. A soldier was charged with her murder. A few months later the soldier's mother, as distraught as the first, came in to collect from my father after her son was hanged at Walton jail.

The seventeen-year-old Leo that my sixteen-year-old mum Ida had met at Coffee House Bridge in Bootle in 1939 was now a young man with prospects. As a couple they were both good-looking, well groomed and fastidious about their appearance. My mother was slim and dark-haired, with startling blue eyes and a soulful, sympathetic face. She burnt with energy. My father was of average height, wavy-haired and athletic, with a natural grace and dignity. They were united by purposefulness, a keen if untutored intelligence and a desire to escape their circumstances.

In September 1939 my father's family gathered around the radio to hear Neville Chamberlain's declaration of war. Out of character, my grandfather Bill cried. My mother wanted to contribute to the war effort, but Grandad Joe insisted she should help him manage the Strand Road canteen instead. (Nanna had opened a second canteen in Bank Hall, which she was managing herself.) Grandad definitely needed my mother's help: he enjoyed the camaraderie of the dockers, and the command of his all-woman staff, but he was a slack manager. My mum had an urge to do things right and well.

She quickly became the driving force at the canteen and licked it into shape as they waited for the real war to begin.

Liverpool's docks were a major strategic target for the Germans. The Luftwaffe used a UK Ordnance Survey map to mark out a bombing zone for their pilots, the boundary of which – we would discover after the war – went right past the front door of the Strand Road canteen, where my mum lived and now worked, just yards off the Dock Road. One of the first bombs to drop on Bootle, in August 1940, fell six yards from the front entrance to the canteen. By a miracle, it landed behind a low concrete parapet which absorbed much of the blast, but it still demolished part of the front of the building. My mum, sheltering with her family beneath the stairs, escaped injury. The next day it was still business as usual at the canteen, but with the dockers entering through a gaping hole in the wall.

Liverpool was now a war-zone. A few months after their narrow escape, another bomb fell behind the canteen – doing yet more damage. Walking home one night, my mum heard a low-flying German plane firing a machine gun at a dockside barrage balloon and saw the bullets smack into the ground in a long line just beside her.

As a member of the Home Guard, Grandad Joe had been issued with a sten gun. He wanted the whole family to be prepared for invasion, so he taught my auntie Joan – my mum's youngest sister, aged eight at the onset of war – to dismantle, to oil and to reassemble his gun.

On his way home from the Pru one day, a hysterical woman dragged my father into her home. An incendiary bomb had dropped through her roof and was sizzling and spitting on her bed. My dad carried the bomb into the street, doused the flames in her bedroom, and saved her home. When he arrived at his own home, there was another incendiary – unexploded – in the back-yard.

In May 1941 eight hundred German planes bombed Liverpool

for seven successive nights. The *Malakand*, a munitions ship, blew up in an explosion so powerful that a four-ton dock winch was blown almost as far as Liverpool FC, two miles away. My father was at home, a thousand yards from the blast. The impact of the explosion on Bootle was devastating. A mass grave was dug at Anfield cemetery for five hundred victims of the persistent, heavy May bombing. The Blitz on Merseyside would claim in all nearly four thousand lives, and many more would be seriously injured. Eighty per cent of homes in Bootle were damaged or destroyed by the bombing. My mother and father and their families, however, were fatalistic and, day by day, unfearful. And they recall with nostalgia the sense of community they experienced in wartime Bootle.

To avoid the bombings, Nanna Anna eventually decided to move her family out of the damaged canteen premises to the greater safety of Southport, to the north of Liverpool, where she rented a house – though they still returned each day by train to Bootle. My mother took more and more responsibility for running the Strand Road canteen. My grandad Joe, though industrious at night in the Home Guard, would drift away from work when the canteen was at its busiest, leaving my mum to cope.

My father was not due to be called up till late 1941 when he would be twenty. But, as the war intensified, he grew restless and resolved to leave the Pru to join up. His first choice was the Royal Navy, but its office was closed on the day he went to volunteer, so he signed up for the RAF instead. He trained as an aircraft engineer, first at RAF Bicester, near Oxford. He serviced the Bristol Blenheim light bombers used for training, and later maintained Spitfires and Lysanders for the high command to fly around the UK.

When in 1943 Leo and Ida decided to marry – against the wishes of her parents – Ida was forced to leave home and forfeit her job at the canteen. She moved in with Leo's family and established a close bond with his mother. Dad obtained leave from the RAF and they married. She converted to Catholicism, though she would never embrace it. My mum's sister Muriel was also thrown out of the family home for attending the wedding. Dad was promoted to corporal, and remitted a more generous allowance to my mum, who rented a flat in Bootle, where she was living when I was born. Dad was granted a day's leave to see his new son, but it would be our first and last encounter for nearly two years, for he was posted immediately to the Middle East. He serviced the RAF's big four-engined Liberator bombers in Egypt. The war in Europe was ending, but the bombers were kept fully operational for fear of Soviet expansionism in the Middle East. At the close of the war in Europe in 1945, Dad was transferred to RAF Lydda in Palestine and promoted to sergeant. Given responsibility for the Vehicle Transport and Maintenance section, aged twenty-four, he was put in charge of seventy men. He was discharged in September 1946, with a good suit and a generous commendation, and made his way home to Liverpool. There he found his beloved mother enfeebled and unwell, afflicted with diabetes. She was so poorly that, one evening soon after his return, he and his sister Eileen watched over her through the night. They thought she was sleeping, but in the morning they realised she was in a coma. She died later that day, only ten days after his return from the war – a cruel and bitter blow after so many years apart.

In his five years at war my dad's abilities had been recognised and rewarded with promotion and increased responsibility; and his understanding of the wider world had grown, as had his confidence. He was ready for life – and determined to do well – in post-war Britain. He rejoined the Pru and was promoted to agent for the Waterloo and Crosby area of north Liverpool.

The Britain to which my father returned was changing rapidly. The Labour Party had swept to power at the end of the war on a wave of radicalism. The problems that families like his had experienced before the war – overcrowding; too little money for a doctor at times of sickness; an education system that didn't allow individuals to reach their full potential; the stark horrors of life for the unemployed – were exactly the problems that Britain wanted a new government to address.

So I was lucky to be starting my life in post-war Britain. Labour's politicians had been encouraged by the work of Keynes to believe that they could manage the economy to full employment. Beveridge had eloquently identified the evils that had to be eradicated by a new welfare state: want, disease, squalor, ignorance and idleness. Bevan would set up a universal National Health Service based on need. The 1944 Education Act would be implemented, opening up effective secondary and higher education for all. Attlee's government would introduce a bold and sweeping programme of reform which would not be matched till Mrs Thatcher's four decades later. It would enable my mum and dad to bring up a family in far more benign circumstances than they themselves had ever experienced. I would enjoy so many advantages that my parents and their forebears had not.

2

Boyhood

When I was born – the first grandchild on either side of the family – I was the centre of attention for the numerous women I was surrounded by. My father was at war and neither of my parents had brothers. There were few other men around, and those that were – like my grandfather Bill – were marginalised. As a result I was doted on by my mum, by my five aunts and by my grandmothers, Anna and Mary. Whenever I needed feeding or cosseting, or to have my nappy changed, or to be taken for a walk in my pram, many willing Liverpool women volunteered a hand – confident, determined and toughened women who between them had survived the Depression and two world wars. At night I slept not in my cot, but with my mum in her bed. I was a fussy infant, always wanting things to be just right for my mum. Those years alone together produced an intense and lasting bond between us.

The family into which I was born may have straddled Liverpool's sectarian divide, but it was united by the Liverpudlian characteristics of wit and cheer, of biting observation, of endless story-telling, of independence of spirit and lack of deference. These qualities were fused with firmness of opinion and a quickness to take offence. My relations were fiercely loyal and intensely family-minded. News about the wider family was a conversational staple. Relatives enjoyed the prefix 'our' – our Billy, our Jane, our Kitty and our John. We could command an army of dockers, labourers, painters, plasterers, carpenters, mechanics, bakers, hairdressers – indeed every kind of trade. But down the generations we had also been involved in running a bakery, a shoe shop, a pork butcher's, a book-making business and canteens. We were positioned socially where small businesses, artisans and labourers lived side by side and shared a common experience and outlook. No one in my immediate family ever created wealth – that is, owned businesses or even a house that they could sell. Even my nanna, better off than anyone else, would have only meagre savings in her building society account when she died. Both sides of my family were stoical, uncomplaining, fatalistic, resilient and self-reliant. They did not think to turn to others for help.

No one in my family had received an education beyond elementary school. They read tabloid papers; enjoyed football, boxing and popular entertainment; kept whippets and terriers; and liked a bet. They showed no interest in politics. But, in a word both sides of my family used, they considered themselves 'respectable' working class. They believed in high standards of behaviour and decorum, in the tidiness of their homes and persons. They kept their front steps scrubbed, their door-knockers polished. They were committed to honesty and to good behaviour. They were never coarse or vulgar. One of the highest insults in my family was to call someone 'common'.

My mum and I lived in a respectable part of Bootle in a rented flat in a late-Victorian house. University Road, in which I spent my early years, is unrecognisable now, vandalised, like much of

Liverpool, by the local authority bulldozer. Only one house remains. Alongside it is a yard protected by a high gate and a wall covered in graffiti. Along the street is a row of decaying garages and an undistinguished brick building: the Bootle Protestant Free Church, founded by the Loyal Orange Institute. Towering above the street are two monstrous sixties office blocks and a multi-storey car park – clashing violently in style and scale with the well-planned, red-brick, nineteenth-century city all around. These fortresses are home to various government departments, including the Mines Inspectorate of the Health and Safety Executive. The civil servants who work there – protected from the people of Bootle by prowling security men – now look down on the street where I spent my early life. At the end of University Road is Bootle's South Park, the gates of which frame Liverpool's Anglican Cathedral looming in the distance.

I can recall my shock when my dad returned from the war, a complete stranger. He is the most gentle of men, but to me at the time he was a gruff-voiced trespasser who threw me out of my mother's bed.

When I was two, the first eagerly awaited pleasure of each day was to push a chair against an old sideboard by the front door, to climb up and pull open the large top drawer where my mum kept a huge miscellany of buttons, combs, scissors, cotton spools, shoelaces and a hundred and one other household necessities. Each morning I was surprised afresh to find a terrible tangle, a disordered mess of objects. I can remember – but did not suspect – the knowing smile on my mum's face as I confronted this disarray. It gave me immense satisfaction to tidy the drawer each day; to bring order to chaos; to create neat, perfect, serried ranks of objects.

We moved out of Bootle to leafy, suburban Formby, an expanding dormitory town centred on an old Lancashire coastal village and connected by the railway to Liverpool. Years later my nanna shared with me another family secret: that of how the Birts came to move out of Bootle.

After the war, Grandad's canteen in Strand Road was losing money. Nanna knew he was in debt because she did his accounts, which he didn't have the skill to do himself. Joe asked for help – a cross-subsidy from the second canteen in Bank Hall that Nanna managed. She went to inspect. When she arrived at Joe's canteen, one of the young women workers was making tea. The woman casually picked up an unopened bottle of milk close to hand – even though there was an already open bottle ten feet away. My nanna admonished her and suggested she use the opened bottle first, but the woman was defiant. 'I take my orders from Joe, not you,' she said rudely. Nanna marched out of the canteen, furious at the slight, resolving immediately not to help Grandad with his debts. When her accountant told her about a nice house in Formby he was putting up for auction, Nanna decided to buy it and to put down a deposit. The sum – several hundred pounds – was exactly what Joe had requested of her. Nanna decided she would let my mum and dad live in the house: they would take over the mortgage and repay the deposit gradually. She told me she had decided my dad was 'go-ahead', that he had prospects. She wanted to back him, to give him and my mother a leg-up out of Bootle. The Strand Road canteen was soon closed and Grandad went to work for Nanna at her canteen in Bank Hall. Thereafter there was never any doubt about who was boss.

One day in 1947 my mum and I travelled on the train to Formby, a strange and unfamiliar place. We came round a corner in Lonsdale Road and there was my nanna, on her knees, polishing the step of our new home – a neat 1930s semi with a garden front and back. We were home-owners. Thus began our new suburban existence in post-war Britain. We were not, however, immediately at ease with our new life. First, my parents had overstretched themselves. My dad's job in the Pru didn't pay enough to cover the mortgage. We had to be frugal and could only scrape by. As a result, the front room in Lonsdale Road would never be furnished: we kept the door closed when there were visitors and hoped no one would ever know it was an empty room. It was my family's guilty secret. Second, although I would not have known the word, I became aware at an early age of class. Our neighbours were on the bottom rung of the middle class – nurses, bank-clerks and junior managers in the public sector, mostly working in Liverpool. My parents were naturally genteel and dignified, and they had a strong sense of propriety, but they were conscious of their own ignorance of the social codes of their new environment. They wanted to conform, to do the right thing, to dress and to speak properly, to achieve respectability – but I was aware that we did not always know how. We certainly wanted to bury our Bootle past: my parents were nervous that the neighbours would frown when the more outgoing and rumbustious elements in our wider family came to call.

My parents built this home painstakingly. My sister Angela Mary was born, who would be my patient and kindly playmate. (She became a teacher, raised four girls, and started a charity.) I attended the local Catholic primary school, Our Lady's, where Angela would eventually teach. I cried inconsolably on my first day apart from my mum.

My mother was fantastically house-proud, cleaning, tidying and washing intensively. Every nook, every corner was dusted; every dish sparkled; every item was neatly slotted in its appointed place. Every day, clothes on the line flapped violently in the gusty wind from the Irish Sea. My father created and tended an immaculate garden – a suburban dream of lawns, dahlias and roses. Like my mother, he never stopped working. When he wasn't in the garden or painting the house, he did paperwork at the dining table. From an early age I was inculcated with a powerful work ethic. My parents were perfectionists. I was taught that if a job was worth doing it was worth doing well. Dad found little time for leisure. When he did, he read G. K. Chesterton or about St Francis of Assisi.

In the early post-war years, we still had rationing and little variety in our diet. I pulled a face at omelettes made of egg powder and the odious daily spoonful of cod-liver oil. Luxury was the arrival each day of the milkman in a horse-drawn cart. He would decant the milk from large churns into bowls we would leave on the doorstep, and Angela and I would spoon the rich cream off the top as a treat.

When we were at home, in the middle of the day we ate 'dinner'. In the early evening we had 'tea'. Before bedtime we had 'supper'. We ate – like everyone else in those years – from a limited and staple set of menus: oxtail soup; sausages with tomato sauce; baked beans, tinned sardines or a poached egg on toast; scouse (a lamb and potato stew with the standard accompaniments, pickled beetroot and HP Sauce); eggs, bacon and fried bread; fried Spam; corned-beef sandwiches. In later years, Dad sometimes had a thin slice of well-cooked steak and, with great curiosity, we would watch him eat it. With every meal there was a pot of strong Typhoo tea to drink, and a great mound of sliced white bread from Scott's Bakery. For pudding there were angel cakes, custard tarts or Eccles cakes rich with currants. I ate voraciously. Between meals there were Trebor chews, liquorice and sherbet, humbugs, mint imperials, gobstoppers and aniseed balls. On days out we enjoyed candyfloss and toffee apples. For a special treat we had coffee made with essence from a bottle and hot milk.

In the 1950s our main entertainment was the radio – a small window on the world beyond Merseyside. We listened every week to *Two-Way Family Favourites*, for the troops still serving in Germany and their families back home; and I was hooked on *Mrs Dale's Diary*, *Educating Archie*, *Life with the Lyons* and *Twenty Questions*. We enjoyed *Have a Go* with Wilfred Pickles, who would tour the country, allowing ordinary people to compete in a quiz for modest cash prizes. Before Pickles put the questions, he would always ask in avuncular Yorkshire fashion: 'Tell us your most embarrassing moment, love.' We would listen to the responses, enthralled. Before he put the jackpot question, he would ask his assistant Mabel, 'How much is on the table, Mabel?' She would respond, to our innocent delight: '£1 17s 6d and a stick of Blackpool rock.' In these unaffected days, the highlight of the week was the unbearably tense yes–no interlude on *Take your Pick*, when contestants were asked quick-fire questions for sixty seconds by Michael Miles and were disqualified if they said yes or no or nodded or shook their heads. I enjoyed reading even more than listening to the radio: I attacked Enid Blyton, *Dr Dolittle* and every volume of Biggles, consuming a book at every opportunity. In the evening Dad often read us poetry. 'The Lamplighter' always brought a lump to my throat.

Television played no part in my early life, but the cinema did – the Three Stooges, Abbott and Costello, Laurel and Hardy. Charlie Chaplin moved me. In 1953 my Dad took me to see *Shane* – in which Alan Ladd heroically comes to the aid of a frontier family – and I was powerfully affected.

One of the strongest memories of my boyhood is of the cold. Only our sitting room was heated, by a coal fire. Beds were warmed with a hot water bottle. On a winter's morning the bedroom window was often etched with ice. I wore a string vest and underpants, which Dad was convinced kept us warm. Once a week we all shared the same bath water. I was the last one in before Dad.

There was always a big gang of children around Lonsdale Road, and I loved to play games with them of every kind – tag and hopscotch; skipping, the girls tucking their skirts in their knickers; bounce–one–two–three and every variant of hide and seek. I would juggle a football and kick it against a wall for hours. In the field close by – where an old white horse called Billy grazed – we played every imaginable ball game. We fished for sticklebacks and tadpoles in a nearby ditch. We searched for conkers, and baked them in the oven to harden them up. We made elaborate paper planes, created complex cradles in our hands with yarn, spun tops. We explored an old, musty stagecoach from a previous century, long abandoned in an outhouse near Billy's field. At home, we played Ludo and tiddlywinks, and I built balsa-wood planes with my dad.

When we were older we explored the pine-forests between Formby and the sea, and the dunes beyond them which bordered the wide beach and protected the land from the pounding grey-black waves of the Irish Sea. From the sandhills, we could see Blackpool Tower to the north – and to the west, the jagged peaks of North Wales. Beryl Bainbridge, one of our greatest writers, lived in Formby at this time and brilliantly captures the mood of the place in *Harriet Said*.

I was not an assertive child. I found it easy to form friendships, but I was quiet and reserved. I never shouted or drew attention to myself and I didn't feel comfortable with domineering or bullying children. My father must have been troubled by my lack of aggression because he tried unsuccessfully to teach me to box, choosing a bigger, older boy from across the street as my opponent. But I was repelled by the idea of hitting and hurting someone.

In my early years, I formed a close relationship with Robert, an open and generous boy, excellent at sport and an easy conversationalist, who lived close by. His family were warm and welcoming, and he and I would chatter for hours in his home or garden. As we grew older I helped him with his maths, and he coached me with my sport. Robert's family introduced me to the lasting pleasures of the Broadway musical.

Even as I enjoyed this existence, something was missing from my life. In the 1950s the world was at peace: the reconstruction of Britain was proceeding at speed, there was full employment, families were stable, there was no crime and there was little to fear. Formby was a kind of suburban bliss – for my parents the promised land. But I found Formby dull. I came alive when I stayed with my cousins in Bootle in a prefab by the railway track, playing in back-entries and by the canal. And best of all I loved visiting my nanna's hot, noisy canteen. I enjoyed the hubbub and the clatter; the banter of the dockers sitting sipping their steaming mugs of tea; the welcoming pats on the head they gave me; being fussed over by the old ladies working in the kitchen; the vast pots of stew bubbling away on the great gas stoves. The canteen was in a cellar. My favourite perch was at the top of the steps, just yards away from the main Dock Road, heaving with traffic – giant carthorses and noisy, hissing steam lorries pulling every kind of load. Ships' whistles and horns pierced the clamour. Chimneys belched thick, black smoke. Engines chugged all around. Dockers and seamen bustled everywhere. The overhead railway clanged by on the other side of the road. The air was heavy with the pungent, acrid smells of cargo from distant lands. I felt comfortable and at home in Liverpool and with Liverpudlians in a way I never would in Formby or with the suburban middle classes. I would never entirely shake off my earliest roots.

Grandad Joe would take me the long length of Liverpool's docks on the overhead railway. Hundreds of ships, great and small, jammed the port. A forest of cranes swung their loads from ship to shore. The warehouses along the Dock Road were a busy hive of activity. Pulleys whirred. It was a magnificent and exciting spectacle. Once Grandad took me to Gladstone Dock to see the great white hulk of the *Empress of Canada* gutted in a fire, lying on her side like a huge beached whale.

When I was seven I had my first taste of success: I was chosen to be the Crown Bearer for the Rose Queen in Our Lady's Church Fête. In the same year I came first among hundreds of entries for the handwriting prize at the Formby Show. Encouraged, I entered a national handwriting competition organised by the *Eagle* comic – along with *Beano* and *Dandy*, my favourite reading. I won one of the third prizes, which, thrillingly, was described as a month's free ice-cream. This turned out to be thirty three-penny vouchers for a Lyon's ice-cream wafer. Unfortunately Formby's shopkeepers viewed these vouchers, proffered by a small boy, with grave suspicion and refused to honour them. I persevered until one kindly shopkeeper did.

At Our Lady's I was drilled in the dogmatic certainties of Catholicism, and I was made fearful of the consequences of wrongdoing. An all-knowing God – we were told – was aware of everything you did and even what you thought. All sins were punished. There were two categories: venial and mortal. Venial described lesser offices, like not honouring your father or mother, or telling a lie. Murder was a mortal sin, but so too was not going to Mass on Sunday. If you died in a state of mortal sin, you went to Hell for all eternity. These ideas took a powerful hold on me as a child, marking me for life, like many Catholics, with a strong sense of right and wrong.

At seven we made our first confessions. I scoured my memory for matters to confess, managing little more than not being as perfect a help to my mother as she would wish. Announcing my imperfections through a grille to the anonymous and invariably Irish priest hidden on the other side, and beyond him to God, was the deepest emotional experience of my young childhood. Afterwards I would skip away, exhilarated, to kneel at the foot of the cross and to say my penance – three Hail Marys or whatever. On Sunday, in a perfect state of grace, sins erased like stains from my soul – which, in my imagination, was a large white egg-shaped object – I would take communion and experience the sacred moment of receiving the host – the small white brittle medallion of bread – on to my outstretched tongue. This did not *represent* – we were taught and I believed – the body of Jesus Christ: it actually *was* the body of the Christ. Communion was a profoundly moving experience.

Catholicism mixed fear and hope powerfully. I shuddered at the barbarity of the imagery, the gory detail of torture depicted in the statuary. In Our Lady's Church, there was Christ exhausted by whipping, by the labour of dragging the heavy wooden cross, by loss of blood from his crown of thorns and from the great nails plunged through his palms and feet. For me as a child the eternal fires of damnation were real and tangible. And one sin made Hell seem a very real prospect: we did not always, as a family, go to church on Sunday. So we were all, I feared, recklessly committing mortal sin and risking hellfire for all eternity.

At Our Lady's School on Mondays we were asked to own up if we had not been to communion, then to raise a hand if we had not been to church. Sometimes I would have to raise my hand: my punishment was to cover my ears when the class next listened to a BBC Schools programme on the radio. My real punishment was to lie awake fearing damnation if I were killed prematurely in an accident. We were offered an escape route – which seemed too easy and which never wholly convinced me. This was to make a perfect Act of Contrition to oneself, which I regularly did, using the words we were taught if we faced the real prospect of imminent death.

I had my first moment of religious doubt when I was six. My teacher, Miss Marsh, told us that a baby that died unbaptised could not go to Heaven, but had to remain in a special place, Limbo, that was neither Heaven nor Hell – and which I imagined as a white, cavernous, featureless chamber – until the Day of Judgement. At six I felt strongly that punishing an innocent child for something outside his or her control was unfair and at odds with the concept of a just God. I had a very real doubt about what the teacher told us; but it did not as yet fundamentally undermine my faith, for I was at ease with Jesus himself, who impressed me with his good sense and his self-sacrifice; and I was comforted by the love and understanding of his mother Mary.

I did well at Our Lady's, always coming top – except on one occasion, when I was beaten from first place by a quiet, undemonstrative boy who would leave school at fifteen and become a window cleaner. I was luckier. One day the teacher asked to see my parents and suggested I needed more challenge in my schooling. She said I should go to the preparatory school of St Mary's College, the Irish Christian Brothers school in Crosby, in north Liverpool.

My parents were hard pressed for money, but they had a strong belief in the value of education, so they stretched themselves to pay the fees for me to go to St Mary's. The school was near the bleak Mersey seafront. Walking to class in the morning, I would see large ocean-going ships, close to the shore, sailing to Liverpool docks. In winter, great foghorns would blare through the sea mist during our lessons. At St Mary's I came first in class again, so the school moved me up a form with boys one year older, which was uncomfortable for a while. I was among the top few in my new class, but I no longer came first. I did, however, win a competition to redesign a nature room at the school, enjoying for the first time the pleasure of working out what was needed for a project and carefully trying to find the best solution.

By tradition, we were a family of Liverpool FC supporters, who were not in the 1950s all-conquering. When I was nine, I briefly turned heretic and went for a year or so to watch Everton at Goodison Park with my friend Philip Mahon, whose family had so crucially helped my father. We once saw Blackpool beat Everton 1–0 thanks to a memorably virtuoso performance from Stanley Matthews on the right wing. But like a prodigal son I eventually returned to the Liverpool fold.

Television was about to become a part of our lives. I had seen sets in shop windows, and one of our neighbours had a TV and invited Angela and me over on a few occasions to see *Andy Pandy* and *Muffin the Mule*. The Coronation in 1953 was my awakening. Excitement was high: at school we were given a commemorative mug and a tin containing a bar of chocolate, and were taken to the circus in Seaforth. On Coronation Day my friends and I went to Delahunty's, the bicycle shop in Formby Village, and the only place in those days where you could buy a TV. There we sat on the hard concrete floor surrounded by bikes and watched the great occasion live. This was something new – the first time I felt part of a great event and of an experience shared throughout the country.

My father continued to strive, changing jobs to better himself. He worked as a sales rep for a soap company, then moved to Firestone Tyres, where he would work for nearly three decades. In the same year as the Coronation our first car, a new and gleaming Ford Consul, appeared in our front path. We went on drives to Parbold or to the beach for a picnic. In the same year my brother Michael – who would become a celebrated photographer – was born upstairs at Lonsdale Road. As a special treat to celebrate, my dad cooked Angela and me sausages on toast for breakfast.

Almost every Saturday in the 1950s we went to visit my nanna. We called on my father's family too, but less often. Nanna was the matriarch. Assorted aunts and uncles and cousins would always be visiting when we were there. She would sit in front of the range, the centre of attention, holding forth, telling long involved stories about her past and about members of the family – news of our Billy and our Jane or of the Minnies and the Maggies. The most common theme of her stories was of someone getting their come-uppance, their just deserts, on account of some wrong committed. My nanna knew how to bear a grudge.

She also loved adventure. Once a week in the summer, Nanna would take Angela and me for a day out. We went on coach trips to North Wales, the Pennines or the Lake District. On one such trip I stood on a road near Whitewell in the Trough of Bowland and was struck powerfully for the first time in my life by the beauty of landscape. We were standing by a mountain stream. I knelt down, cupped my hands and slaked my thirst with sweet, cold water.

My favourite place on the charabanc was the back seat. Most of the day-trippers were older ladies, like my nanna, from Liverpool and Lancashire. I basked in their motherly attention. On the way home there would always be a sing-song, which I loved, of old, popular favourites like 'It's a Long Way to Tipperary' or 'My Blue Heaven'.

When I was nine, Nanna and Grandad took me on a fourteen-day coach tour of Europe. We raced round Germany and Denmark, stopping only at night. I can remember the extensive bomb damage, and an embarrassing episode when we spent a whole afternoon without a stop and my bladder filled and filled till I squirmed with discomfort and anguish. The matronly ladies in the seats in front soon noticed and guessed my predicament. The courier was consulted. He counselled there was no place to stop: I would have to hold out till our destination. I grew whiter and whiter. Grandad slipped off his shoe, and handed it to me. Another row of old ladies turned in their seats. 'Pee in my shoe,' Grandad said, 'I'll tip it out the window. That's what we did in the Army.' The old ladies chorused: 'Yes, go on. Pee in his shoe!' They waited keenly to see me do it, but embarrassment proved an even stronger force than the intense ache of my ballooning bladder. I pushed away the shoe, and somehow contained myself till evening. The old ladies were most disappointed.

Nanna's greatest joy was a day at the races. With me as her companion, she would travel by steam train to racecourses all over the north. She would always end up in a pub, sipping Guinness, with me waiting on the steps outside for what seemed an interminable time. Occasionally she or a kindly stranger – always a man – would bring me out a glass of lemonade. Once I was allowed to the door of a pub in Chester after the races to peer through the smoke at the legendary Everton centre-forward Dixie Dean, serving behind the bar.

Nanna and I went to the Grand National. Once she gave me two shillings to bet on one of the early races and my horse won at 50–1. I took home a large, crisp, white five-pound note, agog at the amount, imagining all the ways I could spend it. My mum had other plans: she took me straight to George Henry Lee's – Liverpool's main department store – and bought me a new mac for £4 19s 6d. I was allowed to keep the sixpence change.

Nanna was superstitious. She believed in luck and loved to gamble. She did the pools each week and backed the horses every day. I was on a bus with her once when she decided to group the six figures on her bus ticket into three two-digit numbers, and to back those matches on that week's football coupon for the three draws. She won four hundred pounds, her biggest-ever win.

Around 1954, Nanna and Grandad gave up the canteen in Bootle and opened an off-licence in Southport. When I stayed there with her, one of my jobs was to take her daily bets to the bookmaker. Off-course betting was unlawful in the 1950s, so Nanna made it clear I had to be careful. I would enter the noisy bookies, fearful of an imminent police raid. Most of the time – or so it appeared to me – I would also carry away her winnings from the previous day's bets. She always seemed to me to be charmed and lucky as well as strong and capable.

As I grew older, I would serve in the off-licence and stack the shelves. In the evening Grandad would allow friends to sit in the back-room around a hot stove and order drinks. Again, I was warned I had to be careful whom I let in, for drinking on the premises was unlawful. Grandad was always on the lookout for the police. I dreaded a raid. Occasionally, a policeman in uniform would come in to buy cigarettes and Grandad would step immediately into the back and – with a gesture – signal his drinking mates to fall silent. We would hold our breaths till the policeman departed.

Nanna took me to Northern Ireland a number of times, once to see Grandad's mother Emma on her deathbed. On our trips, we visited relations in Belfast – my grandad's sisters and brothers and their children. Uncle Tom, solemn and quiet, was an undertaker and drove the hearse. When I was very young, I watched a huge parade with my aunts in Belfast city centre. Men in orange regalia marched by in large numbers. I asked in ignorance why they were parading: my Loyalist aunts sniggered and whispered to each other and did not respond, much amused by the innocence of their Catholic relation from Liverpool.

One summer Nanna took my sister Angela and me on a coach trip around Ireland. On the overnight crossing to Belfast, we had no cabin, so Angela and I tried to sleep sitting up in the lounge while Nanna drank Guinness all night and chattered merrily to a group of Irish priests. Given her views on Catholics, I was surprised she even spoke to them. Every night of the trip she went to the pub. It was Ireland so Angela and I didn't have to wait on the step: we were allowed in to experience at first hand the cheerful delights of an

Irish pub in full swing. My nanna jigged into the small hours, her skirts held high, enjoying the attentions of the many men around, seemingly unconcerned that every last one was a Catholic.

As children my sister and I puzzled why Nanna had married Grandad, a weak and foolish man – but it may simply have been that she had fallen for a tall, brave, handsome young soldier in uniform, seven years older than her, on leave from the trenches.

Grandad accepted Nanna's authority, and was happy to go his own way, positioned rather on the periphery of her life. He would sit apart, regularly clearing his throat and spitting mucus on the fire which sizzled, an action which – affected as I was by my mother's passion for cleanliness and decorum – always turned my stomach. Grandad would also clear his nose on the street, as we walked along together, his finger over one nostril, blowing hard and decisively on to the pavement through the other. He rolled his own cigarettes, smoked a pipe, sprinkled salt on his porridge and had a blackthorn stick. His favourite snacks were onion sandwich and 'chucky egg' – a soft-boiled egg mashed in a cup with salt, pepper and butter, eaten with a spoon. He enjoyed the company of children. As my youngest aunt grew older, Grandad adopted me as his companion. Each week he would buy me the *Eagle* comic so I could enjoy the adventures of Dan Dare and the Mekon. When we visited on Saturdays, the grown-ups would talk and Grandad Joe would chatter to me as he went about his business at the off-licence, using a mallet to drive the brass tap through the cork stopper of his beer and cider barrels, rolling away the caskets when they were empty. One evening he took me out into the yard to watch the Russian Sputnik pass over Lancashire. Grandad was opinionated in a rather cranky way. Whenever we had tinned pineapple, a common dessert in the 1950s, he would assert that we were really eating turnip – that the food manufacturers were defrauding us by flavouring cheap turnip with chemicals and passing it off as an exotic tropical fruit. I think of him still every time I see a slice of pineapple.

Just as in the Second World War Grandad had been keen that my auntie Joan should learn to dismantle and to reassemble a sten gun, so he was keen that I should learn to shoot with an air rifle. We would fire at distant sixpences on a far wall in the back-yard – and, while we were shooting, he would tell me stories, generally of the First World War, which was always on his mind; and of the Blitz in Liverpool. In the 1920s Joe had gone to sea and sailed to South America and back, working as an engineer in the boiler room of the SS *Araby*. He tantalised me with his description of an anaconda which had swallowed a small donkey and looked in silhouette like a bowler hat. I was a good listener and a keen inquisitor.

Keeping pigeons was Grandad's greatest passion. He had a large loft in the yard, home to a hundred birds, which gave off an over-powering reek. In the middle of the week, he and I would carry a basket of pigeons to the local railway station, and place it in a great mound with other cooing wicker containers destined for France. From lunchtime on Saturday he and I would wait in the yard for the first bird to return. Almost always, the bird would perch high on a gutter, looking down on us nervously, stubbornly refusing to enter the loft. Grandad tried every trick. He would send hen birds to France that were incubating eggs, hoping to entice them home to their brood; he had a great wire sieve full of dry corn and would rattle it to lure the hungry bird down; he would coo enticingly, but all to no avail, till the pigeon, in its own good time, finally decided to return to its home box. Then the bird was quickly captured, the ring on its leg removed and inserted into a compartment in a big, heavy chronometer. The moment the compartment was shut, a pin punc-tured a hole in a paper roll and registered the exact second of the pigeon's arrival. Grandad and I then carried the chronometer to the local pigeon club. As we converged on the club-house, so did many other men – as in a Lowry painting – looking exactly like my grandad in their tawny, belted raincoats and their flat caps, and carrying identical pigeon clocks. None of my grandad's birds ever won a race, or even came close. Every week he cursed with renewed frustration.

In 1962, on the fiftieth anniversary of the signing of Carson's Covenant, Grandad Joe returned to Belfast and led a parade of his fellow Covenanters. When he died, in 1973, long before my nanna, the service was conducted by a fiercely eloquent young Presbyterian cleric from Belfast who had tended Grandad in hospital in his final days. The preacher thundered like a young Paisley. He spoke of a sensitive, compassionate, God-fearing Joe who was unrecognisable. His grandchildren stifled their giggles. Only when my nanna surprised us by producing the bluebells hidden in her bag were we moved to emotion – for none of us in his lifetime made any effort to understand what had shaped and disturbed this limited man.

My nanna was a major influence on my life. She gave me a strong appetite for travel and adventure, for the pleasure of exploring the unknown. She had a deep conviction about self-reliance, about sorting things out for yourself, about the value of hard work, about not complaining. She never had any regrets. Unlike me, she believed in fate; that whatever cards fate dealt you would be right. 'In the end,' she would always say, even when things looked bad, 'everything's for the best.'

I keep a picture of the young, beautiful Anna on my desk, looking very like my daughter Eliza. She looked after herself in a council flat in Southport till she was almost ninety, still drinking Guinness every day, and travelling into Southport on the bus to shop and to talk to other little old ladies, many of them, like her, originally from Liverpool. In the late 1980s she had an especially enjoyable encounter with a woman she sat next to. They swapped yarns about common haunts in Liverpool. Towards the end of the journey the other lady handed my nanna an address card. She was surprised because people she knew didn't have cards. On it was her travelling companion's name and details and the description, 'The Mother of Tom O'Connor' – Tom being the amiable Liverpool comedian and game-show host. My nanna had no card of her own but she countered with pleasure: *my* grandson is the Deputy Director-General of the BBC! They were two proud Liverpool ladies.

In the last few years of her life, my nanna lived in a home in Liverpool. On her ninetieth birthday I asked BBC Radio Merseyside if her favourite DJ, Billy Butler, would dedicate 'Danny Boy' to her. He did – and, using the letter I had written, paid her a handsome and lengthy tribute. She was thrilled. Her standing rose with all the old Liverpool folk in the home. She died shortly after, without warning, in her sleep.

At breakfast on the morning I was to sit my eleven-plus, my father said he had been at a pub the night before where he had seen a Liverpool comedian and singer who had greatly impressed him. Dad had obtained an autographed photograph for me. It was Ken Dodd.

I passed the exam, aware that the 90 per cent who had not were doomed to secondary moderns, to leave school at fifteen, and to become – as we saw it – manual labourers. I was glad to be on the right side of this social and educational apartheid. I went on to St Mary's Senior School, one of the 144 bright Brylcreemed Catholic boys in the first year drawn from predominantly working-class homes. We were to be educated by the Irish Christian Brothers, with help from lay teachers.

The Christian Brothers were founded in 1802 by a Waterford businessman, Edmund Rice, whose portrait stared down on us severely from a main corridor wall. They were formed to fight discrimination against Catholics. Rice wanted to help the Catholic poor by equipping 'young people mentally, morally and religiously to stand on their own two feet and to change the society that caused and allowed them to be poor'.

A hundred and fifty years later, in twentieth-century Liverpool, the Brothers were still determined to propel their clever Catholic charges towards better things. To begin with, we would be taught middle-class graces. In the first year, Brother Francis, the head-master – a small, dour, intelligent man with red hair – gave us lessons in politeness once a week. Franco tutored us in an essentially middle-class code of proper behaviour: doffing your cap when greeting an adult and standing up for ladies on the bus. He taught a class of Liverpool lads the polite way to eat: how to tip the soup plate away from you, how not to slurp. We listened in wonder as he explained the proper use of cutlery at a meal – with different knives, forks and spoons for every course. We learnt to our surprise that there was a fish course as well as a meat course, and, aston-ishingly, that there was a specially shaped knife for eating fish. How had we managed at home without one? 'Don't worry,' Brother Francis assured us. 'If in doubt just start on the outside, and work in.' I remember him still whenever I sit down to dine at a grand dinner or state occasion.

Our textbook was a slim volume called *Christian Politeness* – trans-lated from the French in 1832. Behaviour should be decorous, the book preached. Manners and composure – even stillness – are absolutely essential. Every individual should project 'serenity'. Decency and modesty are emphasised. They must be maintained even when blowing one's nose. 'Levity' or 'stupidity' are the worst afflictions. Anger must be suppressed, even when you are insulted. Cleanliness at all times is important: 'Nothing is more intolerable than filthy hands.' Across a century, the book spoke to a class of bemused Liverpool boys: 'Pride and arrogance of mien denote a bad disposition, for they are known to spring from an overweening self-esteem, and they can never be mistaken for dignity or gravity.' Much of Franco's advice went over our heads, but one powerful idea struck home: to consider the interests of other people above your own.

We were not only to be turned into little gentlemen, but to speak like little gentlemen too. Miss Bushell was to give us elocution les-sons. She was a buxom lady with a posture like a thrush: her bosom

stuck forward and her bottom stuck out. The purpose of Miss
Bushell's lessons was to eradicate our Liverpool accents, of which –
it was clear – we ought to be ashamed. Miss Bushell organised
speech choirs in which we recited poetry in unison. I had a solo part
as a member of a speech choir on speech day at Liverpool's
Philharmonic Hall. I played the Walrus in Lewis Carroll's poem,
The Walrus and the Carpenter. I believed I spoke without a Liverpool
accent – 'proper', as we termed it – until I heard, after the event, the
recording made of our performance.

I recited:

> 'The time has come' the Walrus said,
> 'To talk of many things:
> Of shoes – and ships – and sealing wax
> Of cabbages – and kings
> And why the sea is boiling hot
> And whether pigs have wings.'

I did well enough, sounding prissy and posh, until I reached the
word 'wax' in the third line. It came out as a resounding, catarrhal,
unmistakably Scouser 'Whax'!

St Mary's placed a heavy emphasis on rote learning and testing,
underpinned by the brutal punishment the Christian Brothers
favoured. Each evening we had an enormous amount of homework, and facts to commit to memory for the following day's
classes – Latin verbs, French vocabulary, history dates. Everything
was reduced to a list: the seven causes of the French Revolution, the
dates of battles in the Peninsular War, and so on. Most lessons
would start with a test – either written, with another pupil immediately marking the test, or oral, with boys picked at random or in
order to answer questions. Failure to perform was punished with the
strap, which became a central part of our lives. Almost every
teacher had one and used it. The strap was about 14 inches long,

1½ inches wide, and about ⅓ inch thick, composed of black leather strips stitched together. Some teachers administered the strap casually, in a matter-of-fact way, others with relish. One stroke on the hand brought a sharp and intense pain which would last for minutes, driving out all thought. A stinging sensation would continue for hours. Poor performance in a test – or for some petty offence like forgetting your gym shoes, or not wearing your school-cap in the street – would earn perhaps one stroke on each hand. For more serious offences, the punishment was two strokes on each hand: this would leave most boys doubled up in agony, barely able to offer their hands for a second stroke. The most serious offences brought six strokes, a shockingly brutal punishment.

On occasions, the whole class would be strapped indiscriminately for, say, talking while queuing in a corridor, or for making a racket between lessons. Anyone late for school assembly lined up outside Franco's study and the moment assembly ended we would see him move quickly and ruthlessly down the line walloping every latecomer. The Polish woodwork teacher, nick-named Doo-Dah, would strap you if your joints weren't tight, then punch you in the kidneys as a follow-up.

Violence was the constant backdrop of everyday life. Strapology – as we called it – gripped our imagination. Boys would compare and contrast the techniques employed by different teachers, and discuss countermeasures. Some ran their hands under hot water to swell them when punishment was anticipated. Some advocated a hand held high to reduce the arc of the stroke; some that lower was better with the hand tipped downwards; some that you should lower your hand just as the strap landed. But this was a dangerous tactic: a hand pulled away earned an extra excruciating stroke.

Jimmy was a retired sergeant major, too old to teach gym any longer, who had a moustache waxed to two points. He was retained to watch over classes when teachers were ill, or to strap boys on behalf of female or squeamish teachers. But he wasn't so old that he couldn't jump in the air to lend speed and momentum to his strapping. There was general agreement that Brother Brickley – Brickhead – who taught us Latin, was the most effective strapper. Brother Brickley had a pronounced Irish accent, and a menacing and sadistic sense of humour. He looked formidable: his crinkly, dark hair was plastered back, and he was strongly built with a big mole in the middle of his forehead. At the back of his neck he had a perpetual purple neck boil and what looked like a bullet wound. Brickhead would often draw a boy out to the front of the class for punishment by pulling on the offender's sideburns and forcing him to tiptoe out to the front, his victim's face contorted with pain. Brother Brickley called his strap 'Excalibur'. He would lift it high, drooping it over his shoulder and down his back and then whip the strap down ferociously, with all his considerable power, on to the boy's outstretched hand. Every stroke counted with Brother Brickley.

There was a grim fascination in the varying ability of boys to withstand the pain. Punishment was always in front of the class – and generally many times a day – so there was ample opportunity for study. Some quiet boys hardly flinched; conversely, some toughies were severely troubled. One notably well-behaved, sweet-natured boy in my class, who was especially stoical, was once repeatedly beaten on one hand until he cried – with the sole purpose of making him cry. Some boys became flustered, and blustered and stammered out of fear when they were asked a question, and were strapped. Some boys were simply punished because they were insufficiently able. The punishment became fiercer as we moved up the school. The most barbaric was meted out in private to one of my friends, a tough, pugnacious, confident boy who received six strokes on his bare bottom, which was badly marked and bruised.

In 1997 the head of the Irish Christian Brothers acknowledged formally the order's abuse of their charges over many years: 'I apologise and ask forgiveness,' he said. In one Catholic paper, a picture of me appeared alongside Gerry Adams – another Christian Brothers alumnus – to illustrate the story.

I was studious at St Mary's and rarely beaten individually, but I loathed the repressive atmosphere in which I studied. I was not, however, unhappy at school, for I was surrounded by other boys like myself, of comparable ability and outlook, from similar back-grounds, and I loved the liveliness of their company. A Liverpool playground in the 1950s was a stimulating place to be. St Mary's graduates like Roger McGough and Laurie Taylor went on to delight the nation. Every one of my schoolmates has since had a successful career: they are research scientists and IT specialists and media executives and senior public sector managers; but in these days they were just sparky, Liverpool lads. In my former school-friends' company, I am struck now, as I was at the time, by their quick Liverpool wit, their easy laughter, their quiet authority, their decency and moral conviction, their sense of responsibility to others. All confess, like me, that they feel guilty if they are not doing some-thing worth while, if they are not working. St Mary's may have affected them, but it did not scar them.

As we entered our teens, my schoolfriends and I were part of a Catholic universe defined by home, school and Church. In the class-room and corridors, statues of the Sacred Heart or the Virgin Mary everywhere looked down upon us. We stood on the hour to say our Hail Marys. We were taught that people outside our universe – fol-lowing other religions – were beyond the pale. As a result, Protestants I didn't know seemed strange and different. They were labelled 'proddy-dogs'. I could not, however, quite bring myself to believe that my Protestant relations were damned; and I shrugged off this inconsistency along with all the other mysteries of child-hood.

At St Mary's, we learnt our religion – like everything else – by rote. Our guide was the Catechism, which set out in a small book-let hundreds of questions and answers – the rules, regulations and beliefs of Catholicism. The Catechism described a universe of tough, hard certainties, a world of hierarchical obedience to the order of things. We had to learn every answer by heart:

Q   What do you mean when you say that your soul is immortal?
A   . . . I mean my soul can never die.

Q   Why must you believe whatever God has revealed?
A   . . . because God is the very truth, and can neither deceive nor be deceived.

Q   How are you to know what God has revealed?
A   . . . by the testimony, teaching and authority of the Catholic Church.

Q   Does God know and see all things?
A   God knows and sees all things, even our most secret thoughts.

The Catechism encouraged self-discipline and denial: 'We are to deny ourselves by giving up our own will, and by going against our own humours, inclinations and passions . . . We are bound to deny ourselves because our natural inclinations are prone to evil from our very childhood; and if not corrected by self-denial, they will certainly carry us to Hell.'

The Catholicism we were taught offered a grim, joyless prospect of life on earth; and the uncertain outlook of a not-altogether-beguiling life thereafter – forever after. In our early teenage years we accepted this as our dreary, unappetising lot. The Christian Brothers would occasionally talk to us about the possibility of one of us acquiring a vocation to become a priest. They emphasised that a vocation was a calling, something that came to you, a gift from God, and not simply something that emerged from within. I dreaded the prospect of God calling on me.

I had always been tall for my age. I shot up in my teens and played rugby for the school in the second row of the scrum. I did so reluctantly: Liverpool was a football city. But the school played rugby for the same reason we had politeness and elocution lessons – to help us to become upwardly socially mobile, to help create a Catholic middle class. I loved my football and did not enjoy pushing and shoving and having my ears twisted in the rugby scrum. Nor did I look forward to losing my Saturday afternoons. We were already cursed with lessons on Saturday mornings. Other boys went home at noon – or on to Anfield or to Goodison Park – but the rugby team travelled by public transport to play in some distant part of Merseyside, over the water to Birkenhead, or to St Helens where we played hulking brutes who were really passionate about their rugby. We never played Protestant teams. Playing rugby for the school was my first experience of command. I was scrum captain: I had to cajole and hector my team-mates to push harder; to pick themselves up quickly; to hurl themselves back into the mêlée. Though I was reserved and undemonstrative in the hurly-burly of daily teenage life, I had no difficulty asserting myself when the task called for it.

My dad's career continued to prosper. His charm and his appetite for hard work made him an excellent salesman. Firestone Tyres thrived on stretch targets and awarded prizes for success. Again and again he won the top prize. The senior managers at Firestone had been officers in the war, and mostly came from public school backgrounds. My dad was conscious of his poor background and of his lack of education; but that didn't hinder his promotion. His earnings increased as Britain boomed. Harold Macmillan told us we had never had it so good, and this was certainly true of the Birts. We were a proud, model family with our immaculate semi, boasting a gleaming, well-polished car on the front path. Ida and Leo were industrious, caring parents. They had three healthy, well-educated children, who got on well together. Michael, my brother, was nearly ten years younger than me, but no longer a baby. Angela and I doted on him.

In the late 1950s Dad was appointed a manager and we went briefly to live in the north-east. In 1960 he was promoted to a bigger responsibility back in the north-west. We returned to live in Formby and I went into the sixth form at St Mary's. Liverpool in 1960 was a good place to be sixteen.

3

Growing Up

The sixth form at St Mary's was an altogether different experience. There were no beatings. We were treated as grown-ups. The more boisterous pupils seemed to disappear, while the studious and civilised ones remained.

I took maths, further maths and physics in the science sixth. The choice was made for me. During my brief interlude at a school in Middlesbrough, the form teacher told us one day to read our books in class. He went round with the register, squatting down and whispering to each boy. When he came to me he said I was a good all-rounder and that I could do any A-levels I wanted – but science was the future, he said, and since I had the ability, I should do that. And that was that. I accepted his advice with nervousness – for I knew I was narrowing my options – but without further reflection. Harold Wilson would soon talk of 'The white heat of the technological revolution', of which I was now to be a part.

I settled down at St Mary's under the best tutelage I ever had – that of B. B. Cooper, the maths teacher. 'Norman' was a round, cheerful, twinkling man with a squeaky voice, who wore glasses and a blue three-piece suit. He enthused over the elegance and beauty of mathematics and explained the most difficult and abstruse concepts brilliantly. We all respected him for his honesty and commitment. I enjoyed my maths, dissecting complex problems, making the imaginative leap to a solution. Norman also tried to broaden our horizons: he read aloud to us from *War and Peace* and encouraged us to read *The Times*, though we didn't. St Mary's had taught us how to pass exams, but not how to think. Norman inspired us, drew us out, gave us projects: he encouraged us for the first time to learn for ourselves. He asked me to lecture the science sixth on how the newly emerging computers worked, and in particular on the difference between analogue and digital technology. This was 1960. Forty years later, when the digital revolution occurred, the BBC would profit from the insights I had gained from Mr Cooper's farsightedness.

I spent much of my time in the sixth with the small, congenial maths group. For our free lessons, we were assigned a corner of the unheated hut where the Cadet Force stored their rifles. Between us we scavenged from somewhere a discarded dimplex electric heater and a toaster. We spent many happy hours chattering and eating toast. I was nicknamed 'Trib' – my family name spelt backwards. At lunchtime we would disappear to the local baker's. Each of us would buy a whole white loaf, hollow out the inside, go next door to the chippy and fill up the loaf with chips. For the first time, I thoroughly enjoyed school.

I was enjoying my football too. In 1959 Bill Shankly had taken over a Liverpool team in the doldrums. He set about building the first of his great sides, which included St John, Hunt, Melia, Callaghan, Thompson and Yeats. Shankly's team would go on to win the League and the Cup, and in the process turn my schoolboy flirtation with football into a lifelong passion. Dalgleish, Souness and Rush would later intensify it.

I had migrated at Anfield from the Boy's Pen to the Kop – to the seething mass, behind one of the goals, of the most vocal Liverpool supporters. The crowd was packed tight. Everyone stood. At a dramatic moment on the field, the crowd could transport you in a great wave, your feet barely touching the concrete steps, ten yards forward, then ten yards back. The banter in the Kop was as entertaining as the play on the field. But you needed your wits about you. 'Be careful someone doesn't pee in your pocket,' a schoolfriend warned. A favourite trick for anyone caught short after too many pints, he explained, was to pee down a rolled-up copy of the *Liverpool Echo* straight into a neighbour's overcoat pocket.

My schoolmates and I were obsessed with popular music. In the 1950s I had been haunted by the tough and tender perfection of Frank Sinatra's interpretations, and beguiled by the wit and melodies of Porter and Gershwin. But my driving passion in 1960 was American popular music – Chuck Berry, Little Richard, Jerry Lee Lewis, Gene Vincent, the Everlys and Buddy Holly. British popular music never captivated me: our rock never felt like the real thing. BBC radio, too, was remote and boring, except for the Goons. Radio Luxembourg was our station: we listened every night, doing our homework to the station crackling and hissing away, fading in and out on 208 metres medium wave.

We had no interest at all in classical music. I never went to the theatre. At home we took the *Daily Express* in the morning and the *Liverpool Echo* in the evening. I read Beachcomber and Curly Wee and little else. I was unaware of politics. When we did General Studies in the sixth form, I was set an essay on the differences between the Conservative and Labour parties, and I hadn't the least idea what they were. At home I consulted our one and only reference book, *Pears Encyclopaedia*, and copied out the entry.

My friends and I were not much affected by television, though I enjoyed *Candid Camera*, *Maigret* and *Sunday Night at the London Palladium* with the rest of the family. We rarely watched the BBC. Television finally came to life for me with the powerful realism of *No Trams to*

Lime Street on ITV's Armchair Theatre and the gritty naturalism of *Z Cars*. I preferred books: I read avidly, including everything by Graham Greene, Evelyn Waugh and Ernest Hemingway. Reading was my main window on the adult world. I visited the cinema whenever I could: the raw emotion of *Room at the Top* was my first exposure to grown-up passion and sexuality; and *Saturday Night and Sunday Morning* and (later) *Billy Liar* captured a world of young, chippy northern men with which I could identify.

In 1960 my father decided to take the *Sunday Times*, because he thought it would better the family. This was the first serious broadsheet I had seen, and I began to read Dilys Powell on cinema every week. She wrote about a corpus of films, particularly European ones, which I had no hope of seeing in Liverpool. But I was very taken with her conviction and a seed was sown.

The muted sexuality in the few serious films I did see, and the knowing references to intimacy in Graham Greene novels, made me aware of something powerful in human relations. But exactly what it was remained a mystery – for there was no sex education. When we were in our mid-teens we had speculated about the process of reproduction, but we were wide of the mark. We did not even know what a naked girl looked like. There were pictures in books of bare-breasted African women, but a veil was drawn over everything else. Brigitte Bardot was exotic and enticing, but we were too young to see her films. We did not even understand our own bodies. Gradually, however, girls entered our lives. Though I increasingly found the repetition of the Mass dull, and the sermons irrelevant, and I longed for the priest to intone *Ite missa est*, going to church became a good opportunity to look at the girls. Catholic girls, however, remained on a pedestal – cautious, pious, unattainable. This was particularly true of those at our sister school, Seafield Convent, which Cherie Booth would later attend. Seafield girls were the iron maidens, tough and savvy, untouched and untouchable, wearing impregnable corsets beneath their petticoats.

I didn't have a serious girlfriend until I joined Formby tennis club in the early 1960s. Formby tennis club exposed me for the first time to well-off, educated, professional people in numbers – and to their self-confident offspring, many of whom went away to school. I keenly felt my Bootle origins, and I was additionally conscious that the members were almost all Protestant, so I felt doubly stigmatised. The adult members of the club were noticeably cool towards me. I felt nervous and inadequate.

My nervousness turned to resentment when I was exposed to my first girlfriend's parents. Her father had been to Oxford; they were well-to-do, and had a family firm in Liverpool. They had always kept their light-hearted, spirited daughter on a tight rein; but they pulled more tightly when she started going out with me. They did not forbid her to see me outright, but they mounted a skilled tactical campaign, allowing her out only when she was chaperoned, only letting her attend social occasions to which I was unlikely to be invited. Her parents made it clear that they did not regard a Catholic with a Liverpool accent from a Bootle family a suitable match for their daughter. They refused to address me when I encountered them in the street. I felt an outcast. None the less my girlfriend and I found opportunities to meet. We would hang around after school on a track by the railway till the cold drove us home, or walk in the pinewoods at weekends. We were very fond of one another and the relationship lasted for years – but it eventually ended, weighed down by the odium and opposition that two teenagers were unable to overturn. I became very resentful of posh, public school types. I read D. H. Lawrence and identified strongly with his tortured working-class heroes.

In my first year in the sixth form, I was invited to play one of the leading parts in the school play, which was to be George Bernard Shaw's *Arms and the Man*. I was cast as Bluntschli, the romantic hero – a Serbian officer on the run – who wins the heart of the heroine, the fair Raina. A pretty, nervous boy from the third form, rather than a girl from Seafield, was to play Raina. None of us thought this was strange. We rehearsed for weeks. Whenever we reached the climactic scene when the hero and heroine were to come together and embrace passionately, the teacher who was directing the play would come between us and halt the rehearsal: 'We'll do that later,' she would say. 'Carry on with the play.' Just as we were becoming word perfect, and just as tickets were about to go on sale, the play was cancelled. 'Rehearsal is interfering with your revision for the summer exams,' was the explanation proffered. We weren't convinced, but we had no explanation of our own to offer for this surprising cancellation.

In the early 1960s Radio Luxembourg announced it would start a Pop Pools competition. Contestants had to forecast whether a record would move up or down the hit parade or stay the same. The competition caused much excitement at school: here was a subject on which we were really expert. Immediately, I graphed the progress of new chart entrants and worked out their typical life cycle. In the first week of the Pop Pools, I correctly predicted seven out of eight chart movements. The exception was Acker Bilk's 'Stranger on the Shore', which had lingered in the charts for months, but had moved up a place that week against the trend of its long-term decline. The winners – with eight out of eight – had won thousands of pounds. With one prediction wrong, I received a postal order for a few shillings. None the less, I was expectant. In the second week of the competition I correctly predicted eight out of eight record movements. Mum and Dad were overjoyed: we anticipated enormous winnings. Moreover, with my forecasting record, I could become a money machine! At school, news of my success spread like wildfire. Brother Coleman, the normally acerbic sixth-form head, proclaimed at assembly that it was a triumph for science. I was looking forward to becoming rich.

My excited family and I gathered around the wireless the next day to hear how much I had won: it was three shillings and sixpence – barely more than my stake. To general merriment Brother

Coleman announced the miserable scale of my winnings to the science sixth assembly. The Pop Pools were closed down two weeks later.

My first real responsibility was given to me by Mr Kelly, a kindly, effervescent man with boundless energy who taught at St Mary's preparatory school. He formed a St Vincent de Paul Society in the school and invited me to be its founding president. His son Philip was my vice-president. (By an extraordinary coincidence, on the very same day in 1987 that I was appointed Deputy Director-General of the BBC, Phil became editor of *Tribune*, the Labour weekly.)

The St Vincent de Paul Society was a Catholic organisation, started in France in the early nineteenth century, to alleviate the suffering of the poor during the industrial revolution. The Society was the Church's response to secular socialism. Mr Kelly believed in the Society's principles and was opposed to other Catholic societies – like the Knights of St Columba – which he believed were a cover for personal advancement, in effect a Catholic freemasonry.

I devised a programme of activity: I led a membership drive, press-ganging my school set to join; I provided a team of unskilled labourers from St Mary's to help some nuns renovate a big country house they were turning into a nursing home; I organised a rota to visit impoverished, elderly Catholics in their homes in our lunchhour. Each pensioner received a packet of tea or half a pound of butter. At Christmas we held a party for pensioners. Mr Kelly amazed us with an unexpected but brilliant stand-up routine, with risqué seaside-postcard jokes, which the old folk adored.

The Society sent me for a week to the Leonard Cheshire Home in the Pennines near Rochdale where people largely or wholly paralysed with muscular dystrophy or other neuromuscular conditions were nursed. One of my duties was to bathe naked men and to help them use the bedpan. I was shocked by their condition, but moved by their dignity and courage. It was a growing-up experience. I spent all day with adults – whether patients or nursing staff – and they treated me like one too. I was sixteen and everyone's pet, a new and temporary focus for their attention. They drew me into their intrigues, competed for my interest, warned me off each other, and – both men and women – talked knowingly and raucously, tantalisingly and inexplicitly, about sex.

My greatest escapade with the St Vincent de Paul Society was a bold but foolhardy plan I conceived to take a hundred boys and girls from a Liverpool orphanage – aged from two to fourteen – on a day out, with picnic and games, at the beach. My helpers were St Mary's sixth formers, as ignorant as I was about young children's needs and welfare – but nobody stopped us. I led a long straggling caravan on the mile-long walk from the orphanage to Waterloo Station. I felt like the Pied Piper of Hamelin. We took the train to Formby, then walked on sandy tracks for two miles through the pinewoods to the sea, carrying everything with us. There were no contingency plans; we didn't consider the risk of injury or illness or losing a child – but luck was with us. It was warm and sunny, and we had a joyful day. In the evening, we embarked on the long trek back and at dusk returned a hundred completely exhausted but happy charges to the nuns who tended them. The orphans' picnic was an important learning experience for me. I was exhilarated by the success of the day. I had been hugely fulfilled by making others happy; I had taken naturally to being the leader; and I had found executing a complex – if risky – plan most satisfying.

I was growing in confidence. When I was younger, a combination of my religion, my family's social uncertainty and an atmosphere of oppression at school had weighed upon me. Now, in the sixth form, my bright, like-minded fellow pupils and a more relaxed regime stimulated my thinking. Height and sport had made me physically confident. Academic ability and a commitment to hard work had brought success in exams and applause. The result was that I felt ever more free to express my frustrations and convictions, to unleash the determination with which I had been born. I was still ill at ease with toffs but not with anyone else. I was ready to protest against Britain's rigid social hierarchies, to undermine stuffy, distant author-ity. My fellow pupils and I were increasingly outspoken with our teachers – but we were candid rather than rude, questioning rather than rebellious, sceptical rather than cynical. We didn't appreciate it at the time, but we were the children of the 1944 Education Act, the grammar-school generation who would go on largely to sweep away the class-based power structures that had constipated Britain. We would be the vanguard of the meritocracy; we and tens of thou-sands of other bright working-class boys and girls from grammar schools would eventually be propelled into the upper reaches of every public and private sector institution in the country.

Something else was stirring in the playgrounds and schoolrooms of Liverpool in the early 1960s that was peculiar to the city. The many influences on this migrant metropolis – its historic success, the influx of the Irish, the cosmopolitan melting pot of cultures and experiences, the exposure of seafarers to American popular culture and ideas – all combined to bring Liverpool's traditional swagger to a peak. Merseyside's youth was everywhere self-confident, fluent and wry; independent, nonconformist and undeferential; proud, defiant and combative. It was ready for revolution, for self-determi-nation, poised to throw off the yoke of the dull, bland, conforming, stifling 1950s.

I first heard of the Beatles when a girl from Seafield Convent explained to me, with a passionate Liverpudlian intensity, what for-midable, unmatched, innovative talents they were. In the summer of 1962 I had a holiday job as a waiter at a municipal café in Southport when the Beatles came to play at the Corporation's Cambridge Hall. They were still unknown outside Liverpool. I was asked if I wanted to earn some overtime as a bouncer at the concert, keeping fans at bay. My job was to guard the Green Room, which the Beatles would occupy before and after their performance. Before the show, I stood at the door and watched the Beatles talking quietly to each other and to their entourage. There were no problems with fans.

The group's performance electrified me. I felt the sharp shock of the new. This wasn't synthetic, antiseptic British rock. It felt revolutionary. It owed much to the American rock canon I revered – Chuck Berry, the Everlys, Buddy Holly – but I began to see, watching that first concert, and more clearly still in the following months when I became a committed fan, that this was *our* music. Its freshness, power and energy captured my feelings and those of my friends and of my generation. The lyrics spoke simply about emotions we could recognise. The fresh, irreverent, skittish banter of the Beatles on stage was just like St Mary's sixth-form common room. Two Liverpool grammar-school boys – John Lennon and Paul McCartney – had formed a sublime union. Two extraordinary and contrasting musical talents had been brought together, as if by a divine force, at a church fête in Woolton: Paul – energetic, optimistic, steady; John – ironic, sour, utopian. From that meeting in Woolton, an exuberant movement – both musical and cultural – would grow and develop which would give the 1960s their special character, and which would rapidly affect the whole world.

The Beatles did not just promote fine feelings, however. After the concert I guarded the door protecting John, Paul, George and Pete (Ringo was yet to join) from a score of emotional and tearful girls of my own age. I was helped by a fellow waiter, a friend from St Mary's who went on to be a doctor. One of the fans was well known to us: she was the most beautiful girl in Formby. We saw her on the train to school each day. She was in a league of beauty of her own and paid no attention to any of us. No one in my circle had ever spoken to her. She pleaded with the two of us to let her in to see Paul McCartney. The other girls finally drifted away. My friend said: 'We'll let you in to see Paul if you let us have a snog and a feel.' She immediately agreed and led us off to some backstairs. To my shame even at the time, I participated in the encounter despite her inert response. This unedifying experience was soon cut short and we led her back to the Green Room to find that the Beatles had gone. I rushed around in a guilty panic trying to locate Paul and, to my relief, found him at the bar. I retrieved the girl, and took her to Paul, who was with a crowd of admirers. He turned round, recognised me as the bouncer, realised I was there with a purpose and raised his eyebrows questioningly. I explained that I was with someone very keen to meet him and introduced Paul to the apparition at my side. He bowed graciously and, as I departed in embarrassment, they were chatting politely to one another.

Paul McCartney was at that time living in a council house in Forthlin Road in Allerton, south Liverpool. In a tiny upstairs bed-room he and John composed and rehearsed most of the Beatles' early songs. In 1995, visiting Liverpool with my family, I saw that 20 Forthlin Road was for sale and persuaded the National Trust to acquire it. Now painstakingly restored, it is a unique monument to the humble origin of the Beatles, and a nostalgic reminder of the Bakelite, Formica and linoleum of my youth.

In October 1962, the Beatles released their first single, 'Love Me Do'. On the first day it was in the stores, the record was carried rev-erentially into the sixth-form common room at St Mary's where a gramophone had been installed for the day. Everyone gathered round. The mood was solemn and serious. We realised that this music of our streets and our time was going to be part of the main-stream.

Suddenly, everyone in Liverpool was in a group. I couldn't sing, but my old playmate Robert and I and another friend none the less composed a song: 'The Liverpool Wall'. We recorded it in Robert's front room, and we submitted it to a record company, but we waited in vain for a response.

On Saturdays and holidays, we went to clubs – including the Cavern in Mathew Street – which heaved with bodies dancing the Cavern Stomp. We wore narrow, tight-fitting dark trousers with 14-inch bottoms, black rollernecks or a shirt with a thin leather tie, and Chelsea boots. The Cavern's low brick arches dripped with sweat;

the air was pungent with an earthy smell like fungus. I had to leave early: my mum and dad insisted I was home by 10.30 p.m.

When I was in the upper sixth, a check of the class revealed that I had not received the fourth of the holy sacraments – confirmation. I had missed the opportunity during my period away in the north-east. Cardinal Heenan was coming to the local church to conduct a confirmation service and my name was put down. This prompted a religious crisis – for, to be confirmed, I needed to be in a perfect state of grace and I had not been to confession for several years. My faith had weakened. I had found the dogma increasingly unconvincing. We had been given instruction, for instance, in the sixth form on the proofs for the existence of God. My belief foundered on how an all-powerful God could allow suffering, torture and inhumanity. I found the thought of a God standing by and tolerating the Holocaust par-ticularly hard to accept. I increasingly felt that the rigour and rationality of the science I was studying was more likely to explain existence than religion. Moreover my own instincts were also under-mining the moral certainties of my religion: my first fumbling experiences with girls had convinced me that sex was not darkly shameful but natural and joyous. I could not accept that these pleas-ures were sinful. Whatever my doubts, however, I was not yet ready to admit to myself or to others that I was an unbeliever. And years of indoctrination made the prospect of taking communion at the confirmation service in a state of sin a taboo I was not yet ready to break. I was in turmoil.

I put off going to confession till the very day of the Cardinal's visit, past the moment when I could queue and attend anonymously, hiding and whispering my secrets to a priest behind a grille. I knew from the novels of Graham Greene that you could ask a priest to hear your confession at any time, so, during the school lunch-hour, I went to the priests' home and knocked on the door. A young cleric came out to see me. 'Will you hear my confession, Father?' I asked. He nodded sympathetically, showed no surprise and ushered me into a sitting room. He sat beside me. I was wearing my full school uniform, with the vivid yellow stripes on the sleeves and breast pocket signifying I was a prefect. I could not have been more conspicuous, or have felt more embarrassed. I started my confession: 'Bless me Father, for I have sinned . . .' I set out my adolescent breaches of the ten commandments. When I confessed to my sexual experiences, I anticipated a shocked and horrified response from the priest. I expected him to jump up and articulate the dark, raging wrath of God. But this kindly, soft-spoken man was unreprimanding and gentle with me. That evening Cardinal Heenan confirmed me and gave me what was to be my last communion.

My A-level results were good and Cardinal Heenan made another appearance in my life when he presented me with the school prize for physics at Liverpool's Philharmonic Hall. St Mary's had started to succeed in getting boys into Oxford, and my name was put down. What would I study? As before in my life, there was little advice to be had. Mathematics, it was suggested, was the obvious choice.

'What jobs could I do with a maths degree?' I enquired of the careers master.

'You could be a teacher, or an actuary,' he replied.

I recoiled at being a teacher: I couldn't wait to get out of school for ever. 'What's an actuary?' I asked.

'You advise insurance companies on life expectancy – how many people die of what disease and things like that . . .' the teacher said. The prospect horrified me. I pictured dark, musty rooms full of charts and tables of figures.

'What if I do physics?'

'You could become a nuclear physicist.'

I had found atomic science the least interesting branch of the physics we had studied. I felt trapped. 'What else could I do?'

'With your maths and physics you could be an engineer and build roads and dams and bridges.'

That sounded more appealing. None of these options felt right for me, but at least as an engineer, I reasoned, I'd be out in the open air and travelling, and I would have the satisfaction of creating some great structure or edifice. So I settled without enthusiasm for engineering.

In October 1962 I travelled alone to Oxford to be interviewed for a place, and took a taxi to Merton College where I was to stay overnight. It was the first time I had seen old, stone-built buildings of such beauty and in such profusion. As I waited at the porter's lodge, I overheard an encounter between two undergraduates who had just returned from their long summer vacation. One had been to Turkey to visit ancient ruins. The pair spoke confidently, fluently and with effortless, unselfconscious erudition. I was sick in my stomach. There was a gulf of sophistication between me and these people that I felt I could never bridge.

That night, as I was alone in my room on the very top floor, there was a loud clambering noise on the stairs. A cheerful young man burst in unannounced. He was taken aback to see me and apologised for the intrusion. He was the room's normal term-time occupant and hadn't realised it was in use. He too was a public school alumnus and exuded confidence, but he was open and friendly and full of advice. The toilet was a great trek away on another staircase. 'Just pee in the basin!' he advised me. This was a shocking thought for a St Mary's boy, and my mother's son. But in the middle of the night I would be most grateful for his advice.

The next day I faced a stern panel of unsmiling dons from Merton and Balliol in an elegant book-lined study. The school had offered me no advice whatsoever about Oxford interviews: I was wholly unprepared.

'You came through Runcorn on the train from Liverpool?' the engineering fellow asked. 'You will have seen the new bridge there across the Mersey. What sort of bridge is it? Can you explain the stresses and strains in its structure?'

I hadn't the slightest idea what kind of bridge it was. We had never studied bridges. I knew, though, about stresses and strains in structures and stumbled through an unsatisfactory answer.

'Who are your favourite authors?'

I mentioned Waugh and Greene.

'Very interesting. They are both Catholics like you – but their Catholicism marks their work in very different ways. Would you discuss that for us?'

I had never been asked to think in this way. I had simply enjoyed the books, mostly more than once. I floundered. I had nothing to say. Unsurprisingly, neither Merton nor Balliol wanted me. Then I was told to meet a Dr Schultz from St Catherine's College at a laboratory on the Banbury Road. I arrived at the appointed time, but the door was locked. A tall, stringy man with high cheek-bones and an amused, impudent face soon rode up on a bike, pedalling furiously, and screeched to a halt. He introduced himself. Dr Schultz was a laid-back, easygoing New Zealander. He complimented me on my A-level results, then put me at ease by asking about my family and what my dad did. He didn't ask me any questions about science or the arts. The conversation took no more than a few minutes. Then Dr Schultz offered me a place at St Catherine's. I was going to Oxford!

Mum and Dad were thrilled. So was Nanna. No member of our family had ever been to university, let alone Oxford. Nor had anyone else we knew, except for teachers. A story of my success with my picture appeared in the *Formby Times*. People at the tennis club noticeably thawed towards me.

There was a catch. I only had one language at O-level and Oxford required two. I had six months or so to learn a language and I chose Spanish – because I'd found Hemingway's Spain intriguing and exotic. But I had outlived school: I couldn't bear the notion of staying on for another half-year to learn Spanish. And there was a serious complication: my relationship with my mum and dad had become strained. There were the familiar tensions between adolescents and parents. I felt hemmed in by their devoted care and attention, by the constraints they placed on my day-to-day free-dom. These common enough difficulties were compounded when I started a relationship with a German au pair in Liverpool. She was older, bohemian and more experienced than me, and my parents did not approve. For their part, they were afraid that she would lead me off the rails, that my hard-won gains would slip away. Their upbringing had made them cautious and averse to risks. Relations between us deteriorated. I rebelled. For a few weeks I left home and school and took refuge with two old ladies in Southport – Russian émigré friends of my German girlfriend. For St Mary's and all my friends, this was a scandal without precedent. A resolution was proposed. I would go to Barcelona and learn Spanish there, returning to school briefly in the summer to sit the exam. I had adventured with my nanna: I was not afraid to uproot myself to Spain. My dad gave me £100 for the trip. I would have to find work in Barcelona if I needed more.

I took the long journey south by train and woke up one dawn to a dazzling sight: the jagged peaks of the Pyrenees bathed in bright Mediterranean light, covered with lush spring vegetation and dotted with white red-roofed houses. I opened the compartment window to let in the warm air and the strange new smells. This was freedom. I was exhilarated.

I stayed in a cheap *pension* on the Ramblas, the other inhabitants mostly Andalucians working in low-paid jobs; and I set out to enjoy Barcelona. I spent most of my evenings in *bodegas* in the teaming, thriving *barrio* around the Ramblas, chatting mostly to old Spanish men. These noisy caverns had great barrels – as tall as me – full of wine which cost two pesetas a glass. I ate olives and anchovies and calamari for the first time. I went to bullfights, and found them a gruesome but powerful spectacle. In the bars of the Plaza Reál, near the port, I met sailors: black GIs from the American South, and world-weary travellers – one a tough-looking forty-year-old American who told me he was a gold smuggler and drank with me till four in the morning, telling me stories of derring-do.

On Sundays the Andalucians would party, and invite me to join in. They tried, in vain, to teach me to dance the flamenco and to play the castanets. I did succeed in learning to drink from a *porron*, squirting the wine in a long arc into my mouth from high above my head. My heart lifted as the guitars played, the heels of the Andalucians' boots banged against the floor, the singers clapped and shouted and wailed and whooped, and the dancers flounced with dash and passion.

During the week, I explored Barcelona and saw Gaudi's master-piece, Sagrada Familia, start to take on its wondrous shape. I fitfully learned Spanish, attending lectures at the University of Barcelona. I was taken charge of by another British student, Tim Davies, an old hand, who had already been in Barcelona for many months and was due to go up to Cambridge. Tim generously showed me the ropes, the best cheap restaurants, the places to go. He introduced me to his Catalan friends. Tim was responsible for my first avant-garde expe-rience: he took me to see Antonioni's moody classic *L'Eclisse*, an Italian film with Spanish subtitles. For the first time, I articulated to myself that I found cinema magical. Tim, who went on to be an accomplished professional actor, had been active in school drama and had developed critical faculties. I listened, asked questions and learnt from him.

After a few months, my German girlfriend joined me. She was driven to Liverpool's Lime Street Station, to begin her journey to Spain, by the only friend I had at school who could drive, and who had access to his father's car. He was in the third-year sixth, about to go to university. The following morning, when he arrived at school, he was summoned to the head. Someone had talked. His favour to me had become known. He was involved, Franco sug-gested, in an improper and sinful conspiracy. He had 'aided and abetted the commission of a mortal sin'. He was nineteen years old, but that didn't matter – he was savagely and ferociously beaten with the strap. This decent, virtuous, public-spirited man went on to be a senior manager in the NHS.

I returned to a tense home and to what would be my last summer on Merseyside. My relationship with the German girl came to an end.

Relations with my parents thawed. I sat and passed my Spanish exam. Now a strapping youth, 6 foot 2 inches tall, I earned a man's money labouring, laying sewers on a new housing estate, working with an all-Liverpudlian gang. I felt at home with these men of Liverpool. They teased me about going to Oxford, but accepted me as their mascot, as someone from the same background as them moving on to a better life, and wished me well.

I laboured for about two months. On the last day, I was paid not only my generous weekly wage in cash, but all the tax that had been withheld during my time on the site – for me the enormous sum of £40. There was an older man on the gang who had hardly ever spoken. As I was saying my farewells he pulled me to one side, wished me luck with my life and then said calmly and with authority: 'Say nothing to anyone but there's a horse racing tomorrow that will win.' He gave me the details, shook my hand and walked away.

I took my earnings home to my mum. The family tradition of the 1930s had survived into the 1960s: every pay packet went first to my mum, unopened, a practice I had followed in every holiday job since I was fourteen. Mum would keep the bulk of the cash and give me some back, but little more than a bonus on top of my modest weekly pocket money. I explained to Mum about the racing tip. The horse was priced at 8–1. The £40 was a windfall we had not anticipated. I was my nanna Anna's grandson. Nanna taught me to believe in luck, to take a chance. I argued we should put all of the £40 on the horse. My mother made the sensible decision: she refused outright to gamble the hard-earned money. And the horse won.

In October 1963 my dad drove me to Lime Street Station to take the train to Oxford. He waited on the platform for the train to pull out. I leant out of the window and waved goodbye till the lone figure on the platform was out of sight. I had a sense of foreboding: I knew in my heart I would never again live in Liverpool. My mum and dad eventually left Liverpool themselves and moved south when my father was made national sales director of Firestone Tyres. His achievement, given the dire circumstances of his own upbringing, was testament to his character, and outstrips any success of mine. My mum returned to work when all the kids left home, and ended up lavishing her considerable energies and capacity for care on running a large Barnardo's home for children in Buckinghamshire. Firestone Tyres in the UK eventually fell foul of global forces and closed down its operations, bulldozing in the process the Art Deco masterpiece that was its headquarters building in London. Just before it did, my dad left the company and he and my mum opened a health-food store together in Grayshott, Hampshire. In the years after we left Liverpool, the changing pattern of trade with Europe, containerisation, industrial strife, perverse local government, political extremism and riots would tip the city where the Birts and Wilsons had lived for over a hundred years into rapid decline. The Dock Road would empty. The Overhead Railway – symbol of a once thriving city – would be pulled down.

II

OXFORD AND GRANADA

4

Oxford

I soon found my feet at Oxford, for I was not the only boy from a northern grammar school to arrive at the University in 1963. Our numbers had been growing in the post-war years, and St Catherine's College was a particularly comforting domicile. It owed much of its character to its founder and Master, the charismatic and avuncular Alan Bullock.

He was the Bradford-born historian of world renown, author of the then definitive study of Hitler, and who still spoke with a pronounced Yorkshire accent. Bullock had created St Catherine's as a new college two years previously – raising the funding and sweeping aside obstacles in his path with boundless energy, vision and pragmatism. St Catherine's was to be Oxford's largest college, with half its places reserved for mathematicians and scientists. It would reach out and draw in students of ability from every kind of background, who would be taught by a notably open and unstuffy body of fellows recruited by Bullock. St Catherine's was not a typical

Oxford college. We would inhabit one of the UK's few distinguished twentieth-century buildings, now Grade 1 listed. The Danish architect Arne Jacobsen used concrete, brick and glass – the very materials with which other architects of the period blighted our landscape – to create graceful, pristine buildings with light, airy interiors. Jacobsen attended to every detail, designing the gardens, door handles, light switches, furniture, cutlery and everything else to fashion a holistic and harmonious environment. He also incorporated central heating – for me a wonderful discovery, which enabled me quickly to discard my string vest!

I first huddled together at St Catherine's with the other northern scientists. Early on I broke up a fight when a drunken Welsh physicist laid into a haughty public schoolboy in the college bar for no good reason. I had fondly imagined my elocution lessons at St Mary's had armed me with a Received Pronunciation accent, but I had only to open my mouth for someone to say: 'Oh, you're from Liverpool.' (I had the opposite problem when I visited my aunts when I returned home to Merseyside. As soon as I opened my mouth, they said: 'Oh, posh! Airs and graces! La-di-da!') The Beatles were in full flow that autumn, and groups from Merseyside topped the charts every week, so there was no more fashionable place to come from than Liverpool. On those grounds alone I was invited to be lead singer of a band, but I was dropped as soon as they discovered I couldn't sing.

Two weeks after my arrival I went to phone my mum and dad from the call box at Carfax in the centre of Oxford. I arrived simultaneously with two pretty girls and, applying my *Christian Politeness* lessons, stood aside to let them call first. One remained outside the box while her friend phoned, and we chatted. She was American and a painter, newly arrived with her friend to study at the Ruskin School of Drawing and Fine Art on a year out from Carnegie Tech in Pittsburgh. I invited her and her friend to college for a drink after I'd made my own call home, and she accepted. I found she was called Jane and her friend Peggy.

I took Jane and Peggy back to the room at St Catherine's of a donkey-jacketed scientist from Manchester, a gangly beanpole with chronic acne and heavy yellow scales on his teeth. We sang Beatles songs to impress our guests. We were ridiculous, but I didn't quite put Jane off, and we started going out together. I was eighteen and she was twenty. Fearful that she would reject me as too young, I lied and added a year to my age. Jane was from a prosperous professional family in Washington DC, and was unlike any northern girl I had met. She was independent of spirit, tough minded and free speaking, funny and fanciful, generous and warm hearted. She was also more sophisticated in every way than me: she had passionate and certain convictions about art, and opened my eyes to the visual world. She had attended Martin Luther King's 'I have a dream' address that August on the steps of the Lincoln Memorial and spoke fierily about racial discrimination. She knew about and loved cinema and had been in the film society at Carnegie Tech. She played me Bob Dylan, whom she had seen live at the Newport Jazz Festival, and she introduced me to Ray Charles, Fats Domino and the Beach Boys, to black music, soul and the blues.

Jane also introduced me to a notion I'd never encountered before: the idea that you should bathe every day and not just once a week. And she bought me deodorant, of which I had never heard. I was taken aback by her observation that rooms full of young British men gave off a rank odour!

Jane and I set out to experience Oxford – which socially was in transition. The sixties proper had not yet arrived. This was still an Oxford of digs, Morris Minors, little old ladies with hats, meat and two veg at Brown's café in the market and bowler-hatted bulldogs – the University constabulary – patrolling the Broad. Skirts were above the knee, and dark-clothed Juliet Greco lookalikes stalked the quadrangles, but the carefree dolly bird had not yet appeared. One of my former St Mary's friends, a biochemist, kept a test-tube of LSD on a shelf in his room, but drugs were still a fringe activity, not in the mainstream. What we did experience was the emergence of

the pill and, in those seemingly disease-free days, greater sexual
freedom.

After only a few months I felt I had escaped prison. The ethos
and outlook of Oxford were in sharp contrast to the conformity of
Formby and the rigours of my Irish Christian Brothers education.
Oxford offered you space, the chance to grow; it encouraged you to
be yourself, not someone else. It also offered equality. Although
there were rich, supercilious young men in tailored suits, sporty
types from the landowning classes with MGBs, bombastic public
school men still wearing cravats, there was no hierarchy. We were on
the same level. We were all just part of the rich texture of University
life. Class began to fade rapidly as an issue for me: a more meritocratic Britain was already sweeping it away. Oxford also provided
stimulus – a thousand things to do, societies to join, meetings to
attend, the company of my clever, curious, witty, questioning fellow
students. Oxford offered tolerance: it was rational and civilised, it
welcomed diversity and eccentricity. I had found another place, like
Bootle, where I felt at home. At Oxford, I became, at first uncon-
sciously, a liberal. I also began my real education. It would be
completed elsewhere, but here I started to learn about culture and
ideas. Here I took my first tentative steps towards a fuller understanding of the wider world.

Jane and I went to the movies three or four times a week. Oxford
had several cinemas showing commercial movies but the scruffy, run-
down Scala in Walton Street, which showed largely arts films, was our
main destination most nights. We caught up on all the classics – by
Truffaut, Chabrol, Godard, Demy, Kurosawa, Eisenstein, Ford,
Hawks, Hitchcock – that had attracted my interest when I had read
about them in the *Sunday Times*. To stretch Jane's allowance and my
grant, we watched from the front two rows of the stalls, right up
against the screen, where the seats cost only 1s 9d. We saw one of the
greatest films ever made, Bergman's *Wild Strawberries*, from the end
two seats on the left of the front row, looking up and diagonally across
the screen, which towered above us, wholly filling our field of vision.

For the first time, I went to the theatre. Michael Palin delighted us in revue. I saw my first Shakespeare play – *Twelfth Night* – and was enchanted. David Aukin, who would later be Channel 4's film impresario, was a memorable Malvolio. We saw some outstanding performances at Oxford over the next few years, most notably the dashingly handsome Nick Elliott, movingly heroic as John Proctor in *The Crucible*; and the dark-haired wild-child Jenny Reeks as the fiery Patty in *Sport of my Mad Mother*. Neither would become a professional actor, but they would later combine – equally formidably – as ITV's drama commissioners in the 1990s.

At Christmas in my first year, I took Jane to Liverpool to show her the city and meet my family, who embraced her. I confessed to Jane, with trepidation, my true age. She laughed and agreed to marry me.

Ken Dodd, whom my dad had first spotted performing in a Liverpool pub, came to Oxford with his show and Jane and I saw him at the peak of his powers. He subjected his audience to an assault – end-of-the-pier humour delivered at rat-a-tat pace, building to a dazzling theatrical crescendo, leaving us all punch-drunk with laughter. Jane and I met him in the street and – pleased to encounter a Scouser among the spires – he invited us for tea in his dressing room and talked thoughtfully about the theory and philosophy of comedy.

I realised fairly early on that I had made a terrible mistake choosing engineering as my course of study. The Oxford course was generalist: we learnt mathematics, thermodynamics, mechanics, electronics, metallurgy, structures – but, suddenly, none of this engaged me. Jane and Oxford had exposed me to other delights. I knew that engineering was not for me. I stopped attending lectures and practicals altogether. I clung on to my place at the University by spending a painful, joyless day each week preparing inadequately for my tutorial.

I knew what did engage me. A notice went up at St Catherine's inviting someone to take over the college film society. I responded

with alacrity. The society had a camera and some film. A group of
us shot some silly comic sequences to learn the basics of film grammar. I raised my ambitions further: I considered setting up a
progressive University film society as a rival to the stuffy OUFS –
Oxford University Film Society – but the authorities, for once intol-
erant, would not allow it. I decided to direct a movie instead. The
equipment to record dialogue in those days was expensive and out
of reach, so I set out to make a short twenty-minute silent film with
a musical soundtrack. After a fight, OUFS donated film stock they
had been given by Kodak, and St Catherine's gave me a grant to
cover processing and production costs. David Aukin played the lead.
Peter Ibbotson, later to be editor of *Panorama* and a senior BBC
executive, was the cinematographer. I doorstepped a promising
undergraduate composer, Misha Donat – who would later do the
soundtrack for *Charlie Bubbles* and for Lindsay Anderson's *White Bus* –
and invited him to write the music. Jane and her friend Peggy were
responsible for the production design and costumes.

We shot the film in the luscious verdant spring of 1964. David
Aukin, in a billowing white shirt, moved slowly through a pictur-
esque English landscape, pouting and looking pained like Hamlet.
He languished moodily in a punt, trailing his fingers in the water as
he drifted through weeping willows. On his tortured journey David
encountered various women – a vamp who taunted him; a virginal
blonde who ran through the long grass with abandon; an elegant
woman in an evening gown who beckoned him in front of an audience, then slapped him persistently when he reached her.

David's misery was briefly relieved in a lyrical scene – conceived
and shot before any of us saw *Jules et Jim* – where he and a girl joy-
ously ride bikes together in a country lane. David had not previously
ridden a bike, and gamely learnt for the movie. The scene ended,
terrifyingly for such a novice rider, with David hurtling headlong
down Headington Hill, doing his best to disguise his terror from the
camera mounted on the back of an old borrowed van that was
barely able to stay ahead of him.

At the climax of the film, a girl in a white dress first gently strokes a lily, then David's head, cradled in her lap. When the girl starts to manhandle him, David turns – suddenly and mysteriously – into a small toy donkey. All this imagery seemed at the time fresh and pregnant with meaning!

Twenty years later, as a surprise for my fortieth birthday, Jane hired the Scala cinema in Oxford for various of our friends from university days and after, to picnic and to view some of our favourite films from the period. Jane also showed *The Little Donkey*. Twenty years on, the photography looked good and the music was still brilliant, but the film as a whole felt dated, adolescent and derivative. Its crude and crashing symbolism provoked hilarity from beginning to end. I could hardly bear to watch it. Nick Elliott called out at one point: 'Did Ingmar Bergman make *Wild Strawberries* before or after he saw *Little Donkey*?'

In 1960s Oxford, though, the première of *The Little Donkey* was taken more seriously. It was a major event, and drew big crowds. I made a splash. John McGrath – one of the creators of the groundbreaking *Z Cars* and an innovative BBC drama producer – formed a panel to discuss the film with veteran British director and cinematographer Jack Cardiff. Both were exceedingly polite and encouraging. I was taken seriously elsewhere. I was interviewed for *Isis*, the Oxford student magazine, and the noted writer Terry Coleman, who had an interest in student films, came up to Oxford specially to view *The Little Donkey*. He recorded in a full-length feature for the *Guardian* my disapproval of the established film societies at Oxford, and my admiration for D. H. Lawrence. He generously, if ambiguously, described my film as 'memorable' and 'unlike any other amateur film I have seen'. An over-enthusiastic film buff from Kingston Film Society characterised it as 'A visual experience of lyric quality . . . the overflowing, yearning desire for experience; the urge to move into new and exciting worlds; the passionate drive of youth . . .'

The Little Donkey was not an enduring masterpiece, but creating it at least taught me that I could make things happen, that I could get

things done. It was at Oxford that I discovered I could be purpose-
ful, focused and ambitious.

In the summer of 1964 Jane and I went to our first Commemoration
ball, at Magdalen, and wandered around the glorious grounds with
the other young things in our rented dinner suits and ballgowns,
enjoying fine food and drink and entertainment until a misty dawn
broke. The Rolling Stones were the main attraction. They had been
booked before they were famous and had reluctantly flown back
from America to appear when Magdalen had held them to their
contract. The dispute had caused bad feeling on both sides. Ambling
down Magdalen's cloisters before their set, I spotted the diminutive
Brian Jones coming towards me, head down, walking fast, not catching anyone's eye. A tall Guards-officer-type just by me spotted him
too. 'Little cunt!' he proclaimed loudly, with lofty disdain, as Jones, in
his hearing, scuttled by. The Stones, and their audience, were muted
at the beginning of their set. But, as they relaxed into their music,
they melted the audience's hostility. I saw the Stones as white men
singing black music, and never bought their records, but that hot
summer night – as I watched them play in front of an audience of a
few hundred people – I recognised them as superb live performers. I
could never have anticipated that, just three years later, my career
would be transformed by an encounter with Mick Jagger.

    That summer Jane took me to the United States so that we could
earn good money in holiday jobs. She served ice-cream in a soda
bar and I was a hotel photographer in the Catskill Mountains resort
area in upper New York State. On my first night, photographing
guests at their dinner tables, there was a loud bellowing. A commanding figure advanced on me, pointing: 'Get that Beatle outta
here!' It was the hotel's manager. Sheepishly, and with a thousand
pairs of eyes on me, I marched out like a red-carded footballer. I had
to go and work in more tolerant hotels.

    I found my first encounter with American business daunting: it was
far more ruthless and aggressive than anything I had experienced

in holiday jobs in the UK. But I loved America too, for its energy and enterprise, for the sense of individual possibility, for its can-do conviction and determination.

Back in Oxford for a second year, I was commissioned by an art gallery to make a documentary about a young sculptor who was holding an exhibition there. As a result, I met Jonathan Gili, whom I invited to edit the film. Jonathan would become one of Britain's most accomplished documentary-makers. I had been impressed by his work on *Isis*, where, each week, he reviewed every film shown in Oxford. He would watch four or five movies on a Monday, pedalling furiously from cinema to cinema, writing his reviews overnight to meet his Tuesday deadline. Jonathan appreciated, as Jane and I did, the artfulness of the best American cinema. He drooled over *Breakfast at Tiffany's*, as well as the French *nouvelle vague*. Like me, he admired few British movies. Jonathan analysed films with real erudition and insight, and raised my understanding of cinema. He and Misha Donat boldly devoted a whole edition of *Isis* to a close analysis of a single film – Joseph Losey's *The Servant* – interviewing Losey and other key members of the production team.

Jane and I became good friends with Jonathan and his girlfriend – later wife – Phillida. Jonathan's parents, Elizabeth and Juan, often invited the four of us to Sunday lunch at their north Oxford home. Juan, a Catalan, was an antiquarian bookseller; Elizabeth had written a Spanish cookbook. This was my first encounter with a gracious, erudite and sophisticated household. We ate piperade, hare with chocolate sauce, or lamb – red-raw and studded with garlic; and we drank fine Spanish wines. Eating at the Gilis' table was our initiation into good food. Jane and I soon discovered, as would our whole generation, a second Elizabeth, the cookery writer Elizabeth David. We were bowled over by her vivid descriptions of Mediterranean cuisine, placing it in its social and cultural context. Elizabeth David helped make the Mediterranean style of living an aspirational ideal for a generation which craved an exotic alternative to the grey drabness and uniformity of post-war Britain – a Britain where only the chemist sold olive oil.

Towards the end of my second year, I tasted failure. I tried to set up a full, professional 35mm feature film. I wrote a script, a thinly veiled autobiography, and tried to raise the money. I went to see the Boulting Brothers and various distributors. They were courteous but did not want to invest. Then I had a break. The National Film Finance Corporation agreed to put up the bulk of the money. I searched for the remainder, advertising in *The Times* for investors. A South African businessman replied. I met him at his luxury flat in Regent's Park and he agreed to provide the rest of the funding. I began assembling a crew and cast – a mixture of professional and Oxford actors. Bob Scott – who, as Sir Robert Scott, later tried valiantly to bring the Olympics to Manchester – had one of the lead parts. But the South African disappeared and never came through with the cheque. I was inexperienced, had been gullible and had not pinned him down. The film had to be abandoned and a large crew dispersed. I felt chastened and humiliated.

At the end of the summer, after two years at Oxford, Jane and I married in Washington DC. My mum sailed over for the wedding. This was to be my last excursion into Catholicism. My faith had weakened but it had not yet finally expired. Jane tolerated my wish to marry in a Catholic church. Family history was repeating itself. I had to seek Cardinal Heenan's permission to marry a Protestant. Jane experienced the torment of a compulsory summer of instruction in the Catholic faith from a severe and humourless Irish-American priest, who detected our sixties free-thinking liberalism and could not mask his distrust of us. After some years' absence, it was a shock for me to encounter the Church again at its most rigid.

On the day of the wedding I was infused with happiness and optimism. As Jane and I stood at the altar and made our solemn promises, I felt a sudden surge of warmth towards the dour and imposing cleric standing before us. Spontaneously I winked at him. I did it to share my joy, but he hesitated mid-sentence and his jaw dropped. In the priest's look I saw first suspicion, then fury: he interpreted my wink as a disavowal of all our promises – which in a sense it was. That was the moment I became an unqualified atheist. The priest failed to turn up at the reception. After a rowdy American send-off, Jane and I returned to Southampton on the *Queen Mary* to face our final year at Oxford.

I had considered dropping out of my final year, leaving to find a job in film or television. I knew for certain that I didn't want a career in engineering. I had devoted all my time in Oxford to film, virtually abandoning my studies. Alan Bullock, Don Schultz and the college authorities had tolerated this, they said, because they could see I was making my mark on university life. The prospect of re-engaging with engineering was dreadful. But the sense that a job started should be completed, which my parents had taught me, and the fear that I would be letting them down if I didn't obtain a degree, persuaded me to press on. I would have to do three years' work in one. I had a mountain to climb and it would be a character-forming experience.

Jane dropped me off each morning at college in a little second-hand Morris minivan we had bought with money from wedding gifts. I would sit all day in the college library and plough through textbooks on every branch of engineering, occasionally turning to my fellow students for help on an issue that stumped me. I allowed myself one treat each day – an action that would have a significant impact on my later career. Before I settled down to study each morning, I spent an hour in the Junior Common Room reading serious newspapers for the first time in my life. One story drew me in above all others: the crisis in Rhodesia, still a British dependency. The white minority had resisted a vote for blacks. In November 1965 the white leader, Ian Smith, announced UDI – a unilateral declaration of independence. Harold Wilson's government responded with sanctions, predicting that the end of the conflict was 'weeks, not months' away. I became fascinated by the unfolding drama: I followed every twist and turn of the plot, reading every commentary.

This was the modest beginning of my interest in politics. In the mid-sixties, few in my generation at Oxford focused on mainstream political issues. That would come later. There were politicos who debated in the Oxford Union, and we knew who Tariq Ali was when we passed him in the street. We instinctively supported the liberal agenda of an end to hanging and a prohibition of racialism. But not much that we would have called political pressed upon us. There were no causes to fire us up. Vietnam bubbled away, but it was an American issue. Everyone was in work. We knew we would have our choice of job when we graduated. We were unaware of the Keynesian idyll coming to an end, the poisonous interplay between employment and inflation that would explode in the 1970s and dominate our lives. We didn't take in that the planners were destroying important parts of our cities, bulldozing communities and building ghettos. We were concentrating instead on having a good time.

My final exams loomed. The biggest test would be the practicals. I had done no laboratory work at all for three years. The engineering department decided that I alone in my year should have two extra practical exams in addition to my written papers. A few other miscreants would have one. I presented myself early one summer morning. I was escorted down to the basement of the engineering laboratory and shown a massive turbine towering above me hissing steam. I was handed a short piece of paper with an instruction: 'Measure the specific entropy of steam at 600°F and 150 p.s.i.'

A year in the library had given me a grounding in theory, so I understood the question. But I had never operated such a fearsome machine, and I am notoriously impractical with physical things. My first concern was not to blow myself up and the whole building with me. None the less, I had three hours as well as an exam to pass, so I set out to determine from theory and by deduction what all the knobs and levers and valves and gauges were for; and I busked my way intuitively through the billowing steam and the clanging and the banging to a graph and an answer that I handed in when my three hours were up.

On the second day I was presented with a soldering iron and a pile of transistors and condensers and switches and wires, and asked to build a radio set with particular characteristics. At the end of the three hours Don Schultz, my tutor, who was invigilating, came over to me with a great smile on his face. He picked up the imaginative electronic contraption I had built and held it up by a loose wire at arm's length, as if it were a rat. The whole room collapsed in hysterical laughter.

I fared better in my written tests. After the final exam, I leapt in the air, relieved to be free at last. On this, my last Oxford day, I punted down river with my mum and dad, Jane and her parents, and picnicked in the sun. Later in the summer, I was thrilled to learn I had got my degree, genuinely proud of my self-taught Third.

In the spring of 1966, as I studied for my exams, I had also been looking for a job. John McGrath took me under his wing and arranged for me to meet someone in a small film production company in Soho who offered me work. But the prospects for the British film industry were not good, and television seemed much more appealing. Jane and I had bought a television in our final year. Two broadcasters stood out for quality and innovation – the BBC and Granada TV. We had particularly enjoyed the BBC's Wednesday Play, and Granada's series based on the short stories of D. H. Lawrence. I applied to both organisations. A fallback plan that I considered was to join the police. I was drawn by the prospect of adventure, but put off by the ethos and quickly rejected the notion.

At the BBC I was interviewed by a dry and dusty but kindly man from personnel in a three-piece suit who put me forward for the prestigious general trainee scheme. I reached the last ten or so. I then faced a panel not unlike the one I had encountered three years earlier at Merton College, but this time even fiercer. I easily held my own on the arts but stumbled during a long and testing cross-examination on editorial policy. What should the BBC's response be, I was asked, if it were faced with convincing research demonstrating that a substantial proportion of its audience held racialist views? Should the BBC make racialist programmes? It was an ingenious question and I was out of my depth. I couldn't on my feet resolve the tension between the instinct to be democratic on the one hand, to reflect all views, and on the other the desire to be civilised and to denounce racialism. I still had had little exposure to this kind of argument, and it showed. I was very disappointed but not surprised to receive my letter of rejection from the BBC.

The interviews with Granada were an altogether different experience. Mike Wooller, one of Granada's senior producers, conducted the first interview in friendly, relaxed but attentive fashion, and let me make my case. Invited to Manchester for a long day of interviews, I was shepherded into a huge committee room with perhaps fifty others, some of whom I knew from Oxford. We were called out individually for interview. Every few hours Mike Wooller would read out a list of ten names and without sentiment would tell the failed candidates that they could go. This was a cruel cull, but I felt a giddy surge of excitement each time I survived. It made me want the job even more. The main interview was with a large panel including Denis Forman – Granada's Managing Director – and David Plowright – editor of *World in Action*. I was given an easy platform to express my views. I was confident and outspoken. They were clearly impressed that I had made two films, and that Terry Coleman had written about me prominently in the *Guardian*. The modish movie of the moment was Karel Reisz's *Morgan – a Suitable Case for Treatment*. The panel was impressed by the film, but I cockily disparaged it. The Oxford film set didn't value British films of this kind. The interviewing panel didn't resent, indeed they seemed to relish, a contrary viewpoint. I stayed in at the next selection and was taken to the executive floor to meet what appeared to me to be two decidedly old Jewish gentlemen, Sidney and Cecil Bernstein, in a wood-panelled room. They were gentle. They wanted to know about my family experience, about growing up in Liverpool, about what my dad did – just as Dr Schultz had three years before. Half an hour later I stayed in at the final cull and was offered a job at Granada as a production trainee, starting in the autumn.

I enjoyed my last months of freedom before work. Joseph Losey came to Oxford to film Harold Pinter's screenplay *Accident* with Dirk Bogarde, Stanley Baker and Michael York. Jonathan Gili knew Losey from writing about him, and he and Phillida were offered work as extras. Jane, described at the time by Phillida as a striking beauty, was stopped in the street by an assistant director and offered work too. Jonathan and Jane drew me into the production. I had only just passed my test but I agreed to drive the props vehicle – a great rusting hulk of a Bedford van which swayed frighteningly on the gentlest curve and seemed almost to have no brakes. Then I became an extra. I can be seen in the final film playing football in a purple shirt on a distant lawn in Magdalen. Jane, Jonathan and Phillida had foreground scenes. Jane was in a small group that Pinter coached to provide background dialogue.

We accumulated just enough money from all this activity to go to Greece. A friend borrowed his father's two-seater Triumph Vitesse, and offered Jane and me a ride. The three of us took turns to drive and to be jammed on to the narrow, uncomfortable back shelf. Driving dangerously, around the clock, through Germany, Austria and Yugoslavia, we reached Athens in forty-eight hours. Then we took the ferry to a still undeveloped Mykonos. Our money was tight. There was only enough for yoghurt and honey at breakfast, fruit for lunch and a modest dinner, and we had to walk everywhere on the island. We soon became tanned, fit and slender.

At the end of September we drove back to Manchester to begin a long life of work.

5

Having a Nice Time

I was one of nine production trainees who started at Granada Manchester in October 1966, most of us intent on a career in television drama. My colleagues were a jolly and lively-minded group. I became closest to Nick Elliott, whose work as an actor I'd long esteemed at Oxford, and whom I would come to enjoy for his merciless candour about himself and everyone else. Other close friends were Andrea Duncan (later Wonfor), a friendly, unaffected Geordie; and Andy Mayer, who had been president of the Cambridge Footlights, and whose permanently benign, impish and quizzical expression always lifted my spirits and prompted a smile.

The main purpose of Granada's well-regarded course – presided over by a conscientious and meticulous director, Dick Everitt – was to give us a thorough grounding in studio production. We spent time with each of the many technical sections involved in making a television programme, and we were given formal instruction by Dick on the craft of studio direction. In the mid-1960s, videotape editing was in its infancy, and most studio-bound programmes were recorded as live without editing. Marshalling three or four cameras and two sound booms which cast long shadows was a planning as well as a creative challenge. Each camera had multiple lenses on a rotating turret, and there was an audible clang (which viewers could hear at home) whenever the operator shifted from one lens to another. The cameras were connected by cables to the studio wall. Each camera covering a scene had to be released at just the right moment if it was to reach the next scene by the time it was needed.

Dick Everitt showed us how to use transparent plastic protractors to select the right lens; and he demonstrated how we should rehearse our moves with little cardboard cameras attached by string to a drawing pin on a paper floorplan, to guard against our camera cables tangling up on the floor – the ultimate directorial sin!

The production trainees were widely resented within Granada. A director's job was the big prize for a camera operator or a floor manager, and this great gang of mostly Oxbridge twenty-one-year-olds was not only inexperienced and ignorant but was also standing in their way. We did several studio-based exercises of increasing ambition during the course and our tentative instructions were invariably greeted with heavy sarcasm.

Our course focused on drama. But one day, out of the blue, we were asked to write a five-minute news script and to illustrate it with cardboard captions. A hard-bitten old newspaper journalist was to supervise us. The other trainees protested: our expertise was in drama and the arts; few of us had any interest in current affairs. I wrote a script about the one story I had really followed – the Rhodesia crisis – and my relative expertise was noted.

In order that we might appreciate and savour Granada's roots, Sidney Bernstein insisted that all the trainees should spend one week working in a Granada cinema. Andy Mayer and I were assigned to the Granada Walthamstow in east London. The manager was unsure what to do with us, but he began by showing off to us his extensive model train set, which ran through his office and out

'But we have nine trainees to place,' came the counter. '*Someone* has to go to *World in Action* – and you're the only trainee who has any interest in current events at all!' I became a reluctant and untutored addition to an experienced *World in Action* team, many of whom had been journalists for decades. On my first day I was bemused when asked to extract some routine information from the Home Office. An older researcher took me in hand and explained that large organisations like the Home Office had press offices that could answer my queries.

David Plowright, *World in Action*'s executive producer, soon gave me a programme of my own to research – on what sort of religious and ethical teaching was needed in state schools. He impressed me greatly with his challenging and systematic probing of the programme proposition that emerged from my research. He was a slightly shy and reserved but dogged ex-newspaperman from Scunthorpe. I came to know him as a decent, moral and straight-dealing man, with a deep conviction about getting stories right. He finally gave the go-ahead for the programme I proposed. I found helping the producer Ingrid Floering to shape the film that emerged immensely enjoyable. When it was transmitted, the programme was well received. Working on current affairs didn't seem so bad after all.

In the spring and summer of 1967 the big story was about Mick Jagger. A huge squad of police officers had raided a party at Keith Richard's home and found drugs, including four amphetamine tablets in Jagger's jacket, for which he did not have a prescription. During his trial in June, Jagger spent three nights in Brixton – one of the most forbidding of Britain's jails – and was manacled during his trips to and from court. He was found guilty and given a three-month sentence, but was released on bail pending an appeal.

Jagger's case was a cause célèbre. The prosecution was seen as persecution. The inadequacy of the trial and the disproportionately heavy sentence inflamed the young. It was suspected that the Stones were a target because they undermined respect for authority, because they were hedonistic and free living. It was this assault on our values and attitudes – and not drugs – that was the battle line for the young.

There was an unexpected twist to the tale: a stuffy, donnish pillar of the establishment, William Rees-Mogg, editor of *The Times*, borrowed a line from William Blake and wrote an editorial entitled 'Who breaks a butterfly on a wheel?' Rees-Mogg argued that Jagger was being pilloried for his beliefs rather than for his crimes. He defied convention himself by writing about a matter that was still before the courts.

David Plowright agreed to my suggestion that *World in Action* should try to mount a programme on the affair. Jagger was hard to reach. He had many journalists trying to get to him, and was defended by protectors on all sides. I spoke to his lawyers, to his management, to anyone I could. I hassled hard. I had some advantages: I was twenty-two years old, convincingly sympathetic on the issues; and I could offer peak-time exposure on ITV on the nation's highest-rated current affairs programme. Jagger and his manager, Andrew Loog-Oldham, finally agreed to see me. I suggested that Jagger was bound to win the appeal, and proposed that we should mount a programme to mark the occasion. I wanted, I said, to do something that would reflect the new outlook of the young in form as well as in substance, that would be an emblematic sixties event. Jagger was non-committal. His main concern was that he might be going to jail, a prospect he dreaded. Nothing was resolved.

Days passed and I heard nothing. I decided to be bold and inveigled Jagger's private home number from one of his coterie and called him direct. Jagger answered. I pressed him to take the notion seriously. He invited me round to his Harley House flat on the Marylebone Road to discuss a way forward. We continued our deliberations at the recording of the twin-sided single 'We Love You/Dandelion' which he was planning to release to coincide with his appeal. Jagger finally agreed that we would make and broadcast the programme on the day of the appeal, but only after the outcome was known. We considered a pastoral setting away from the city, in the English countryside, something of a party, with friends milling round. We finally settled on a conversation between Jagger and Rees-Mogg and a panel chosen to represent the establishment, retaining the notion of a country backdrop.

The appeal was heard on a hot, cloudless day in July. Jagger's sentence was quashed by the Lord Chief Justice. The press conference was held at Granada's offices in Soho. When I started taking charge, Allen Klein, Jagger's burly American co-manager, demanded brusquely: 'Who's this guy, Mick?' I escorted Jagger to Battersea heliport in a white Jaguar driven at speed by a stunt driver to shake off the press. Jagger's girlfriend, Marianne Faithfull, was waiting for us at Battersea, sporting a tiny, eye-catching mini-skirt, which showed off the whole length of her famously long, shapely legs. In the helicopter, Faithfull sat between Jagger and myself – jammed tightly between us on the small bench-seat behind the pilot. We flew out along the Thames, then swung north, flying low over the lush Essex countryside. I drank in the glories of the midsummer panorama, but Faithfull's attention was directed elsewhere: she launched herself at Jagger – pawing him, kissing him passionately, writhing, her pert bottom grinding against my flank on the tight seat. I tried to concentrate on the view.

When we landed at our destination – the magnificent seat of the Lord Lieutenant of Essex – I escorted Mick and Marianne to a bedroom. I told them they could freshen up and rest before the interview, which was in a few hours' time. I had misinformed them: when I went downstairs John Shepherd, the stylish Granada director who had acted as a sympathetic mentor to me during the ups and downs of the project, told me there had been a change of plan. The live transmission link to the network was unreliable. To be on the safe side, we had to record the interview immediately, and send the tape by car to London. Where was Mick, Shepherd asked? I returned nervously to the room, and knocked on the door. There was no reply. I knocked again. Still no reply.

'Mick, it's John.'

After a long pause, a weary response: 'Yer?'

'I'm sorry, Mick. You have to come right away . . .' I explained why. There was another pause.

'OK.'

Mick soon emerged in a flowing white shirt to confront and confound the representatives of the establishment assembled on the lawn. The Labour government of the day would not participate. However, a previous Labour Home Secretary, Frank Soskice – by now Lord Stow Hill – had agreed to appear. John Robinson, the Bishop of Woolwich, represented the Church. Rees-Mogg had insisted on having a Catholic on the panel, so an ancient white-haired Jesuit intellectual, Father Corbishley, was an inquisitor too. Soskice and Robinson sat on a garden bench, Rees-Mogg and Corbishley behind a small patio table. The gentle late-afternoon breeze ruffled Jagger's hair.

This panel of upper-crust gentlemen spoke slowly with careful diction and complete courtesy: 'Mick, do you think the society that you live in is one that you ought to rebel against?' one asked. 'Where would you draw the line where freedom ends and constraint begins?' another reasonably inquired. Jagger never quite gained his normal fluency in the interview – he appeared tranquillised. But by the end of the programme he had more or less set out his position. He mainly just wanted to have as good a time as possible, he said; but he *was* rebelling, things *were* wrong. The law shouldn't intervene in personal matters. Heroin was a crime against yourself, not society. Suicide and homosexuality had been crimes quite recently, even if they were no longer. The law could change, but it was too difficult to instigate change. Power was in the wrong hands. Coloured people – as Jagger termed them – argued with peaceful means in America, but got nowhere. Politicians got bogged down and achieved little.

I sat on the grass by Jagger and the group, out of shot, listening to this discourse. I was a little numb after an intense day and a busy few weeks; but I was also pleased that an idea I had proposed and driven had come off, that I had broken a mould, that there had been a dialogue between generations, however fumbling, and that my second-ever television programme would make such a splash.

The newspapers the next day brimmed with coverage of the interview as well as the appeal. Granada was thrilled to have created such a stir, and I was immediately summoned up to Manchester to see David Plowright to be congratulated and to be promoted to director.

I came down to earth with a thud. As the most junior of Granada's directors, I was assigned to the least challenging programmes. I cut a feature film into twenty-minute chunks for a children's series. I directed *What the Papers Say*. I worked on *All Our Yesterdays*, and the producer didn't like the way I edited the archive film.

My lowest point was a programme called *Time for a Laugh*. Cecil Bernstein had bought a job-lot of old cartoons. Thousands of individual spools were piled high in a Granada cutting room, uncatalogued, under the supervision of Granada's oldest and most enthusiastic but least creative film editor. My job was to manufacture cheap fillers for the transmission schedule of five, ten, fifteen and twenty minutes' duration, composed of cartoons linked by the amiable folk singer and guitarist Wally Whyton. I spent months diving at random into the cartoon mountain. I would view the *Felix the Cat* or *Popeye* episode I'd grabbed, and I would keep on searching through the other cartoons until I could concoct a programme with a spurious theme linking one cartoon with the next. I would then phone Wally who would create a link by writing a new verse to some old song. On studio day we would process these programmes through the studio rapidly, like cars on a production line.

I took pleasure from new friendships at Granada if not from my new work. Nick Elliott had been assigned to do the television equivalent of national service on Granada's live nightly local magazine programme. He was having hair-raising experiences of his own:

one day he featured the word's largest dog which bent down and bit off – live – the head of the world's smallest dog. Nick and I also started watching Manchester United. I remained at root a Liverpool fan, but in the following years we watched Matt Busby's Best/Law/Charlton/Stiles/Crerand team play the most enchanting and inspired football I would ever see.

Nick and Andy Mayer both married – Gilly and Tess respectively – and settled near Jane and myself in Altrincham. Nick bought a red Mini and drove us all to work. Our journeys were full of laughter and gossip, and terror – for Nick was the most daredevil of drivers.

On one of our death-defying rides Andy and I idly conceived an entertainment show we thought we would both like to watch. We christened it *Nice Time*, and submitted the idea to David Plowright, newly promoted to Granada's head of programmes. David commissioned a pilot, then three series over the next two years, which I would produce. It was a blessed relief to be able to say goodbye to the cartoon mountain.

Nice Time was a fast-paced show with around twenty short items in half an hour, linked by brief, silly sketches. It was presented by Kenny Everett and Germaine Greer – in their first television roles – and by the veteran Jonathan Routh. Later, Sandra Gough – Irma Barlow from *Coronation Street* – joined the team.

Nice Time was a celebration of working-class humour and popular culture, which used real people to entertain. It began each week with a musical item: a choir of George Brown lookalikes singing 'My Way'; or a percussion group of teeth tappers; or some George Formby impersonators with ukuleles singing 'I'm Leaning on a Lamp-post'; or an ensemble of ventriloquists' dummies mouthing 'The Legend of Xanadu'. Every week Jonathan, Kenny and Germaine visited the markets and fairgrounds of Bury, Bolton, Blackpool and other northern towns and asked fat ladies in bloomers to tell us about their first kiss; or gentlemen pensioners to improvise a western shoot-out; or a group of holidaymakers to march and to whistle 'Colonel Bogey'; or men in a pub to strip naked a shop-window dummy. We would ask people what most annoyed their spouse; or to play on a drum kit; or to make a clay pot on a wheel. We asked very young children to tell us the largest number they knew; famous architects to build sandcastles; and northern window cleaners to reveal the secrets of what they saw.

Nice Time involved real people in other ways. A gang of French students who spoke no English were shown films of vaudeville comedians acting in the English music-hall tradition. Then they were dressed in loud jackets and straw hats and asked to read out well-known gags in English – which they did with gallic panache but with the emphasis hilariously and unknowingly in the wrong places. We mounted competitions: the camera would track down a long line of men in the studio dressed as vicars. Only two were real; viewers were invited to guess which. Jim Callaghan, Patrick Gordon Walker and other politicians told jokes. We assembled TV treats: we showed a sixty-second montage of Bobby Charlton's best goals; or of Elsie Tanner's most angry moments. Leslie Halliwell – the renowned film authority – selected the most entertaining sequences for us from musical cinema – songs from Eddie Cantor or Jimmy Durante or dance sequences directed by Busby Berkeley. In an item true to the period, *Nice Time*'s curvaceous, scantily clad bikini girl – Kenny's studio assistant – was put on a rotating pedestal for sixty seconds and ogled closely by the camera. At the end of the programme each week, we organised a surprise: 'If you live in Gas Street, Bradford,' Kenny would say, 'look out of the window and you'll see a big removal van. Go and bang on the door and a big brass band will march out and play for you for an hour!' And this really would happen – though it was something different each week, like an elephant to ride.

Our most successful item ever was a much publicised national competition to discover the worst male and female singers in Britain. Thousands applied: Tom and Phoebe won. They were a supremely self-confident couple who could belt out a song with real relish and power – but they were wholly, sublimely, resonantly off-key. Their 'Cinderella, Rockafella' duet brought the house down every time.

Nice Time was an immediate success in its late-Sunday-afternoon slot, appealing both to working-class taste and to the progressive young. Kenny and Germaine became instant stars. The programme was also a succès d'estime. Philip Purser, the long-standing critic of the *Sunday Telegraph*, declared *Nice Time* to be one of the best three television programmes of all time. Len Deighton, on the other hand, wrote to Sidney Bernstein suggesting that those responsible for the programme 'must be the worst people in the world'.

Nice Time was both a great comedy machine and a complex logistical operation. We had a large team of young writers supplying ideas for items and how to shape them: Michael Palin and Terry Jones before *Monty Python*; Graeme Garden and Tim Brooke-Taylor before *The Goodies*; Clive James, Mick Sadler, Fred Metcalf, Chris Allen and Gillian Reynolds before their distinguished careers had taken off. A large team of researchers made things happen, with Marian Nelson as the lynchpin. Claudia Milne, later a force in the independent sector, started her TV career as a researcher on *Nice Time*. The average age of the team was twenty-two. Life seemed like one long party.

But there were more than a few hiccups. The programme's success brought me more contact with senior Granada executives. I was summoned to see Granada's Managing Director, Denis Forman. Denis, unlike David Plowright, was a grandee with a strong sense of his own importance, and with little sense of silly sixties fun. The great man had had an idea. *Nice Time* should create a perfect, luxury environment for . . . a hen! We should research what a hen would most like and *Nice Time* should provide, in Denis's words, 'for its every whim'. I jumped to it and passed on the idea to my bemused team.

Nice Time's researcher came up with few insights about a hen's deepest desires, but we did our best and in due course Granada's designers produced a spacious plywood construction with an area for the hen to sleep and rest in, with soft flooring and clean hay; a dining area with a multiple choice of all the food a hen might find delicious; and a play area with various perches and obstacles to keep a hen's body exercised and its mind stimulated.

The nation's smartest young team of comedy writers was called into play. They were stumped. They could come up with no elegant way of developing the item, of giving it a beginning, a middle and an end. But needs must. A voice-over script of some sort was cobbled together. A plump and pretty hen was selected and introduced to her flat with a fanfare in front of a live studio audience. The hen, however, stood rooted to the spot, terrified. Various attempts were made to shoo her around her choice, luxury accommodation. But she wouldn't budge. Then she collapsed and died. Thankfully, Denis had been too busy to see the item. He beamed with pleasure when I duly reported to him what a great success it had been.

Later on we had a surplus of *Nice Time* T-shirts, and decided to give them away to our viewers in one of our end-of-programme events. As *Nice Time* became more successful, these events were drawing sizeable crowds, so we realised we had to limit attendance in some way. We devised our worst idea ever: viewers would receive a T-shirt only if they produced a dog. We pinpointed a small street in Wigan. Germaine duly waited there with a member of the team and a small van full of T-shirts. The announcement of the giveaway was made on air. Within minutes, about five hundred people, mostly children and men with flat caps, turned up with a great assortment of every kind of dog – Jack Russells, Alsatians, spaniels, boxers, Pekinese. They all converged on Germaine, desperate to claim their prize, holding up their yapping pets in her face in support of their claim. In the press of the crowd, the dogs became over-excited, snapping, snarling and growling at each other and at any human close at hand. The T-shirts were quickly snatched away, but more dogs and more people kept arriving. A full-blown dog riot – with fighting on a grand scale – was now in progress. The front fences of a whole row of houses were trampled, then the gardens. A kindly couple gave Germaine refuge and a brandy. Quickly recovering, she called me at home in Altrincham.

It was a Sunday afternoon. I had never smoked cigarettes and hardly drank alcohol. I have only ever smoked pot about half a dozen times, but this particular afternoon, with the dog riot in progress, had been one of them. As Germaine explained the situation to me, her words were almost drowned by a cacophony of barking in the background. My brain was fuzzy, my thinking slow. I could barely focus on a course of action. I took Germaine's number and encouraged her to stay put. Soon Granada's duty officer was on the line: the police and the press were already complaining. Struggling to frame a thought, I finally agreed a line of regret and a statement that we would compensate all the residents. The police escorted Germaine to safety and the crowds eventually dispersed. Germaine never complained about our miscalculation: for her it had been a great adventure.

Jonathan Routh brought experience to the *Nice Time* team. He also extended Jane's and my social horizons, and added to the joy of our lives with his abiding eccentricities. Jonathan lived in succession with two rich partners – Bobby Hamlyn, Paul Hamlyn's former wife, and Olga Deterding, the oil heiress. He often invited us to parties at their homes on Sundays. Jonathan introduced a warrenful of white rabbits to Bobby's house which would hop everywhere while we were served Black Velvets – a combination of champagne and Guinness. When he left Bobby and moved to Olga's, he introduced a completely convincing flock of stuffed sheep, which appeared to be grazing her thick pile carpet. Jonathan scattered raisins around as his parties progressed.

Then there was Kenny Everett. It emerged that he and I had parallel lives. He was born Maurice Cole in Liverpool in 1944 just fifteen days after me, the son of a tug-boat captain. After failing his eleven-plus, he went to the Catholic secondary modern a few hundred yards from my school, St Mary's. Kenny was uncomfortable and ill at ease at school – not one of the lads. His parents, like mine, moved to Formby. On leaving school he worked in a bakery, then in an advertising agency. Kenny also worked by himself, alone in his bedroom with his own tape recorder, making comedy tapes which he submitted to Radio Luxembourg, which recruited him. Kenny was an audio genius, able to weave comedy, effects and music together seamlessly. He had admired the DJ Jack Jackson, as had I. He progressed to the BBC which would fire him, shamefully, in 1970 for a harmless jest on air about the wife of the Minister of Transport. He had fantasised that she must have had to bribe an official to pass her driving test.

Kenny treated me as an elder brother. When he was recording *Nice Time*, he generally stayed with Jane and me in our flat in Altrincham, and we would chat into the small hours. In a frivolous moment in 1969 he proposed and lost a silly bet, and wrote out a cheque with a flourish payable to me for a million pounds – post-dated to 1999. The big struggle in Kenny's life was over his sexuality, and he shared that struggle with me. He gradually came to appreciate that he was attracted to men, but his upbringing made him uncomfortable with this. Like me, he hadn't even known about homosexuality when he was growing up. (When as a teenager I first heard words like 'queer' and 'poof' and 'faggot', I recognised they were disparaging but didn't understand what condition they referred to.) Kenny saw his homosexual leanings as an affliction. He took LSD – once with John Lennon at Weybridge – and pronounced himself cured: he proclaimed he now found women attractive.

Kenny started going out with Lee Middleton, a warm, maternal woman of plain good sense, a jazz singer who had been married to Billy Fury. They announced they would marry. It would be a great sixties event. Jane and I attended. Kenny and Lee were driven from the registry office to the party at their home in an open carriage pulled by a pair of white horses. Kenny was dressed in a pale, tight-fitting suit with a loose collar and a neck-scarf, and carried a single long-stemmed rose. Lee wore a white lace dress and a floppy, wide-brimmed hat, and carried her little Chihuahua dog. There was a mêlée of Kenny's friends in attendance – including a couple who, even in our innocence, we realised were transvestites. Someone laced the punch with acid, but Jane and I were warned, and avoided it.

Long after we stopped working together, Kenny and I continued to meet, lunching regularly throughout his life. One day around 1980, he finally broke out: he showed me a shockingly revealing picture of his Russian boyfriend Nikolai sitting naked on the toilet. He soon became outrageously and publicly gay, on and off the screen. Shortly before he died of Aids in 1995, aged fifty, he confessed – with a look that combined both a gleam of mischief and a tear – to having the fondest feelings for me. He regretted he wouldn't live long enough for me to cash his million-pound cheque.

I was bowled over immediately when I first encountered Germaine Greer at lunch with Andy Mayer at a steak house in Manchester when she came up to Granada for her *Nice Time* audition. Andy had worked with her in the Footlights. Germaine had an instant impact on everyone she met: she was tall, striking, funny, energetic, impulsive, caustic and shockingly honest – a formidable and ferocious life force. She was both an entertainer and an intellectual whirlwind with pronounced and considered views on a giddy array of issues great and small. She had not jumped at the chance of presenting *Nice Time*. She had finally agreed because of her admiration for Andy, and because she thought *Nice Time* would break new ground, and create 'happenings'.

Germaine was in the first rank of academics. She had done her masters at Sydney, and her Ph.D. at Cambridge on 'The Ethics of Love and Marriage in Shakespeare's Early Comedies'. She was enthralling when she spoke about literature. After Cambridge she went to teach at Warwick University. Kenny would sweetly pick her up where she lived in Leamington Spa on his way up north in his little red Fiat. This unlikely duo got on well together. He enjoyed

playing Germaine his favourite new music. She liked him because
she thought he was subverting the radio medium.

In Sydney, Germaine had been in a group of anarchic libertari-
ans. She found Britain and especially Cambridge sleepy and tried to
shake them up. The year before I met her, she had created a stir
with an article in *Oz* magazine, newly launched in London, on her
experiences of English sexuality: 'In Bed with the English'.
Germaine was the first counter-culture intellectual I had met. She
knew the historical antecedents of a movement with which I had an
instinctive sympathy. She liked to stir the pot, to challenge everything – but with reason and passion, never with bile or hate: she was
naturally good-hearted and tolerant. Germaine introduced me to
Richard Neville, the Australian editor of *Oz*, who became a friend.
I used to visit the *Oz* offices with her, which were home to a small
army of nonconformist individualists – older leftists who had
marched with CND, and younger activists who had emerged in the
late sixties, fired by disappointment with the Wilson government,
and by Vietnam. *Oz* itself, however, was much more rooted in the
mainline youth movement of the time in the celebration of a new,
freer lifestyle.

When Germaine was in Manchester, she took a room above the
saloon bar at the city's social epicentre, the Brown Bull, a scruffy
pub by a railway viaduct about half a mile from Granada's studios.
The Brown Bull was home to the free-living elements of the
Manchester United team, led by George Best; the *Nice Time* gang;
and various of Manchester's shady characters. All these groups were
allowed to drink at the Brown Bull after hours. On studio days, *Nice
Time* partied there. Once, the police mounted a late-night raid and
Germaine gave shelter in her darkened room to a large part of
Manchester United's forward line.

Germaine came to work one day with a surprise. She told us
that she had just married a builder called Paul de Feu. We had had
no warning of this. Her marriage lasted just three weeks. She soon
rebelled against the transition from lover to chattel, describing

marriage as 'sanctioned cruelty'. She went back into action and
wrote a paean to groupiedom entitled 'The Universal Tonguebath'.
She began to think about, then to write, the book about women that
would sweep the world and which would establish her as an icon of
the age – *The Female Eunuch*. I still have the proof copy she gave me
to read at the time.

During these momentous years, and amid the mind-stretching frivolity of *Nice Time*, our first child, our son Jonathan – or JJ to us –
was born, eight weeks earlier than expected, and weighing only 2lb
7oz. In the late 1960s, only a few babies survived at that weight. Jane
and I watched over JJ's fight for life in his incubator in Wythenshawe
Hospital in the most upsetting weeks we would ever experience.
Like many premature babies, he would be slow to grow, to develop
and to speak; but he would eventually turn into a beefy, sunny-
natured and academically brilliant man. My mum and dad and
nanna Anna came to Manchester to celebrate the first grandchild
and the first great-grandchild.

Germaine may have been writing *The Female Eunuch* when we
were working together, but feminist ideas were not yet current. I
behaved as a typical male of my period. There was no question that
my career would take precedence; that Jane and I should move to
Manchester when I was offered a job by Granada; and that I would
not be expected to change JJ's nappies or to take my share of
responsibility for looking after him. Soon Germaine and others
would change fundamentally and for the better how the world
thought about these issues.

Nice Time had its moment, then it came to an end: Kenny and I
and the others had new horizons to explore. For the very last *Nice
Time* ever, we mounted our most ambitious item: we revived – at
Tim Brooke-Taylor's suggestion – the historic backwards-walking
race, over the spine of the Pennines, from Macclesfield to Buxton, a
distance of twelve miles. We meant the race to be funny, but it
turned into a sombre, spectacular and thrilling sporting marathon.

Hundreds of athletes completed, each with a guide walking forward. The winner eventually struggled – backwards – exhausted, continuously falling, near to collapse, urged on by a large crowd, up the long steep hill into Buxton's town centre.

We held the party to celebrate the end of *Nice Time* – the end of my quintessential sixties experience – on a glorious summer's day in 1969 in the spacious grounds of a large country house near Oxford. We dressed in our sixties finery; we gambolled; we played games. Most of the team got drunk. A happy, splendid group, who had had a wonderful time together, laughed the afternoon away. I declared to Andy that I had had the best time doing the programme that I would ever have in my whole career in television.

At sunset, as we all began to make our way home, I suddenly saw Andy departing spectacularly – shooting along the top of the garden's high stone wall at 25 m.p.h., without any apparent means of support. In fact, though we couldn't see it, he was sitting on top of a Mini, driving along on the other side of the wall, his feet on the bonnet, his legs obscuring the drunken driver's vision. It was a fitting epitaph for an era in which we'd careered along to television success, buoyed up by some exciting creative talent, more than a dash of devil-may-care boldness and deep-seated camaraderie.

My own future had been settled. To my surprise, David Plowright had offered me, along with Gus Macdonald, the editorship of *World in Action*. I had been nervous about accepting: I was only twenty-four years old, and my experience of journalism had been limited to working on *World in Action* for just a few months. David talked me round: he said he wanted me to bring to the series the confidence and imagination that I'd demonstrated on the Jagger programme and with *Nice Time*. I had proved, he said, that I could create and manage a large team and a complex operation. Gus would bring the journalistic experience. As Gus put it, I'd supply the levitas, he the gravitas. I finally agreed, touched by David's faith in me.

At the end of the summer of 1969 – when man first walked on the moon, and on the final weekend before I joined *World in*

Action – Jane and I went to the last great event of the sixties: the first of the two spectacular Isle of Wight pop festivals.

We went in style. I was now earning good money. I wore a green suede jacket with snakeskin lapels, a Liberty print shirt with large rounded collars, trousers of a blue Scottish plaid and green boots with Java pythonskin toecaps I'd had made at Granny Takes a Trip on the King's Road. Unfortunately, I had to squeeze into this wonderful outfit because expense account living was beginning to make me chubby. Jane had boots from the same source made of a patchwork of brown and natural-coloured leathers overlaid with great gold stars. She wore a green embroidered kaftan and had her hair cut like Jane Fonda, whom we saw backstage. I had my hair to my shoulders, cut by Iain of Scissors in the King's Road (who cuts it still). In the previous few years, we'd first had a souped-up Mini, then a TR4. We drove to the Isle of Wight in our new Ford Mustang.

We had bought tickets in advance but worked a scam with friends to get into the backstage area and the press enclosure, which was bang in front of the stage. We had a magnificent close-up view. We saw and heard over that holiday weekend some of the best music of our time at its mature peak, including Bob Dylan, the Who and the Band. Two hundred thousand people attended. The mood was happy and peaceful. Men, women and children wore beads, necklaces and garlands of flowers. A naked woman walked on the heads of the crowd. This was the last summer of sixties innocence. A far bleaker decade was around the corner.

6

World in Action

As Gus Macdonald and I took over the helm of *World in Action*, the mood of the times was darkening. Protest, particularly over Vietnam, was intensifying, the youth movement radicalising. Britain's economy was deteriorating, its industry riven by union strife. Northern Ireland exploded in my first weeks on the programme.

Under David Plowright's leadership, Granada's documentary and journalism stable, including *World in Action*, had become the most pioneering and innovative in British television. *World in Action*'s early brashness had matured into hard-edged revelatory journalism. And Jeremy Wallington, one of the founding members of the *Sunday Times* Insight team, had been brought in to invent investigative journalism on television. The breakthrough was a *World in Action* in 1967 which demonstrated vividly how Rhodesian sanctions were busted. Granada had also been more alert than any other broadcaster to the significant cultural shifts of recent years — for instance, filming the Beatles at the Cavern and the Stones in the Park; being there in 1968 when Che Guevara's bullet-riddled body was brought in from the Bolivian jungle; chronicling the anti-war riots in Grosvenor Square.

Gus and I continued to plot the key litmus events and movements. We made editions about the values of hippies, the emerging women's movement, and contemporary notions of homosexuality – in a profile of Quentin Crisp. We made a powerful programme about the trial of the Chicago Eight, that year's cause célèbre for the alternative society which I had followed closely with Leslie Woodhead, the most talented of all Granada's directors. At the Democratic Convention in August 1968 there had been a mass demonstration of radicals and hippies in favour of the anti-war Presidential candidate, Eugene McCarthy, over the establishment Hubert Humphrey. Mayor Daley's Chicago police rioted. Hundreds of demonstrators were injured and many arrests made. The leaders of the different factions were put on trial – a rainbow coalition including Yippie anarchists Abbie Hoffman and Jerry Rubin, anti-war activists Tom Hayden and David Dellinger and Black Panther leader Bobby Seale. Each day during the trial, Bobby Seale was gagged and manacled to his chair in the dock because he refused to accept the jurisdiction of the court. Leslie won unprecedented access to the defendants and their legal team, and made an extraordinary film that captured the moment: the transition from the soft hedonism and anarchy of the mid-sixties to the tough, demanding protest politics of the late sixties.

I went with a team to the United States in November 1969 to make a film about one of the climactic anti-war events: the march of around three hundred thousand protesters on Washington. Nixon's government feared violence on an enormous scale. The massed ranks of the National Guard assembled to counter them. In the days before the march the protesters camped all over the city in community spaces and the offices of sympathetic groups. We filmed a myriad of factions – pacifists, liberals, leftists – getting ready to unleash their anger and let loose their convictions. The youth movement was becoming a ferocious and challenging force. The march, when it happened, was an extraordinary spectacle. At its climax, a large group of demonstrators massed in the centre of Washington attempting to put government buildings under siege. An agitated cordon of police with truncheons blocked their way. I was with a crew filming the front rank of demonstrators at government buildings on Constitution Avenue, who were becoming progressively more threatening. Suddenly the police fired a massive fusillade of tear gas. The air was instantly dense. Thousands of people – including me – turned and ran, sprinting through at least a hundred yards of thick, billowing gas, unable to see more than five yards in front; trampling on fallen, screaming demonstrators; gasping for oxygen, but sucking in only gas; feeling utter pain and panic.

Another special quality of Granada's programme-makers was their alacrity in harnessing new technology and production techniques: they had embraced the new lightweight cameras and fast film, and had learnt from US pioneers of fly-on-the-wall documentary-making, like D. A. Pennebaker (with whom I later worked). Gus and I employed these techniques in an edition which followed around a persistent offender on the first day of his release from prison, and veteran film-maker Denis Mitchell made a brilliant observational documentary for us about the Rev. Ian Paisley going about his business in the community and in his church.

The most original and experimental programme of the series was made by Leslie Woodhead, who had obtained an account – smuggled out by Swedish Amnesty – of the interrogation of a Russian dissident, General Grigorenko, who had been wrongly diagnosed as mentally unstable and confined to a Soviet psychiatric hospital. Leslie and I wrestled with what to do with the riveting insights the transcripts provided, and finally agreed to do the obvious, though it had not been done before: to reconstruct Grigorenko's experience with actors – to make a drama-documentary. Leslie would continue to pioneer this important programme form in the years ahead.

Being joint editor of *World in Action* was a real learning experience for me. With *Nice Time* I had learnt how to run a large team and a complex operation on a weekly turnaround. On *World in Action* I learnt how to assess the strength of a journalistic idea; to juggle multiple stories; to respond to sudden opportunities; to have the courage to kill a story that was going nowhere; to spend all night in a cutting room with an exhausted production team trying to bring shape and coherence to an ill-produced programme against an imminent transmission deadline. I learnt to have confidence in my analytical powers, and to follow my creative and journalistic impulses to help fashion strong programmes.

I learnt a great deal, too, from Gus Macdonald, who had a formidable array of skills I came to admire greatly. Gus was a few years older than me. He had been a shipyard apprentice in Glasgow, and had led a strike. He had been chairman of Gorbals Young Socialists, and then circulation manager of *Tribune*. He began freelancing as a journalist, then leapt into a staff position on the *Scotsman* before being recruited to *World in Action*'s investigation unit. He had lived at the sharp end in a way I had not and was worldly beyond his years. Gus was also a politico, at ease within the power structures, and not a sixties rebel. Nor was he a firebrand: he naturally looked for the reasonable way forward in any dispute – whether on the team, or between workforce and management (he was active in the union). He was funny and fluent in conversation and had brilliant powers of oratory, with the ability to sway mass meetings. A real operator, he networked across a range of liberal-left groups, national and international, and through them he found stories and gained entrées. Above all Gus was a salesman. Whereas I had the natural sixties tendency towards candour, a readiness to identify difficulties and reverses before successes, Gus greeted everyone with a pithy three-bullet-point summary of *World in Action*'s current triumphs. He was the first person I knew to perfect the soundbite.

In 1970 *World in Action* won a prize, and Gus and I went to collect it. We had been voted – by the readers of the new, upstart newspaper the *Sun* – Britain's best current affairs programme. Prime Minister Harold Wilson would present our award. We were told to wear dinner suits with black ties. Mindful of our radical credentials, Gus and I agonised over this. I compromised by getting a tailor who made outfits for pop stars in Carnaby Street to create for me a big, stylish suit out of black velvet, and a shirt and tie both made of a brilliant yellow Thai silk. Gus wore an ancient, heavy, black-and-white herringbone tweed suit, and he stuck out even more than I did.

When we arrived at Grosvenor House on Park Lane for the awards ceremony, which was to be broadcast live on ITV, we were met by a pair of tough, no-nonsense, middle-aged Australian executives from the Murdoch stable, which owned the *Sun*. They barked at us that only I should go on stage to receive the award and that Gus should remain in his seat. They could offer no rationale for this course of action, but were stubborn in their insistence. Gus and I conferred. We had been told that both Murdoch and Wilson were nervous of *World in Action* in general, seeing it as a den of leftists, and of Gus in particular, who was active in a media ginger group, the Free Communications Group. We speculated that either Murdoch or Wilson or both were afraid that Gus would embarrass the Prime Minister with a political speech. We determined to stand our ground. I informed the *Sun* executives that it would not be fair to Gus if only I were seen to win the prize, and that if they called my name alone I would remain in my seat and not go up on stage. The negotiations continued until the ceremony started. The *Sun* executives finally yielded and Gus and I both went up together – graciously and unprovocatively – to collect our award from the Prime Minister.

I made a mistake and I learnt a lesson. David Frost had emerged in the 1960s as a precocious screen talent. He had started as the face of satire on *That Was the Week That Was*, but had moved on quickly, embracing serious interviewing and business. He brought together the consortium, for instance, that had won the LWT franchise. Frost was prolific: in the UK he made programmes at the weekend for his fledgling LWT, and he flew across the Atlantic every week to make five long weekday programmes for a US network. He was a social force to be reckoned with too: his power breakfasts at the Connaught for major political, industrial and entertainment players attracted a great deal of attention, especially when the Prime Minister, Harold Wilson, attended one.

The hard-edged journos on *World in Action* felt that Frost had betrayed his satirical heritage, that he had signed up with the mighty when he should have kept his distance. We decided to make a programme about Frost and to draw out these issues, which, Gus and I agreed, I would produce. It would chiefly be a fly-on-the-wall observational documentary. The issues would emerge from our filming: Frost would hang himself. Our *World in Action* programme would also look into the allegations that had surfaced in *Private Eye* that David had abused his position as a founder of LWT to win preferential deals to supply programmes from his privately owned company. The researcher and I talked to various executives who had left LWT in one of the upheavals that had characterised the company's early history. They supported the claims made in *Private Eye*, although – now that they had left the company – they no longer had access to documentation to verify their allegations.

Frost agreed that we could follow him around on both sides of the Atlantic for a week. We asked sharp questions of his research team about his journalistic commitment; and of David himself – en route to a black-tie reception at Downing Street – about consorting with the establishment. But, while the fly-on-the-wall filming behind the scenes was entertaining, it did not reveal the story we had set out to tell. David and his team came over as serious-minded and professional, and they were convincing about their journalistic bona fides. I interviewed David at the Algonquin Hotel in New York, and put to him the allegations of impropriety, which he vigorously denied. We had no evidence to sustain them, so the interview fell flat.

David insisted we should come to his office in London, which we did, and he opened his files to us. We were able to see any contract we wanted. We were able to establish a clear audit trail in his business arrangements back to before LWT started. Our film was a damp squib with no edge. We had been gullible and we hadn't done our homework or thought things through. In addition, Denis Forman was irritated that we had set out to make a programme hostile to the interests of another ITV company without alerting him. He insisted we abandon the film. David was disappointed that a programme that had shown him in such a good light was never broadcast. I learnt a lesson from this unhappy episode that I would never forget: allegations had to be bottomed out; they had to be sustainable.

Stephen Clarke taught me a valuable lesson too. Stephen was a serious-minded producer on *World in Action* who investigated a series of derailments on British Railways and established that they were caused by the instability of a particular kind of goods wagon, which was ubiquitous across the system. It was a dry and complex story and Gus and I were sceptical it could be told on television. Stephen insisted it could – and, with models and graphics, mounted a gripping programme with a compelling narrative. The programme was a revelation to me. I discovered that, with television, difficult and complex issues could be explained and addressed visually.

I felt in my element at *World in Action* innovating with new forms, moving the medium on, chronicling the radical agenda. Granada's programme-makers themselves, picking up the mood of the times, were also radicalising and instinctively on the side of the underdog. (We had been comfortable making programmes about Northern Ireland's oppressed Catholic minority and resented the ITA – the broadcasting regulators – requiring us to make programmes explaining the Loyalist point of view.) Yet I felt uneasy. I was becoming increasingly aware of the mainstream issues pressing upon us. Britain's economy was declining relative to those of other countries. Union disputes had been growing, but reform blocked. I was acutely conscious that no one on the team – including myself – had the ideas, insights or understanding to swim in the mainstream, to explain what was happening. I was becoming increasingly aware that most of our work highlighted problems, never solutions. Moreover, I was not entirely happy working as *World in Action*'s editor. Jane, JJ and I had moved to London just before I was appointed to the programme, so I was working in Manchester during the week, and returning to London – if I was lucky and there was no programme crisis – at the weekend. On top of all this, I was still only twenty-five and I had a strong feeling that I had become a programme executive too early in my career: I wanted to work a little longer as a programme producer. Gus had a similar feeling. David Plowright agreed we could both go back to pro-gramme-making after our first year as editors.

At the end of the summer of 1970, Jane and I went to our second Isle of Wight pop festival. The sweet spirit of the previous year had evaporated. A far bigger number – around five hundred thousand people – attended. The island bulged. Activists demanded that the festival should be free, and attacked and breached the perimeter fence. A steady stream of abuse, much of it in German, French and Dutch, was aimed at the press enclosure. I listened to the Doors with my back to the stage, watching out for the beer bottles and cans that were regularly hurled towards us. The atmosphere was so oppressive that Jane and I returned to London, and thus tragically missed Jimi Hendrix, who died of a drug overdose the following month. In the course of that year there was another pop tragedy: the Beatles were gradually breaking up, riven by personal, creative and business dif-ferences. I felt a gaping hole had opened up in my life – a real heartache, as if my youth was over.

In what would be my last year at Granada, I had a brief to make spe-cials. With Andy Mayer, my main collaborator on *Nice Time*, and a talented troupe of actors, I experimented with improvisation to pro-duce an hour of comedy – which had charm but no punch – called

Flat Earth. And I tentatively crossed to the mainstream for the first time with two political programmes, the first a profile of newly elected Prime Minister Edward Heath, which I made with *World in Action* reporter Malcolm Southan. Little was known about Heath, either the man or his political touchstones. We had access to him sailing on his yacht, *Morning Cloud*, and were able to conduct long interviews. His mother had been a maid and his father a carpenter who had ended up running his own building business. Heath's formative experience had been in Spain during the Civil War, where he was machine-gunned; and in Germany, which he visited before the outbreak of the Second World War. He saw totalitarianism as arising from mass unemployment, which needed to be averted at all costs.

Heath emerged from our programme as a decent centre-ground technocrat who wanted opportunity for all, and in particular an effective state-run educational system. He also came over as an internationalist who believed that a stable Europe required an EEC with Britain as a fully participating member. Our programme certainly did not in any way anticipate that the post-war dream was about to explode on Heath's watch – with inflation and public spending rocketing, and Britain with electrical power for only three days a week. Heath spoke sincerely to the concerns of my parents' generation, but not to mine: I found it difficult to relate to him at any level. Personally, he was dry as dust. On his yacht he was a decisive but monosyllabic captain. He sought and took advice from his expert crew, but, when it came to relaxing with them after the race or dining in port, there was little camaraderie in evidence: they were definitely not a jolly bunch of pirates.

I spent some time alone with Heath myself – one evening, for instance, sitting with him watching the sunset over the Solent. He was very self-contained and had less small talk than any other public figure I have ever encountered. Offered a softball conversational gambit – whether political or 'Isn't the sunset beautiful?' – he was perfectly happy to respond, 'Yes,' and then to lapse into a long, stony silence.

I encountered Heath many times over the years that followed, and many times exhausted my small talk on the long journey from reception to the studio. He never ever showed any sign of remembering meeting me before. When I joined the BBC he invited Jane and me to a Sunday lunch party at his beautiful home in the Cathedral Close at Salisbury. There were about sixteen guests in all, including the young Nicky Campbell, then a Radio 1 DJ. When the final guests had arrived and the room had filled, Heath insisted on introducing everyone. He indicated Nicky and said, 'He's the Deputy Director-General of the BBC,' and pointing to me, 'He's a Radio 1 DJ.' No one laughed, for everyone realised that that was what Heath really thought. In 1997 I encountered him again when I was invited to Hong Kong to witness the ceremonies transferring sovereignty from the British to the Chinese governments. Everyone attending was caught without shelter in a tropical downpour so total that it soaked us to the skin. After the state dinner, an assortment of British great and good – much amused by their common predicament – boarded an unlikely vehicle, a red double-decker bus, to take us back to our hotels. The last one on the bus was a lumbering, sodden, dripping Edward Heath who heaved himself on to the back seat among the bantering crowd, neither acknowledging nor saying a solitary word to anyone.

One night when I was editing the Heath programme, I was called to Queen Charlotte's Hospital in Hammersmith for the birth of our second child. In the early 1970s, husbands weren't prepared in advance for the wonder and drama of childbirth, and I had missed JJ's emergency birth – so it was an especially stirring and moving moment when Eliza emerged, her dark hair matted, screaming assertively. My lovely, determined, sensitive, companionable daughter had been born – and thankfully without difficulty or complication.

In 1971 my spirited friend Richard Neville, editor of *Oz*, whom I'd met through Germaine Greer, and his collaborators Jim Anderson and Felix Dennis were put on trial, charged with obscenity and indecency offences over an edition of *Oz* edited by schoolkids. I had discussed with Richard how Granada could respond to the *Oz* trial, which was another cause célèbre to rival Jagger's a few years previously. Richard, a charming and cheerful showman, turned the trial into theatre, a showcase for his ideas. The three male defendants posed for photographs dressed as schoolgirls in fetching gymslips and boaters. The fund-raising had been fun too: Jane and I attended a wild, ticketed party hosted by Keith Moon at his home. John and Yoko recorded a song, and donated the sales. David Hockney contributed pen-and-ink portraits of the three defendants unashamedly naked.

At the trial, John Mortimer – the liberal standard-bearer – was counsel to Felix and Jim. But Richard Neville was his own advocate, defending himself with dash and eloquence. Geoffrey Robertson, a shy, quiet Rhodes scholar at Oxford, looking like an angelic sixteen-year-old choirboy, helped to plan the defence. (Geoffrey was later transformed into a fiery, crusading QC, fighting for free speech and defending unpopular cases all over the world.) Ronald Dworkin, George Melly, John Peel and others spoke up for the defence from the witness stand. The trial was presided over by the old-world figure of Judge Argyle, who ended the proceedings with an outrageous summing-up – condemning, for instance, 'the astonishing claim that homosexuality is not a perversion'.

Oz was satirical and subversive, promoted sexual liberation, and offered a platform to an assortment of radical ideologists. It was also dense, impenetrable and – with tiny print superimposed over complex graphics – sometimes barely readable. But the magazine was fun and fresh and never took itself seriously. I admired and identified with Richard, and was always enormously stimulated by his company. Neither of us had any answers to life's problems yet, but we knew what we liked and didn't like. We didn't want police acting like gauleiters, suppressing the opinions of the young. We wanted free expression. We bridled against stuffy, out-of-touch, unaccountable institutions. We hoped for a more open, honest, tolerant society, more freedom for individuals, more space to stretch. We didn't yet understand how to achieve these goals, but in the event the liberal values and notions of our generation would indeed change the world, generally for the better, in the decades ahead.

Richard, Felix and Jim were found guilty of some, though not all, of the charges. They were remanded in jail for psychiatric and other reports, and shorn of their long hair. In court, awaiting sentence, Richard said to Judge Argyle, 'If you jail us today, your Lordship, you will show the world that your generation – while it appears to listen with every courtesy – is in fact deaf.' Argyle immediately sentenced Richard to fifteen months' imprisonment, and recommended that he be deported thereafter. The crowd outside the Old Bailey, which included John and Yoko, immediately rioted. There was widespread outrage at the severity of the sentences. Relief came when a higher court granted bail. I was asked to stand surety for Richard – for the sum of £100 – and was glad to. I went with Geoffrey Robertson to Wormwood Scrubs to collect Richard and his fellow defendants, and I took them all out to an Italian restaurant in Notting Hill for an escapees' lunch. In November, the Lord Chief Justice presided over the appeal and found that Argyle had given 'serious and substantial misdirection'. The main conviction was quashed, and, though the minor charge stood, the sentence was suspended. The *Oz* defendants were free. David Plowright did not chastise me – as he reasonably might have done – for standing bail for Richard; but he did rule that my independence was in question and that I could not now make the intended programme on the *Oz* trial.

Richard returned to Australia, but I was always pleased to see him over the years on his intermittent visits to London. His ultra-liberality was tested when Jane and I and the kids visited him on a cold day in the Blue Mountains outside Sydney. Richard offered his own favourite woolly hat for JJ to wear on a walk. We owned up that JJ had head-lice, a common problem in his south London primary school, but explained that he was being treated for the condition. Richard hesitated for only a fraction of a second before generously repeating his offer, which JJ gratefully accepted.

Twenty years after the *Oz* trial, I encountered Judge Argyle in bizarre circumstances. As the BBC's Deputy Director-General, I was asked to present the prize in one of the main classes at Cruft's, the dog show, which we broadcast. Invited to lunch beforehand with the panjandrums of the dog world, I was surprised to be introduced to the demon Judge, by then retired and a leading light in Cruft's. Argyle turned out to be a cheerful old buffer, with tweedy country values and dogmatic *Daily Telegraph* opinions. I did not reveal to him as we chatted that I had once stood bail for the most notorious defendant in the trial that had made him famous.

What turned out to be my last programme for Granada created a political sensation in the autumn of 1971. I produced a *World in Action* which registered a radical movement, almost at its germination, that would have a profound impact on British politics over the next two decades: the awakening of the left as a force within the Labour Party.

Parliament was about to vote on whether the UK should join the EEC. A powerful group within Lincoln Labour Party was arguing that their MP, Dick Taverne, should vote to reflect the local party's anti-European convictions, and not his own pro-European sentiments. I turned up in Lincoln with Malcolm Southan and Brian Lapping. Brian was new to television, having joined Granada from *The Economist*. He had a serious, academic bent, and would go on to make some of the best and most serious factual programmes on British television – like the Hypotheticals series and *Death of Yugoslavia*.

The *World in Action* team opened the lid on a cauldron of frustration, resentment and dissidence in Lincoln. Some in the party saw Dick Taverne, a middle-class intellectual, as aloof and remote from the concerns of working people. Moreover, Taverne was associated with the policies of the Wilson government – raising prescription charges, wage restraint, and attempting to curb trade union powers – which the activists had despised. The political and personal antipathy to Taverne was intense, and seemed bound to erupt publicly: the vote over Europe would be the catalyst. We suggested to all sides – and they agreed – that they should come together and that we would film the meeting. The simmering pot finally boiled over. All the leading players took their gloves off. We witnessed an extraordinary, angry, passionate, uncompromising battle for the soul of the Labour Party, with deep convictions expressed on all sides, and personal resentments spilling out. We had unprecedented footage of politics in the raw, a leading MP on the ropes. The programme had a huge impact. Here was the first powerful evidence of the Labour Party changing in a fundamental way. Lincoln did indeed prove to be a watershed. Dick Taverne became the first Labour MP to be successfully deselected by his local party. He went on with others to found the breakaway and ultimately doomed SDP.

The most charismatic and articulate opponent of Taverne in our programme was the constituency chairman, Leo Beckett, a local shop steward. I got on with Leo particularly well, and found him an appealing figure, not because of his politics but because he was the sort of warm, honest, salt-of-the-earth working-class person I'd grown up with, and with whom I felt very much at home. When Taverne was deposed, Lincoln Labour Party chose in his place Margaret Jackson, who married Leo and became Margaret Beckett. In the following decades, whenever I visited the Labour Party conference on broadcast business, I would generally encounter Leo, who would be escorting Margaret. He and I would always be pleased to see one another. Leo took avuncular pride in the rise through the broadcasting hierarchy of the young twenty-six-year-old producer he had first met in Lincoln. Once in the 1990s, after I'd become the BBC's Director-General, Leo said to me: 'Margaret says, "You shouldn't be seen talking to that John Birt: he's very unpopular!"' He twinkled at me defiantly: 'And I said to Margaret:

"I've known him since he was a lad, and I know he's a good person! I *will* talk to him!'"

One night when I was filming at Lincoln, I received a call from David Frost. He had been impressed by my Jagger programme, by *Nice Time* and by my stewardship of *World in Action*, he said. Would I consider moving from Granada to LWT to produce his next series? The circumstances in which I had met Frost – making the aborted *World in Action* on him – had been uncomfortable for me. They had been trying for David too, and I was surprised and uneasy at his approach. I had been persuaded, however, that Frost had done nothing wrong, so I explored the proposal. In addition to the Frost series, LWT offered me dramas and documentaries to direct, and a big pay rise. I was tempted. Granada was an exciting creative hothouse, riding high, but living and working in London for a Manchester-based company had not been easy. Moreover, Granada was bulging with talent – whose main complaint was that there were too many producers chasing limited slots and funds. LWT, on the other hand, was a greenfield site: under John Freeman, the company had finally stabilised after a disastrous roller-coaster beginning; but it had few staff producers and it was making little programming of note. I sensed an opportunity to grow unencumbered in a new company. Moving to LWT would be a risk, but I decided to take it.

I was sorry to say goodbye to Granada, and particularly to David Plowright. Under his and Denis Forman's creative leadership, Granada would continue to innovate. Brian Lapping would take Granada's journalism into the mainstream with programmes of real weight and authority. The doughty, puritan, plain-speaking Ray Fitzwalter would prove a brilliant upholder of the *World in Action* flame. Brian Moser's *Disappearing World* would provide an extraordinary chronicle of tribes and communities around the world facing extinction. Denis Forman's inspired championing of *Brideshead Revisited* and *Jewel in the Crown* would help to redefine classic drama adaptation on British television.

But eventually Granada tipped into decline. In the 1970s and 1980s, *World in Action* became racked by dissent as many of the young radicals on the programme turned into surly activists and opened up a battle front on the programme itself, preparing accusatory dossiers about the programme's management and demanding worker rights. Able, dedicated executives like Gus Macdonald and David Boulton found themselves in the firing line. One producer on *World in Action* bought a gun and conducted secret target practice at the weekend in the Pennines to prepare for the coming revolution. Union activism in Granada generally introduced restrictive practices and undermined management and creative endeavour as it did in other ITV companies. The bold business expansion of the Granada group eventually turned sour, and executives from outside broadcasting were brought into the business to sort it out. David Plowright refused – as he saw it – to collaborate in destroying Granada Television's creative heart, and as a result he had to leave the company he had worked to build for over three decades. Denis Forman stayed on. I organised a dinner of tribute to David at the BBC for all of those he had championed and with whom he had been close.

In 1998, after thirty-five years, *World in Action* broadcast its last edition. It had long since lost its originality and ambition, as ITV's commitment to serious programming waned, and as the pressure to entertain intensified.

III

LONDON WEEKEND
TELEVISION

7

Adventures with Frost

In producing the Frost series, I moved firmly into the mainstream of national and international events for the first time, and I landed on my feet – for working with David Frost was like being a gambler on a roll. The news agenda dealt us some strong opportunities, and we seized them.

In the first week of our series, in January 1972, Bangladesh finally won – with the support of the Indian Army – its year-long war of independence with Pakistan. Sheikh Mujib Rahman, the Bangladeshi leader, was released from prison by the Pakistani authorities and peevishly flown west to London, rather than east to his new homeland of Bangladesh. The world's press besieged Claridge's – where Mujib stayed overnight – before doing an about-turn and flying to Dacca. With typical boldness and directness, David Frost drove over to Claridge's, waded through the press cordon, straight past the security guards, to be warmly welcomed by Mujib's aides – who, it turned out, watched regular re-broadcasts of

David's programmes on the sub-continent. He was ushered in to meet Mujib, who immediately agreed to give him his first interview as head of state. There was a catch, however: Mujib would not speak to anyone in the media before he had once again set foot on his native soil. David could have a world-first television interview, if he travelled to Bangladesh the following week to conduct it.

I set off immediately for Dacca with two film crews in tow. We flew to Calcutta to be told it was almost impossible to enter Bangladesh from India. The roads were impassable, the bridges damaged by war. Calcutta itself was bulging with refugees: everywhere we went, there was the heart-rending sight of families camped by the roadside. Few planes were flying, and there was a mighty waiting list for places. I spent a day hustling for seats, using David's name shamelessly. Two senior airline officials, both earnest Frost fans, agreed to jump me and my crews to the top of the queue. I also arranged to lease an aircraft to fly us out after the interview. As I was about to board our flight to Dacca with my team, one of the officials told me that the plane was carrying too much freight, and that it was likely our equipment would be off-loaded. I pressed a wad of cash upon him and begged him to ensure by whatever means that our equipment stayed on the plane. Looking nervously out of the window I was reassured by a smile and a thumbs-up from my new friend. As the plane started to taxi there was a shriek from a US network news producer at the front of the cabin: 'Stop the plane! That's our equipment!' he shouted, pointing at a pile freshly off-loaded on the tarmac. No one paid him any attention. The plane took off. I looked the other way.

In the immediate aftermath of war, Dacca was in chaos. When David arrived, a few days after me, we were picked up at night and taken by the cabinet secretary in his official car to meet Sheikh Mujib at his private residence. There were soldiers everywhere. As we came to the street where Mujib lived, a police guard barred our path. The cabinet secretary ordered the driver brusquely to carry on, and the policeman jumped out of the way. I looked back to see how he would respond: I watched in horror as the police guard drew his gun and pointed it at our fast-retreating vehicle. I cried to David to duck, and threw myself to the floor. I waited for a shot to ring out, but nothing happened. After a few seconds, I looked up tentatively to see the crestfallen figure of the guard, the gun hanging at his side, looking sheepish and uncertain.

The interview was delayed by a day. Telephone communication was unreliable, so I went to the airport to cancel the only plane I had been able to lease – a 150-seat airliner – to take us back to Calcutta. I asked the pilot to come back and collect us the following day. Before the plane could take off, I was approached by an immaculate, pukka-looking major from the Indian Army: 'I understand, sir, that that plane is yours and it is about to return empty to Calcutta. I'm trying to get my men back. May I use it?' I readily agreed and enjoyed the sensation of watching the Indian Army march with all their weaponry on to the only airliner I would ever have temporary command of.

We duly filmed the interview, returned to London on the morning of transmission and raced to edit our programme in time for broadcast. The moment we finished, the film was rushed across London by David's driver to reach LWT's studio exactly thirty seconds before the broadcast was due to begin. It had been quite a week, but we had a world scoop, and Mujib's claims about the scale of the Pakistan Army's massacres of the Bangladeshi people dominated front pages all over the world. We were back at work the next day.

Two weeks later we were in the pit village of Blaenrhondda, in South Wales. The miners' strike was three weeks old, and there was no sign of it ending. Within a month, deprived of power, British industry would begin a three-day week, and household blackouts would become an everyday part of our life – marking the dread beginnings of the seventies proper. I decided to take the then novel step of broadcasting our programme not from the formal confines of a television studio but from a miners' club. On the morning of transmission, officials from the NUM had taken David and myself down the local mine to impress on us the difficulty and danger of their work. Thousands of feet below the surface we crawled on our hands and knees, along the narrow claustrophobic tunnel adjoining the gleaming coal-face, our heads bumping against the low roof. We returned to the pit-head black all over with coaldust. In the evening David talked on the programme to hundreds of miners, drinking at tables, sitting in a fug of tobacco smoke. The miners spoke fiercely and expressively, leaving no doubt about their solidarity and their determination to stay on strike as long as it took to win. The programme made for original, atmospheric, revealing television.

Later that night, I was awoken from the depths of an exhausted sleep in my hotel in Cardiff by David's driver with news of Bloody Sunday: thirteen people had been killed on the streets of the Bogside in Londonderry by British Paratroopers. In the two years or so since Northern Ireland had first imploded – and British troops had moved in to protect the Catholic community – the position had further deteriorated. Attempts at reform by the Stormont government had faltered: Ian Paisley and William Craig obdurately blocked change; and the newly formed Provisional IRA stepped up its campaign of terror. Internment was introduced to deal with the escalating paramilitary violence. It was against this backdrop that the Parachute Regiment fired on a civil rights march in Derry's Bogside.

I decided we would mount a discussion in the heart of the Bogside. No outside broadcast facilities were available in Northern Ireland, so I immediately decided to ship over LWT's own units on the ferry. I was nervous at first that we would face hostility or threats, but there were none. At lunchtime in a Derry hotel on the day of the recording, I walked through the wrong door and surprised John Hume, the local SDLP MP and civil rights leader, lunching with a small group in a private room. I caught all the tension and apprehension in his face as he looked up anxiously at a stranger bursting in. That night, we recorded our discussion in a school in the

Bogside. We were told that half the Derry brigade of the IRA was in the audience. The discussion was tense, solemn and serious: it was evident that the crisis in Northern Ireland had materially deepened. We moved our outside broadcast unit to Belfast and talked to a studio full of Loyalists, one of whom protested at the label 'Bloody Sunday' and said, rather, it was 'Good Sunday' because the British Army had at last 'taken its gloves off'.

I flew without a break to what was then called Salisbury in Rhodesia. Ian Smith had agreed to give us a rare interview. I was to meet the plain, dry, unflappable man who had first prompted my interest in politics. Rhodesia was in the news because a new settlement between Smith and the British government was under consideration. Faced with Frost's awkward questions, Smith repeatedly contradicted himself, or suffered a memory loss: he claimed he didn't know that Judith Todd – the former Prime Minister's daughter he had detained – was being force-fed. Nor did he know that Daniel Madzimbambuto had been detained for thirteen years without trial, though he did know enough to correct David's mispronunciation of the detainee's name later in the interview.

A few weeks later, dizzy with travelling and exhilarated by the drama of events, David and I were back in Belfast on the day that Edward Heath imposed direct rule on Northern Ireland. A nervous Independent Television Authority ordered that we should keep Nationalists and Loyalists apart in separate studios. Ulster TV's studio crews and technicians had ideas of their own. The imposition of direct rule may have been a landmark in Northern Ireland's history, but Ulster's staff refused to work on the programme unless they were paid a huge multiple of their normal hourly rate. I was being blackmailed. I faced a gigantic bill wholly out of line with my budget. I asked if all the crews could be assembled. I addressed them and argued passionately that they should not abuse their power. I reminded them of the crucial importance of the day, and of their critical social responsibility as broadcasters. They were stony faced and unmoved, and responded that unless I paid up they would go home. Their lack of idealism appalled me, but I paid the danegeld – as I would again and again over the coming years.

Elizabeth Taylor celebrated her fortieth birthday in Budapest where she and Richard Burton were filming *Bluebeard*, a twilight-of-career potboiler. David had persuaded them both to record an interview with him for his US series, and asked me to direct it. Burton proved sharp and fluent in the interview, Taylor muddled and incoherent. She was slurring her words, and seemed very much the worse for wear. After the recording, we were invited back to their penthouse suite for drinks. David, Neil Shand (the US producer) and Burton plonked themselves at one end of a thirty-foot-long L-shaped couch. I sat at the other end, furthest away from Burton and next to Taylor. I was just out of reach of the conversation, but I could hear the lively Burton, hungry for stimulus, up with the news, anxious to engage. I felt trapped. Next to me was the still-beautiful apparition I had considered, as an adolescent, to be the most rav-ishing woman in the world. I should have been thrilled, but I was deeply uneasy. Taylor was barely comprehensible, her attempts to intervene in the wider conversation abruptly rejected by Burton. She hadn't the slightest idea who I was, yet we were here for the evening.

Eventually she had no choice but to fasten on to this young stranger to her right. She began a rambling, repetitive monologue about her fortieth-birthday gifts, and especially the large diamond Burton had given her, which had prompted worldwide media atten-tion. After an hour of this brain-numbing monotony, she asked, 'Would you like to see my diamond?' I nodded. She took me by the hand and led me to her bedroom. At this point David and Neil looked up in mild surprise at our unexplained exit. In Elizabeth Taylor's bedroom, already open on a chest, was a casket spilling over – as in Aladdin's Cave – with jewellery of every description. Taylor picked out the enormous birthday diamond and held it to the light, examining it adoringly. 'Isn't it beautiful? Isn't that the most beautiful object you've ever seen?' she burbled. I waxed on as best I could about the jewel. 'But isn't that the most beautiful object you've ever seen?' I found something else to say. Soon it was clear I was stuck in a time warp. Transfixed, hypnotised by her illustrious gem, she repeated the same question to me in the same words about ten times, and I did my increasingly uninspired best to answer it ten times. Then she showed off her other prized baubles. After half an hour or so, again holding me by the hand, she led me – by now in a stupefied silence – back into the main room. Burton didn't blink or show surprise at our prolonged absence in the bedroom, but David Frost and Neil looked nervous, suspicious and quizzical.

At the end of an interminable evening, we bade Burton and Taylor farewell. They escorted us to the lift and waved us off. The moment the lift doors closed, David and Neil turned on me: 'What happened? What happened?' I told them I was too much of a gentleman to say.

Over those hectic months, David and I combined to produce a series which created a real stir, which chimed week after week with the big stories of the moment, and was required and compulsive viewing. Working with David was a tonic for me – he and I had much in common, particularly a willingness to take on a challenge, and to blast through to a result – but he raised my game. He boosted my confidence, gave me powerful encouragement to follow my instincts. I learnt from him in other ways. He had a great television and journalistic brain. He could master a brief quickly and focus on what mattered – the key facts that sharpened an issue, that would engage an audience. He would cram all his insights, quips and briefing material on to a single buff cardboard folder with a thick felt-tipped pen, every square inch crowded with information laid out chaotically and, to any other reader, incomprehensibly. But this single folder would be David's sole aid during a live interview or studio discussion.

David was larger than life: he seemed to inherit from his formidable mother an unbreachable conviction that nothing could go wrong. He pushed a deadline further than anyone I have ever known. He appeared to feel he could defy time, that events would inevitably and miraculously march with his needs. He was ready, for instance, to receive an outside phone call on an unrelated matter with minutes to go before a live show, or to prepare till the last possible second, showing neither nerves nor fear. David felt he could command any space. Once, driving his large Rolls-Royce, with me as his only passenger, he held up traffic in every direction at the complex five-way junction at London's Brompton Cross by embarking on a multi-point turn in the very centre of the junction, in the middle of all the traffic lights. He smiled gleefully at the bemused, honking drivers he was holding up in all five directions.

David was also a sunny, relentlessly positive optimist. After every programme, he would proclaim with manifest sincerity: 'That was one of the best shows we've ever made.' He was upbeat about people, too, never bitchy and intensely loyal to the team with whom he worked. David was lively and beguiling company, acute and well informed, with a ready wit and an unexpectedly fanciful, surreal streak of silliness. He had the gift of intimacy, of making any companion feel special. He was not self-important, pompous or grand. Famously, he would remember the names and other details of people he had met only briefly. I once saw him greet by name a secretary he had encountered only once before – fifteen years previously. David had a natural desire to draw everyone into the big, happy, extended Frost family. He was not a party political animal. He wanted the good, well-meaning guys from every party to be in his gang.

David's talent and drive enabled him to become the only television presenter so far, from any country, to be known and appreciated globally. I enjoyed working with this able adventurer, and years later I would do so again.

8

Weekend World

When I was working on *The Frost Programme*, Cyril Bennett, LWT's Controller of Programmes, asked me to launch the programme that would have by far the greatest impact on my life – *Weekend World*. Cyril had explained that LWT wanted, at this juncture, to honour its last-remaining franchise promise and launch a third current affairs programme on ITV, alongside Thames's *This Week* and Granada's *World in Action*. *Weekend World* would run for around ninety minutes at Sunday lunchtime, from the start of autumn to the end of spring.

I did not immediately jump at the chance, for I was keener to extend my experience as a TV professional than to return full-time to current affairs, and my contract with LWT was to direct dramas and arts programmes as well as two series of *Frost*. But Cyril pressed me: he argued that this was my chance to put my stamp on something new and enduring. Moreover, he would substantially boost my pay. I relented above all because I had had an idea, or at least the germ of one, that I'd wanted to develop.

When I was editor of *World in Action*, I had felt frustrated by our inability to understand and explain the UK's deepening problems. I had a particular conviction that I wanted to make the news comprehensible to ordinary people of the kind I'd known in Liverpool, to satisfy those like me who were curious but unversed in current events. Here was my chance to try. I produced a treatment for Cyril with Nelson Mews, a burly, gentle-mannered and experienced Australian journalist, who had worked on the *Sunday Times* Insight team and with me on *The Frost Programme* – a person of sound good judgement who would prove unflinching under fire.

John Freeman was then LWT's Chairman and Managing Director. He was an austere man of great authority, widely held in awe, who spoke and wrote immaculate, characterful English. He had been a Labour rebel; a minister in Harold Wilson's government; the legendary interviewer on *Face to Face*, editor of the *New Statesman*, and Britain's Ambassador in Washington. He had generously admired what I had achieved on *The Frost Programme*, but he did not like my treatment for *Weekend World*. He was worried that the programme would be too expensive and insufficiently appealing. He emphasised the need for ratings.

Cyril Bennett had been a journalist himself, but his heart was closer to show business, and he admired American sophistication. He pressed me to consider creating a relaxed and urbane lifestyle programme, focusing on people and places, modelled on *New York Magazine*. But Cyril could always be persuaded by argument and conviction, and there was only one programme I was interested in making. In the end, Cyril – with typical big-hearted generosity – backed my vision, and put his own aside.

I set out to recruit a team. Cyril pressed me to poach David Dimbleby from the BBC, but I wanted programme-presenters with expertise and authority in specialist fields. I also liked the idea of creating some new stars. From their writing I was attracted to Peter Jay, economics editor of *The Times*; Mary Holland, who covered Ireland for the *Observer*; and John Torode, the trade union specialist from the

Guardian. They would provide insights into the key subject areas we would be covering. I managed to recruit some able young print journalists to work in support. Nick Elliott, my old friend from Granada, and David Elstein, a young, fiercely clever current affairs producer from the Thames stable, were the mainstays of the team. But a number of other people I targeted were happy in their current jobs in newspapers or TV, and saw no reason to take the risk of joining a new and untried programme. As a result, I started a demanding ninety-minute weekly series with an insufficient number of tested people.

Christopher Hitchens was one of the youngest members of the team, but there was no doubting *his* talent. (Later Chris would be an acclaimed political commentator in the US as well as in the UK.) Chris was a charming, skilled and informed debater at team meetings, but he didn't relish the hard routine grind of television production – of actually making something complicated happen – and he was a poor timekeeper, often arriving at work hours late wearing a dishevelled, threadbare, brown velvet suit, and looking ashen faced, hung over and exhausted. He took chastisement without rancour, head bowed, looking back at me doe-eyed and disarming. Christopher would move on with my best wishes to more suitable and congenial work after *Weekend World*'s first year.

Assembling a team was not my only difficulty: ITN resented *Weekend World*'s aspiration to review and analyse the week's news, fearing we were trespassing on their territory, so they refused initially to give us access to that week's news footage. It took many meetings with the editor, Nigel Ryan, and high-level lobbying before they reversed their position.

The IBA were also nervous: they feared that a multi-item programme with strong presenters and reporters would lack item-by-item balance. They fired a warning shot. John Freeman wrote: 'Big brother will be watching us.'

Coming up to our first edition, Cyril Bennett was in an agitated state. At his best, Cyril was lively and astute, firing off wisecracks like the smart New Yorkers he so admired, but he could be unpredictable

under pressure. He wrote an eccentric note to me and Geoffrey
Hughes, my departmental head:

> The story, as of today, as far as I am concerned, is
> Asians/Uganda.
>
> 1.   What the hell is going on there?
> 2.   What does it mean here – in this country? . . . I have
>   watched the ITN news bulletin at 10.30 pm on Saturday
>   23 September, and I still don't know . . .
> (i)   *They* (black men) live and work in this country; they 'are
>   after my women, my job, my house'. It is that
>   fundamental.
> (ii)   They (black men) are doing something in a place called
>   UGANDA. To and with white men in both places.
>   WHAT and WHY?
>
> As it is the first programme, I am sending the Chairman a
> copy of this memo – for information only. I will be interested
> in his view. Matter of record that he has some experience as
> journalist and editor. Unless and until I hear from the
> Chairman to the contrary, please proceed as formally
> instructed.
> If not, 'I will do the damn story myself' – cf. Walter
> Burns, *The Front Page* by Ben Hecht.

Geoffrey Hughes tactfully and bravely queried Cyril's assumption

> that an experienced producer of John Birt's calibre can be
> *instructed* as to the content of the programme . . . I make no
> comment, except to remind you that, as a very successful
> producer of *This Week*, you did not welcome such
> instructions from above, nor did you need them.

On the memo from Hughes, Bennett wrote in his own hand: 'I never had anyone of my calibre "above".' Cyril was placated, however, and never pressed his point again. Hughes had won me the space I needed.

The first *Weekend World* was transmitted on 1 October 1972. I was twenty-seven years old. The programme had items on Ugandan Asians (*not* addressing Cyril's questions), Northern Ireland and prices and incomes policy. There was a biting commentary on the week's news from Peter Preston of the *Guardian*, and – to leaven the mix, in an echo of *Nice Time* – a bizarre interview with the delectable Fiona Richmond, who took men to bed and reported her explicit findings in *Men Only* magazine.

Contemporary rock accompanied the opening and closing titles of the programme – an instrumental by Mountain, who grew out of the 1960s super-group Cream. The programme's logo and graphics were designed by a shy, shuffling and untidy young designer called Martin Lambie-Nairn (who went on to become British broadcasting's leading brand designer, creating the logo for Channel 4, and rebranding the BBC during my time as Director-General).

The first *Weekend World* was a muddle of influences and ideas, but it did seem fresh and new. Bennett's written verdict after the first edition was: 'Peter Jay is a star.' And he reported that Lew Grade, the ATV chief, had phoned him to say that he had enjoyed the programme, and concurred with Cyril's assessment of our lead presenter.

In the first year of the programme we had a rich agenda to cover. Watergate revelations mounted, and we explored them with live drama reconstructions of witness testimony. Nixon fought and won a second term, and I made a film in Cheyenne, Wyoming, with the legendary D. A. Pennebaker as part of our coverage. Heath put a freeze on wages and prices; the war in Vietnam escalated; Britain joined the EEC; Ulster was paralysed by a general strike. Sharp weekly comment on *Weekend World* came from, among others, A. J. P. Taylor and Auberon Waugh. And we lightened the content with items on George Best, Chuck Berry and the Liverpool–Everton derby. On April Fool's Day we played a trick on Peter Jay. He and I wrote, as usual, the opening sixty-second live introductory link to the programme, but I asked Eric Idle from the *Monty Python* team to impersonate Peter and to perform it – dead straight – instead of him. At noon Peter prepared to deliver the opening link, but his jaw dropped in shock when he saw Eric Idle, at the very same moment as our viewers, perform the opening in his place.

Julian Mounter – a *Weekend World* reporter who later became Director-General of New Zealand's public service broadcaster – flew to South America to do the first interview with the survivors of an aeroplane accident in the Andes who had resorted to eating the dead crash victims when their food supplies were exhausted. The survivors said they would not discuss cannibalism directly. 'So what did you do when the chocolate ran out?' Julian asked, and they told us the story straight.

Weekend World was being generally well received, described by Sean Day-Lewis in the *Telegraph*, for instance, as 'in some ways the best current affairs programme on TV'. More importantly for LWT, after the company's stuttering and controversial start, praise came from where it most mattered: Sir Brian Young, the IBA's Director-General, gave the Authority's verdict: 'Its success will never be measured in ratings . . . but the distinction which the programme's lively and serious approach to news adds to our schedule is something that the [Authority's programme] committee values.' This observation alone guaranteed *Weekend World*'s future within LWT.

Towards the end of the first series in 1973, Cyril suddenly announced to me that he and I must seek Rupert Murdoch's view of *Weekend World*. Murdoch was a leading shareholder of LWT, who had bought his way into the company at the moment of its deepest crisis following an infamous appearance on *The Frost Programme*. Murdoch had been interviewed by Frost in front of a hostile studio audience after the *News of the World* had published Christine Keeler's memoirs, and had suffered an onslaught. Spitting with fury at the end of the show, Murdoch had stormed out of the studio vowing: 'I'm going to buy this place.' He set out to do this, but he had not long been the driving force at LWT before the IBA intervened with an ultimatum – which had paved the way for John Freeman to take over as Chairman and Managing Director. Murdoch had remained a shareholder but was sidelined, enabling John Freeman finally to stabilise the strife-ridden company.

As Cyril Bennett and I drove over to Rupert Murdoch's office for the meeting, I became aware of his intense agitation. With the self-confidence of youth, I wasn't nervous at all. Murdoch was accompanied at the discussion by Larry Lamb, the editor of the *Sun*. Murdoch was laid back and made no strong impression on me. He seemed not to have watched *Weekend World*, but Larry Lamb certainly had, and Murdoch indicated that Lamb would do the talking. He did, promptly and energetically mounting a sharp attack on the programme from a tabloid journalist's perspective, dismissing out of hand its high-ground ambitions. I was furious and battled back, refusing to concede an inch. Cyril was tense and silent. Murdoch seemed mildly amused by the row escalating before him. Plainly, he didn't care about *Weekend World*: he seemed, though, to derive some voyeuristic enjoyment from my feisty and unyielding defence.

I could defend *Weekend World* to the editor of the *Sun* in good conscience, and the programme's first season was being widely admired, but I was not happy with the programme myself, since it still did not match my original vision. We had made too modest an advance in explaining the key stories of the day. I had not been able to meld the disparate talents in the team into a coherent force. We had interviewers who could interview with insight, who could shape a group discussion in the studio or on location. We had film directors and reporters who could combine to make a short, polished film on a particular story. There had been minor breakthroughs: we had analysed Tiny Rowland's business affairs with great clarity, and skilfully investigated the causes of the crash of Concordski, the Russian supersonic passenger jet. We had been inventive, contemporary and enterprising – but we were still imprisoned by current orthodoxies. We had not broken out and found new ways to grapple with key events and issues. I remained frustrated. The breakthrough finally came at the very end of the first series, in our last two programmes. One, produced by Nelson Mews, was the first pull-together of all the evidence that had emerged about Nixon's complicity in the Watergate affair. The ninety-minute programme was an eye-opener for everyone who saw it, bringing coherence and clarity to a jumble of inchoate and incomprehensible allegations. The story was plainly told, with pieces to camera written around expert explanatory material on film and graphics. But the programme made for compelling viewing and was highly praised.

The second breakthrough programme, a week later, was a review of the major political and economic events of our first tempestuous year. This contained a long and acute analysis, authored by Peter Jay, of the economic problems that were plaguing Britain, and their political consequences. As with Watergate the previous week, the programme drew together seemingly disparate events or trends – many of which we had covered during the year – but showed how they were connected, or were a consequence of one another. It clinically laid bare the underlying forces that were propelling events. Here was raw, convincing diagnosis and a sharp identification of the hard choices ahead for the UK. I felt elated: at last we had broken loose and were offering the journalism I had long craved, providing something of real democratic value.

I returned after the summer to edit my second series of *Weekend World* confident that I could now see a way forward. I had already weeded out the weaker members of the team and recruited some strong journalists in their place – most notably David Cox, who would go on to be a visionary editor of *Weekend World*; and I had promoted the most able of the junior members. I resolved – and announced – that we would henceforth generally cover only one subject per edition, and that we would overhaul our whole approach, placing rigorous analysis, rooted in original research, at the centre of our production process. Each element of our programme would illuminate a single point in a coherent, logically told story.

This decision to introduce a no-holds-barred full-frontal focus on key issues occurred at a critical moment. It was the autumn of 1973. We did not know it but we were essentially at the beginning of a crisis in the UK which would last for the whole of the 1970s, and which would not play out fully until the end of the 1990s. A cascade of events was unleashed that autumn: the Yom Kippur War broke out between the Arabs and the Israelis; the price of oil rose (doubling in a single day in December); the power workers and the miners took industrial action; a state of emergency was declared; the UK stock market crashed; Britain was put on a three-day week; public spending was cut; industry was paralysed; a balance of payments crisis erupted; Heath called an election to settle who governed Britain, which Wilson won; and the miners were awarded a 35 per cent increase in pay. A newly defined *Weekend World* was in just the right place at just the right time. Week in, week out, we analysed these extraordinary occurrences, putting ourselves firmly on the map in the process. The programme instantly became required viewing for opinion-formers. No other media body, print or broadcast, had our capability or focus, or our commitment to stay on board the roller-coaster of events. It was the most exciting period I ever experienced as a journalist. For decades afterwards, strangers would regularly come up to me and say that *Weekend World* had changed their lives, that it had given them a weekly tutorial that helped them understand the world.

The responsibility for our success was clear. As well as Nick Elliott and Nelson Mews, we had a hard core of capable producers and analysts, notably Jane Hewland, an old Granada hand of New Zealand origin and obsessive brilliance; and Julian Norridge, a quiet, steady and systematic graduate of the *Evening Standard*. My main contribution was my mathematician's ability to dissect and to probe and to bottom out an argument; and my stubborn insistence on persevering through many drafts until I was content with the rigour and clarity of a script.

Weekend World introduced new production processes, which, understandably, were not popular with some of our programme directors and reporters. In the first series, we had sent out film-makers to cover an issue, and subsequently found ourselves trawling through their footage for insights – much as I had done on *World in Action* – and trying, and often failing, to introduce coherence into films in the cutting room in the middle of the night. Now, the pro-gramme-making process started with a long period of research, talking to everyone involved with an issue. An outline script was then written before experts were interviewed and sequences filmed to illuminate particular points. Directors and reporters were sent off with a clear specification of the story their film should tell. These sequences became known as 'pea factories', named after the first of the genre, which had indeed been filmed in a frozen-pea plant. This process brought a leap in coherence, but – initially at least – a decline in the team's morale. The directors and reporters had lost the freedom of the road; they had forfeited much of their discretion. It was no surprise, therefore, that after a few months I faced a minor revolt and a stormy team meeting. But I had an iron conviction that we were now finally on the right track, and I rode out the storm, recognising that *Weekend World* would not be stable until all the team broadly shared my perspective – a state of affairs that would eventually come to pass.

Another production innovation was the introduction of animated graphic sequences to illustrate abstract connections or complex arguments about the economy. In these pre-digital days, every one of the twenty-four frames per second was drawn and shot individ-ually. Normally, it would have taken weeks or months to shoot a short cartoon sequence. We brought the time down to days, utilising some of London's best animators, and grew more and more ambi-tious with our cartoons. For a major programme on the economy, we planned for the first time not one but many such films, and assembled a legion of animators from all over London to make them. Each separate sequence featured the same northern factory with smoking chimneys and workers moving in and out and performing various tasks explained by the commentary. A standard guide-drawing was issued to each animator. Hours before transmission all the work was brought together. The cartoons were not without their quirks: one of the designers was a talented animator of Chinese origin, and all the workers and factories looked similar, except his. His northern workers had almond eyes, and his factory had smoking chimneys, but looked like a pagoda, with the edge of its roof curled up towards the sky.

We discovered, too, the convenience of archive film, obviating the need to send expensive crews abroad, and offering tailor-made pictures to support a commentary against a tight deadline. *Weekend World*'s most notorious use of archive – which became a standing joke on the team – was of the only known film in existence of an Arab worker in headdress turning a wheel in the desert on an oil pipeline. This archive film was used over and over again during the economic crisis of the 1970s to illustrate the notion that the oil-producing countries had turned off the oil-tap.

Weekend World interviews were meticulously planned, like chess games. We were not in the hardball school of interviewing – throwing quick-fire, aggressive questions to unbalance or to discomfit the interviewee – an interviewing technique which puts a high premium on the most basic of all political skills: dodging the question. The *Weekend World* school, started by Peter Jay and myself, refined and systematised by David Cox and Brian Walden, was to precede an interview with a compilation setting out fairly the context in which the politician was working, and the difficult choices he or she faced. We moved away from the notion that there are risk-free 'right' answers, accepting that all political options have downsides. This approach was far harder for politicians to dodge. Evasion was much more clearly exposed. It soon became apparent that – for a politician – thirty minutes with Jay (and later Walden) was a real heavyweight bout, and only the best were up to it. Real insights about government or opposition thinking increased enormously – famously so when Mrs Thatcher revealed for the first time on the programme what her approach to trade union reform would be. As a result, *Weekend World* interviews were routinely reported on the front pages most Mondays.

Working on *Weekend World* was punishing for everyone. The key members of the team would be up for most of Saturday night each week, refining scripts and packages. Sometimes we would work for most of Friday night too. Takeaway Chinese or Indian food was our staple diet. Most weekend dawns, trays of cold, congealed leftovers were lined up outside the office, awaiting the arrival of the cleaners. We would return home after our lunchtime transmission on Sundays, exhilarated but exhausted – in my case to a welcome from two affectionate young children eagerly awaiting their absent father. I would play with JJ and Eliza for as long as possible before tiredness overcame me and I sank into a deep twelve-hour sleep. We all had Mondays off, except for phone calls, and we would try to make a family day of it. On Tuesdays, the cycle started again.

In November 1974, *Weekend World* transmitted an interview by Mary Holland with David O'Connell, a leading figure in the IRA. The IRA had been conducting a long and gruesomely effective campaign of bombing in mainland Britain, notably at Aldershot, Guildford and Woolwich. A stern-faced O'Connell threatened that IRA bombing would continue unless Britain released IRA prisoners. Additionally, he demanded that Britain should declare its intention to withdraw from Northern Ireland, and allow the whole of Ireland to come together to determine its own form of government.

His remarks provoked outrage in the press, and a flood of angry calls to LWT's switchboard. Four days later the IRA committed a particularly horrible atrocity, bombing two pubs packed with young people in Birmingham's city centre, killing seventeen people and injuring many others horrendously. It was the worst attack yet. I felt physically sick when I heard the news, not only for the scale of the outrage but also because I knew waves of revulsion would sweep over *Weekend World*. I realised we would be contaminated by our association with O'Connell's ruthless threats.

There was an onslaught in Parliament. Gerry Fitt, the SDLP MP for West Belfast, asked Home Secretary Roy Jenkins 'to prevent such broadcasts happening again'. Enoch Powell demanded that the Director of Public Prosecutions should take action against us. Lord Hailsham suggested that during the interview O'Connell had perhaps issued an encoded order to bomb to an IRA cell. Alan Beith and Keith Joseph argued in more reasoned terms that the IRA should be denied such a platform in future. Brian Walden, himself a Birmingham Labour MP, was a rare voice of support: 'Do not let us be so foolish as to deny ourselves an understanding of the mind of the enemy.'

LWT was rattled. We had been through due process. John Freeman and Cyril Bennett had agreed we could conduct the interview. The sturdy, clear-thinking David Glencross and other members of the IBA's staff had come into LWT to vet the interview before transmission. But everyone was uncomfortable with the public response. John Freeman wanted a balancing interview with Paisley or some other Loyalist figure the following week, but I resisted, since this would have had little journalistic relevance. LWT's legal adviser wrote a note of all the general provisions in law, including treason and sedition, which interviews with the IRA might fall foul of. John Freeman immediately issued a ban on such interviews in the future and set out other prohibitions. I was asked to enforce this order but not to share its existence with the – by now nervy and defensive – *Weekend World* team. I protested, and fought hard for the journalistic imperative not to be fettered, to tell the whole, relevant story, however unpalatable. I wrote at length to the IBA and to LWT's senior management, laying out a full and comprehensive analysis of the Irish conflict. I argued that British and Irish politics were in great flux; that the IRA was only one of the many forces in play; but that – from time to time – it was critical to establish its position.

I had, too, to defend Mary Holland, who had interviewed O'Connell for *Weekend World*. In the late 1960s Mary's sympathies and connections had been obviously nationalistic and, as a result, some suggested her journalism was tainted. But, working closely with her, I knew she was a formidable reporter – well connected to every strand of significant opinion in the whole of Ireland – and a true sophisticate with a deep understanding of Ireland's intricate politics, and a commitment to telling the full, fair story. Her chronicling of the Irish conflict on *Weekend World* had been magnificent, and I resisted all hints from senior LWT managers and board members that she would be better on another beat.

I was rescued from a difficult confrontation within LWT by the Independent Broadcasting Authority, who issued new guidance on interviewing the IRA, making clear that such interviews were not ruled out. John Freeman immediately withdrew his note of prohibition. The O'Connell episode was my first – but certainly not my last – significant experience of the inevitable, legitimate and yet insoluble tension between on the one hand the journalist's desire to paint a complete picture of the world, and on the other the offence and even outrage that this can cause.

In 1974, after two years of editing *Weekend World*, I began writing an article for *The Times* that would make me notorious. Britain remained in crisis, and I had developed a fervent conviction that television news and current affairs programmes reported the symptoms of crisis but were failing fundamentally to diagnose the reasons or to identify a remedy. I set out to explore my frustrations on paper. Jane Hewland helped me to order and refine my arguments. She pressed me to pull the key paragraph from the body of the early drafts and to put it first, which I did:

There is a bias in television journalism. It is not against any particular party or point of view – it is a bias against *understanding*. And this bias aggravates the difficulties which our society suffers in solving its problems and reconciling its difficulties.

The article went on to argue that the main forms of television journalism – short news items, half-hour films on single subjects, studio discussions – presented a chaotic kaleidoscope of the world, a bewildering cacophony of soundbite snippets and disputation, and didn't grapple with or clarify the underlying issues. Moreover, TV journalism was putting pressure on politicians to deal with the symptoms of crisis rather than the crisis itself:

> . . . suppose there is something in the view held by growing numbers of politicians and economists that, if we can find no effective method of restraining general levels of pay (at the moment through the Social Contract), then it will not be possible much longer for us to reconcile four central features of our society: Parliamentary democracy, full employment, stable prices and free collective bargaining. The country might soon have to decide which to forgo. Such a choice would impose extraordinary strains on the political process. For this reason, if for no other, television and the press must ensure that the options available are fully and sensibly debated.

When I showed Peter Jay the article, he loftily awarded me high marks, commenting, 'This is a very good article indeed. Also the most meteoric political education since the younger Pitt!' Peter suggested we should work together on two further articles, identifying first how the green-eyeshade culture of journalism – which we foolishly rooted, by way of example, in Gateshead – was an impediment to progress; and second, how the whole system of broadcast journalism could be reformed to remedy the problems I had identified.

We proposed a system of news with expert, informed, specialist journalists at its heart; and a portfolio of programmes dissecting and debating the real problems of the UK and the wider world.

My article was published in *The Times* in February 1975. I had not imagined for a moment that my first-ever article would cause a ripple, let alone attract wide public attention. In fact, its publication provoked a furore, which intensified when two further articles – written jointly by Peter and myself – appeared shortly after. Our article on hackery, which with hindsight I can see was insulting and elitist in places, inflamed many established reporters. The old war-horse Llew Gardner wrote of the 'overweening pomposity' of the 'superior pair' and 'their awful elitism, their smug conviction'. Mike Nicholson protested our 'monstrous snobbery'. The mild-mannered Denis Tuohy suggested that viewers needed to understand with their 'heart as well as their head. The job of television journalism is', he wrote, '. . . to be a mirror more often than a blackboard.' Other voices feared we were proposing a powerful, monolithic broadcasting news machine which could be tightly controlled, with editorial lines fed down from the top. This was my first experience of unpopularity, of the price paid for taking on received wisdom or entrenched interests. I was surprised by the snarling hostility. In my innocence, I had expected a fairer hearing. The opposition, however, did not dent my conviction in any way. I saw our opponents as conservative defenders of the status quo. Nor, I was relieved to discover, did the opposition trouble me greatly.

Whatever support we lacked on the front line of journalism, however, we gained in spades in high places. The Chairman of the IBA, Lady Plowden, and the Director-General, Sir Brian Young called in the panjandrums of ITV news and current affairs to justify themselves at a conference with Peter and myself and leading officers of the Authority. The executives were polite, but plainly irritated that Peter and I had been taken so seriously. The most enthusiastic convert was the BBC's Chairman, the confident, towering Sir Michael Swann. In a lecture he said of Peter and me: 'they have produced a very perceptive article. They have succeeded in crystallising thoughts that have been troubling a great many people.' Swann went on to embrace much of our thesis in detail. Peter and I had a private meeting with him where it became clear that the BBC's radically minded Chairman was considering inviting us into the BBC to put our ideas into effect.

At Swann's request, we prepared a detailed, no-holds-barred analysis of BBC news and current affairs programmes. In an early draft, later sanitised, we airily castigated *Nationwide*, for instance, as 'A useless programme that should be abolished or reclassified as light entertainment'. In the paper for Swann, we were dismissive of the contribution made by most BBC news and current affairs programmes to overcoming the 'bias against understanding'. We argued that the BBC had lost its way, and we set out a blueprint for reform. We dubbed our approach – in a pre-echo of Tony Blair – 'The New Journalism'. We proposed uniting all the BBC's news and current affairs components into a single department:

> The whole of the news-and-current affairs department
> would be organised into two parallel echelons under the
> head of the department. One would consist of programme
> editors and those, like producers, exercising the editor's
> delegated responsibility. The other would consist of
> journalists. They would be organised into subject teams
> headed by subject editors, such as a political editor, a foreign
> editor, an economics editor and so on.

Twelve years later, I would be invited into the BBC as Deputy Director-General to introduce just this reform, and Peter would become the BBC's economics editor in a new order. But in 1975 BBC executives vigorously resisted our ideas, both in public and behind the scenes. Brian Wenham – at that point the BBC's head of current affairs – accepted that a merger of news and current affairs was 'one day' inevitable; but he conceded nothing else, sheltering behind a pettifogging, bureaucratic defence of the status quo. In particular, he stood squarely behind the BBC's flock of general – non-specialist – reporters, and the value of the first-hand evidence that they could gather. Peter Jay's sharp rejoinder to Wenham was: 'A building cannot be understood as a pile of bricks.' We felt we were in a dialogue with the deaf. Alasdair Milne, then Director of Programmes for BBC Television, invited Peter and me to lunch, but he must have been acting under orders, for he made no attempt to disguise his hostility to our ideas. Subsequent to these events, Milne appeared unwilling even to recognise my existence. At industry occasions, he wouldn't even nod to me. Once, when Jane and I went to see David and Carina Frost's first-born, we arrived at the same time as Alasdair Milne, the only other guest. We all celebrated the new baby, but Alasdair wouldn't acknowledge Jane or me in any way at any point.

The former Director-General of the BBC, Sir Hugh Carlton-Greene, wrote to me to say: 'I find myself in almost total disagreement with your paper.' Sir Charles Curran, the Director-General at the time, stuck the knife in at a Royal Television Society conference:

I go all the way with them in seeking more explanation. I stop at the point where they seem to want to do things *to* the audience rather than *for* them. I will show the audience the man who wants to wash their brains – or even two of them or as many as may present themselves. But I will refuse to be in the brainwashing team myself, or allow my own people to be in it.

The BBC's Chairman was plainly at odds with his over-hysterical Director-General and his senior management team, so it was no surprise that our talks with Swann simply fizzled out. I was disquieted at the time by the smug and cynical complacency of the BBC executives I encountered as a result of writing the 'bias against understanding' article, by their support for the status quo, and by the absence of any sense on their part that the BBC was there to inform the people at a time of growing national crisis. The BBC's lack of seriousness of purpose – in sharp contrast to the intense idealism of my colleagues at LWT – registered strongly with me and would affect my attitudes later.

One former BBC executive did stretch out a welcoming hand. The doyenne of BBC current affairs, Grace Wyndham-Goldie – by then retired – invited me to tea in her Kensington flat. She plainly relished the dialogue and offered warm support for the direction of change I proposed. Other less surprising figures wrote in support, including Joe Haines from Downing Street; Sir Keith Joseph from the Centre of Policy Studies; and Denis MacShane from the NUJ. There was interest from overseas. America's largest circulation magazine, *TV Guide*, printed my article. The *Reader's Digest* asked me to summarise the whole thesis in twenty-five words. I was embraced by academia, and invited to give lectures at home and abroad – one, curiously, to a group of elderly benefactors at a university in Texas. I was asked to debate Peter's and my ideas on television. I was confident and outgoing when ad-libbing at team meetings in the workplace, but I had had no previous experience of the cut and thrust of public discourse, or of giving prepared addresses to large public meetings, and I quickly discovered I had a lot to learn about presentation.

Peter Jay was *Weekend World*'s key asset. He had been tutored in public affairs from an early age by his father, the Labour politician Douglas Jay. There followed seemingly effortless moves to Oxford, to the Treasury and to *The Times* as its economics editor. Peter was just thirty-five when I first approached him, an intellectual of unmatched power, with a deep understanding of politics and foreign affairs as well as the economy. He had formidable analytical capability, and was effortlessly able to define a single powerful theme on which to hang a complex story. Much of the skill for myself and others on *Weekend World* was in translating Peter's densely packed ideas into plain and simple language for our viewers. He would then mark one's translation, and correct one's grammar, frowning and tutting as he did so. I still think of Peter every time I am about to split an infinitive or end a sentence with a preposition.

Peter led a busy life working both for *The Times* and *Weekend World*. Sometimes William Rees-Mogg, the paper's editor, would assume he was with me, and vice versa. In fact, I learnt decades later that Peter was often attending to his beloved boat in St Katharine's Dock, where only Nelson Mews, a fellow sailor on the team, could ferret him out in an emergency. Peter would sweep grandly into the office on Saturday afternoons to read over the script, to plan his interview and to make a series of ex-cathedra pronouncements – then fly away again.

Peter had been uneasy with the prevailing Keynesian orthodoxy in economics for some years, uncomfortable that each successive economic cycle brought higher and higher rates of both inflation and unemployment. From the late 1960s he had followed the arguments of Milton Friedman and other US economists that there was a connection between inflation and the amount of money in circulation, and that there was *no* longer-term trade-off between inflation and unemployment – ideas that undermined the whole post-war approach by both main parties to running the economy. Peter began to write about these radical notions in *The Times*.

He also knew or spotted many of the UK's other key thinkers in political, economic and social affairs, and we drew a fair number of them into *Weekend World*'s orbit – David Watt, Sam Brittan and Philip Windsor, for instance, were regular contributors. In October 1973 Jane Hewland went to see the twenty-nine-year-old London Business School academic Terry Burns about a programme on inflation, and Terry began appearing routinely on *Weekend World*. Terry and I were of the same age and of similar background: he was an ever cheery, tousle-haired, football-obsessed northerner and one-time Catholic, and the son of a mine worker. He and I and our families became close. We both had small houses near Brecon in Wales. I can remember puffing up a steep hill in Radnorshire in the 1970s while Terry patiently explained to me the significance of different monetary measures. In 1979 he would become chief economic adviser at Mrs Thatcher's Treasury, and later its permanent secretary – and would be at the heart of Britain's economic reform over the next two decades. During the 1970s and 1980s other economists would make a substantial contribution to *Weekend World*, most notably Alan Budd, himself later a chief economic adviser at the Treasury; Bill Robinson, who became a special adviser to Norman Lamont as Chancellor; and Gavyn Davies, who was a Labour Party adviser and became a Goldman Sachs economist and finally Chairman of the BBC.

Jane Hewland went one day, at Peter's suggestion, to interview another illustrious economist, Michael Stewart; but by mistake she had arranged to see a different Michael Stewart – the former Labour Foreign Secretary. He told Jane he was willing to have a shot at answering all her complicated questions about monetarism, though he didn't really know much about it!

Weekend World was a key centre of economic debate in the UK in the 1970s. As Britain tumbled from the enormous Heath/ Barber boom of the early part of the decade to incomes policies, to a floating pound, to massive industrial unrest and to inflation in mid-decade at almost 30 per cent, it was clear that the post-war economic consensus was breaking down and that something was needed to replace it. *Weekend World* was able to throw these issues into sharp relief. We always scrupulously invited the Keynesians on to our programmes, but the monetarists manifestly had the best tunes. I started attending seminars at the Institute of Economic Affairs run by Ralph Harris, a far-sighted prophet of free-market thought. I was one of a small group invited to see the ultra-confident Milton Friedman speak there. By the mid-1970s *Weekend World* was regularly floating the notion that governments could control inflation but not unemployment. It was the price set for labour – particularly by the trade unions – that would determine the level of unemployment, *not* governments. These were unpalatable ideas for all those – on both left and right – who had been affected by mass unemployment in the 1930s; and they were especially unpalatable for socialists captured by the romantic and progressive idealism of the trade union movement. But the new monetarist ideas were increasingly accepted by key individuals in both main parties. Sir Keith Joseph, the Conservatives' free thinker, spoke out in Preston in 1974. Peter Jay had a hand in drafting the historic speech to the Labour Party conference in 1976 given by James Callaghan, Labour Prime Minister and Peter's father-in-law, in which he proclaimed that:

> We used to think that you could just spend your way out of a recession . . . I tell you in all candour: that option no longer exists; and that in so far as it ever did exist it worked by injecting inflation into the economy. And each time that happened the average level of unemployment has risen. Higher inflation followed by higher unemployment. That is the history of the last twenty years.

Callaghan had been Wilson's first Chancellor. I met Wilson when he did major interviews with Peter Jay for *Weekend World*, and many times at social gatherings after he left office. He was always buoyant and confident, happy to tell long stories – some of which I heard many times – which chiefly featured Wilson himself in a heroic light, or having the last word. Wilson was a skilled party political manager, and an effective day-by-day operator in government. But he and Heath were the last, innocent and unknowing custodians of the post-war policies that accelerated the decline of the UK, and precipitated and intensified the crisis of the seventies.

When Callaghan succeeded Wilson as Prime Minister in April 1976, my family and I were soon invited to tea with the Callaghans and the Jays at Chequers. Eliza, just five years old, slipped into the swimming pool and the Prime Minister jumped in to pull her out.

Then, and on other occasions, Callaghan sought my opinion and I offered him my advice. As a broadcaster with a commitment as well as an obligation to impartiality, I should not have done, but I didn't think much about the issue at the time. Callaghan was kindly and tolerated his daughter and his son-in-law's friend. He arranged for me to be invited to market-research seminars at Downing Street, and sent me draft texts of broadcasts to critique. He also asked me to provide drafts of possible speeches for him: the main drive of my advice was to press Callaghan to be brutally honest with the British people about the depths of the crisis in the UK, and to explain that a long journey lay ahead before we could escape it. In one draft speech, I wrote:

> Even if we do our best, the next years will be hard. Next year unemployment will get worse and living standards will drop further. The year after that we may – I stress 'may' – pull out of the dive and level out. Not until 1979 is there even a prospect that living standards will start to rise again. Only then can we start the long slow climb to stability and to prosperity. We will not approach our destination during this decade. In the Eighties, we may.

And:

> If you are a worker, I would like to see you taking more of an interest in how the firm is run rather than simply what is in your pay packet. Let us see pressure from you for wise investment; pressure for the clever marketing and exporting of your firm's products; pressure for more modern and efficient management; pressure for more productive use of labour and machines; pressure for the humane phasing out of wasteful over-manning or restrictive practices.

Both Peter and I advised Callaghan of the critical importance of television as a means of communication at a time when most

politicians still focused on print media. I suggested fireside chats to
the nation; live evening interviews with leading journalists; and a
conscious attempt to appeal to the young as well as to the old. I even
proposed that the Prime Minister should acquire contact lenses. I
told Callaghan he should seek to define and reinforce an image and
not just make arguments. I put some of my views in writing:

> The image might be: the genial, contented and dependable
> man who is not afraid to celebrate family values; who wants
> to see his children and their children well cared for and
> happy; who, by extension, wants to be the father of the
> whole nation – all classes, ages and races; and who sees
> worrying about the economy or industry as a means to an
> end, not as an end in itself.

Callaghan listened to my views and advice courteously, but never
really acted on anything specific I suggested, though he seemed to
like receiving suggestions about what to say in a speech or broadcast.
In my experience, in the end he always sat down and wrote what he
wanted.

Invited once to a meeting with Callaghan and a posse of his advisers – I was far and away the youngest person present – I was the last
to enter his first-floor study at Number 10. The Prime Minister sat
behind his desk. Everyone else quickly bagged a couch or a chair. I
eased myself into the one remaining armchair. 'John, that's my seat!'
Callaghan boomed, standing up to claim it. Red-faced and feeling
distinctly adolescent, I slid embarrassed on to the crowded couch.

I attended the recording, on the eve of the 1979 general election,
of Callaghan's last address as Prime Minister. Downing Street was
quiet and deserted. Callaghan was dignified, but for the first time I
realised that he himself held out no hope of winning.

I met Sir Keith Joseph many times in the 1970s, often lunching
alone with him. His anxious, pained honesty and his openness to

fresh ideas made him an appealing companion. He combined social compassion with an avowal of the advantages of free markets. He was a key influence on the set of ideas that would encourage both main parties fundamentally to refashion their policies – first Conservative, then Labour – over the next two decades. Meeting and talking to Joseph, and spending time at the Institute of Economic Affairs, I realised that the mainstream right was thinking harder and more convincingly about how to rescue Britain from crisis than most on the left, still wedded by tribal loyalties to state ownership of industry, and to the virtuousness of trade unionism. Sir Keith Joseph had been the foremost radical thinker among the Conservatives, but he baulked at assuming the leadership. He paved the way for Mrs Thatcher to take over the party in 1975.

It is hard to believe now, but when she was first interviewed on *Weekend World* by Peter Jay in 1977, as leader of the Opposition, Mrs Thatcher was nervous and tentative. She brought her daughter Carol to accompany her on to the studio floor, explaining that she wanted Carol to appreciate what a trial a long television appearance was. After the programme I sat alone in the hospitality room with Peter and Mrs Thatcher for about an hour. In the following years, I would see her completely dominate such occasions, barely tolerating an interruption to the fiery monologues that were her hallmark. In 1977 she listened rapt and respectfully – and in awe – as Peter set forth *his* views of what needed to be done to put Britain right. It was not at all clear at that point that she was a convinced monetarist with her own plan of action.

For me, the 1970s were the grimmest period of my adult life. High inflation gave way to the IMF crisis; *The Times* went unpublished for a year as Duke Hussey presided over a long printers' strike; the winter of discontent brought rubbish piled high on the streets and bodies unburied. At moments in the 1970s everyone I knew felt a sense of helplessness, in sharp contrast to the ebullient optimism of the previous decade. Britain appeared destined for continuing decline. The trade unions seemed all powerful. Inflation made everyone feel vulnerable. Where would the crisis end? Most people squirrelled away a huge stock of candles. Peter Jay had a complicated lighting rig at home powered by car batteries for use in an emergency. Jane and I hoarded abundant supplies of tinned food. We talked half seriously of moving to the United States; and we also half joked that we would be among the first to be shot when all the steely Trotskyist sects took over.

One Trotskyist group displayed a keen interest in me – the WRP, the Workers' Revolutionary Party. They were active in Tooting where we lived near the Common. Out of curiosity, I started taking the WRP's daily paper at home. It always made interesting reading. Their heroes – like Gaddafi and Scargill – were everyone else's villains. But their commentary was intelligent and informed, their perspectives arresting, if unpersuasive. The WRP were excited to have a media executive on their newspaper delivery list, and sent many apostles to turn me to their cause. They never got beyond the doorstep, but their persistence became unsettling. One day Jane answered the door to a beautiful woman who said: 'I'm Kika Markham. Is your father in?' We invited Kika into our kitchen, aware she was a luminary of the WRP, as well as an actress of talent. She pressed on me the WRP's intricate views on the issues of the moment, presumably hoping to see their perspectives reflected on *Weekend World* the following Sunday. In return, I was polite but forthright, and explained that I did not want to be, and never would be, a convert. I didn't hear again from the WRP.

Jane and I watched the 1979 election coverage at home with friends, including Jonathan and Bel Dimbleby, who lived near us in south London. Mrs Thatcher's clear-cut victory left us all feeling despondent. We knew it was the end of an era. At 3 a.m., we bade the Dimblebys a gloomy farewell. Twenty minutes later the doorbell rang. It was the Dimblebys again, looking even more dejected. For them, the first event of the Thatcher era was a flat car battery. For me it was scrabbling around in the dark and cold trying to locate and to attach jump leads before we could finally see them on their way.

My feelings about Mrs Thatcher winning were not entirely rational. I had ended the 1960s a libertarian, more interested in lifestyle than mainstream politics and the economy. In the 1970s I had met some of the sharpest and best-informed minds in the country. Two people in particular – Peter Jay and Terry Burns – had had a profound impact on my thinking. I had become a convert to free-market mechanisms. I was deeply sceptical that the state could run business. I abhorred the increasingly ugly abuse of power by the trade unions, not least in my own industry. I could see that my unthinking conviction in the 1960s that the state could solve every problem, that public spending could rise and rise, was ill founded. On the other hand, I remained passionately committed to the well-being of ordinary working people, and often thought of my nanna and grandad, whom I still visited regularly, and of my many cousins in Liverpool, some of them unemployed. My values had not changed. I had joined the Labour Party in the early 1970s as my interest had shifted to mainstream issues. I wasn't at ease socially with most Conservatives. I knew which tribe I belonged to. I had a personal attachment to the Callaghans and their family. I knew that Callaghan and Healey had no illusions about what needed to be done to put Britain back on track. But I also knew that the reform agenda was long and difficult; and that, whether the trade unions were confronted or cajoled along, they remained a major obstacle to reform, and a tough challenge for a Labour government – as the horrendous winter of discontent in 1979 had shown. In the years ahead, I would come to believe that Mrs Thatcher's unique qualities were Britain's salvation. But it took me some time to reach that position.

Years after his election defeat, I encountered Jim Callaghan again at Margaret Jay's home in County Cork in Ireland. Through his eighties, he still maintained a lively and dispassionate political perspective, and was most engaging company. One day, we sailed in

Peter's ocean-going yacht to a remote and entirely deserted beach for a barbecue. We remembered everything except the fuel for the fire. Peter was infuriated. I scoured the beach for dry driftwood. Jim and his wife Audrey pottered around, helpfully looking for tinder while Peter scowled. I built a windbreak with stones to protect the flame, but I could barely light a match before it was blown out. Eventually, and with one of my last few matches, I created the tiniest spark on a piece of half-dry timber. I flapped frantically to nourish the spark into a flame. Peter stood and watched and conducted a gloomy running commentary. He suggested that my task was hopeless, and forecast failure. Jim Callaghan, on the other hand, stood watching attentively and offering continuous encouragement. After an eternity, the fire took hold and we had our barbecue after all. Peter remained grumpy.

I maintained responsibility for, and a keen paternal interest in, *Weekend World* until I left LWT fifteen years after the programme's birth, but as I moved up the ladder in LWT I passed the editorial baton in succession to Nick Elliott, to David Cox and to Hugh Pile. In 1977 Peter Jay went to Washington as Britain's Ambassador and gave way to the idiosyncratic but brilliant Brian Walden, who interviewed with crystal clarity and scalpel precision. Matthew Parris – a man of translucent honesty and gentle wit – eventually took over as *Weekend World*'s third and final presenter.

Weekend World's early pioneers were replaced by a generation of fiercely bright, policy-minded young things, who were drawn to the programme like moths to a flame. David Cox emerged as their spiritual leader. Tall, fragile, nervy, intense and quirky, David none the less inspired all with his acute insight, his assured scepticism and the incredible rigour and depth of his analysis. The second generation on *Weekend World* made the programme a true powerhouse of thought in every key policy area. Recruitment was taken seriously and became infamous. Large boards would cross-examine candidates in great depth about a question of the moment, testing their understanding and knowledge. For years afterwards, people would come up to me at parties and complain – reasonably enough – about the mauling they had received. But recruits like Glenwyn Benson, David Aaronovitch, Nicholas Evans, Michael Wills, Bruce Anderson, Charlie Leadbetter, John Lloyd, Samir Shah and many more, all thrived and prospered in an atmosphere of pure intellectual inquiry, where individual preconceptions and party allegiances were left at the door.

These later generations had the zeal of converts. Whereas the early pioneers had needed advice from experts, the SAS-like latter-day Weekend Worlders were often experts in their own right, and were ready to take on the pundits on their own territory, irritating them, hassling them in interview until the punditry was refined, and fitted neatly into their finely crafted scripts. They sometimes drove an analysis to an injudicious extreme – famously concluding at the end of one edition on tensions in the Middle East that when the snow melted on the Golan Heights a world war would be inevitable. Overall, though, these later *Weekend World* brigades were dazzling and capable, and produced remarkable and insightful journalism. They picked apart every move that Mrs Thatcher made – union law reform, the Falklands War, her battle with the miners. They monitored the rapid decline of Labour under Michael Foot, the slow climb-back under Neil Kinnock, the emergence of the SDP. They plotted, step by step, economic reform in the USSR.

The Weekend Worlders eventually moved on to occupy key positions throughout the media and politics. One such was Peter Mandelson, Herbert Morrison's grandson, who had been a young researcher for an MP before joining LWT. On *Weekend World* Peter was exposed to a wide range of ideas and contacts. When he returned in 1985 – to everyone's surprise – to a Labour Party seemingly at rock bottom and unelectable, he was a different person, taking new techniques and ideas with him. In his time on *Weekend World* he had learnt the value of rigorous analysis, how to think through a proposition to the end, and how to structure an argument. He had toughened up intellectually. One of the last programmes he made at *Weekend World* was an edition analysing the challenges for the major parties. He used the ideas about the Labour Party on the programme as the basis of his interview with Labour's National Executive.

Greg Dyke also worked briefly on *Weekend World* as a producer, where he had had an argumentative relationship with David Cox. When Greg left LWT for TV-am, David Cox wrote on his leaving card: 'Fuck off, Dyke, and don't come back!' When Greg returned to LWT, years later, to succeed me as Director of Programmes, one of his first acts was to abandon *Weekend World*. Its spirit lives on, though, in the comradely diaspora of people – like me – for whom working on the programme was a profound learning experience. *Weekend World* gave me and others a crash course in understanding the world from some of the key and most innovative thinkers of the times, whose ideas were to have an impact not just on the UK, but on the international scene. That grasp of ideas, particularly the intellectual roots of both Thatcherism and Blairism – would help me critically when I moved later to the BBC. And *Weekend World* introduced me to a set of people – some of whom became close friends and rose to key positions in the main parties and in the civil service – who would be vital contacts in later life, not least because we had bonds of trust founded on shared notions as well as common experience.

Weekend World was my pivotal, formative, growing-up experience in the worlds of television and politics.

9

The Blossoming of LWT

LWT in the 1970s became a hotbed of talent and ideas. The company sizzled with creativity and debate, punching way beyond its weight. It seemed to attract people who challenged received wisdom not only on how the country should be run, but also on broadcasting itself. And for the most part LWT had the distinction of being a contented company where personal relations were marked by honesty and mutual respect. John Freeman set the tone – rational, fun, caring. My years of programme-making at LWT would be the happiest of my working life.

The origins of LWT's success went right back to the Pilkington Report in 1962 with its devastating critique of ITV's lack of range and ambition. Later, new leadership in the IBA – the flinty, scholarly, former head-teacher Brian Young and steely and committed colleagues like Colin Shaw, David Glencross and Clare Mulholland – resolved to raise ITV's game, to enhance its public service commitment. ITV's revenue boom of the 1970s gave them their chance.

The IBA insisted that the extra income ITV was attracting should be spent on expanding local programming and on innovation in every factual area. The IBA's new policy drive proved critical to my career, for I rode the wave that Brian Young created: in 1974 Cyril Bennett made me head of current affairs, adding local programmes to my remit, alongside *Weekend World*.

My first new venture was with Barry Cox, another former colleague from Granada's *World in Action*. Barry was a solid, hunky man, honest, candid and self-critical, level-headed, tolerant and generous of spirit – his first instinct was always to give others credit in preference to himself. Barry had a persuasive vision: that London as a city was undergoing profound social, economic and cultural change; that it was awash with stories; and that it merited a current affairs programme all its own. I was an immediate convert to this simple but novel idea. *The London Programme* was born, and, in the years that followed, helped to define London. It chronicled the decline of the city's traditional industries; it asked what should be done about Docklands; it assessed the risk of a devastating flood; it reported on sink estates and juvenile crime; it raised questions about the effectiveness of local government; and it offered a platform for London's politicians, including the budding Ken Livingstone. *The London Programme* reported on social strife in Brixton, Hackney and Tottenham. It had editions on IRA cells in London; the decline of Fleet Street; the National Front; industrial clashes at Grunwick; and the death of Blair Peach in Southall. Importantly, in programme after programme, it focused on corruption in the Metropolitan Police, and made reform inevitable. A moustachioed, long-haired Peter Mandelson was briefly a foot-in-the-door reporter on *The London Programme*, hounding landlords who harassed tenants.

Next I started *The London Weekend Show*, aimed at a young adult audience. We set out to capture London's vibrant youth culture, and to address issues of interest to our target audience. To produce *TLWS*, I recruited another old friend from Granada, Andy Mayer, with whom I'd collaborated on *Nice Time*. Having also enjoyed Janet

Street-Porter's clear and forthright views on LBC each morning on my way to work, I tracked her down in Los Angeles and offered her the job of presenter. *TLWS* quickly uncovered Ian Dury, punk music, the Clash and the Sex Pistols. The programme broke taboos, unveiling issues hitherto undiscussed, like teenage lesbians and incest. The stylish, forceful Janet was an imaginative creative entrepreneur. She had trained in the 1960s as an architect and was well plugged into the avant-garde. She was a superb networker with an extraordinary capacity to connect with anyone in London producing interesting and original work in music, design, fashion or the arts. Janet understood what young people were thinking and what excited them. When she moved on to be a producer, she brought into LWT the young, and – at the time – slender Danny Baker, who had been editor of *Sniffing Glue* magazine. Danny presented *20th Century Box*, which was shot moodily in black and white. The programme allowed young people to tell their own stories. It also spotted Spandau Ballet and Depeche Mode, the New Romantics and new town electronic music.

Janet nurtured in her years at LWT not just Danny Baker but a succession of bright production talents, including Charlie Parsons, Sebastian Scott, Tracey McLeod and Alex Graham. In a taut but fruitful collaboration with Jane Hewland, Janet went on to create in the 1980s the seminal breakthrough youth programme, *Network 7* – a rebellion against mainstream TV and a programme of panache and energy which challenged every broadcasting convention in storytelling, lighting, camerawork and graphics, and which changed television for ever, influencing all youth programming that followed. Janet's and Jane's pioneering work would have a profound effect on my later thinking.

As the 1970s progressed, I grew my hair to my shoulders and wore wooden clogs. I took up David Bowie, Neil Young and the Eagles, and still went to pop concerts and the movies whenever I could.

As I rose up the LWT ladder and our disposable income increased, Jane and I bought a house in Wales, just north of Brecon.

Like many of our friends in the period, we began to develop a keen love of the great outdoors. LWT rewarded hard work in the year with generous time off, so we had long summer holidays to develop our interests. Richard Mabey's *Food for Free* was our guide: we collected wild strawberries, made jam from raspberries gathered in the forest, and wine from elderflowers plucked from the hedgerow. We made cheese with milk from the local farm, and hunted crayfish under stones in mountain streams. We attended local eisteddfods in remote chapels, listening to recitations and to hauntingly beautiful Welsh baritones singing into the early hours of the morning. Every Saturday in the summer there was a local show to visit, with proud farmers competing for best-in-show with their clean and well-brushed livestock. There were guess-the-weight sheep competitions; tugs-of-war between bashful youths from the local pubs; and prancing Welsh cobs – their owners red-faced, and their bellies wobbling, as they ran their muscled, snorting charges around the ring. Displayed in the show marquees were winners of the biggest vegetable competition, or the prettiest flower arrangement, or the most finely carved walking stick. In the early evening, there were trotting races with the riders sitting on little sulkie carts behind their steeds, tearing precariously round the rough makeshift course, accompanied by wry and sardonic commentary on the booming, echoing loudspeaker. Jane was made president of our local sheepdog trials, which drew entrants from all over Wales.

The little community where we lived was full of children. JJ and Eliza played out all day, every day, during the summer months, adventuring in the hay barns or the woods. In the evening we arranged rounders or football with players aged from three to seventy-three, and played on until the Welsh light faded well past ten o'clock. Once a year we had our village sports day with competitions for both children and parents. Jane invariably won the ladies' welly-throwing competition. Each year I came third in the sprint and always felt a thrill of pride when my name duly appeared in the *Brecon and Radnor Express*. In August we would escape to

Pembrokeshire and walk the coast-path or play games on the long, empty, out-of-the-way beaches. Mr Jones, our gardener, was a retired shepherd from Abergwesyn steeped in country lore. He made tables from logs, whittled love spoons, forecast the weather from the movement of sheep on the hill and fished the pools in the brook which ran through our village down to the Wye, returning to share with us a bag bulging with sweet, succulent little trout. He would tell us yarns of a boyhood in Wales in the early 1900s, poaching salmon, being a shepherd out on the hill all night with only a pony and his flock for company.

I became a keen walker – an enthusiasm, along with football, that would bind together many of my generation. I explored the open hills of Breconshire and Radnorshire, which at the time I had all to myself, seeing only one other walker in my first ten years on the hills. Jane and I began taking walking holidays, first hiking over the back of Wales with Terry and Anne Burns, from the border with England to the Irish Sea. We learnt through our mistakes how to keep ourselves and our backpacks dry when it rained all day; how to charm farmers' wives in remote mountain places – where we were marooned at night – to cook us dinner to restore our strength. Anne Burns, born of the steadiest Welsh stock, once acted completely out of character at the end of a tiring week on the Pennine Way, suddenly announcing that we would cross the racing, turbulent Tees a short distance above High Force, the largest and most spectacular waterfall in Britain. And we would do this not by walking to a distant bridge, but by wading perilously across the fast-flowing river, carrying our thirty-pound packs, only just managing to remain on our feet and not to be swept away. Anne lost her boots, and we watched them bobbing up and down, heading for the plunge over High Force and onward to the North Sea, never to be seen again.

In 1976 Cyril Bennett called all his key programme-makers to a conference at Selsdon Park in Croydon. To everyone's surprise he announced that Brian Tesler, LWT's Deputy Chief Executive, would take the chair. Brian had recently been brought in by John Freeman – over the head of Cyril – from Thames, where he had been Director of Programmes. Conferring with my fellow programme-makers in other LWT departments would be a novelty, for Cyril liked to operate alone. There were no company meetings; we barely knew one another. Michael Grade, for instance, had joined LWT a few years before as head of entertainment, and he and I had offices on the same floor, but we had never moved beyond exchanging pleasantries in the corridor.

Current Affairs at LWT was thriving, but much of the rest of the company at that point seemed to be in the doldrums, and ITV's weekend schedules – compared with the BBC's – appeared dull. JJ and Eliza were now aged eight and six. As a family we sat and enjoyed together *Jim'll Fix It*, *Dr Who*, *The Generation Game*, *The Two Ronnies* and *Dad's Army* – all on the BBC – rather than anything on ITV. LWT's early peak-time successes, including *Upstairs Downstairs* and *Please Sir*, were not being replenished. The IBA's recent review of LWT had been mixed. Rather brazenly, I offered to give a paper at the Selsdon conference and Cyril readily agreed. My somewhat stern keynote speech argued that LWT needed reinvigoration, more ambition, elbow-room and experimentation; that better-educated, more prosperous viewers needed more challenging peak-time programmes than LWT and ITV were offering: 'the average Briton, and especially the younger Briton, is more sophisticated, independently minded and confident of his intelligence . . .'.

The conference prompted an honest debate. Cyril admitted he had failed to innovate in recent years and had chosen the soft options. Michael Grade, who might have bridled at my candid, forensic analysis, instead endeared himself to me and to his other colleagues by owning up to being embarrassed by his trite and pedestrian comedy, *Yus, My Dear*, and by the general lack of ambition of LWT's entertainment department under his leadership. In the evenings, Cyril and Brian Tesler went off to bed early and the rest of us stayed up and talked. We had a hilarious time and bonded in a wholly unexpected way. I particularly enjoyed the company of Michael Grade and John Bromley, LWT's head of sport. Cyril had hired most of us, and we discovered we had a lot in common – we were an open, outgoing, fun-loving group.

The conference took off. There was a tangible release of ideas, energy and good cheer. Cyril seemed deflated but he was – as ever – unresentful and generous of spirit. The only wrinkle, which we noted in private, was that Brian Tesler had dominated the conference from the chair, and that he had not given Cyril much space in which to shine. But LWT's programme-makers left Selsdon Park on the Saturday full of hope for the future.

That night Cyril fell to his death from the sixth floor of his small Westminster flat. I was devastated. I had reached thirty without suffering the premature death of anyone close to me. And I had been deeply fond of Cyril, who had championed and supported me. He was an agoniser, a man of instinct, not particularly analytical, who had left his East End school at fourteen; but he was no pushover: he would tease away at a proposal until he was satisfied. He was a delight to deal with – warm, welcoming and full of good show-business gags. He was also modest, realistic and often pessimistic. On the night of his greatest triumph, when LWT had cleaned up the BAFTAs a few years before we entered the doldrums, all Cyril could say was: 'You win some. You lose some. Let's see if you still love me next year!'

Why had Cyril died? Was it suicide? The *Evening Standard* had a picture of the building from which Cyril had fallen and the lurid headline: 'In TV you are only as good as your last ratings'. Had I and all the other programme-makers upset him by our increasingly energetic and cheerful display? Had he felt left out or left behind? Had he felt upstaged by Brian's over-domineering performance? The programme heads and Pam Shand – Cyril's long-term personal assistant – gathered together for mutual comfort. My outward emotions were initially held in check but I was seething within. The dam broke at the funeral. Cyril's other boys, his key departmental heads, and I turned up as a group – looking, to one observer, like a Mafia family. When the first handful of earth thumped on the coffin lid, I sobbed uncontrollably on John Freeman's shoulder.

In the following days, the hostility to Brian grew. The programme heads demanded a meeting. We wanted to discuss why Cyril had died; and how LWT would treat his dependants. We pressed that Cyril's office be demolished: we didn't want it to be used by someone else. We asked to be consulted about the succession. It occurred to no one that Cyril's replacement would be one of us. I did much of the talking. Brian was calm and considerate; and in a meeting that went on for many hours he allowed us to discuss all these matters, maintaining his poise. A fuller picture emerged, from Brian and others, of Cyril's deep despair over his private life; of a new contract which had recently been agreed with Cyril, and which had been awaiting his signature. During that meeting – and in subsequent days – I gradually came to the realisation that my suspicions of Brian had been unfair, that my behaviour had been immature. At the coroner's inquest it emerged that the sill of the window of Cyril's flat was markedly low. Cyril had been expecting his driver to call for him. He may have leant out of the window to check that his car had arrived, become unbalanced and toppled out. Perhaps. We shall never know.

Michael Grade and I were unlikely comrades – his rich, vaudevillian background contrasting in every way with mine – but mutual grief drew us together: he was as upset as I was to lose Cyril. Having massaged the egos of many stars as an agent, Michael was good – as he himself termed it – at 'dressing-room talk'. But there was more to him than that: he had a real sensibility about other people and their needs. I had previously been sniffy about Michael because – unlike me and my capable team – he was not a programme-maker; he had not come up the hard way; Cyril had plucked him straight from the agency business to run LWT's entertainment department. Michael hadn't painstakingly bottomed out a programme idea as a director or producer, blended together the multitude of different talents that make up a television programme team, showing an understanding of the precise, unique ability of each one, moulding the group into a fighting force, wrestling with creative failure, and arguing into the night to put it right. His appeal was that he was modest and honest about his handicaps, quick-thinking and street-smart, and – like Cyril – a natural comedian always up on the latest gags.

I expected Brian Tesler to appoint an outsider to replace Cyril. I told him truthfully that I had no interest in the job myself: I had no appetite at all at that point for scheduling ITV peak-time; and I was grieving too much to contemplate succeeding Cyril. My ambition, rather, was to take over the rest of LWT's factual output. Brian readily agreed to that and soon confided in me – to my astonish-ment – that he planned to make Michael Grade Director of Programmes. Brian explained: 'Michael is a lousy head of enter-tainment, but I'm certain he will prove a good Director of Programmes.' I was doubtful, but I offered my support.

In the event, Michael unleashed much of the pent-up creative energy at LWT that had been apparent at the Selsdon Park confer-ence, and began to improve LWT's programme performance. He had a lot of new money to spend. He expanded drama and enter-tainment, and he supported me without question as I took over all of LWT's factual programmes. I put Nick Elliott and Barry Cox – by now proven editorial leaders and managers – in charge of Features and Current Affairs respectively. The next years saw an extraordinary blossoming in LWT's factual output.

Nick and I began work on a template for the new Features department. As Nick grew in experience, he kept me and everyone else on our toes with his increasingly blunt, shockingly honest and occasionally fiery opinions – but as a collaborator he had excellent, confident, creative judgement, and was enormous fun to work with. He and I agreed that the charming and idiosyncratic arts pro-gramme *Aquarius* had not survived Humphrey Burton's return to the BBC, and we had similar aspirations for the arts to those that had prompted *Weekend World*. I was especially keen that we should plunge into the mainstream, make programmes about the major artists of the time, and extend the somewhat prissy television arts agenda to the popular arts like film and rock. I wanted a successor to *Aquarius* that would expose serious art to a wider audience, that would aid everyone's appreciation of work of quality, that would offer context and insight. I thought we should aim for a tone that was inclusive and unfussy, avoiding the superior, elitist air that was currently the hallmark of arts programming on television. Nick and I scouted around for someone to run the programme and settled on Melvyn Bragg, whose plain no-nonsense books programme for the BBC – *Read All About It* – had impressed us: the charming, knowledgeable, unpompous northern writer embodied the virtues we were seeking. *The South Bank Show* was born – though, for a brief moment, it was almost called *Imagine*.

Melyvn brought zest, ambition and enterprise to his work, and, collaborating closely with Nick, created one of British television's most enduring successes. He went for the heavy hitters. He had credibility in the arts world, could open doors, and was adept at putting artists at their ease and encouraging them to talk revealingly. In the first years we made editions on Ian McEwan, David Hockney, David Edgar, Dave Hare, Dennis Potter, Satyajit Ray, Karajan, Hal Prince, Ingmar Bergman, Woody Allen, Jonathan Miller, Joseph Heller and Ted Hughes. We were definitely in the mainstream. We made some of the most ambitious and successful arts programmes ever – powerful, long, revealing films, for example, on Laurence Olivier and David Lean. Early in its life, *The South Bank Show* had an extraordinary, spectacular triumph which LWT, ITV and the BBC could barely believe: we won television's premier international prize – the Prix Italia – in the three successive years in which ITV was eligible to enter, with programmes on MacMillan's ballet *Mayerling*, on William Walton and on Benjamin Britten. From a standing start, we could not have ridden higher.

Through Melvyn I met some significant British creative spirits. I struck up a friendship with David Lean after the film we made, and visited him often before he died at his grand converted ware-house home in Wapping. We talked about contemporary film, and the state of Britain – a subject which fascinated him on his return after years of self-imposed exile. One evening Melvyn held a dinner at his Hampstead home attended by Beryl Bainbridge, Alan Bennett, John le Carré, Iris Murdoch – and me. As these astute observers of life were quick to note, I was the only one among them who was not a world-famous writer; but they did appreciate that I was Melvyn's boss! I sat next to Iris Murdoch at dinner, whose work I had much appreciated in adolescence. Without any preliminary pleasantries, she immediately set about cross-examining me. In a quiet voice, she began by asking me to define precisely what I wanted from my work and from my per-sonal life, and she ended by asking me if I believed in God. She pressed me further and further until I answered to her satisfaction. I felt she had reached down deep inside me and interrogated my soul. I had never told anyone so much of a personal nature about myself so quickly.

At the end of the evening, when we all stood up to say goodbye, the whole group indulged in the standard luvvy practice of warmly embracing each other, as if we were the oldest of friends, with loud smooching smacks on both cheeks. The whole group, that is, except Iris Murdoch, who stood shyly back, and *we* all held back from her too: she was too august, and in any case so much older than the rest of us, for such familiarity. Rather, everyone shook her hand awk-wardly, and bade her farewell. Melvyn, an attentive host, established that Iris had no car and was going to walk out to find a taxi. But then he had another idea: 'No, John will be driving back to South London through Kensington: *he* will take you home.' So I found myself once more with Iris Murdoch, this time with her in the pas-senger seat. On the journey we *did* make small talk at last – about mutual friends, the Gilis. I pulled up in due course outside Iris's home in an elegant square. I expected her to open the car door immediately and get out, but she lingered. There was a long pause, then she leant over and kissed me sweetly and gently on my cheek before opening the door and departing.

Nick Elliott's Features department enlivened LWT's education and religion programmes. Michael Braham brought grown-up journalism to religious affairs with the current affairs series *Credo*. We provoked massive controversy by assessing the historical roots of Christianity in *Jesus, the Evidence*. Fundamentalists protested. York Minster was struck by lightning and some blamed LWT. A month later, the Bishop of Durham stirred another storm when he said on *Credo* that he did not believe in the Resurrection of Christ.

Clive James presented a lively guide to healthy eating, exercise and living – *How to Stay Alive*. We made documentary series on Stalin and Islam. Peter Jay did a series of hour-long interviews with some of the world's great thinkers, including Isaiah Berlin, James Meade and Bernard Williams. James Meade was an old, distinguished economist who would later be awarded the Nobel Prize. He had worked with Keynes as a young civil servant on the historic 1944 White Paper, which had set the post-war economic mould. At lunch after the interview Meade asked me about myself, having read my 'bias against understanding' article. I revealed to him my youthful frustration with conservative institutions. I complained that there was no appetite for taking up my more radical ideas. He counselled sagely: 'Ideas are a market, like any commodity. Bold ideas frighten people. They don't understand them. But my experience of life is that when things go wrong it is the people with bold ideas – like Keynes – that everyone immediately turns to for help, whether they understand their ideas or not! Be patient!'

Barry Cox was the producer and I the executive producer of another ground-breaking programme, *Saturday Night People*, which, alongside *Nice Time*, also reached the short-list of Philip Purser's all-time favourite programmes. *Saturday Night People* was journalism for laughs. It was presented by Russell Harty, Janet Street-Porter and Clive James, still a TV novice. Each presenter made short, funny films reporting on some true-life story. The whole panel would then respond to each report, the discussion crackling with witty repartee. Janet and Russell were already well established, but *Saturday Night People* made plain that Clive James would be a major presenter in his own right.

Barry and I worked with the illustrious director Stephen Frears on a drama-documentary which told the story of the IRA cell captured in the Balcombe Street Siege in December 1975. Subsequently, Stephen and I went to dinner with Johnny Rotten of the Sex Pistols to persuade him to make a film with us. We got nowhere. Rotten took an instant dislike to me. Conversation was tense. He disagreed with everything I said. We only just avoided a row. At the end of dinner, standing in the middle of the crowded restaurant, strikingly outlandish – with spiky hair and torn clothes and with every eye upon him – he proffered his hand, as if he had regretted his behaviour and was making a placatory gesture. I softened and put out my hand. Immediately, before we could touch, he withdrew his, put his thumb on his nose, wiggled his fingers at me, stuck out his tongue and jumped away in giant prancing steps.

Barry, Nick and I put real time and effort into recruiting talented people to LWT's Features and Current Affairs department, which was now expanding rapidly. We also continuously monitored the progress of every individual in the department, and took a view annually on how best to develop them by moving them around. We had a stern system of programme quality control. Scripts had to be shared well in advance of transmission with Nick and Barry, who checked them for rigour and coherence. I watched every single programme myself when it was broadcast and conducted a lengthy post-mortem each week with Nick and Barry. All the time we trawled for new ideas and notions; we strived to innovate.

We were a very comradely and social department. We enjoyed each other's company in and out of the workplace. We partied at any excuse. Every Friday lunchtime some members of the department played football. The game was instituted in the mid-1970s and continued into the next century. Generations of able and not-so-able, young and not-so-young footballers played to win. I played in midfield or defence. I was not particularly skilled but I was very enthusiastic, and I was always willing to abuse my seniority by bossing my fellow team members second by second to maintain a balanced formation. I loved playing in a team, especially on those all-too-rare occasions when individuals move miraculously in combination, as if united by some sixth sense, to produce a seamless move of elegance and beauty. At such moments the comradeship, the sense of fellow-feeling, the pleasure of co-operation was intense.

When we first began playing together, all the players were journalists from the Features and Current Affairs department, but gradually friends and colleagues from other departments and TV companies invited themselves. My laid-back hairdresser Iain started to play with us. Howard Davies, a terrier on the pitch and eventually in financial regulation, became a loyal attendee. I carried Howard off the field twice with what looked like career-threatening knee injuries; but, like a movie monster, he never gave up and always came hobbling back in the end. David Frost, Melvyn Bragg and Michael Grade put in occasional appearances. Greg Dyke, Roger Bolton and I were among the most stalwart attendees. The gossip in the showers and the changing room afterwards – about LWT, the industry and politics – was delicious. Women and unsporty men from LWT felt – reasonably enough – excluded. But, for those who did participate, Friday football was a strong bonding experience. Over the decades, a freemasonry of dozens of one-time Friday footballers emerged, some playing every week, others absent for years before reappearing, always to be welcomed back.

Media football teams traditionally had a liberal transfer policy. In my early years at LWT, I regularly turned out for the *Sunday Times*, and I sometimes played with staff from the communist newspaper, the *Morning Star*. One day John Peel turned up to play. When I tackled him, he fell and broke his wrist. I was distraught and took a large pineapple into Broadcasting House the following day as a peace offering. I once turned out for the *Morning Star* in their strip for a game against a team from a visiting Soviet warship. Team pictures duly appeared in the *Star* and in *Soviet Weekly*. I imagined MI5 staff poring over the pictures with heavy suspicion.

In 1977, my personal assistant of many years – the intensely loyal, bubbly, enthusiastic Marion Toberman – left to be a full-time mother. Katie Kay, who had been a secretary on *Weekend World*, took her place. Katie is a vivacious, blonde Yorkshire girl with a shrewd wit and a delicious sense of fun who would administer my affairs smoothly and effectively for the next twenty-three years, reining me in when I overdid it. She and Barry Cox became partners, eventually marrying and settling in Hackney. Two young lawyers moved in next door – Tony and Cherie Blair – and the four became close friends. When Jane and I went round to Barry and Katie's for parties, I always enjoyed chatting to the personable, approachable and curious young lawyer with a winning smile, bouncing a baby on his knee. And I felt comfortable with Cherie too, for we were of the same stock – she was from Liverpool and had been to Seafield, St Mary's sister school, just across the road.

ITV was awash with money in the 1970s. By the end of the period, the IBA's drive to expand serious programming had finally transformed ITV. If you were an ambitious and experimental factual programme-maker, ITV offered at least as many opportunities as the BBC. The 1970s were arguably a golden period for ITV, and not just LWT. Brian Lapping and Roger Graef produced innovative work at Granada; there was *The World at War* and *Rock Follies* from Thames, and *Johnny Go Home* from Yorkshire; and ATV produced many fine documentaries. The ITV companies also used their funds in the 1970s to invest in diversification as well as in programmes. LWT bought into several companies – including Hutchinsons, the publishers, and a travel company – but lacked the skill to transform itself into a rapidly expanding conglomerate. The unions extracted their own share of their spoils in the period, and in the process began to suffocate the system. In the early 1970s a landmark agreement had not only increased pay but introduced ludicrously rigid terms – the notorious golden hours – to an industry where flexibility was essential. Any technician with less than a ten-hour break between shifts would start work the following day on a generous multiplier of his or her basic rate. The baseline for the multiplier on the subsequent day would be the previous day's already inflated rate, and so on. Pay could rise day by day in giant steps. With such high rewards, corrupt practices began to emerge. The union restricted recruitment to boost overtime; it denied management the opportunity to use outside facilities to meet peaks of need, ensuring that the extra work was done on overtime. Extra work was voluntary, and in some union sections at LWT a system operated whereby only those already on a high overtime multiplier would volunteer for extra work. One year an LWT videotape editor earned in excess of a hundred thousand pounds at 1970s prices. The joke at the time was: 'What's the difference between Sheikh Yamani (the Saudi oil minister) and an LWT videotape editor? Answer: Sheikh Yamani doesn't get London weighting.'

Programme-making at LWT increasingly took place in a union war zone. Nick, Barry and I were managers in a climate where the trade unions became ever more forceful and constrained us at every turn. Crews became hard to work with: *The Good Food Guide* was in every film unit's car, and the timing of the lunch break was often determined by the availability of tables at the restaurant of their choice. One of the most distinguished British programmes of all time, Granada's *Disappearing World* – which chronicled remote tribes and peoples – was allowed by the union to have a small unit on location in the jungle only on condition that the remainder of the crew was housed – doing nothing – in a hotel in Latin America. In a fantasy of the absurd, one ITV company had to fly an electrician to the United States, even though the director said he would film without lights. The union had insisted on an electrician being on the crew 'in case'. Given that he was obliged to have an electrician, the director changed his plan and proposed after all to make use of the extra crew member he had reluctantly acquired. The electrician promptly refused to do the work. He was not there to work but 'in case'. Another electrician would be needed if lights were to be used. The dispute was resolved only when a second electrician flew out.

At LWT, the union film crews determined who would work on which programme. They constantly tried, generally successfully, to place LWT camera operators in roles – shooting major filmed dramas, for example – for which they had neither the experience nor the competence. Later, I would have to abandon a major film drama series at huge expense after the first week's shooting, because the quality of some of the lighting and the camerawork was so risible: parking meters were prominently framed in one shot of what was a period drama.

In 1975 earnings at LWT rose by 47 per cent in a single year. Over the decade as a whole, restrictive practices and crew sizes grew. Any unusual programme requirement was negotiated with the union. Line managers like me would often deal directly with shop stewards, meeting them, negotiating with them where they worked – say in a videotape booth. The director of personnel would be brought into any serious dispute to buy LWT's way out of a problem. A ransom demand – a common occurrence – to complete an over-running show in the studio usually needed his intervention. Towards the end of the 1970s a standard crew for the simplest factual filming would generally consist of nine people – two camera, two sound, electrician, production assistant, reporter, researcher and director. New technology – lightweight electronic cameras and digital editing – stayed on the shelf, its introduction obstructed by the unions. In 1979 a strike kept ITV's screens blank for eleven weeks before the companies surrendered. Pay rose again 40 to 50 per cent over the following eighteen months. Acknowledging that the TV unions were a destructive force, greedy for money, frustrating creativity, raising costs and reducing the number of programmes made was not easy for a generation of programme-makers – like me – imbued with the notion that the union movement was progressive. The first brave, outspoken voice in the late 1970s was that of Jeremy Bugler – a writer for the *New Statesman* who later worked at LWT. A kindly man with a soft and gentle manner, Bugler laid bare the horrors of the industry for all to see.

Not long after Mrs Thatcher came to power, I encountered Denis Thatcher at a party. *Weekend World* had just mounted a live interview with her at Number 10. It was a simple, straightforward broadcast, but over a hundred LWT technicians had been accredited with Downing Street security officials. Mr Thatcher was protesting about this shocking statistic at the party, berating the unions and overmanning. He denounced the *BBC*, however (and not LWT!), for its failure to manage the size of the crew at the interview. I blushed but did not own up, and allowed the BBC to take the rap.

The union's stranglehold in ITV would be maintained until Mrs Thatcher finally changed the industrial climate. First Thames, then TV-am, would run services manned by managers during a strike, maintaining their advertising revenue and breaking the union's long-held power. By the 1980s I had grown hard-hearted about unionism. And by the time I left LWT I would finally have put in place a detailed but secret plan to enable the company finally to take on the unions, and to eradicate their restrictive, uneconomic practices.

In the 1970s, broadcasting was dominated by the debate about how to use the fourth channel. The discussion began as I was leaving Granada at the beginning of the decade, prompting me to think for the first time about the structures and purposes of broadcasting. The ITV companies were lobbying for control of the channel, but I doubted that ITV's leaders had the vision to pioneer a second channel of their own. ITV's schedules at the time seemed to me to be over-rigid, ITV programming middle aged, and innovation rare. I joined forces with David Elstein – the precocious, maverick current affairs man – to offer a view on the proposed new channel. David and I proposed first to the IBA, then to Sir John Eden – the broadcasting minister in the Conservative government – that the controller of the fourth channel should be independent, commissioning programmes from all sources on merit alone; that an independent production sector should be encouraged; that ITV should hold the monopoly to sell advertising both on ITV and on the fourth channel; and that a levy on the ITV companies should fund the new channel. We wrote to Eden to say:

> [The] need is for the creative forces within the present systems to be liberated from the restrictions imposed by the requirements of the institutions which presently employ them . . . A programme controller running the fourth channel with departmental heads (but not departments) might be able to back hunches and allow ad hoc production units to form in a way that is just not possible within the present institutions.

The Birt/Elstein proposal was remarkably close to the structure for Channel 4 finally adopted a decade later, but no one at the time paid much attention to two young Turks, neither of us yet thirty. (LWT was remarkably relaxed about one of its own middle managers organising letters of protest to *The Times* and lobbying openly against the company's interests and ITV's official line.) More public attention was paid, rightly, to the ideas of Anthony Smith, the true begetter of Channel 4. David and I had bridled at the current system but had had no wider vision of the fourth channel's purposes, while Tony Smith had. He was an idealistic man of boundless energy and persistence, a BBC producer of exceptional talent, whose credit I had long ago noticed at the end of programmes I had admired – most notably *24 Hours*. Tony had left broadcasting to become an academic at St Antony's College, Oxford, and to write about the media. His vision for the fourth channel in its earliest expression – dubbed a National Television Foundation – was essentially of a political notice-board: he wanted a democratic opening up of the airwaves, greater plurality of expression. He wanted 'an imp in the mechanism'. He argued that the fourth channel should be a lean organisation, which would allot resources to producers and others who arrived with an idea, a grievance or a cause. He favoured individual expression, but wanted space for community groups; for the TUC and the CBI; for Parliament; for the best of European broadcasting. Funding would come from sponsorship and from government grant. Tony Smith's considered vision chimed with my 'child of the sixties' instincts towards openness, and I found the breadth of his thinking about the role of the media inspirational. But as a programme-maker I was nervous that his prospectus lacked the stuff of creativity, that the channel he argued for would be worthy but dull and sterile, even if he himself was manifestly not.

Working during the 1970s in the potent creative milieu of LWT, I eventually came to a different vision, which would stay with me. I saw much broadcasting as clichéd and formulaic. I bridled increasingly at the prevailing notion of mass programming, of serving a homogeneous audience of people with uniform tastes. I had an alternative perspective: I saw society fragmenting into innumerable groups, each with its own defined passions, interests and concerns – and with a unique and distinct need for information, entertainment and stimulation. Above all, I felt this about my own generation, whose needs were rarely met by television. I also felt keenly that the ethnic minorities and other groups – like gay people – who barely surfaced on the UK's airwaves, were under-served. Janet Street-Porter's pioneering work had mined a rich seam and shown what young people were doing with their lives, how they were expressing themselves. These minority programmes of Janet's were surprising, full of the unexpected. They were educative, yet unleashed energy. I sensed potential like this in every aspect of our national life. I felt television had still not unlocked the full creativity of Britain.

In the late 1970s, I prepared a series of articles and lectures in which I set out my ideas. In 1977 I wrote:

We define ourselves by our interest in where we live, where
we work, where we or our children are educated, what class
we belong to, what sports or games we play or watch, what
hobbies we have, what arts we participate in or inspire us,
what religion we believe in, what racial or ethnic group we
belong to and what political, economic and social systems we
favour . . . Our minority interests increasingly dictate how we
spend our time and money. The next step in the
development of our broadcasting system should be to set
about serving as many of these minorities as possible.

In 1978 I wrote:

the variety of wares television puts on display is severely
limited . . . We labour under the same difficulties that would
be endured by those, in an imaginary country, who ran one
of only three newspapers, or chose the films, plays or music
for one of three chains of cinemas, theatres or concert halls,
all of which were obliged to display the same wares on the
same day throughout the country.

In 1979 I gave a lecture at the Edinburgh Television Festival, by
now emerging as a ferocious annual parliament of producers and
industry activists where ideas and careers were launched or
quashed. I argued that television barely catered to the Beatles generation, hardly understood its needs and values, was censoring its
ideas. Television was ignoring the new ethnic minorities, excluding
important and significant views, failing to serve a divided, diverse
society. I tried to offer hope for the future:

In the long term, though, a solution presents itself to all the
problems raised here; to all the problems of censorship,
control and access denied. Inside this black plastic tube are
two strands of glass fibre cable, each only as thick as a piece

of cotton. Down each strand a laser beam can carry 80 channels – 25 times the capacity of our present wire*less* system. A thin cable, the diameter of any household cable, containing just 12 strands of fibre optics, could carry 1000 channels. If we want it, we now have the technology to create a television publishing market as open as the print publishing market is. Anyone with a camera and a video-recorder would be free to publish a programme at any time, and to charge the price they wanted for it. The viewer's set would be metered and the producer reimbursed.

The *Observer* described me as 'hero of the week' for this far-sighted if premature vision, one of the last occasions I would be lauded by the British press. Tony Smith wrote generously to say: 'It's the most charming, clearest and best-argued presentation of the pluralist position which I've heard. It challenges the established institutions and the self-conscious ultra-radical fringes equally.'

That same year I put some of my ideas into practice, starting the London Minorities Unit and putting Jane Hewland in charge. We would move beyond Janet Street-Porter's seminal work on youth programming to cater for London's ethnic minorities, its gay community and eventually the older audience. Trevor Phillips and Samir Shah were the lynchpins of *Skin*, which authoritatively unveiled the concerns, interests and texture of the Asian and black communities for the first time on British television. Michael Attwell produced *Gay Life* and steered us through the intense politics of the gay community – some of whom bridled at a programme that reported on them rather than offered them a platform. And Michael too steered us past homophobic resistance from some in the wider community, including on LWT's own board. These programmes were all I'd hoped for – fresh, bursting with passion, incredibly revealing.

The battle for control of the fourth-channel-to-be intensified in the late 1970s. The government-appointed Annan Committee supported

Nanna Anna and Grandad Joe at their Southport off-licence, sometime in the 1960s

Grandfather Bill at some point in the 1940s. He was the agent of much misery in my family

Grandmother Mary, a pious and selfless woman, in 1942

My father and mother, Leo and Ida, in 1942. They had met as teenagers at Coffee House Bridge in Bootle

With brother Michael and sister Angela in Formby in 1956

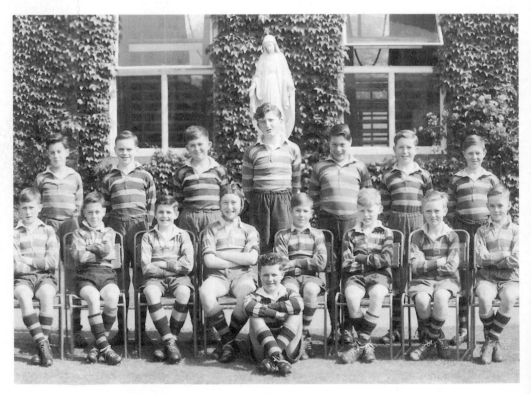

St Mary's College, Crosby, Under 12 rugby team (middle of front row)

Oxford University Film Society requests the pleasure of your company at the first showing of John Birt's
"The Little Donkey."
Afterwards a discussion will be held between the guests &
Jack Cardiff
John McGrath
Junior Common Room St Catherine's College, Oxford 8.30 p.m. Friday 4th June Please bring this invitation with you.

An invitation to the premiere of *The Little Donkey* in 1964

With fellow St Catherine's students in 1966 (on the left)

With Mick Jagger in 1967, at the time of his trial for possession of drugs

The presenters of *Nice Time*: Jonathan Routh, Germaine Greer and Kenny Everett, 1968

Oz trial defendants James Anderson, Felix Dennis and Richard Neville, 1971. I stood bail for Richard (Popperfoto)

With Harold Wilson and Gus Macdonald at the *Sun* Awards, 1970 (News International)

Right With President Nixon, 1977, at the time of his celebrated series of interviews with David Frost

With David Frost at a pit in Blaenrhondda during the miners' strike, 1972

Peter and Margaret Jay off to Washington – the *Weekend World* goodbye party, 1976. Peter had been the programme's key asset

Left The idiosyncratic but brilliant Brian Walden interviewing Margaret Thatcher on *Weekend World*, 1980 (London Weekend Television Ltd.)
Top With Michael Grade in happier times, 1981 (London Weekend Television Ltd.)

Centre With Nick Elliott (left), Barry Cox (right) and Katie Kay (foreground), 1981
Bottom left With David Lean and Melvyn Bragg, 1985 (London Weekend Television Ltd.)
Bottom right With Cilla Black, 1987 (Granada Media)

With Jane in Pembrokeshire, 1981

With Eliza and JJ in Kenya, 1982

With Tony Blair and Katie Kay (right foreground) in France in 1990

David Frost presents the prizes to the Go-Kart race finalists at Jane's fiftieth birthday celebrations: Christopher Bland (1st), Peter Mandelson (2nd), Ian Hargreaves (3rd) and Jane (1st lady), 1993

Terry Burns on a walk we took together in the Brecon Beacons, 1979

Ascending Annapurna, 16,000 feet
up, in the Himalayas, 1992

A surprise encounter with a BBC
outside broadcast truck on a walk
in the Radnorshire hills with
Andrew Turnbull in 1992

Walking across Provence with former BBC Director of Corporate Affairs
Howell James (left) and Laurie Taylor in 1994

Tony Smith's vision and advocated what they dubbed an Open Broadcasting Authority. The ITV companies counter-attacked, led by the big barons Paul Fox and Denis Forman. I wrote to Labour Home Secretary Merlyn Rees, whom I knew from my days on *Weekend World*, urging him not to give way and make the fourth channel the creature of ITV. The pivotal figure in the debate turned out to be Willie Whitelaw who – when he was shadow Home Secretary – had supported the case for pluralism. With the change in government in 1979, Whitelaw became Mrs Thatcher's Home Secretary and settled the issue, proposing a Channel 4 independent of the ITV companies, but regulated by the IBA, and funded not as the Annan Committee had proposed, but on a similar basis to the one David Elstein and I had suggested nearly a decade before. Sir Keith Joseph supported Whitelaw, and David Elstein played a vital part in the final as well as the first act of the saga by persuading the main broadcasting union not to resist independent production. And so Channel 4 was born.

Whitelaw's visionary decision would be critical to the general opening up of the whole of British broadcasting over the next twenty years. A thriving independent production and facilities sector would finally put the in-house departments on their mettle, competing on quality, innovation and price. Many of the stifling rigidities of the existing structures would end.

Channel 4 would now be a reality. The last question to be settled was: who would run it? Jeremy Isaacs was the obvious answer. He was twelve years older than me. He had the seniority, experience and support. I admired him greatly: he had not only been a distinguished programme-maker – most notably responsible for *The World at War* – but an adventurous and innovative Director of Programmes at Thames. And he had a wild, audacious streak, which endeared him to radical programme-makers. I reasoned that Jeremy was likely to be appointed – but he might not be, for his rebelliousness might put off the faint-hearted. All-round general management was not his strong suit, and he might frighten off the conservatively minded as well. And Jeremy was unpredictable, and so might make a mistake. I decided to stand against him. The period of expansion of Features and Current Affairs at LWT was clearly coming to an end. I was ambitious for a new challenge. I did not expect to be appointed to run Channel 4. I had no illusions at all, but if Jeremy stumbled I was probably the best-placed alternative. I felt I had made a major contribution to the battle of ideas about broadcasting in the 1970s, and had run a successful and pioneering department. Even if Jeremy did not stumble, I would be putting down a marker for the future that I wanted a place at the top table.

I prepared thoroughly, collaborating chiefly with Rod Allen, ex-editor of *Broadcast* – who produced LWT's media programme *Look Here* – and Sue Stoessl, head of research at LWT. Over a period of months we worked out a prospectus, a rationale for Channel 4 rooted in my recent writings about minorities, but we also went further, trying to nail down the scheduling, financial and organisational issues. John Freeman fondly and formally supported my candidacy. In preparing my manifesto, however, I became too immersed in the detail. My passionate conviction made me zealous. My application was over-earnest. At the interview with the shadow board, I felt I demonstrated a real command of all the issues, but I was far too serious. Brian Tesler, a member of the panel – and effectively ITV's representative on the Channel 4 board – had to come to my rescue. He assured his colleagues after the interview that, contrary to the impression I had made, I was in fact a relaxed colleague and keen on fun. Being over-serious when there was important business afoot would be a mistake I would make again until I became better versed in high institutional politics.

Channel 4's board *did* in the event have some worries about Jeremy's maturity. He had offended Brian Tesler, when they worked together at Thames, by mischievously flicking balls of bread from one table to another during an industry awards dinner. And Jeremy had famously handed over material on the RUC's treatment of IRA suspects – which had been banned by the IBA – to the BBC's

Nationwide. These issues were aired. Channel 4's Chairman Edmund Dell had the gravest doubts about Jeremy, and I became his first choice to run the network. Dell wrote to me later to say, 'I was not impressed by Jeremy,' adding that I was the 'outstanding candidate'. But the board as a whole finally did select him, and I think they were right to do so. In retrospect, I don't think – at thirty-six – I had the necessary level of experience to start a brand new network.

Channel 4 went on to break the mould of British television for the better. At its finest, the network's programmes exhibited a wonderful eccentricity. It gave space to dissonant voices and talents which might not have broken through in the established, entrenched broadcasting organisations. It stimulated and prodded. Over the following decades, however, Channel 4 produced few programmes of exceptional, enduring weight and excellence. It would have few entrants in a pageant of great programmes made in the twenty years since its inception. As a channel, it would prove high on stimulus, but low on creative achievement.

I had genuinely not expected to be made Chief Executive of Channel 4, but the process of applying was long, and the competition intensified my interest. My hopes had also been raised by the doubts over Jeremy. I took Edmund Dell's call in a noisy kitchen at home in Wandsworth one Saturday morning with Radio 1 blaring in the background. Dell was most generous and flattering about my abilities, but when he told me I had not got the job I was deeply disappointed. Though normally buoyant, I became low and directionless, lost without a challenge. Michael Grade came to my rescue and gave me a new lease of life. In addition to my existing responsibilities, he asked me to be LWT's link to Channel 4, and to pull together all of LWT's own proposals to make programmes for the new network. Working with all of LWT's programme departments, I produced a vast portfolio of offers. On the basis of my genuine and unfaltering commitment to Channel 4, I established a good working relationship with the top team – Jeremy, his affable

Controller, Paul Bonner, and his senior commissioning editor, the ebullient life-force Liz Forgan, whom Jeremy had recruited from the *Guardian*. LWT began with a huge commission from Channel 4. From its launch, and for many years thereafter, LWT would be the network's largest supplier of programmes from any source.

LWT launched on Channel 4 the factual magazines *Black on Black* and *Eastern Eye*, for the black and Asian communities, both programmes tremendously appreciated by their target audiences. We made *Saturday Live* and *No Problem*. We produced Jim Callaghan's memoirs, we mounted the trials, with leading lawyers, of Richard III and Lee Harvey Oswald. We made scores of arts, books, music and history programmes.

The most lasting consequence of my work managing LWT's contribution to Channel 4 was, however, more industrial than creative – for some key financial discoveries made during the process would herald major changes later, first in ITV, then at the BBC. I needed to be sure that LWT was selling its programmes to Channel 4 at a profit and not a loss, so I first had to work out how much it would cost LWT to make its programme package for the new network. To help me uncover the answer, I had the help of a brilliant young LWT accountant Christopher Turner. Our task would prove enormously difficult, for LWT, like other ITV companies, knew and monitored the direct cash costs of making programmes – cash for scripts, presenters, programme teams, location expenses, set build and so on – but the facilities and support services used by a particular programme were managed by a separate division within LWT, outside the programme division's control, and allocated to programmes by administrators. The true cost of all these facilities and support services consumed by an individual programme – including pay, overtime, the cost of capital – did *not* appear on the programme's budget.

Christopher Turner and I set out to understand the cost of individual resources – for instance, a fully crewed studio for a day – and then to assign them to the programmes that used them. In other words, we tried to discover for the very first time in the history of British television the true, total cost of individual programmes. Our findings amazed us and were not believed by many in the industry for some years. When the full costs of all the staff and their golden hours and the under-utilised plant and the excessive overheads were added in, every kind of programme was costing many times more than its direct cash cost. The figures were startling. But, armed with this information, we negotiated a good price for LWT's contribution to Channel 4.

As we were building our relationship with the new network, LWT's own franchise came up for renewal, and the IBA also advertised a new breakfast franchise. LWT's programme department convened at a Brighton hotel to consider the company's bid. My Features and Current Affairs department prepared long and hard, and put on a brilliant display for me and the rest of the conference. Jane Hewland was in particularly scintillating form. Michael Grade wrote afterwards:

> I cannot tell you how exhilarated I was by you and your
> department's contribution to Brighton – quite breathtaking.
> We may laugh sometimes at the serious way you approach
> these kinds of problems – but the end results viz Brighton
> are really quite amazing. I suspect that not only is yours the
> most talented programme department in television but the
> most organised and best led. Absolutely terrific!

Many of my good friends – Peter Jay, David Frost and Nick Elliott – combined to bid for the new breakfast franchise, branding themselves TV-am. Peter and David asked me to read and to comment on their bid, the heart of which was a high-minded 'mission to explain'. They sent me a souvenir copy of the final application inscribed: 'With warm thanks from your disciples!' I conducted a mock interview for them a few days before the real thing in front of the full Authority. As I drove to the rehearsal I heard the news on the radio that John Lennon had been shot dead. I churned inside. I felt a dreadful loss. A thrilling icon of my generation had been cruelly stolen away.

The news cast a sombre cloud over the day's proceedings. At the rehearsal, the TV-am team, including its galaxy of stars, performed disastrously – as they were the first to realise. They had not established who among them would address each particular area of questioning. No one was articulating simple, clear, coherent propositions. No overall narrative emerged. I was merciless in my criticism. A few days later the same group swept the IBA off its feet with its glamour, intellect and brilliance, and walked away with the franchise. I joined in the euphoria but was sorry I was now going to lose one of my trusted henchmen, the trenchant Nick Elliott. Peter Jay invited me to come aboard – as Managing Director to his Chairman – but, though I was attracted to the idea of working with such close and admired friends, TV-am's remit was too narrow to engage me. It was a lucky escape: the company tragically foundered not long after its launch and Peter Jay and other good friends were lost overboard.

On the day I returned from my summer holiday in 1981, Michael Grade asked to see me, and escorted me up to Brian Tesler's office. There Michael told me he was going to leave LWT to work for a production company in Hollywood. Brian immediately interjected to say he would like me to succeed Michael, and that I should consider whether I wanted to. Michael added that I was his recommendation.

I was distressed at the thought of Michael leaving LWT. We had had a good few years together, and we had become close. I had felt even more affection for Michael when I appreciated just how deprived his childhood had been: like my grandfather Bill, Michael had been deserted by his mother and effectively by his father, who had lodged Michael with his adored grandmother to be brought up by her. I had been in New York with Michael – forced to share a bedroom with him because of a slip-up over hotel bookings – when the call came through to tell him that his grandmother had died, and I had been moved to see, momentarily, a little boy lost. I had seen Michael grow in the job. He had acquired new skills and worked out how to apply his entrepreneurial and deal-making abilities in fresh fields. He had gamely learnt to accommodate broadcasting's liberal elite, who had trounced him on his first fumbling outings at the Edinburgh Television Festival. It had never occurred to me that Michael would leave LWT, and, therefore, I had never considered that I might succeed him. After a few days' reflection, though, I finally decided to accept Brian's offer. Peak-time entertainment was a long way from the centre of my interest, but applying for the Channel 4 job had persuaded me I needed the stimulus of new horizons.

I organised Michael's send-off with John Bromley. We, his four Controllers, ambushed him one day, flew him by helicopter to Heathrow and boarded a plane to Paris. There we held a magnificent dinner in his honour. We were all sad to see him go. I would encounter Michael again – and far sooner than I realised – in much less happy circumstances.

10

Nixon, Kissinger
and the Shah

In the late 1970s and early 1980s I joined up with David Frost again – on leave of absence from LWT – to work on three programmes of some historic significance: the television memoirs of Richard Nixon, Henry Kissinger and the Shah of Iran. As a result, I found myself dealing and negotiating with people toughened by power and their experience of world events.

The Nixon Interviews were the last delayed act of the Nixon presidency – which had ended with his resignation in 1974 – and the long-awaited dénouement of the Watergate scandal. They would be the first and only times Nixon would ever submit himself to cross-examination about his presidency. Much was at stake.

David had outbid NBC for Nixon's memoirs, offering more time, four ninety-minute programmes, and more money, a fee of $600,000, than NBC. When David went to sign the deal with Nixon, he placed a cheque for $200,000 alongside the contracts – the first down-payment on the fee. The moment the papers were signed, the former President reached out to pocket David's cheque. Nixon's agent – the famously street-wise Swifty Lazar – interrupted sharply: 'Please: let *me* have that!' He held out his hand. 'It's made out to me,' responded Nixon plaintively, holding the cheque closer. Lazar raised his voice: 'Give . . . it . . . to . . . me . . . please.' A sheepish Nixon reluctantly handed over the money. Swifty would later fall out with Nixon after he was reported as saying: 'Listen, I'd represent Adolf Hitler if there was money in it!'

David, typically, had taken a huge risk. He had signed a contract without having first assembled the necessary funds – around two million dollars – to cover Nixon's full fee, as well as the massive cost of a major television production. Nor did David yet have an outlet for the interviews in the States, for the major US networks had turned their backs on the series as they would not cede control of a news programme to an outsider. Undaunted, David set out to create a network of his own, and to attract investors. He hoped to distribute the series to independent television stations – unaffiliated to the networks – and to raise revenue by selling the advertising. This would all prove difficult, and would place David under great strain as he balanced the editorial and business needs of the project over the next two years – for neither investors nor advertisers queued up to be associated with the disgraced President. One advertiser said: 'Half of the advertising industry would never have been seen dead with Richard Nixon. The other half is embarrassed that they were.' After paying the production's bills with his own money for many months, David eventually attracted Polygram and Jimmy Goldsmith's Banque Occidentale as lead funders. The first intrepid advertiser was a company called Weed Eater from Houston, Texas. It would be a long haul, but David would, eventually, come out slightly ahead on overall costs.

In 1976 we assembled a team of US journalists to research the interviews, leaning on the veteran commentator Joe Kraft for recruitment advice. The lead journalist was Bob Zelnick, square built with a wide, friendly face, brought up in the Bronx, a former lawyer turned reporter who had worked for US public radio. (After the Nixon interviews, Bob would go on to work for ABC News for many years, chiefly as its Pentagon correspondent, later to become Chairman of the Department of Journalism at Boston University.) Bob Zelnick was a true intellectual, with a powerful academic mind and formidable knowledge of every major policy area. He was also the very best kind of American journalist, with a deep moral commitment to high professional standards of accuracy, fairness and integrity. I worked side by side with Bob for months – sometimes for twenty hours a day – and he and I established a close bond.

The team began a long period of research into Nixon and his record. We wanted our series to stand the test of history. We resolved to be thorough and tough with Nixon, but also to be fair.

Nixon had had a small-town upbringing. He was a man ill at ease with himself, and with a chip on his shoulder. He was at once hardworking, earnest, studious, ungregarious, paranoid and sly. Throughout his time in politics, he had hit back hard when cornered. He was a talented but flawed man. He had little interest in domestic policy and was certainly not a free-market ideologue: he had no compunction, for instance, in introducing pay and price controls. Rather, his obsession was with foreign affairs, and he had taken significant strides as President towards making the world a safer place. He ended China's isolation; he brought a thaw in relations with the Soviet Union; he negotiated major arms-control agreements; and he reduced tensions in the Middle East.

These achievements had to be set, however, against the running sore of Vietnam. The war overshadowed Nixon's presidency, deeply divided America and created widespread dissent on the campuses and in the cities. I had seen Washington under siege while making a film there for *World in Action*. The smell of revolt had been in the air. Nixon's regime had waged war on his opponents: Daniel Ellsberg – the former US government employee who had leaked confidential papers on the Vietnam War to the *New York Times* – had had his files stolen from his psychiatrist; the Brookings Institute was

fire-bombed in an attempt to destroy sensitive papers; Nixon's political enemies had had their income tax scrutinised; reporters seen as
hostile were wire-tapped. Against this backdrop it was not surprising, therefore, that five Nixon supporters had broken into
Democratic Party offices in the Watergate building in Washington
DC to plant bugs. The break-in had been planned by Nixon's re-
election committee – CREEP – headed and run by close Nixon
loyalists. Our task on the Nixon interviews was to paint this vast
canvas. We wanted to do justice to the former President's achievements and to debrief him for history – but we also wanted to
cross-examine him about his personal guilt in respect of Watergate
and other political skulduggery.

For our Watergate research we waded through a mountain of
material already on the public record, particularly the tape recordings of conversations in the Oval Office. In the process of our
research, we uncovered further tapes pointing to Nixon's culpability.
The tapes had been buried – undiscovered by reporters – in court
records. They gave us ammunition Nixon wouldn't be expecting.
Bob Zelnick and I sought and received off-the-record assistance on
our Watergate programme from one of the key lawyers who would
have prosecuted Nixon if he had faced an impeachment trial in the
Senate. And we were also given advice by Bob Woodward – one of
the *Washington Post* reporters who had helped topple the President –
on how best to approach Nixon on Watergate. Woodward was a
model journalist, utterly clear about what was proven and not
proven about Nixon. He and Bernstein would become iconic and
spawn many imitators, but few with their scrupulousness.

It was proving difficult to agree firm dates to record the interviews
with the Nixon team. They said they were worried because some
Watergate legal actions were still outstanding. Moreover, Nixon was
falling behind with his memoirs. We were fearful, however, that
these might not be the real reasons, that Nixon had developed cold
feet. I flew to San Clemente in California, where Nixon lived and

worked, to try to resolve matters. I met Jack Brennan – the ex-Marine colonel who was Nixon's chief of staff – and staff member Frank Gannon in the austere, functional, prefabricated offices that had once been the Western White House. We were a contrast in style and attitude: my hair fell nearly to my shoulders, and I had a natural affinity with the protesters who had marched on Washington. Brennan and Gannon wore crew-cuts and were strait-laced, hard-talking men of Republican stock. Anyone who had immersed themselves in the Watergate transcripts, as I had, would be wary of any Nixon staff member, and I certainly was. Moreover, these were the staunchest loyalists, those who had stayed the whole course, remaining on Nixon's team long after his resignation. I talked with Brennan and Gannon for six hours. They offered me neither food nor drink. I wilted, but stayed the course and estab-lished to my eventual satisfaction that the Watergate sessions would go ahead, that the prime reason for the delay really was that Nixon wanted to do justice to his book. I took a chance and flew a kite: I shared with them my own conviction that, to clear the air, the series needed to start with Watergate. Until Watergate was out of the way, I argued, no one would pay any attention to anything else Nixon said about China or any other policy matter. To my surprise, Brennan and Gannon didn't demur.

A few weeks later, David reached final agreement with Brennan: we would record our twenty-eight hours of interviews in March and April of 1977 in a private home near San Clemente, and we would start transmitting the following month, in May.

David had an ingenious ruse for charging some broadcasters around the world a premium price for the right to show the inter-views. Nixon had agreed, without considering the consequences, to record four additional hours of interview – for exclusive showing in Britain, France, Italy and Australia – focusing on issues of particular interest to those countries. David's scheme was unwelcome to me – as producer of the main series – as I feared the extra programmes would be a distraction both for Frost and for Nixon. The notion was that each of the participating broadcasters would produce its own hour, with me retaining oversight. In the UK the BBC bought the interview, and I went to Lime Grove for a meeting over lunch with Brian Wenham, the BBC's head of current affairs, and his team, to discuss their approach. Wenham behaved like a monarch surrounded by courtiers. He seemed to find the Nixon enterprise a great joke, an excuse for frivolity, his team laughing in chorus at his every jibe. He obstructed my attempts to steer the conversation towards a proper discussion of what Nixon should be asked about in the British hour. Instead, he either tried to pry gossip on Nixon out of me or merely pontificated. I was affronted by the experience, which confirmed all my prejudices about the BBC's unsystematic, unserious approach to current affairs, in sharp contrast not just to the LWT school of journalism but to the conscientious team of American reporters beavering away on the project in the States.

The other foreign broadcasters took their hour of interview with Nixon much more seriously than the BBC. The Italians in particular produced page after page of abstruse analysis and questions covering US–Italian relations since the Second World War. I blanched when I read them. The only remark made by Nixon we could track down about Italy was his infamous 'I don't give a shit about the lira!' The exact terms of the first Italian question are lost from my memory, but they went something very like:

> Mr President, in 1947, when you were on your way to the Middle East, your plane had a brief stopover in Italy for fuel, and you held a meeting with Foreign Minister Paganini. Can you confirm that at that meeting you discussed the future of the iron and steel agreement and its implications for Europe?

Bob Zelnick and I doubled up with laughter when we read the proposed question. I was certain Nixon would not be able to answer from memory this or any other of the esoteric questions on the Italian list. I tried to address this difficulty.

We had always resolved to let Nixon's team know in advance the general – though not the precise – areas of questioning that we would cover in each day's interview, for we wanted Nixon to be focused and prepared, if not forearmed. But Bob and I decided, pragmatically, to go further with the Italian hour and the other overseas programmes and to slip Nixon's team the *actual* questions that David would ask. However, we didn't tell the Italians, or anyone else, what we had done. Nixon subsequently revealed a complete mastery of every question put to him in the additional foreign hours. In response to the first question on the list, Nixon said something along the lines of 'Yes, I remember very well my meeting with Signor Paganini. We touched down in Rimini in the late afternoon. It was in September 1947. He and I discussed . . .' The Italians were most impressed. During the French hour, the cheroot dropped from the mouth of the silky suave producer from Paris when Nixon – again tipped off – demonstrated total recall of the circumstances surrounding France's suspicions that America was trying to exclude de Gaulle from the nuclear club.

As Nixon began to appreciate just how much mugging up he would have to do for the foreign hours, he approached them with an air of glum resignation. Just before the taping sessions were due to begin, the hand-picked production crew – who would work on all the sessions – were assembled in San Clemente to meet the former President. Nixon went down the line of thirty to forty people, one by one, shaking hands with each crew member. Like Edward Heath, Nixon had little small talk. He woodenly asked each person their name, what they did, and where they came from. 'I am Herbie Smith, Mr President. I am a sound assistant, and I come from Santa Monica.' This typical exchange was duplicated over and over again, with dreary repetitiveness, right down the line. Last in the row was a sunny Dane with a sing-song accent who would be directing the outside broadcasts: 'I'm Jørn Winther, Mr President, and I live in Pasadena – but I come originally from Denmark.' Nixon looked abject and walked away muttering: 'Well,

I was worried about the Italian and the Australian hours. But the *Danish* hour!' He was quickly put out of his misery.

The production team was quartered at the Beverly Hilton Hotel in Los Angeles. For the many months of preparation, Bob and I survived on room service during the day, but most evenings, around 10 p.m., we headed off for sustenance to the Japanese quarter of LA, where Bob introduced me for the first time to what would become one of the great loves of my life – sushi. There were few if any sushi bars at that time in London, and they were still a rarity in LA. Except for one evening when Candice Bergen turned up, the clientele of our sushi bar was solely Japanese, and no one spoke any English. It had a friendly, raucous atmosphere, with constant catcalling between the sushi chef and his regulars – among whom Bob and I were soon counted. Each evening we were greeted on arrival by a roar of welcome from the sake-sozzled diners. Bob and I would wolf down impeccable, succulent Pacific fish until we could eat no more. Sometimes – late night, post-sushi – I would drive alone up to the hills above LA and along Mulholland Drive, and look down on the spectacular lights of the city spread out below me, or explore the palm-lined boulevards of Beverly Hills, Hollywood and Santa Monica and their architectural glories, which Raymond Chandler's novels had first taught me to appreciate. Two newly released classic albums – the Eagles' *Hotel California* and Stevie Wonder's *Songs in the Key of Life* – played endlessly on the radio as I savoured the city of angels in the early hours.

The time for taping the interviews drew near. David would be interviewing Nixon every Monday, Wednesday and Friday over a period of nearly two months, with a week off in the middle. We prepared meticulously, mapping out which issues we would cover in which session. We planned to cover domestic policy, foreign policy and Vietnam in the early sessions, leaving Watergate and other sensitive issues until towards the end. We worked on our tactics. David, Bob and I would brainstorm, trying to identify how Nixon would respond to a question, plotting our responses like chess moves. Bob, it would turn out, had a high success rate in predicting Nixon's replies. I would cry 'Bingo!' in the control room, again and again, as Nixon answered right on cue during the tapings, as if he were reading a Zelnick script.

The first sessions on Vietnam did not go well. Nixon gave long, unfocused, meandering answers. David was feeling Nixon out, not wanting to put the project at risk by showing his mettle too early. One or two gems were buried in the early interviews, but I was fearful that, even edited down, overall the material lacked punch. An early assembly of a possible first programme demoralised us. The team was nervous. We felt the eye of history and of America on us. We feared that David was not taking control and was not driving the interviews hard enough. There was some plain talking between us all. David felt strongly that we were over-reacting and resented our criticism. For a few days relations were tense.

Nixon's answers were so long winded in the early interviews that we soon faced a further problem: we were beginning to drift seriously behind our timetable. We pressed Nixon's people for more time, but they were adamant: a contract was a contract – Nixon would not budge from the time allotted. David and I decided we had to confront the issue. We held a meeting with Brennan and Ken Khachigian, another of Nixon's aides. I said we could no longer do justice to all the issues in the time remaining: we had to cut our losses, drop some key subject areas and leave Nixon to cover them in his memoirs. With brazen effrontery I said we would leave out détente with the Soviet Union and the normalisation of relations with China, Nixon's greatest triumphs. 'China must go,' I said, preposterously. Nixon's Chief of Staff went white. 'How much more time will you settle for?' Brennan asked. 'Four hours.' Nixon relented and conceded the extra time.

Relations between the Nixon and Frost teams as the tapings progressed were more relaxed than I had anticipated. Ken

Khachigian in particular had a nice line in banter. David once, in error, left behind a briefcase containing some research material for the interviews. Ken called to say: 'Thanks for leaving the briefcase. It saves us a fire-bombing!' Ken asked Bob one day how he was handling press enquiries on a particular matter. Bob responded: 'I don't give a shit. I stonewall, I cover it up – anything that will protect our plan!' Nixon himself was generally disconnected and sombre. He found it hard to relax or to strike the right note. One Monday, as he sat down on the set, he said to David, in everyone's hearing: 'Have you done any fornicating over the weekend?' On another occasion he noticed David's shoes and commented: 'They tried to get me to wear shoes like that, but I thought they were too effeminate!'

The Frost team was tense as we approached the Watergate sessions, uncertain how well we'd do, unclear how Nixon and his staff would respond. We all – and particularly David – immersed ourselves in the tapes. David has a superb retentive memory, and soon had a masterly grasp of who said what to whom and when. We agreed our tactics: we were not going to throw poison darts which made David sound tough but which Nixon could easily fend off. We weren't going to waste time on fishing expeditions, looking for something that might be there, but of which we were not certain. We would ignore all of those many areas – for instance, whether or not Nixon knew in advance of the Watergate burglary – where there was suspicion of his complicity but no proof. We would focus only on those charges where there was real evidence of criminal behaviour on Nixon's part. In addition, we researched the many abuses that had occurred under previous presidents, and were prepared to support a line of argument that, under Nixon, abuse of power had become institutionalised and of unparalleled scope; and that Nixon was enmeshed personally to an unprecedented extent. And, recognising that Nixon was a skilled and experienced lawyer, we didn't want to be out-legalled: we became authorities on his position in law; we acquainted ourselves with the actual statutes that he had transgressed. Bob Zelnick's own legal training was critical here.

At midnight on the night before the first momentous interview on Watergate, I put a personal note under David's door. I wrote:

> It is not a conventional interview: you are exchanging interpretations of the known facts; you should talk almost as much as he does. Most importantly, don't be tempted to put brief and 'pointed' questions that elicit long and vague answers: when he paints a picture that you know to be false, respond by painting, at the same length he does, the alternative picture as you understand it. Always keep firmly in mind that Watergate is a difficult subject for a mass audience to follow and at each stage it is your responsibility to point out clearly to the audience the implication of any question, fact, event, statement or admission that you consider relevant. Stay cool and firm, but be polite: only raise your voice if and when you are pushed to. And, finally, keep up the pressure at all times: you will win only if you can, so to speak, sprint the mile.

The next morning the whole of Nixon's support team came to the taping for the first time – Ray Price and Diane Sawyer as well as Brennan, Gannon and Khachigian. (Diane Sawyer went on to be one of ABC News's biggest stars; Ken Khachigian to be a speech-writer for Reagan.) One of the Frost team remarked: 'Wow! Today we have *all* the President's men.'

That day's session on Watergate – and the one that followed – would be David's greatest hour as an interviewer, demonstrating his utter command of his material, his resourcefulness under pressure, and his powerful self-confidence. As soon as we began, it became clear that Nixon's defence would rest on what he claimed were his benign motives for his actions, and on his highly self-serving interpretation of the law of conspiracy. We had correctly predicted this tactic. David took charge. Nixon was visibly taken aback when David firmly contradicted his eccentric interpretation of the conspiracy statute. He was further shaken when we played in the new evidence from the unpublicised tapes we had uncovered. He was even more rattled when, again and again, David's intimate grasp of the evidence became clear. One of the most telling moments was a quick-fire sixteen-point rebuttal by David, with chapter and verse, blasting Nixon's contention that he was innocent of agreeing to pay hush-money to one of the conspirators.

During this critical exchange, I watched Nixon on the control-room monitor as emotion passed in waves over his hollowed, angular, pitted face: he reeled, he blinked, he winced with the pain of David's assault. For two taut, tense hours, David took Nixon systematically through the evidence on a string of charges. Nixon dodged and weaved, but his account was unconvincing. The Frost team was transfixed by the drama of the occasion, admiring of David's performance, and thrilled by the success of our preparation and tactics.

The moment the session ended, however, my immediate concern was with the Nixon camp: how would they react? I was fearful that Nixon would walk away, the interviews unfinished. I sought out Jack Brennan, Nixon's chief of staff. 'That was a disaster,' were his first words to me. Nixon's whole crew gathered around – not, as I first thought, to protest, but to share with me their own distress. 'He made himself look like a common criminal,' Ken Khachigian snapped. Diane Sawyer soon revealed the underlying reason for their disarray: Nixon had not yet apparently either written or even prepared the Watergate section of his book. Nor had Nixon's team prepared him for that day's interview on Watergate as they had the earlier sessions. Nixon's staff had no more known in advance how he would handle the charges against him than we had. They plainly thought – and this came as a revelation to me – that he had the wrong stratagem for Watergate. Just like the Frost team, Nixon's aides wanted full disclosure. Only that, they calculated, would enable Nixon to put these terrors behind him, and to build a new life.

Nixon had always been punctual for the tapings, but he was twenty minutes late for the second Watergate session, and arrived looking haunted and drawn. The atmosphere was highly charged. In this second session, we were due to take him further down the charge sheet, and to ask him about his relations with two key aides – Haldeman and Ehrlichman – whom he had had to fire. We also planned to ascertain whether he would finally own up to criminal conduct and express contrition for his acts.

As the interview began, Nixon was still defensive, but some of the fight had gone out of him, and he became more emotional as we moved closer to the events preceding his downfall. His voice broke when he talked about firing his aides at Camp David. But he still evaded any admission of wrongdoing. His chance was slipping away and he was going nowhere. I groaned with frustration.

Then I noticed Jack Brennan on the set, waving a piece of paper, seemingly at Nixon. We stopped the tape. Nixon returned to his private room and David and I cornered Jack in a small corridor by the stairs. On Jack's piece of paper was scrawled: 'Let him talk.' It had been aimed at David. Emotions were running high: Jack was passionate; David was tearful; I was impatient. Jack insisted that Nixon was being held back by David's prosecutorial style. If David would only pipe down, Jack said, Nixon would eventually steel himself to go further. 'But will he say he was guilty of a crime?' I pressed. 'I don't know,' was Jack's response. 'That he was guilty of impeachable offences?' 'I don't know.' I was unimpressed, and didn't want the interview to lose its tightness and momentum: 'Sorry, Jack,' I said, 'David must continue to cross-examine him.'

Jack retreated to speak to Nixon. I pressed David not to be deflected. Brennan returned: 'I don't know what he's going to say, and I don't think he does either. But you must give him a chance!' I responded over-aggressively, determined that our control of the interview would not slip away: 'Jack, we won't plea-bargain.' David was more placatory: 'We'll give him a chance, Jack, but if he doesn't come through, I shall have to press him.' 'OK,' said Jack, 'and if it doesn't work, we'll try again next week.' '*No*, Jack.' I insisted. 'Don't let him believe he has another chance. It's now or never!'

Brennan departed to bring Nixon back to the set. I took David to one side: 'Don't get caught up in the emotion. What happens next is going to be pored over by history.'

Nixon began slowly, but over the next few incredibly tense minutes – under prompting from David – Nixon made a number of critical admissions and statements. He admitted his mistakes had been 'horrendous'. He said: 'I brought myself down. I gave them a sword and they stuck it in. And they twisted it with relish. And, I guess, if I'd been in their position, I'd have done the same thing.' On Haldeman and Ehrlichman, Nixon said:

I will admit that acting as a lawyer for their defence, I was not prosecuting the case. I will admit that during that period . . . as the one with the chief responsibility for seeing that the laws of the United States are enforced, I did not meet that responsibility. And, to the extent that I did not meet that responsibility, to the extent that within the law – and in some cases going right to the edge of the law – in trying to advise Ehrlichman and Haldeman and all the rest how best to present their cases – because I thought they were legally innocent – that I came to the edge. And under the circumstances, I would have to say that a reasonable person could call that a cover-up.

Now we come down to the key point – and let me answer it in my own way: how do I feel about the American people?

Nixon explained what he had said at a dinner with close supporters on the night before he resigned in 1974:

'I'm sorry; I just hope I haven't let you down.' That said it all. I had. I let down my friends. I let down the country. I let down our system of government and the dreams of all those young people that ought to get into government, but think it's all too corrupt and the rest. Yep, I let the American people down. And I have to carry that burden with me for the rest of my life. My political life is over. I will never again have an opportunity to serve in any official position. I can only say in answer to your questions that while technically I did not commit a crime – an impeachable offence – these are legalisms. As far as the handling of this matter is concerned, it was so botched up; I made so many bad judgements – the worst ones, mistakes of the heart rather than the head . . . But, let me say, a man in that top job, he's gotta have a heart. But his head must always rule his heart.

The moment the interview was over, both teams gathered round the two principals in jubilation. I hugged David: he had been brilliant. I shook Nixon's hand vigorously. Nixon may have baulked at admitting he had committed an impeachable offence, but he had owned up to all the elements of a crime. Any jury would have convicted on his testimony. And he had spoken with powerful and affecting emotion. This was the closest Nixon would ever come to expressing contrition and to admitting culpability for Watergate.

The remaining interviews in the weeks ahead were businesslike. In the end, we had enough material for four long, revealing and electric programmes on every subject that mattered – powerful programmes on Watergate; on foreign affairs and Nixon's dealings with Mao and Brezhnev; on the impact of the Vietnam War at home and abroad.

David held a big party at Chasen's – then Hollywood's leading show-business restaurant – to view the first programme on Watergate as it was broadcast. Hugh Hefner turned up. Joseph

Cotton, star of *Citizen Kane*, sat at my table. After the programme, Hefner invited David and myself – along with our partners, Caroline Cushing and Jane – to go back with him to the Playboy Mansion East, near Sunset Boulevard. I had spent months working intensively in a dark and dull hotel room, so it was a curious contrast to be escorted round the bright and ostentatious Playboy Mansion and its extensive gardens by its proud owner. We saw Hefner's pink flamingos wading in his lake; we spied the hideaway jacuzzis in shadowy grottoes; we were shown, tucked away in the grounds, discreet cabins with mattresses on the floor and gymnasium-style contraptions to aid sexual acrobatics. Hefner himself was engaging and erudite, a sharp reader of politics and a gracious host. We were offered anything we wanted from twenty-four-hour room service: 'There's no menu. Ask for anything. We'll have it!' Hefner introduced us to a great bevy of willowy, busty, blonde beauties and to his other guests. David was deservedly very much the centre of attention.

Our programme was a sensation. We had had the largest audience ever for a news broadcast, with fifty million viewers in the United States alone. We dominated the front pages for days. We held the biggest press conference I have ever attended, with something like a thousand journalists participating. Congratulations came flooding in. Carl Bernstein said we'd done a fine job. The lawyer who would have prosecuted Nixon phoned to say we could not have done better. Dick Salant, head of CBS News – who had passed on the opportunity to acquire the series – generously commented: 'One of the best, most interesting interview broadcasts I've ever seen.' The esteemed TV critic of the *New York Times*, John O'Connor, encapsulated the general verdict: 'a programme with extraordinary impact. Frost proved to be thoroughly prepared, extremely effective and frequently brilliant . . . persistent without being abrasive; clear-headed without being vicious; compassionate without being sentimental.'

Bob Zelnick and I went to San Clemente to say farewell to Nixon. He greeted us cordially and treated us seriously. He waved away any discussion of the interviews. They were already behind him. He wanted, rather, to talk about the American century; to share with us his fear that – under President Carter – America's willingness to use its power was waning. Talking about the nuclear deterrent at one point, he made an observation that stuck with me: 'Always keep your enemies uncertain about your intentions.' Nixon underlined his conviction to us that communism would continue to grow in influence. I asked him how long, as a system, he thought it would survive. With my newly acquired free-market convictions, I suggested that it might collapse under the weight of economic as much as democratic pressure. Nixon paused, seeming not to have considered the question before. Then he asserted that communism would last for another five hundred or even a thousand years. It was as if the man who had made his name first as a cold war warrior, then as a cold war manager, couldn't bear the thought of the old enemy disappearing.

As we were getting up to go, Bob asked Nixon if he had felt betrayed by his own Vice-President, Spiro Agnew, who had lied to Nixon about his own transgressions: 'Who gives a crap?' came Nixon's pungent response.

I didn't meet Nixon again until the early 1990s – just a few years before he died – when he gave a speech in London at a dinner for leading politicians, industrialists and editors. I encountered him before the dinner, standing alone at his table. Approaching him, I said: 'Mr President, you may not remember me, but I'm John Birt: I produced the interviews you recorded in the 1970s with David Frost.' A moment of pain passed over his face. Finally he growled: 'Don't remember you at all. That's in the past. I don't ever think about those interviews now.' Then he turned away.

Later, speaking without a note and with unfaltering fluency, Nixon talked brilliantly for half an hour about contemporary foreign affairs issues. He tailored his remarks to his British audience, including witty, apposite and esoteric examples from British history. He was rewarded with a standing ovation. Jim Callaghan was one of the first to his feet. Nixon was being taken seriously again. He had cleared the air. There *had* been life for him after Watergate.

In 1979, a few years after the Nixon interviews, David Frost and I combined again, this time to work on Henry Kissinger's television memoirs for the NBC network in the US.

We had been approached by Nigel Ryan, a vice-president of NBC News, a debonair, straight-backed, upper-class Briton with whom I had previously tangled over my 'bias against understanding' article in *The Times* when he was editor of ITN. NBC was in a scrape, Nigel explained. The network had recruited Kissinger as a consultant when he left office, provoking massive criticism from those who felt that he would be incapable of commenting impartially on the Carter administration – the successor regime to the Nixon/Ford presidencies that Kissinger had served as Secretary of State. An NBC special on Euro-communism had been seen as an uncritical platform for Kissinger's views, and had embarrassed the network. If the Kissinger memoirs were produced by NBC with a staff interviewer, Nigel explained, they would lack credibility. On the back of our Nixon success, David and I were now needed to restore NBC's reputation for independence and integrity.

We created a team to prepare for the interview, including Les Gelb, a noted foreign affairs specialist; Walter Pincus, a reporter from the *Washington Post*; and Willie Shawcross, the British journalist who had written the definitive analysis of Kissinger's role in Cambodia in his book *Sideshow*, using America's new Freedom of Information legislation to extract a huge amount of revealing and damaging data about Cambodia from the Pentagon. We kept Willie's role on the project secret.

From the beginning, we laboured under time restraints on what – it was soon apparent – was a misconceived project. NBC wanted a single one-hour special, compared with the six hours we had had for

Nixon's memoirs. They had initially agreed with Kissinger to tape two ninety-minute sessions, which had subsequently been reduced to two forty-minute sessions. This reduction, we discovered late in the day, was the quid pro quo for Kissinger withdrawing the right – ceded to him under an extraordinary and unprecedented contract of which we had been unaware – to review the editing process on our programme *at all stages*, though NBC still retained ultimate editorial and executive control. David protested directly to Kissinger that two forty-minute recording sessions for a sixty-minute programme was a straitjacket. 'I want you in a straitjacket,' Kissinger had rejoined. Given these demanding time constraints, David and I decided that our best approach would be to start each section of the interview with a long, challenging, scene-setting question, then follow up quickly with rapid-fire question and answer.

This would be the first occasion on which Kissinger would be held to account on Cambodia. The central charge against him was that his and Nixon's decision to expand the war from Vietnam to Cambodia had precipitated the greatest horror visited on one society in our time – the genocidal atrocities of the Pol Pot regime. Self-evidently, America did not bear the blame alone – the Khmer Rouge had to take prime responsibility for its own bestiality, and the North Vietnamese had not respected Cambodian neutrality either. But without America's intervention Cambodia's ruler, Prince Sihanouk, might have prevailed and held the fragile peace. In addition, we would question Kissinger about other international issues, including the Vietnam peace negotiations, the attempt to overthrow Allende's regime in Chile, and the failure of the US to stop its ally Pakistan committing genocide in Bangladesh.

As we had done with the Nixon interviews, David and I and the team prepared our tactics, hypothesising about Kissinger's likely response to each challenge, preparing our counters and follow-ups, working closely with Willie Shawcross. We anticipated that Kissinger would be commanding and formidable. In the event, he was not. Kissinger was on the back foot from the very beginning of the first section of the interview – on Cambodia – and he never regained his balance. David was firm and confident, rattling Kissinger more than once with his mastery of the record. Kissinger looked shifty, smouldering and surly. He seemed not to have considered his tactics at all, or to be prepared for a tough cross-examination. He was not defending his policy with any conviction. And it was clear he was not going to recover.

The phone rang in the studio control room where I was supervising the recording. Nigel Ryan listened to the unidentified caller, then finally spoke: 'I agree: Frost is too tendentious. I'll get a message to him.' But Nigel couldn't: David wasn't wearing an earpiece, and Nigel jibbed at stopping the recording.

The interview continued, and became testy. David, alert to the time constraints, was interrupting when Kissinger answered at length. Nigel Ryan's phone rang again. Again he listened for a long time. Finally he said: 'I agree. We should not transmit this interview. We will get Frost to do it again.' Immediately, I told Nigel that we would never do that. Ryan's phone rang a third time. He listened to his caller without responding, then left the studio. We later discovered from NBC News executives friendly to us (because of their hostility to Kissinger's contract) that Nigel Ryan had just been ordered on the phone to fire Frost summarily, and to substitute an NBC staff reporter in David's place. Indeed, even while the interview was progressing, we were told that the call went out to track down NBC staff reporter Edwin Newman. If found, Newman was to be brought straight to the studio and – in the stuff of nightmares – he was to retape, there and then, untutored and unprepared, the Cambodia interview! This madcap scheme was soon dropped, however, and Newman was duly spared the ordeal of a lifetime.

I watched Kissinger storm out of the studio the moment the interview ended, at the head of a phalanx of tight-lipped aides. I congratulated David, before informing him of the shocking events I had just witnessed in the control room, of which he had been blissfully unaware. Nigel Ryan soon joined us: 'Kissinger's very angry. He says he won't return for the second interview tomorrow. And he won't be interviewed again by you, David. I'm trying to persuade him not to be hasty.' Nigel withdrew.

An hour later we all met again in the office of Les Crystal, the number two at NBC News, for a meeting that was to last six hours. Crystal began by accusing David of endorsing the views of Kissinger's critics: 'The job of a reporter is to ask tough questions, not to argue!' David and I held our ground, but after hours of disputation we could not bridge the gap between the two sides. We were summoned finally to the office of Bill Small, President of NBC News. Small declared he too had been 'a tough journalist' (the word 'tough' was to recur over and over again in the harangue that followed). But we had been out of bounds with Kissinger, we had been rude to him, we had hounded him, we had interrupted a former Secretary of State. Small elaborated on his theme: a tough question was OK, provided the interviewer sat quiet and listened before moving on to the next 'tough' question. Follow-ups were not part of Small's vision of the television inquisitor's armoury.

David and I counter-attacked: NBC must recognise its journalistic responsibilities, the value of the reporter testing and challenging authority; the network must cease kow-towing to Kissinger; it must tell him there could be no concessions; the poor quality of Kissinger's responses in the morning's interview on Cambodia had been powerfully revealing, and must be aired. But we went round in circles: we were not getting through. Finally, Small declared himself: he wondered out loud if any of the morning's material was usable, adding that in any case that would be Tom Tomasawa's decision, not Small's or ours. Tom – an NBC staffer, and not David and me as previously agreed – would be editing the programme according to NBC's own editorial criteria, and Small said we should all simply support and uphold whatever Tom decided. Our friendly NBC allies later drew wry amusement from the elevation of the able and likeable – but quiet and unassuming – Tomasawa to be the ultimate referee of this treacherous editorial combat.

We rejected the suggestion and put a counter-proposal on the table: first, Kissinger should lift the restrictions on the recording time. Second, we made a concession (wrongly, I now think): Kissinger had felt he had not had time to answer the opening question on Cambodia; we would record the first answer again, but we would not pull back from cross-examination.

Our bitter argument with Small and his colleagues continued to go round and round in circles, but it gradually dawned on David and me that NBC was still negotiating; that they were unwilling to precipitate our departure from the project. NBC was stuck between a rock and a hard place, between us and Kissinger. They wanted both parties to stay on board, but we were all at an impasse. Small turned to his colleagues: 'Have you mentioned the question that I myself suggested?' 'No, there hasn't been an opportunity,' a nervous executive replied. We waited expectantly. Small paused, enjoying his moment in the spotlight: 'Without giving Kissinger any warning, you ask him to draw a pen portrait, in just a few words, of some of the key figures he met in public life – Mao, Chou, Brezhnev, Nixon, Agnew, Haldeman, Ehrlichman.' Then Small paused for dramatic effect. What was coming, I wondered? 'Then you give him the final name. You say: Kissinger!'

We had spent all day and late into the evening in meetings with NBC when we should have been completing our detailed tactical plotting for the second interview the following day. We had been put seriously off our stride. The next morning, I arrived early at David's flat to the news that Kissinger had been phoning Nigel Ryan since 6 a.m. Kissinger had agreed to extend the second session from forty to eighty minutes; he accepted our proposal to redo the first question and answer; and he demanded copies of all the documentary evidence we had referred to on Cambodia. This latter demand posed no problems for us, for all the material was already on the public record.

David and I set off for NBC's studios, resolving that, from our point of view, the rules of the game had not changed. Pope John

Paul II was visiting New York that day and we were delayed by heavy traffic. 'Where are the papers for Kissinger?' Nigel demanded on our arrival. We hadn't appreciated they had been wanted immediately. We searched for the documents, but we couldn't find them – they were possibly at David's office. The floor manager appeared to tell us Kissinger was ready for the interview. We continued our search for the lost papers. Tom Tomasawa came in: 'Dr Kissinger is waiting.' We explained the delay. 'Don't worry,' Tom said, 'we're now going to record Cambodia in the third session.' 'What third session?' we enquired – the first we had heard of it. Before Tom could explain, Nigel Ryan came in looking pale and said: 'Kissinger says he will walk if you don't come now.'

The second interview began nervously, David and Kissinger both wary. Unlike the previous day, David was driving without a firm route map; he hadn't had time for last-minute swotting. Nor was he in the right frame of mind for a major interview. Kissinger's own confidence began to blossom. Eventually, David too began to find his feet. There were some revealing exchanges, but none of the previous day's electricity. In the control room, the relief among the NBC executives was palpable: 'Things are going well,' Nigel remarked. Les Crystal only half listened, spending his time instead on the phone arranging a helicopter to take Kissinger to Washington.

At the end of the interview, Crystal and I emerged from the control room as Kissinger walked by. 'Well done!' Kissinger proclaimed, wrapping his arm around him. I joined David in his dressing room. Kissinger walked in beaming and magnanimous, offering a few husky words of peace and reconciliation. He was in a rush, he said, but he was looking forward to the third session: 'Ten minutes on Cambodia; ten on China; and five on whatever *you* want to raise.' He whisked away.

Ten minutes on Cambodia? David and I sought an immediate meeting with Ryan and Tomasawa: 'What does Kissinger mean: ten minutes on Cambodia?' we demanded. NBC, we were informed, had agreed – without consultation with David or me – that

Kissinger could return to all the ground covered on Cambodia in the first session. Kissinger was concerned in particular about four questions and answers where he had been wrong-footed into making damaging admissions or into giving unconvincing answers, because – Kissinger claimed – David had used information of which he, Kissinger, had been unaware. Kissinger wanted to see the documents, and then to redo his answers. Tom told us that Kissinger had demanded an undertaking from NBC that, in the event the documents were not provided, the questions and answers to which they related would be excised. 'We did not agree to that,' Nigel reassured us. Brave Tom corrected him: 'Nigel, when Kissinger asked if we agreed it, we said nothing. I'm sure he left convinced we had.'

David and I withdrew to consider our position. Kissinger's objective was all too clear: he was determined to remove his embarrassing performance on Cambodia. There had been no trickery on our part in putting the questions: aided by Willie Shawcross, we had simply done our research and been well informed. Even if Kissinger had been unaware of the detail to which we had referred, he should have been able to mount a more convincing general defence of his overall actions in Cambodia. This had been Kissinger's first cross-examination on the subject, so there was a clear public interest in seeing the hesitancy – as well as the substance – of his responses. If we recorded more on Cambodia in a third session, there was nothing to stop NBC using all of the new material to replace the embarrassing segment. We could not be confident of NBC. Their handling of the dispute thus far had sapped our trust in their editorial integrity.

On the morning of the intended third session, David and I sent a letter to NBC stating that we would not participate under the conditions NBC had agreed with Kissinger. Nigel phoned to conciliate: he was prepared to reopen discussions with Kissinger, who was waiting at NBC's studios to complete the interview. Bill Small phoned: he was less conciliatory: 'Are you going to get over to the fucking studio? Yes or no?' David said no. Small put the phone down on him. An intermediary then warned David that, if he did not tape the session, he would not work for NBC News, or any part of the NBC Network, ever again. Moreover, NBC could pull strings at other networks. David didn't budge. The last call was from Nigel: the whole deal was off.

We were deflated. We gave the story to the *New York Times* and to the *Washington Post*. I was most impressed by the professional integrity of the reporter from the *New York Times*. He was determined to get the story right: he took nothing I said at face value; he cross-examined me rigorously on every point over a period of hours; he cross-checked the whole story in detail with the NBC executives involved; and he came back to me on many points for clarification. (I wish I had encountered more of his like in the years to come.)

David and I had lost our baby. Someone else was editing our material for an early transmission. Our friendly sources at NBC told us that – stung by the hostile media coverage – the pendulum at NBC News had swung again: the network had turned once more to protecting its reputation rather than its relationship with Kissinger. We were told that Kissinger had called Nigel Ryan thirty-five times in just a few days; and that Ryan had informed Kissinger that his damaging testimony on Cambodia would remain in the transmitted programme. Our NBC friends predicted that we would approve of Tom Tomasawa's edit. They were right.

We watched our prodigal programme with our production team in a room at the top of one of the twin towers of New York's World Trade Center. We had quibbles, but it was a powerful, revealing programme, and it remained *our* programme. We had just about survived the entrapments of NBC's ill-judged arrangements with Henry Kissinger. As for Kissinger himself, as one NBC executive remarked: 'Henry showed about as much respect for the independence of NBC as he did for the neutrality of Cambodia!'

The last quintessential figure of the 1970s with whom David conducted a major interview was the Shah of Iran. The Shah had been

overthrown in 1979, and had fled Iran to be replaced as leader by
Ayatollah Khomeini.

In exile, the Shah had been parked by the Carter administration
on Contadora, an out-of-the-way island off the Pacific coast of
Panama. The Shah was an assassination target, so he was being protected by the Panamanian authorities. In practice, this meant that
when the Shah came anywhere near us he was surrounded by a
dozen or so muscled, sulky young men in jeans. They looked like
drug-cartel hoodlums, except that each carried a large, gleamingly
new executive briefcase containing an automatic weapon. The head
of security was a jolly, menacing giant of a man like a character
from a Graham Greene novel, who exposed a large gold tooth
whenever he laughed.

The Shah was dying of cancer, and we did not know how long he
would live. It was touch and go, we thought, whether the Shah
could survive the interviews. (In the event, he died six months later.)
His cheeks were hollow, his shirts loose around the neck. The key
adviser on the Frost team was the donnish, mild-mannered Andrew
Whitley, who had worked in Iran both for the *Financial Times* and for
the BBC's World Service. Andrew's nightly reports, beamed into
Iran by the BBC, had been widely applauded for their authority,
sober insight and accuracy; but they were also considered by the
Shah and his aides to have helped precipitate the regime's downfall.
I witnessed a poignant moment as the Shah met Andrew for the first
time, greeted him graciously, then walked on, remarking unacri-
moniously to an aide: 'He is one of the main reasons we are here.'
(Andrew went on to work for the UN, and became an administrator
in East Timor.)

The interviews with the Shah were bought by the US network
ABC – so my old friend Bob Zelnick, an alumnus of Frost/Nixon,
came down to Contadora to liaise with us on ABC's behalf. Bob had
the unedifying job of plundering our interview not for history but
for soundbites for ABC News's nightly programme on the Iran
hostage crisis, which was then running.

The Frost team addressed the difficulties posed by the Shah's illness: it was distasteful to put a man with little time to live through a hostile grilling. None the less, we had to press the Shah to give his account for history. He had been carried away by fanciful ideas and notions of imperial grandeur. In addition, he had pushed Iran too far, too fast, investing the inflated revenues from the oil-price hike of the early 1970s in an over-rapid development programme for Iran, which had brought millions from the countryside into the sprawling and expanding cities. The Shah's modernisation process was bungled: the infrastructure couldn't keep pace with the population growth; the sewage from the rich flowed downhill to the tenements of the poor; power cuts were rife. There was an economic downturn and inflation rose. The influential merchants of the bazaars became disaffected when the Shah created state monopolies of key imports. His links with America were becoming generally unpopular. The new and religiously conservative urban proletariat was affronted by the westernisation of the professional classes in the cities – who, in their turn, resented the Shah's overweening arrogance. Unease turned to dissent. The Shah cracked down, bringing allegations of torture and suppression, and finally provoking an uprising. Asked about a particular mistake in this long saga, the Shah didn't deny it. He gave a Gallic shrug: 'When things go wrong, *everything* is a mistake.'

In the interview sessions, the Shah was calm, dignified and regal. He was more open than we anticipated to the thesis that he had pushed Iran too far, too fast. He acknowledged that Savak, his secret service, may have used torture; but he was not ready to admit to the huge scale of bungling, corruption and suppression that his critics alleged. Overall, I felt the interview was flat. For the first time, David and I found it hard to agree on our approach. I wanted David to press the Shah further and harder, and there were tensions between us for a while.

After the recordings, I was due to return home via New York on the same plane as the Shah's restless twenty-year-old son, Crown

Prince Reza, and his personal entourage. When we all arrived at the airport, we were told that the plane from Panama would be delayed for seven hours. The security people immediately whisked us away to a seedy, run-down hotel in the jungle, not far from the airport, with verandahs and shuttered windows. We were ushered into a steamy room without air conditioning, but with a large rotating fan suspended from the ceiling. I expected Sidney Greenstreet and Peter Lorre to walk in at any moment.

I sat at the one and only table with the Crown Prince, two of the Shah's advisers from a New York public relations firm and the large, gold-toothed Panamanian head of security. As he sat down, the Panamanian's shirt parted, revealing an ample belly and a revolver jammed down the front of his trousers. The Crown Prince announced that we would play poker. The rest of us blanched at the thought of gambling with one of the richest young men in the world. But no, he said, we would play not for money, but for matches. Boxes were located and pooled, and we were each given a hundred matches as chips.

I had never played cards with anyone who wanted to win more, not even my nanna Anna. The Crown Prince threw himself with relish into the game, permanently on the attack, willing himself to win every hand – which he very nearly did. Two hours later, he had all five hundred matches, having knocked the rest of us out of the game. He hoarded his pyramid of matchsticks as if they were the crown jewels, cupping his hands around them, his eyes gleaming with triumph.

I flew back to London. My period of working with David Frost – the most enterprising and able interviewer of his day – was over. And so was my experience as an active programme-maker, for I would soon move up the ladder at LWT to an executive position and never again make a programme myself.

II

Director of Programmes

When I succeeded Michael Grade as LWT's Director of Programmes in 1982, at the age of thirty-seven, I was halfway through my career in broadcasting. My sixteen years as a producer and departmental head at Granada and LWT had been pleasurable and exciting, and, with the brief exception of the brouhaha over 'bias against understanding' in the mid-1970s, had brought me little experience of contention or conflict. Leading small groups of able and creative people, it was not difficult to identify a common goal, to persuade a team that we were all on the same side. The second half of my broadcasting career would be very different. I would find myself reforming and reshaping institutions in Mrs Thatcher's, John Major's and finally Tony Blair's Britain, taking on the forces of inertia – the comfortable, entrenched interests that stop all organisations developing and responding to new needs and circumstances. This period of my life would prove at least as stimulating and rewarding as my time as a programme-maker but, by contrast, would bring me difficulty, pain and strife.

Michael Grade stayed on for a brief handover before setting off for Hollywood. The first meeting I attended with him and LWT's schedule managers brought me abruptly face to face with the realities of my new job. The meeting was shambolic: it had been called to consider a new ITV quarterly schedule. 'What have we got?' Michael asked LWT's about-to-retire scheduling manager, who responded with a short, bedraggled list of LWT programmes, and a few from the other major ITV companies. Michael cursed: 'Is that all? We can't make a schedule with that rubbish!' He ranted about the other companies and their inadequacies – as both he and Cyril Bennett had done in front of me many times before. Then Michael sketched out a rough, meagre schedule, demanded to know which movies in stock could fill the holes, and closed the meeting. The initial euphoria brought on by the thrill of a new job evaporated. As we all walked out of the meeting, I murmured to Warren Breach, who was about to take over as LWT's scheduling executive: 'It won't be done that way in future.'

Michael may not have been a long-term planner or a master of process, but he had good instincts and had definitely improved LWT's own contribution to ITV's weekend schedule. A bold attempt to use Bruce Forsyth to link a pot-pourri of formats to fill Saturday night had proved a damp squib, but Michael had recruited powerful executives to run the Entertainment department – David Bell, Alan Boyd and Richard Drewett – and some programmes had emerged – notably *Game for a Laugh*, *Russ Abbott* and *A Fine Romance* – which were valuable building blocks for the weekend schedule. Michael was denounced for his enterprise by the BBC's Alasdair Milne as running LWT like 'the Mafia with a chequebook'. Away from peak time, Michael had commissioned some masterly plays from Alan Bennett and Dennis Potter. And he had fought LWT's corner vigorously at the weekly Monday-morning meetings of the five controllers of the main ITV companies: LWT, Yorkshire,

Thames (the London weekday contractor), Granada (serving the north-west) and Central (for the Midlands). I sat open-mouthed a few days into the handover as Grade viciously abused Mike Scott of Granada in very personal terms for the inadequacy of his company's contribution to the next quarter's weekend schedule. LWT had long considered itself to be ITV's David, fighting the Goliaths of the BBC and the rest of ITV, while the other companies regarded LWT as a tiresome thorn in their sides. But although – with a stronger contribution from LWT – ITV's weekend schedules were improving, they were still threadbare on most nights for much of the year compared with the BBC's; and they performed badly with the audience in LWT's own region, where the company's ratings position was weak. Within days of starting my new job, it was clear to me that both LWT and ITV faced huge problems. Here was a massive drawer to sort!

The heart of LWT's difficulty was the London split. Alone among the fourteen regions of ITV, the London franchise was divided between Thames in the weekday and LWT at the weekend. All the other companies had a monopoly of TV advertising in their areas, and their revenues, unlike the London companies', were not dependent on the strength of the schedule. LWT's share of London revenue in the battle with Thames, on the other hand, broadly corresponded with LWT's share of the London audience. As a result, Thames and LWT competed hard to offer the strongest schedule, made up both of their own programming and that of other network companies. Thames drafted ITV's weekday schedule, LWT the weekend. Nigel Ryan, whom I had last encountered in New York in the course of the Kissinger fiasco, had recently become Thames's Controller, and therefore my arch-rival.

Yorkshire Television was run by the industry's vastly experienced bull-elephant Paul Fox. Paul had a balanced view of ITV and made a range of programming – from the prestigious to the popular – including programmes for the weekend; but Paul was LWT's only ally. Relations between LWT and both Granada and Central had been terrible for years. Both companies were preoccupied with producing ambitious programming, particularly factual programmes, of real excellence; but neither was interested in helping ITV to counter the wicked competition in weekend peak time of the BBC's quality popular programmes like *The Generation Game*, *The Two Ronnies* or *All Creatures Great and Small*. Central and Granada were making the peak-time programmes that captured their fancy, increasingly oblivious of the needs of the audience or the schedule. They were not acting irrationally. They were responding to pressure from the IBA to make intelligent, challenging programming; and their monopoly of television advertising in their regions gave them the security to pursue such a strategy without commercial cost.

There was an additional difficulty: ITV's bedrock had been the old industrial working class, particularly in the north, and as it went into decline, so did ITV. Soon after I took over as LWT's Director of Programmes, we established that the proportion of Londoners working in professional and skilled jobs had grown to over 50 per cent of the population, and was rising. These younger, better-educated and more prosperous groups seemed to like smart, clever television – like *Minder* – and increasingly recoiled from much of ITV's traditional, undemanding fare. A north–south divide was emerging in ITV, with viewing of ITV in the south declining fast. If the trend continued, ITV would soon have fewer viewers than the more intelligent BBC1. A few years later, in 1985, when Peter Mandelson left LWT for the Labour Party, I shared my insights and LWT's confidential market analysis with him, suggesting that the Labour Party and ITV were each in long-term decline – and for similar reasons. Each faced the same massive challenge of reaching out to a more prosperous, better-educated Britain.

I set out not only to strengthen LWT's programming but also to bring new direction to ITV. It would be an uphill task. I started in my own back-yard, with LWT's Drama department, which had become a loose agglomeration of directorial talents, and needed strengthening, management and leadership. I offered the job of

head of drama to the stalwart Nick Elliott – at that point still destined for TV-am – and he accepted. Nick's was a controversial
appointment, for LWT's staff had their heart in show business, and
they had long resented the growth of my Features and Current
Affairs leviathan, with its legions of snappy young journalists. The
staff had greeted my own appointment as Director of Programmes
with suspicion. Nick, they reasoned, was one of my own, a journo
untried in drama. But I knew that Nick was a true thespian from his
time at Oxford. And with his excellent creative judgement, he would
manage his way to success – which he did, becoming over the next
two decades British broadcasting's most successful drama commissioner. But Nick had a sticky start, with hate-mail so vile we had to
bring in detectives to investigate.

Nick had other early problems to contend with: an industrial dispute over advertising greatly reduced LWT's expected revenues
from Channel 4. As a result the company was obliged urgently to
reduce both its network and its programming costs. I had been
bequeathed by Michael Grade a large stock of untransmitted
drama, so, to economise, I had no alternative but to transmit from
stock, and, as a result, commissioned little new drama in my early
years as Director of Programmes. This would not be the last time in
my life when I would follow a spend-spend-spend predecessor and
have to cut-cut-cut. Nick soldiered on stoically through these difficulties, standing his corner against the LWT malcontents, never
complaining or regretting his decision not to join TV-am, until more
normal times returned. By the end of my period he had triumphed,
either creating or developing the sound foundations of a new ITV
weekend schedule – including the long-running hits *London's Burning*
and Agatha Christie's *Poirot*. On the way he had produced a series of
successful single dramas like *Blue Money* and William Boyd's *Dutch
Girls*; he had had one-off popular series like *The Charmer*, with Nigel
Havers; and he had produced a fine adaptation of J. G. Farrell's
Irish novel, *Troubles*. Nick had also created an international action-
adventure potboiler, *Dempsey and Makepeace* – about which we did not

necessarily boast to our friends! – but which became an anchor of ITV's Saturday-night schedule. LWT stumbled over the adaptation of every journalist's favourite novel – Evelyn Waugh's *Scoop*. We got the casting wrong, and were justifiably panned. But I really came to like *Scoop*'s steely producer Sue Birtwhistle – a fellow mathematician – who would go on to achieve great things on my watch at the BBC. For Channel 4, Nick produced Jane's mother's favourite book, *Mapp and Lucia* – E. F. Benson's delicious comedy about rivalries in a small English town. Geraldine McEwan, Prunella Scales and Nigel Hawthorne played the lead roles. For fun, Nick and I produced an exquisite ice ballet with Torville and Dean for the Christmas schedule – *Fire and Ice*.

I paid a lot of attention to the buying and placing of bought-in films and series in the schedule. I found that more viewers were at home on Sunday and Monday than on any other nights of the week and – as a result – ITV started scheduling mini-series very successfully across those two evenings. We discovered the ratings power of the avenging female. Our greatest success was a turgidly made Australian series called *Return to Eden*, about a plain woman whose rich husband attempts to murder her by throwing her to the crocodiles in the Outback. Horribly mauled, her face disfigured, she is rescued by a handsome plastic surgeon who rebuilds her face and makes her the most beautiful woman in the world. Her murderous husband unknowingly falls for her all over again, and she exacts her vengeance. *Return to Eden* won huge and happy audiences, mostly women!

I changed the balance within LWT's Entertainment department. David Bell, the head, was the outstanding producer of variety shows of his generation. His programmes had verve, polish and glamour, an unmistakable gleam all of their own. David had been producing glittering specials for LWT with major entertainers like Tommy Steele and Stanley Baxter; but I soon established that such programmes were enormously expensive and not particularly popular.

A single Stanley Baxter special had needed twenty-seven costly days in the studio. To David's disappointment, I abandoned these programmes and encouraged him instead to modernise the live variety form on Sunday nights – which he did brilliantly and successfully with *Live from Her Majesty's*, hosted by the commandingly professional Jimmy Tarbuck.

Alan Boyd, the acknowledged master in the UK of people shows, had come over from the BBC to create *Game for a Laugh*. Alan and I went on to introduce a number of programmes to the weekend schedule which would become ITV stalwarts, like *Surprise, Surprise*, but our greatest triumph together was *Blind Date*.

One of LWT's scheduling managers drew my attention to the runaway success in Australia of a dating game, *Perfect Match*. We quickly obtained a tape. The programme's appeal was immediately evident and we acquired the UK format rights. But there was a problem: even though *Perfect Match* had been transmitted in Australia at 5 p.m., the programme was explicit and raunchy. The dating pair were encouraged to go the whole hog and to share their experience with the audience. I knew this would never be acceptable to the Independent Broadcasting Authority, so Alan and I worked closely to sanitise the programme for a British audience. In the event, David Glencross at the IBA was even more nervous than I had predicted. Alan and I brainstormed about the rules. In LWT's version, we would be spoilsports: the winning couple would travel to and from their date in the span of a single day; and they would go their separate ways and return to their respective homes by nightfall. They would be chaperoned at all times by a stills photographer. In their debrief in the following week's programme, they would be encouraged to talk about personality. We would steer well clear of sex.

Alan suggested we should go even further: he was convinced that we could allay the IBA's fears by casting a host who would take away the risk altogether that the programme would be seen as a passport to sex – we would have a camp presenter! Alan duly cast in the pilot a young comedian in the Frankie Howerd mould. This proved a disastrous miscalculation. The presenter's unprovoked stream of gay innuendo not only put sex centre-stage, but also got in the way of the strong, central message of *Blind Date* – heterosexual attraction.

Alan and I agreed we had to think again, but I was committed, unfortunately, to showing our pilot tape to the IBA. Seeing it intensified their nervousness. Despite my reassurance that we would find a new presenter, the IBA concluded that our programme was manifestly not a family show, and definitely not suitable for early Saturday evening, which was a big blow. In the middle of this troubling dialogue I caught Cilla Black on Jimmy Tarbuck's talk show for LWT. It was a rare appearance as she had done little television during the years that she had been bringing up her children. Cilla was fresh, unaffected and deliciously, naturally funny. I saw in an instant she was the right presenter for *Blind Date*. She was everyone's favourite aunt, lively and knowing, wanting the young folk to have a good time – but not too good a time! Cilla agreed to do the show, and the IBA was placated. Cilla was a sensation, and *Blind Date* went on to staggering success, and to be the main pillar of ITV's Saturday schedule for decades.

I hugely enjoyed my experience of entertainment as an ITV controller. Growing up in Liverpool, I had always watched and enjoyed the peak-time entertainers with my family, so I felt particularly comfortable in the company of my delightful Scouser contemporaries Jimmy and Cilla, who became friends. I held occasional scouse lunches at home to which they came, along with other expats like Anne Robinson, Roger McGough and Robert Runcie, former Archbishop of Canterbury – whom we termed the Proddy-dog leader. My mum and dad prepared the meal: chip butties, scouse with pickled beetroot and HP Sauce; jelly and evaporated milk. Jimmy always returned for seconds!

I was less successful with LWT's situation comedy. Humphrey Barclay was the company's intense and committed comedy head.

He had produced much work of quality. Some of his comedies – like *Hot Metal*, a satire on Fleet Street – played successfully for LWT in the upmarket slot at 10 p.m. on Sundays; and he made a brilliant contribution to Channel 4 with our black comedy *No Problem*. But most of Humphrey's peak-time sitcoms had proved too delicate for the rough battlegrounds of the weekend schedule, and had been neither greatly watched nor – our research showed – much appreciated by their audiences. Humphrey did help create two successful peak-time comedies in my time – *Me and My Girl* with Richard O'Sullivan and *The Two of Us* with Nicholas Lyndhurst; but my relationship with Humphrey deteriorated as I rejected proposal after proposal from him as being insufficiently strong for peak time. Then we both made a mistake: he offered me a series called *Bottle Boys*, and I accepted. This coarse, witless production about milkmen embarrassed both of us. Humphrey resigned.

The most thrilling, sublime and important entertainment programme of my time as Director of Programmes at LWT was *Saturday Live*, which we made for Channel 4. Ninety minutes long and very definitely live, the show was produced with breathtaking ambition by Paul Jackson, and directed exhilaratingly by Geoff Posner from LWT's largest studio, with wild, imaginative sets and a studio floor heaving with a large, mobile, stand-up audience. *Saturday Live* definitively established a fresh generation of British comedians. On the programme Harry Enfield invented the sublime Stavros and the quintessential 1980s character Loadsamoney; Dawn French and Jennifer Saunders redefined the double act; Stephen Fry and Hugh Laurie introduced delicate wit and verbal dexterity; Ade Edmonson and Rik Mayall created mayhem; and Ben Elton demonstrated that he was a comic genius.

Ben would turn up the day before transmission and belt out on his typewriter an acute, observant twenty-minute comic monologue about current events and the ironies and eccentricities of contemporary life, and he would deliver this text word-perfect the following evening in his inimitable motormouth style. I came greatly to admire not only Ben's writing and performing brilliance but his decency. More than any other of the many presenters and performers I encountered in my time in broadcasting, Ben was never self-important; fame never went to his head. He remained thoughtful, modest and caring of other people.

LWT was the home of ITV's main sports operation, headed by John Bromley, a jolly rascal of a man who maintained his good humour with me despite my blunt challenge to ITV's traditional sports policy. Audiences for *World of Sport* on Saturday afternoons were fading fast. The BBC had a stranglehold on most quality sport and there was little of excellence or appeal in ITV's flagship sports programme. I pressed for, and won acceptance for, a new policy for ITV – to abandon *World of Sport* and to schedule sport on the network only when it was live, quality and exclusive. We would invest in British athletics, snooker, boxing and football.

Football was the big issue. Recorded match highlights on ITV's *The Big Match* and the BBC's *Match of the Day* were increasingly dull, and both programmes were faltering. Football on television needed refreshing. When Michael Grade returned to the UK in 1984 to become Controller of BBC1 (Hollywood had not worked out for him), he and I conspired to win a historic breakthrough. We agreed not to accept a new package from the football authorities unless it contained live league football for the first time. I was particularly uncompromising: I had identified the true commercial value of football to ITV and had told John Bromley that I would not accept a package without live games and unless the price was reasonable; and my valuation was well below what others in ITV were prepared to pay. (Throughout my time in television – in both ITV and the BBC – I would see otherwise prudent souls throw all caution aside when bidding for sports and film rights as if their own personal worth was somehow validated by the monstrously over-inflated price being placed on some asset.) I wrote to John Bromley: 'Their [the League's] proposition that football increases

ITV profitability is ludicrous. Taking football as a whole, and including production costs, the opposite is the case: we will save money if there is no football!' I told John that if the League did not accept ITV's offer, 'I will immediately take football out of LWT's budget for the next year.'

Michael Grade and I held firm. When the 1985–6 season started, there was no football on British television. In effect, there was a football strike. When the football authorities saw that the broadcasters were serious, a satisfactory deal was finally struck, and in September, in an historic move, the first live league game was broadcast on British television – a move which would do much to rekindle excitement in our national game over the next decade.

The final strengthening of LWT's schedule from the company's own resources was instituted by my old department – Features and Current Affairs – now led by Barry Cox. LWT's weekend time-slot had been extended by the IBA, after keen lobbying by LWT, to include early Friday evening. To launch our new slot, Barry and I decided to build on the pioneering factual entertainment format he had developed with *Saturday Night People*, but this time the journalism would be popular and accessible. The *Six O'Clock Show* – as we labelled it – would be presented by the gentle, sardonic Michael Aspel, and produced by Greg Dyke.

A late arrival to journalism at LWT after a job in community relations, Greg had risen to be deputy editor of *The London Programme* after a sticky patch on *Weekend World*. He had not thrived on the programme. With his short attention span, freewheeling spirit and quick-thinking intuitive intelligence, Greg was not suited to *Weekend World*'s deep study, its take-no-prisoners rigour. But he was a regular Friday footballer, and I had greatly enjoyed the company of this breezy, ebullient, unpretentious firecracker, with his amusing, opinionated, indiscreet and ceaseless chatter on every issue of the day. Greg was particularly scathing – as the producers' union representative – about the ease with which LWT's management caved in to his outrageous demands. Barry and I thought that Greg had just the personality and outlook to run *The Six O'Clock Show*. It would be a significant shift for him from serious current affairs; but we judged he was talented enough to make the leap. We cast Janet Street-Porter and Fred Housego (and eventually Danny Baker) alongside Aspel.

The first two pilots were a disaster, and Barry and I were seriously worried that we had a major flop on our hands. We resolved to move Greg to another programme if the third pilot was as bad – but we didn't have to, for Greg won through, the programme suddenly coming together as a brilliant, lively-minded and amusing take on London, bursting with chirpy, smart, Cockney wit. *The Six O'Clock Show* was a ratings triumph – quickly becoming the most watched early-evening programme on ITV, and it provided a splendid launch-pad for LWT's Friday schedule. Unfortunately, the programme's success was quickly noticed by the rest of the industry, and Greg was soon wooed away from LWT to improve the fortunes of the ailing TV-am.

As I strengthened LWT's own programming, I set out in parallel to improve the competitiveness of ITV's weekend schedule in other ways. First, I had to learn the art of scheduling. I was lucky: the best tutor in the UK was close at hand. Brian Tesler, LWT's dapper, fluent Managing Director, had been a programme Controller for twelve years – first for ABC Television, then for Thames. Brian was a legend for his formidable brainpower and analytic capability, who had gained a congratulatory First at Oxford – but instead of a career in the City or in the Foreign Office, he had devoted himself to his great passion, show business. He had thought harder about peak-time programming than anyone else in broadcasting, and, with forensic skill, could pick apart any would-be popular programme and identify why it would or would not succeed. Brian's critiques could be a tour de force, and were often devastating, especially for a stumbling, inarticulate drama or entertainment producer. Brian had also developed the *science* of TV scheduling. He had studied audience flow across the day and the week. He explained how to create the right inheritance for a new programme; or what the weaknesses of the opposing schedules were and how they could be exploited. He identified the importance of understanding every programme's unique viewing profile – the mix of people of different ages, genders and social classes who watched it. Finally Brian emphasised the need to look not just at *how many* people had watched a programme but whether they had actually *appreciated* the experience.

I soon realised that neither LWT nor ITV had properly exploited Brian's body of knowledge, so I began creating systems and processes that would build on his insights. And I set about becoming a master myself of audience data and trends – there was much to grasp, for there is probably more data available about British television viewing than any other form of human activity anywhere in the world. I was aided in my drive to transform ITV's weekend schedule by a passionate and tireless young executive and Clint Eastwood fanatic called Warren Breach; by Sue Stoessl, the industry's top researcher and a shrewd authority on audiences in her own right; and by Jane Larner, from a consultancy called TAPE. (Suzanne Hatley joined the group later, when Sue Stoessl moved to Channel 4.) TAPE was a company that advised networks in the US and Australia about the popular appeal of programmes, and had been used by both Cyril and Michael. Jane had a mischievous outlook, a dirty laugh and an unsentimental eye for the true appeal of a programme and where it should be scheduled.

We set out as a group to make LWT's schedules strong on every weekend night, and across the whole year. We introduced routine weekly meetings and systematic analysis. In an industry that had traditionally planned a quarter ahead, we created an ideal long-term schedule, across three years, and plotted and manoeuvred our way towards it. Every decision – short, medium or long term – was scrupulously considered. We brought rigour to the evaluation of film packages, sports rights and programme offers from the other companies. The team ensured I was the best-briefed ITV Controller ever. I would turn up to meetings carrying three or four plastic bags bulging with files. In a group where bluff assertion – and often false claim – was the rule, I would invariably have in my head or in my brief the killer facts, the clinching arguments, the precise numbers. This irritated my fellow Controllers, who would ridicule the approach. 'John can put it in his hopper and come up with the answer!' they would say. I infuriated my colleagues even more when I asked them to focus on the needs of the weekend. I analysed each company's contributions and showed them how little impact they had had historically on ITV's weekend peak time. One year, Granada had supplied no programmes at all. I was given a not-so-polite hearing and then ignored.

This was a problem I had to crack. I took decisive and provocative action. First, I refused to schedule manifestly inappropriate programming from Granada and Central in weekend peak time. I placed Granada's *Shades of Darkness* – one-hour adaptations of nineteenth-century tales of the supernatural – at 10.30 p.m. on Friday when the rest of the network played the series at 9 p.m. I consigned Central's *Pictures*, a 1920s pastiche, to the same late-evening slot. I refused to place *On the Line*, about machinations in the car industry, at peak time at the weekend. This angered the group. Even without such incitements, the Monday programme controllers' meetings remained, as they always had been, deeply contentious and unpleasant – famous for slanging matches, intimidation and threats. When he was a controller, Brian Tesler had had to take Valium before participating. Attending the programme Controllers' group was certainly a growing-up experience for me. Unlike the others, I never shouted; I argued calmly; and I never made threats for the sake of it, only warning the others of actions I fully intended to carry out, a principle I stuck to. Unsurprisingly and understandably, Paul Fox soon complained to Brian Tesler about my intransigence: 'You must do something about your boy John. He never compromises. We had our disagreements with Michael Grade, but Michael always compromised in the end. John won't!'

ITV companies exchanged their programmes through a barter system, each swapping its portfolio of offers for programmes of equivalent financial value from the other companies. Everyone put their programmes in what was called the 'pot' and in return could show programmes from the other companies without charge. ITV companies had swapped programmes historically on the basis of their *cash* cost. The work I had done with Christopher Turner had identified the huge *total* cost of LWT's own programmes when over-head and facilities charges were included. I proposed – and it was accepted – that ITV's programmes should be swapped on the basis of their true total cost. I then worked out that LWT would be no worse off if we moved away from the barter system, if we *sold* our programmes to the rest of ITV rather than put them in the pot, and if we bought only those programmes from other companies that we really wanted. I was ready, in other words, to withdraw LWT from the ITV network system founded thirty years before, and to intro-duce a regime of willing buyer, willing seller. Brian Tesler supported my stratagem, and he and I went on to explain the seriousness of our intent to Central and Granada: unless they produced a better-balanced portfolio of programmes, LWT was ready to quit the network. At Granada, we faced David Plowright (my old and admired champion) and Mike Scott; and at Central, Bob Phillis and Charles Denton.

Brian and I were given a courteous hearing, insufferable though our effrontery must have seemed. And we began at long last to talk seriously with Central and Granada about planning for the long term, and strengthening the weekend schedule with appropriate programming. In due course, Central would produce some valuable peak-time entertainment for the weekend, like the brassy *The Price is Right*, the classic *Shine on Harvey Moon*, the sublime *Auf Wiedersehen Pet*, and the inspired *Spitting Image*. I wanted Granada to move one of its two weekly editions of *Coronation Street* to Friday night, but Mike Scott decided instead to create a new soap for the weekend. Unfortunately, the result, *Albion Market*, was ill-conceived and roundly rejected by the audience and I had to withdraw it quickly from its slot. Overall, though, we were beginning to make progress.

Using LWT's insights about the real, bloated cost of ITV's programme-making, I analysed how ITV was spending its money and came to the remarkable and barely believable but robust conclusion that only 13 per cent of ITV's whole programme spend was being invested in peak time. The wave I had ridden in the 1970s – ITV's vast and admirable expansion of factual programmes, and a huge investment in local programming by fifteen separate companies – had been overdone. Moreover, I concluded that ITV's major regions – TVS, Anglia and HTV – were an untapped resource. They had mushroomed financially, but had no clear and commensurate network role, producing only a modest amount of ad-hoc network programming.

I made a stinging presentation to the IBA, laying bare ITV's skewed financial priorities, arguing that ITV was killing the goose that had laid the golden egg, and suggesting that ITV needed significantly to readjust the balance of its spend towards peak time. Some members of the IBA were shocked that the person who had given them *Weekend World* and ambitious arts, education and religious programmes was framing such an argument. And, not liking my message, some of the IBA's own staff set out to undermine my figures – but their understanding of ITV's finances lagged way behind LWT's, and they foundered. There was no immediate and fundamental shift within ITV following my controversial presentation, but the climate of opinion did gradually change and, over the next few years, ITV did begin to invest more money in peak time, and the major regionals – whom I courted – did eventually make a much bigger contribution to the ITV network schedule overall. My reward from Anglia in Norwich was many marvellous adaptations of P. D. James's Inspector Dalgleish novels, and, from HTV in Wales and the west, *Robin Hood*. I worked with Andrea Wonfor of Tyne Tees, who had been a production trainee with me at Granada, on the concept of *Highway*, a religious *Down Your Way* made by ITV's regions, with Harry Secombe as the presenter. *Highway* transformed the quality and appeal of ITV's early Sunday evenings and made Harry very rich. For years after, this warm, funny and genial man gave me a special hug of welcome and gratitude whenever I encountered him.

I was bolder still with TVS. I wanted to place a strong controller at the helm of this large, rich south of England company with a hitherto unspectacular programme record. Greg Dyke and I still played football together most Fridays and had become closer. He had confided in me that he wasn't happy at TV-am, so I asked Brian Tesler to propose to TVS that they should take on Greg, and that, if they did, LWT would pave the way for a bigger network role for TVS. Greg was duly appointed, and TVS became a major supplier to ITV of weekend drama and entertainment programming.

All of these many measures – strengthening LWT's own programmes, a better contribution from the majors, drawing in the regionals – taken together soon created a far more powerful weekend schedule for ITV than I had inherited. LWT's historically weak position was being remedied. Its schedule would become more powerful still in subsequent years as Nick Elliott's drama portfolio grew in strength.

I discovered something basic about myself in those years in the 1980s working as an ITV Controller: I was not prepared to tolerate the blatantly unsatisfactory; I had a compulsion to sort things out, a willingness to take the harder path. I had made some necessary but difficult changes within LWT, and I had ruffled feathers throughout ITV. I had been very successful and forced a great deal of change. But I had also made life difficult for many people: I had been involved in continuous confrontation, standing against the consensus, opposing the established way of doing things, refusing to be a good old boy – one of those dominant personalities in the system who huffed and puffed and elbowed a bit, but ultimately fitted in with the pack. I had broken the mould before – with *Nice Time* and

Weekend World — but always with start-up operations on greenfield sites, which didn't threaten anyone much. Reforming mature systems like LWT and ITV was altogether unhappier work. But I learnt about myself that I could live with unpopularity more easily than chaos, and about most other people that they tend to put those priorities the other way round.

Being LWT's Director of Programmes hardened my ideas as well as my resolve. I became hostile to entrenched interests of all kinds, whether unions or ITV's unappealing, complacent, sitting-tenant companies. I longed for more open, transparent and competitive systems. When Mrs Thatcher attacked vested interests, I cheered within. I believed ever more strongly in open-market mechanisms. I was happy to be given an incentive by my share options to create wealth at LWT, to improve efficiency and effectiveness.

In 1984, when I was forty, JJ and Eliza composed a song for my birthday. The chorus went:

> Daddy we love you
> You're forty today
> You're handsomer than Melvyn
> Much cleverer than Peter Jay
> Daddy we love you
> You're forty today

At my family birthday dinner, which included my mum and dad, Jane made everyone dress in black tie except me: as the guest of honour, I was to wear white tie and tails. The doorbell rang, and Jane motioned for me to answer it. A tall, incredibly glamorous young woman was on the doorstep. This was the age of the strippergram and, thinking quickly, I whispered nervously to the lithe and slender beauty that she should bear in mind that my mum and dad were with me. But she marched right in, and boldly announced to the assembly that in an hour's time she and I would dance together to the music of Fred Astaire singing 'Top Hat'. We rehearsed alone. My teacher was a professional dancer. She had worked out the choreography cleverly – which was helpful because my brain doesn't seem to connect to my feet when dance steps have to be learnt. While she tapped and twirled around me, I had little to do but feign being debonair, and to repeat some simple steps. Sixty minutes later we made our debut. We brought the house down, and earned an encore.

Though our liberal convictions were under assault on all sides in Mrs Thatcher's Britain, Jane and I held stubbornly to our view that the kids should go to state comprehensives in the Tooting/Clapham area of south London where we lived. Jane, a Labour appointee, became the chair of governors of the local comprehensive that Eliza attended. Our children benefited from the rich mix of cultures in their schools and the friendships they made, and went on to achieve high academic excellence at university; but the rough and tumble of inner-city London comprehensives, and their relatively less challenging educational environment, was sometimes difficult for two kids from a prosperous, socially privileged, professional home inculcated with liberal, civilised values. JJ saw the state system through; but at a late stage in her secondary education we relented and finally transferred Eliza to a local private school.

In the early 1980s, John Freeman brought Christopher Bland on to LWT's board – on which I also sat. Christopher was both commercially and politically sharp. He had grown up politically alongside Geoffrey Howe, Leon Brittan, Michael Howard and Norman Lamont at Cambridge and in the Bow Group, which he had chaired. He had started his working life as a consultant, then created his own wealth by buying and developing businesses. He was dry on economics, and wet on social issues. He became a GLC councillor, then chairman of schools at the ILEA. In 1972, when he was thirty-four, Christopher Chataway made him Deputy Chairman of the IBA, where he caught the eye of John Freeman. It was easy to see why, for Christopher cut to the chase at board meetings – he always did his homework, and put over his points powerfully, directly and sometimes ferociously. Christopher was sceptical about LWT's bloated costs and the effectiveness of the company's commercial diversifications. He made plain he thought LWT was unbusinesslike and was paying insufficient attention to its shareholders' interests.

In 1984 John Freeman summoned me and – in his usual genteel and gracious way – explained that he had decided to step down, and that he wanted to consult me about his successor. I was shocked: John Freeman had always seemed such a fixture – a steadying, guiding, supporting hand; I had had no warning that he intended to go. There were two candidates, John said: Christopher and a second member of the board who was likeable and able, and who was also rigorous but who always spoke with restraint and unfailing courtesy. Playing for time, for I had not previously considered the choice, I thought out loud, weighing impartially the pros and cons of the two candidates. Unusually, and out of character, John Freeman interrupted me when I talked about Christopher, adding to my pros and countering my cons. It was immediately clear who was to be Chairman. John Freeman had seen, wisely, that LWT needed a dose of Christopher.

Christopher was hugely enjoyable to work with – amusing, decisive and quick to learn. Like me, he loved his fun, and organised jolly escapades for his friends, which Jane and I soon became – tennis weekends, or canoe expeditions on the Dordogne, or, later, gathering in the grape harvest at Château Bland. He was passionate, open and honest, with a great generosity of spirit. Christopher also had a famously short fuse. He could, for instance, become exceedingly agitated about time-keeping – even a minute's unpunctuality would draw steam from his ears. And when annoyed, he could suddenly and unexpectedly bite you badly. It never happened to me; but inadequate, slow or inarticulate people – as well as the successful and powerful – could suffer a terrible, searing mauling. But the volcano would subside as quickly as it had erupted, and his honest wit and infectious drive would quickly reassert themselves, and carry people with him.

Christopher wasted no time as LWT's new Chairman. First, he sorted out and sold off the company's unsuccessful subsidiaries; and he and I worked together to bring some business discipline to LWT's programme sales company. (I learnt at Christopher's side a great deal about business – he was good at demystifying key financial precepts in clear and simple language.) He, Brian Tesler and I focused hard on identifying LWT's restrictive practices and pinning down our inflated costs. We began to discuss a strategy for taking on the unions, and reforming our working conditions. I investigated secretly with Warren Breach and his scheduling managers how – in the event of a strike – we could transmit a service using management or overseas labour, and how we could continue to collect advertising revenues.

For years I had felt helpless in the face of union power, but now Mrs Thatcher had enfranchised managers like myself. She was now in her second term, and in her ascendancy. In the mid-1980s, Labour appeared a lost cause. In 1980 it had chosen Michael Foot, who proved unelectable and gave way, following a second Conservative victory, to Neil Kinnock. Kinnock continued to face impossible odds. Leftist extremism was rampant, not least in my own home city. Attending the party conference in Bournemouth in October 1985, I saw Kinnock speak out powerfully against the Militant Tendency – causing Derek Hatton to walk out. I met Peter Mandelson immediately afterwards, flushed with success, exhilarated that Kinnock had taken off the gloves. But I can remember feeling that Peter's moment of hope was unwarranted, that Labour's challenge was impossible, that Mrs Thatcher was all powerful. She had won a victory against the odds in the Falklands; she had ousted the wets in her own party; she was pushing through trade union reform; she had powerful like-minded allies in Nigel Lawson, Geoffrey Howe, Norman Tebbit, Cecil Parkinson and David Young. Above all, six months earlier she had emerged the victor from the climatic battle of the 1980s: the bitter, divisive, year-long miners' strike.

After the strike, with Mrs Thatcher indomitable, Alan Peacock – an eminent, super-dry, free-market professor of economics – sat down with his government-appointed committee to consider, ostensibly, whether to fund the BBC from advertising, but in fact to examine the whole future of broadcasting. The Prime Minister was determined to shake up the BBC and to make all of broadcasting more competitive. Whereas the agenda of the Annan Committee, the previous broadcasting inquiry, had been how to nurture and to develop public service, Peacock's would be a vigorous market-oriented scrutiny. Peacock was much influenced in his deliberations about broadcasting's future by the strong free-market axis of *Financial Times* commentator Sam Brittan – a member of his committee – and Peter Jay, an informal adviser. In the background, a muscular Cabinet group – dominated by free-marketeers Mrs Thatcher, Chancellor Nigel Lawson and Industry Secretary David Young, with policy head Brian Griffiths in support – considered the issues in private. Home Secretary Douglas Hurd was on the committee too, but in a wet minority of one. ITV was woefully unprepared for what lay ahead.

When the Peacock Committee reported in 1986, its most far-reaching recommendations centred not on the BBC – its intended primary focus – but in the event on ITV. For ITV's incumbents, Peacock's proposals were devastating. With only a modest genuflection to programme quality, Peacock proposed that the ITV franchises should be auctioned to the highest bidder. The ITV companies would be sitting ducks: they could be outbid in auction by any efficient, lean, credible competitor – with no expensive studio complex or entrenched union practices to fund – who could provide programming at a fraction of the incumbents' costs. I attended the infamous Downing Street seminar in 1987 to discuss Peacock – chaired by Mrs Thatcher (by this time, I had left LWT for the BBC).

The ITV companies were in complete disarray, wholly incapable of asserting their value as public service broadcasters in terms likely to appeal to the Iron Lady – or indeed of articulating any kind of compelling or persuasive case at all. Had I remained in ITV, I doubt I would have done any better. Although I was far more aware of Tory thinking than the fat cats of ITV – because of my time on *Weekend World* – in truth I had not made the leap that Mrs Thatcher's radicalism might apply in such an extreme form to my own industry. I would have expected – and welcomed – ITV being opened up to competition in programme-making and in facilities provision; but I had not anticipated that ITV's genuine programme capabilities could be valued so lightly.

ITV's chillingly poor performance at the Downing Street seminar was an experience I would never forget: it greatly affected my future actions at the BBC. I resolved not to be caught as unprepared as my former ITV colleagues when the BBC's time came. But, when Mrs Thatcher famously referred at the seminar to television 'as the last bastion of restrictive practices', LWT was well on the way to doing something about it. Christopher prepared with typical boldness for the forthcoming franchise competition by binding in LWT's top forty executives with a share incentive scheme – which would become infamous – motivating them to reduce costs and to see off a rival bidder. LWT's staff was soon halved and the company's costs reduced massively. The scheme would make all my former LWT friends and colleagues multi-millionaires.

Christopher's second stroke of brilliance was to steer one of Mrs Thatcher's favourites, the predatory Michael Green, away from eyeing LWT's franchise and towards Thames. Michael Green and his partner Mike Luckwell had once asked to see Christopher, Brian and myself to enquire if they could buy a controlling interest in LWT. I had never heard of Michael at that point and was astonished by his chutzpah – at the time I thought it was an impertinence for someone with a small, if highly rated, business and no broadcasting experience to want to buy his way into a large and creatively successful ITV company. Nothing came of Green and Luckwell's ambition at the time, but Christopher made sure he never let this sharp-toothed predator out of his sight and kept in touch with Michael during his various failed attempts to buy into Thames. At the franchise round, Christopher and Michael Green agreed to share a joint London news operation – which Thames refused to do – if Green's Carlton were successful in its bid for the London weekday franchise, and thus greatly reduce both companies' costs. Carlton duly went on to unseat Thames.

My own role in LWT's bid to regain its franchise, from my new vantage point in the BBC, was to read the final draft, to declare it 'of outstanding quality' – which indeed it was – and thus to persuade Christopher to put in a low and, in the event, winning bid for the franchise on the grounds that LWT would meet the exceptional quality test in the bidding process. (The quality tests had been finally strengthened in Parliament by David Mellor, then a minister in the Home Office, acting on his own initiative in daring defiance of Mrs Thatcher's wishes.)

LWT won its bid; but, irony of ironies, was taken over in 1994 by the old enemy, Granada, after a bitter fight and a vigorous defence by Christopher and his colleagues. One of the two most powerful programme traditions in ITV took over the other – but in the process, LWT's freebooting spirit was crushed, and it would cease to be the potent force it had been in the industry for so many years. Christopher fights to win, and he hated losing to Granada. He was visibly discombobulated, and for a while, before his true character reasserted itself, grew an untidy beard.

In the period when Professor Peacock was putting the television industry under intense scrutiny and I was still at LWT, the BBC veered from drama to drama, its internal divisions laid bare for all to see. Management and Governors were at war, the staff volatile. A full-blown crisis erupted when the Governors decided to ban *Real Lives: At the Edge of the Union* – a documentary which included an interview with Martin McGuinness, the Sinn Fein leader, at home in Derry. In October 1986 Marmaduke Hussey – one-time Managing Director of *The Times* – was appointed Chairman on a reform ticket by Margaret Thatcher and Douglas Hurd. Within months, the Director-General Alasdair Milne was fired, provoking a media frenzy. Michael Grade – with whom I had remained close – phoned to tell me he was going to apply to succeed Milne as Director-General. Would I help him prepare? I was preoccupied with ITV's problems and had not thought deeply about the BBC's, but I said I would do my best. I conducted a mock interview with Michael alongside Bill Cotton, Managing Director, Television; and Michael's policy thinker, Peter Ibbotson, who had been the cinematographer on my Oxford film, *The Little Donkey*. Michael would be in competition with Jeremy Isaacs, Paul Fox, Brian Wenham and others.

The battle for the succession dominated the news. No one in broadcasting could talk of much else. On the evening the Governors were due to make their decision, Jane and I waited in my LWT car – nervous with anticipation – for the phone to ring with news. Late into the evening, Michael Grade called, disappointed, to tell us that Michael Checkland, the dark-horse accountant, was the surprise victor.

A few days later my phone rang at home. It was Paul Fox. He was still at Yorkshire Television, but he was an intermediary, he explained, for the BBC. Would I like to be the Deputy Director-General of the BBC? I was momentarily surprised that an ITV executive was trying to lure me to a rival. He explained he was speaking on Michael Checkland's behalf. The notion that I might assume high office at the BBC had never crossed my mind. I had just accepted an offer from Brian and Christopher to become LWT's Managing Director on Brian's retirement, which was imminent. I was happy working at LWT. Generous terms, including valuable share options, had been offered. I was due to appoint my successor as Director of Programmes and to spend the autumn at the Harvard Business School to enhance my business skills and to gird my loins for the union and franchise battle ahead. I didn't quiz Paul; I said I would think about it. In fact, I didn't focus very hard on the question: I assumed I would be one of many candidates under consideration, and I was disinclined to be part of another media circus. Three days later, Paul rang again, this time a little agitated, obviously rattled that I had not returned his call. Suddenly it became clear from his words that I was the only person in the frame. I agreed to meet Michael Checkland.

Our rendezvous was the bar at the Howard Hotel, across the river from LWT's South Bank studio block. Checkland wasn't a man about the industry, and he and I hardly knew one another. I was expecting a long discussion but – typical of the man, as I would learn – he got straight to the point. He wanted me as his number two; he was an accountant; he needed an editorial person as his deputy. BBC news and current affairs were a big problem, under disparate management, of uneven quality and out of control: the whole area needed sorting out. He had the funds to build a grand new building in which to place a united News and Current Affairs directorate, currently scattered across London. He was minded only to be a one-term Director-General; if I accepted I was the most likely person to succeed him. I would be paid £80,000. Would I accept?

Checkland's pitch took just minutes. I was taken aback: I pressed for more detail, but he didn't have much more to say. I was doubtful. I had been an ITV Controller for five years. I had spread my wings and rekindled my interest in drama and entertainment. I no longer wanted just to be involved in journalism. If the role were simply to look after the BBC's news and current affairs, I told Checkland, I wouldn't be interested. No, he reassured me, I would deputise for him across the whole span of his responsibilities, and in all editorial areas, not just journalism. I would be involved in all the key strategic decisions. This undertaking would prove critical. How was I contracted at LWT, he asked? My services were provided through a company, I explained. That wouldn't be a problem, he assured me. Lots of people at the BBC were contracted that way. Was I a member of any political party? Yes, the Labour Party, but I had not been active for some time. That wasn't a problem either. I said I would reflect on the offer.

Michael Grade soon phoned to press me to come: 'You are just what the BBC needs.' Mike Checkland was a good guy, Grade suggested, who would turn over the place and do away with, as Michael saw it, Alasdair Milne's vile and arrogant legacy. I pondered the significance of Grade's call: I would have expected him to be sensitive to me leaping to a position two rungs in the BBC hierarchy above him; but, magnanimously, he seemed not to be.

I convened a conference with my parents and the kids. If I went to the BBC, I would probably lose all my existing share options – worth, roughly, five years of BBC pay – as well as the prospect of additional capital in the future. My family were excited and awed by the offer, but some urged caution: I should think twice before giving up wealth, happiness and security for the high risk of working for an organisation in turmoil. Jane and others emphasised the challenge and importance of new responsibilities, the chance to help an ailing BBC, the opportunity to discharge a major public service. I was torn; but the next morning I awoke to the realisation that I would forever regret a missed opportunity if I did not accept the offer. The BBC was the most important broadcasting organisation in the world. I greatly admired its creative programme tradition – so many of its programmes over the years had moved, educated or inspired me. The organisation was in trouble; I could not turn my back on it. With a heavy heart, I recognised I had no choice but to move to the BBC. My family gave their unqualified support to the decision.

I told Checkland I would accept, and arranged to meet Hussey and his Vice-Chairman Joel Barnett. It was not an interview – the decision had been made – rather, a brief and cheerful rah-rah welcome. Hussey and Barnett seemed almost rapturous I was coming. Every candidate for the director-generalship, they said, had advocated uniting News and Current Affairs, improving the quality of the BBC's journalism, battling for high editorial standards. I was the man to sort it all out. They had consulted widely and everyone they had spoken to had said I was the outstanding person for the job.

I felt tearful when I told my close colleagues at LWT that I was departing for the BBC – all too aware I would be leaving behind a centre of real originality, a rational, civilised, supportive company, full of well-motivated people and good friends. Christopher was irate I was leaving and rowed with Hussey about my departure date. The news of my appointment exploded across the front pages: 'BBC turmoil as outsider becomes No. 2', 'BBC braced for Birt shake-up', 'Bold move that brings a spark of hope to the battered BBC'. I asked LWT if I could keep my share options, but the board ruled, as I and my family had anticipated, that they must be forfeited.

I had long before decided in my own mind that Greg Dyke should succeed me as Director of Programmes at LWT. He had proved tough, savvy and a doughty ally at TVS; he had a natural, unfeigned commitment to popular programming, and he and I shared a common view of the industry and how it should be run. I pressed Greg's claim without difficulty on Brian, and without much difficulty on a more sceptical Christopher. During the handover, an intensive series of briefing meetings was arranged for Greg. He disconcerted the scheduling team by listening but not taking notes, and endlessly doodling Plutos on a pad.

I went to visit my nanna Anna, now eighty-seven. As usual, I took a crate of Guinness with me. Nanna was no doubt pleased by her eldest grandson's elevation to Deputy Director-General of the BBC, but she certainly didn't say so. That wasn't her way. She believed in fate, that if things happened they were ordained to happen. She believed that everything, in the end, was for the best.

When I left LWT for the BBC I was forty-two years old. With many programme successes now under my belt, I had great confidence in my creative capacity, my ability to spot talent, to take

12

BBC News

In my first few days at the BBC I scored a goal at Wembley on Cup Final day. David Frost had organised a seven-a-side of assorted soap stars and celebrities to play in a charity match in front of eighty thousand Spurs and Coventry supporters just before the 1987 Cup Final. As in a boyhood dream, I found myself at the centre of defence alongside World Cup hero Bobby Moore. I had to mark Daley Thompson, a Rolls-Royce of an athlete who scorned my defensive efforts with two spectacular goals. With just a minute to go, Bobby Moore controlled, under pressure, a long difficult ball with his chest, and pushed a short, precisely weighted pass to me. I hit a long first-time ball to snooker ace Dennis Taylor on the wing, looked up to see that the other side's defenders had deserted their posts to attack our goal, and ran the length of the field into the hole behind them, arriving just as Dennis crossed the ball. I doubt it was his intention but the ball flew goalward. The goalie punched it out to land just by me, to my left. I knew enough to shoot straight

away – even if it were on my weaker foot. I mishit the ball, yet it
bobbled slowly but inevitably beyond the goalie's outstretched arm,
just inside the far post. I had scored! I was rewarded with eighty
thousand desultory cheers.

I was unprepared for the BBC. From the outside I had held the
organisation in awed, if qualified, respect. On the inside it was not
what I expected. At LWT my office had been flooded with light
from a huge picture window with a panoramic view of the Thames
and London, in some ways symbolic of LWT itself – an open,
straightforward, outward-thinking company, keen to embrace and to
understand the world. At the BBC my office was modest and
cramped, gloomy and dimly lit, with small windows. It was adjacent
to the office of Michael Checkland, the Director-General, to one
side of the prow of the great liner of Broadcasting House that
points along Portland Place. My office had an odd wedge shape,
narrowing to a point. The interior of Broadcasting House was as
dull as the exterior was elegant, with long, bare, scruffy corridors
decorated with noticeboards and fire extinguishers.

LWT had been full of contemporary, alert, fun-loving men and
women. The centre of the BBC was dominated by sober, careful,
grey-suited, middle-aged, middle-class men. Most of the early meetings I attended were male-only, the list of attendees an alphabet
soup of initials like MDXB, DDRR, CRAXB. It was MDR who
attended and spoke, not Brian Wenham, the head of radio. The culture at the centre was closer to the civil service, to the Church or to
the common room of a minor public school than to the media villages of Covent Garden or Soho. In the first few days, when
discussing how to respond to a letter of complaint, a stuffy, disdain-
ful member of the Secretariat explained to me: 'Oh, the BBC
should never admit wrong. It should never apologise!' When I said
we should, and did, there was sullen resentment.

The centre of the BBC seemed stuck in the 1950s, and, as someone whose values and attitudes had been formed in the 1960s, I

stood out. In a world where people bent over backwards not to declare themselves, where they were shifty and evasive when pressed for a view, I said what I thought. I gradually realised I was at a court, where information was the currency, swapped in whispers in shadowy corners – a world of nods and winks, of constant jockeying for position, of issues settled out of sight; a world of intrigue, calculation and plotting; a world in which Machiavelli himself would have felt at home. For the first time in my working life, I found myself without the necessary skills. Within days of my arrival, I read casual remarks I had made at small meetings, with only a few people present, in the next day's papers. My modern clothes were obviously a cause of great fascination too, as detailed descriptions of my attire began appearing in the media as well. A strange folklore began to build around me. I was dieting when I arrived at the BBC, eating only fruit and cottage cheese for lunch, and so I was soon labelled a vegetarian, then a Buddhist. My father began to be described as a railwayman.

I was the first outsider to join the BBC at the very top for decades, and I was as welcome as a Protestant made Pope. There were no niceties at the first Board of Management I attended. Brian Wenham was supercilious and made sarcastic jokes aimed directly at me. John Tusa, Managing Director of World Service, eyed me suspiciously. (Wenham and Alan Protheroe, Assistant Director-General, soon took early retirement.) Hardly a soul made me feel welcome. I soon felt solitary and isolated, and was grateful for the consoling support of Katie Kay, who had made the journey over from LWT with me.

The BBC had just suffered a nervous breakdown. For the first time in its history, the Director-General had been violently dismissed, following years of guerrilla warfare between the Governors and the management. The BBC had been under ceaseless assault from the outside, following a series of bitter, divisive rows over programmes. Only a few weeks before, for instance, the Special Branch had entered the premises of BBC Scotland and taken away material from a series called *Secret Society*. The BBC felt violated and defence-less. I met senior executives strung out, nerves stretched beyond endurance, uncertain what the future held for them personally, or for the constant, unchanging, cradle-to-grave world of the BBC they had comfortably inhabited for so long. Wherever I went, I was told that staff morale was at rock bottom, an observation that would be much repeated in a different context over the years ahead.

The Governors were the most confident and assured group around. After years of frustration, they had just struck decisively by deposing the old regime, and introducing the new. They did not feel to me like a representative group. They were overwhelmingly small-'c' conservative, ranging from steely through bombastic to cranky. Though newly appointed, Duke Hussey led his Governors with authority and understanding, playing on the group's prejudices. His key alliance was with his Vice-Chairman, Joel Barnett, who had been Chief Secretary to the Treasury in Callaghan's Cabinet. They were both natural schemers, and generally got what they wanted.

The miracle was that in this paranoid, backbiting, untrusting, ungenerous environment, the BBC still made good programmes. The powerful creative incubus that had been at the heart of the organisation since its inception – and had produced many of the wonders of the broadcast world – could not be suppressed; and exceptional talents all over the organisation were still flourishing and producing remarkable work of the kind that had long made me admire the BBC. But I quickly came to appreciate that the BBC's performance was very patchy. Alongside innovation, manifest weak-ness had been tolerated and allowed to fester. There was little sign of the strong, involved, creative management of the kind I had experienced at both Granada and LWT. And in those early weeks, the BBC appeared slack to me in other ways. Katie soon spotted how soft the whole place was. She noticed how much less hard everyone worked compared with ITV, how often offices were deserted long before six, and how frequently our late-afternoon calls remained unanswered. It was quickly apparent that this bloated, bureaucratic monolith was wasting licence-payers' funds on a massive scale.

It was also apparent that there was no all-embracing cross-BBC strategy, no overview from the centre of how well each of the BBC's component parts was performing. Pronounced weakness was not being confronted. The operating divisions behaved as baronies, with keep-off signs discouraging interest from the centre. The Board of Management was a meeting of Mafia clans, not a team working for a common purpose. The organisation's processes were slack. Important issues were not fully dissected. Decisions were made casually in the absence of a full analysis. There was no organised flow of information coming to the centre, identifying difficult issues. Meetings were chatty and casual. The whole way the BBC was managed was shockingly amateurish, much less professional than ITV, itself hardly outstanding. What seemed to be at the front of everyone's mind was the politics of the organisation itself. The notion of public service had not been lost at the BBC, but it was muted in many quarters. From the beginning, I was struck by how little overt idealism was in evidence compared with Granada or LWT, both of which had taken their essential character from old, hard-edged leftists – Sidney Bernstein and John Freeman.

Three people stood out against the crowd. The first was David Hatch, the brilliantly funny, cheerful and genuine Director of Radio, who at Cambridge had been a member of *Beyond the Fringe*. David brought a tireless, honest intensity to managing radio, applauding the good, unafraid to offer a penetrating, carefully argued critique of the weak. And he was a decent and generous man who saw immediately how unwelcoming the BBC was to me and reached out with sympathy and support, sending me a steady stream, over the years, of funny, pithy, candid billets-doux. David did this despite Radio's opposition to forging a unified News and Current Affairs directorate, which I would lead. He wrote to Michael Checkland after my appointment to say, '. . . I must place on record my heartfelt objection to the proposal to relieve this

Directorate of responsibility for News . . .' But, having written his note, David put his feelings to one side.

The second person to make an early impression on me was Patricia Hodgson, the Secretary of the BBC, who – at Hussey's instigation – as part of her job had helped prepare secretly for Milne's dismissal. For this she was scorned as a Judas by her colleagues. Patricia had a deep understanding of the unique character and politics of the BBC. She was focused and energetic, and, unlike other corporation-lifers, alert to the world outside the BBC. She was also an extraordinarily smart operator, with an acute sensibility to every kind of individual, to their flaws, vanities and convictions. She was sharply attuned to the early difficulties of my position.

The third person to stand out from the crowd was the Chairman himself, Marmaduke Hussey, a battle-hardened ex-Guards officer, a product of Rugby, Oxford and the English upper classes. He was a great gangly 6 foot 6 inch toff, who would have been entirely at home as the Colonel of the Regiment, or as a country squire. He had lost a leg in action in the war, and walked with the aid of a stick and an artificial limb. Hussey was friendly and unpompous, with a powerful, cheery, larger-than-life personality. His favourite form of discourse was the monologue. As a regular visitor to his office, I was treated to long, scathing, gossipy diatribes – full of barrack-room expletives – aimed at the world in general and the BBC in particular. He was on a perpetual hunt to uncover fresh examples of the BBC's incompetence, foolishness or wickedness, and he delighted to share them with me. Hussey had spent months investigating *Maggie's Militant Tendency* – a *Panorama* alleging that some Conservative MPs were extremists, which had resulted in an expensive and humiliating legal action for the BBC. As a result of his investigation, Hussey had concluded that the BBC was out of control editorially, and that it had poor processes for handling legally sensitive programmes. Nor was he impressed with the overall quality of the BBC's journalism. He observed in his first meeting alone with me that no one had told the BBC's journalists that they were not doing

well. All of the candidates for the director-generalship had agreed
on that. That was why I had been appointed. He said he, Joel
Barnett, Mike Checkland and I had five years to restore respect for
the BBC. Hussey had taken on the Germans; he had fought the
print unions in a year-long strike when he was Managing Director
of *The Times*; he positively relished the prospect of the battle ahead
for the BBC. He would be the field marshal. I would be his general
on the first main battleground, which was to be news and current
affairs.

Historically, BBC News had been split into four, discretely managed, unrelated and uncoordinated units: TV News and TV
Current Affairs were separate departments in Television; the political reporters at Westminster were managed from the centre; and
radio News and Current Affairs were integrated, but managed by
Radio. As a result, there was no single and coherent overview of the
BBC's journalism. There was also a consensus that BBC Television
News had a mid-market tabloid agenda; that it lacked quality and
authority; and that it lagged behind ITN in its dynamism and professionalism. I soon picked up, though staff at the centre spoke in
hushed tones of the matter, that the Television Service had completely lost control of Lime Grove – the battered studio complex in
west London where Television Current Affairs was situated, and
where reporters regarded themselves as untouchables.

I had my own views about BBC journalism from the outside –
many of them developed over ten years previously when I had written the 'bias against understanding' series of articles with Peter Jay,
after which we had engaged in a dialogue with the BBC's then
Chairman, Michael Swann. I had felt – and still felt – that BBC
journalism overall was just not serious enough, and did not engage
the issues that mattered. The BBC's journalists were overwhelmingly generalists, few having the authority – like those I'd worked
with on *Weekend World* – that comes from real expertise, from long
immersion in a specialism. And BBC current affairs was not always

impartial: too many journalists were willing to offer their own opinions rather than undertaking rigorous, open-minded exploration of
all sides of an issue. The BBC's journalistic tradition overall was
descriptive rather than analytical. Moreover, the BBC had not yet
come to terms with Thatcher. For ten years or more, LWT had
been in the thick of the political and economic debate about what
was wrong with Britain. The BBC's journalism, on the other hand,
was still trapped in the old post-war Butskellite, Keynesian consensus. Many BBC people found it hard to think of Mrs Thatcher as
democratically legitimate, perceiving her as an aberration. LWT
had been on the South Bank, within walking distance of
Westminster, Covent Garden and the City, and was exceptionally
well plugged into what every kind of group in the capital city was
thinking and doing. By contrast, many of the BBC's journalists and
programme-makers seemed trapped in their West London prisons.
Unaware of the swirl of ideas around them, they may as well have
been four hundred rather than four miles from the centre of one of
the world's most vibrant cities.

The BBC's journalists, though, were not just considered off the
pace by commentators on the right. Neil Kinnock, the Labour
Opposition leader, asked to see me when I was appointed. He laid
into the BBC's journalism with typical vim and vigour. He made no
partisan points: he spoke not as Labour's leader but as an ultra
BBC loyalist, which he would remain. Kinnock didn't just attack the
lack of *quality* of the BBC's journalism: he complained with fiery
conviction about its inefficiency – he told vivid tales of over-manned
news and studio crews, of unnecessary duplication. And he criticised
the management capabilities of BBC Television (though he was
kind about Radio).

Mrs Thatcher herself was far more polite. Not long after my
arrival, she invited Michael Checkland and myself to lunch one
Saturday at Chequers. We talked from noon to late afternoon,
ending with tea in the drawing room. She referred to us throughout
as Mr Checkland and Mr Birt. As we ate, I saw the odd sight of

ordinary bobbies with helmets, but with rifles slung over their shoulders, continually patrolling the grounds outside. I knew from friendly sources that Mrs Thatcher thought the BBC drew more than its fair share of leftists; that it promoted its own not the public interest; that it fell short of the standards to which it should aspire; that it was an unquestioning platform for every kind of vested interest; that it was unpatriotic; and that the licence fee was an unjustifiable tax enforced by criminal sanction. I knew she had been heard to say: 'I never listen to the *Today* programme. It was particularly bad this morning.' I knew that Denis Thatcher saw the BBC as part of the enemy ranged against his beloved Margaret. I also knew that she had a succession of Blimpish figures who regularly rang and wound her up about the BBC. But over lunch that day she was on her very best behaviour, and kept her prejudices contained. She revealed that she watched BBC2 and named programmes she had enjoyed. She fired a warning shot about Radio 1 and local radio: 'It's all pop,' she said. She worried about satellite and cable channels importing sex and violence. She reminded us we were the *British* Broadcasting Corporation; that we should aspire to the highest standards; that we must not bend, or become too popular.

What she most wanted to do, however, was to hear *our* views about the BBC. Michael Checkland talked fluently about a self-reliant, better-managed organisation. Bravely, he confronted an issue that had plagued his predecessor, Alasdair Milne. He told Mrs Thatcher directly that the BBC would not be putting on *The Falklands Play*, an account of the war, written by Ian Curteis, which showed her in a heroic light. He explained that Michael Grade thought the play insufficiently strong creatively, and he supported that decision. Mrs Thatcher paused but did not respond. She turned to me: she wanted to hear my perspective on the BBC's culture, and clucked approvingly when I shared my insights with her about an inward-looking organisation largely cut off from the intellectual ferment around it. 'Marxism is at the root of debunking journalism,' she asserted. I parried, accepting that much journalism assumed that a problem identified was a problem for the state to solve. I argued that there were other powerful influences on our national culture: disputation – undermining your opponent's case – was at the heart of our Parliamentary, debating and judicial systems. The anarchist tendency, exemplified by *Private Eye* and its renegade public schoolboys, enjoyed throwing everything up in the air. And the self-confident Oxbridge tradition of we-know-best commentating was a literary rather than an analytical tradition. There were many reasons why British journalism did not really grapple with Britain's problems.

Mrs Thatcher engaged, she was interested, she argued back. She didn't flinch when I made the same speech to her that I had already made to Neil Kinnock: that I wouldn't be content until the BBC was giving MPs of all parties a harder time; until we had journalists of real authority and expertise testing politicians rigorously about their policies and ideas. 'We'll keep you on your toes, Prime Minister!' She laughed. 'I don't mind that,' she said. Mrs Thatcher was punctilious – then and on other occasions – in always talking as Prime Minister and not as party leader. She would never once complain to me – even if she did to others – about a BBC programme. She emphasised always the BBC's duty to be fair to all sides.

I spent the early months after my appointment listening to all the key players among the BBC's journalists, and spending time – often a whole day – with a programme team. I was generally greeted on my rounds with sullen suspicion – hardly surprising, given that I was an outsider, and given the unsettling dramas preceding my arrival. I formed two powerful impressions about the people: one was that there was a huge cohort – chiefly in their forties or fifties – for whom news and current affairs were a process. They covered and responded to events. They were competent and experienced, but they had long since ceased to think enquiringly. They were in a groove, serving time. They were mostly male and macho, and drink played an important part in many of their lives. The place was awash with Australian Chardonnay. The second, and contrary, impression was that among these listless legions were many glorious individual exceptions, generally in their twenties and thirties – a younger generation, in both radio and television, of a different hue. *Newsnight* and the *Today* programme in particular seemed to have produced a corpus of people of energy and confidence who had maintained their originality of thought. But they were not in positions of power.

Most staff in News and Current Affairs, I found, were looking at the issues through the other end of the telescope from the Chairman, the Governors, and much established opinion. These groups may have regarded BBC journalism as being in urgent need of widespread improvement and reform – but the journalists themselves didn't, nor did they even seem to appreciate that they were at the top of everyone's agenda. They thought the journalism was just fine. Their own agenda, which I understood and with which I sympathised, was that they had felt insufficiently supported when Mrs Thatcher and Leon Brittan had protested about *Real Lives*, and when Norman Tebbit had attacked the BBC's coverage of the US bombing of Libya in October 1986. They were understandably mistrustful of the Governors and of senior management. They felt vulnerable. Neither side had faith in the other.

I had other early realisations: on arrival I had asked for a copy of the BBC budget for the general election of 1987. I had been in charge of ITV's coverage and was curious about the comparative cost. I was astonished to be told there was no budget of any kind. Elections cost what they cost, I was informed, with no hint of embarrassment. The election programmes got made: the bills got paid. This was my first clue to the true state of the BBC's financial management.

I commissioned a financial analysis of the current cost of the four component parts of BBC News and Current Affairs – each under separate management. At LWT, I had been used to tip-top financial support, to computerised spreadsheets. At the BBC I was presented with the analysis I had requested by a young, inexperienced accountant on a single piece of paper with a row of rounded numbers written in *pencil*. Network Television's accounts were particularly impenetrable. I would never uncover the true cost of the departments I inherited. It would take years – and the introduction of skilled, outside accountants – to make even a credible estimate.

Even without sophisticated analysis, it was clear that the Television service had starved News and Current Affairs of resources. The most striking manifestation of this was the paucity of overseas bureaux. BBC TV News had fallen way behind other world broadcasters. NBC, for instance, had twenty-five established overseas bureaux in the late 1980s, BBC Television News just five. The BBC had no television bureaux at all on the European mainland – nothing whatsoever in Paris, Brussels or Bonn. Network Television's lack of vision, as well as its financial incompetence, scandalised me.

I was also surprised to discover that the BBC had only a few, rudimentary editorial guidelines. In ITV I had been used to working within – and constantly referring to – the IBA's comprehensive editorial code when dealing with the tricky editorial and ethical issues that programme-makers in every field constantly encounter. In the absence of a BBC bible, inconsistent case law was being established day by day all over the organisation. Again, Network Television emerged as an unmanaged, lawless place, increasingly disconnected from the BBC's ancient tradition of editorial care and integrity. Michael Grade, for instance, caused great upset at the centre shortly after my arrival when, as the Aids scare intensified, he offered Richard Branson free airtime to advertise Mates condoms.

The overall impression I formed of the BBC in my early months was of a vast organisation with no governing brain or nervous system, which had expanded and grown and multiplied organically, with powerful instincts but with no guiding thought. The BBC was unmanaged and undisciplined in a way I would not, from the outside, have thought possible. I had taken on infinitely more than I had bargained for. With a sense of trepidation, and friendlessness, I set out to reform and to modernise one part of this enormous, uncontrolled leviathan, BBC News.

Two months after I arrived, I brought together the senior managers from all four parts of the news empire into one place, for the first time ever. The four-day conference – the longest I would ever convene – was held in a run-down hotel not far from the M25 near Leatherhead. Our deliberations were accompanied by the ceaseless nerve-jangling hum of distant motorway traffic.

I was Daniel in the lions' den, and the mood was nervous and sombre. To launch the conference, I spoke at length, setting out my first impressions and convictions, and a vision of what I hoped a unified and united BBC News and Current Affairs directorate could achieve. Informed reporting strengthened democracy. We would aim for the high ground. Our journalism would be about the significant stories that really had an impact on people's lives. We would recruit a corps of specialist journalists with real expertise. We would be authoritative. We would create a portfolio of programmes that would allow us to focus on what really mattered. We would seek more investment. We would formulate a comprehensive and coherent set of editorial guidelines. We would reassert the principle of impartiality as a touchstone of BBC journalism. Many BBC television current affairs programmes I had monitored had rushed to judgement. They had emotional, value-laden commentaries taking sides on matters of public dispute. In a *Panorama* I had just seen, the reporter had used the phrase 'beyond belief' to describe a contentious issue, when he should have stayed cool and kept his distance. A series of allegations had been characterised as 'an appalling litany'. The audience had not been presented with all sides of the argument, they had not been allowed to make up their own minds. Some BBC reporters increasingly appeared to want to tell the audience what to think. I wanted judicious journalism, not reporters preening themselves, full of half-baked opinions and their own sense of self-importance. I wanted all the arguments to be weighed. I wanted to see greater rigour in the BBC's programme-making process. News and Current Affairs decision-makers needed to get out of their offices and into the wider world, and to expose themselves more to the flow of ideas. We would make difficult pro-grammes – we were not afraid of sensitive subjects, of challenging authority, of putting powerful people under scrutiny – but tricky programmes must be vigorous and must have proper legal and edi-torial scrutiny. I made clear I had television journalism in my sights, and that radio journalism needed refreshing but that it had not lost its way.

As I amplified my criticisms and approach, I was listened to in stunned silence. Over the next days, there was a nervy and stilted discussion of the issues I had identified. After the conference, a shock wave went through the BBC's centres of journalism as the firmness of my views became known. My new colleagues later told me the journalists had felt no one could touch them. Suddenly they feared I could. There was a welter of tales and speculation, increas-ingly hostile to me.

I shared the essence of my thinking with the senior BBC jour-nalists because openness and frankness had always been my way. Could I have been more stealthy? Some of those who joined me later on the perilous adventure – and who completed the journey to a successful conclusion – argue that the scale of the change needed was so great that sooner or later my aims would have been clear anyway; and that, without the initial shock of candour, change would have been even harder. Others argue that I could have done more at an early stage to signal to those who would be the young officers of the revolution what their place would be. I wasn't, how-ever, yet certain who my officer class were; and in part I wanted to use the conference to identify those who could join me on the jour-ney. What is clear is that given the scale of change needed in a paranoid organisation which had already experienced the intense traumas of Alasdair Milne's BBC, all paths ahead were hard. Under any scenario, sooner or later – when my plans became clear – there would be a howl of outrage and bitter resistance from the many whose jobs were threatened or whose working lives would be fundamentally changed.

I set out to form a senior management team. The key player was Ron Neil. Ron was solid and sturdy in both appearance and outlook, a Scot of principle and integrity, with an open mind. He always introduced himself by saying, 'Ronald Neil, that's my name,' but everyone called him Ron. From my vantage point in ITV, I had long ago noted his programme credentials: Ron was a real television professional who could combine all the elements of programming with a sure touch. He had a deep commitment to craft excellence, to the quality, clarity and precision of language, to finding and backing people of ability. He had launched *Breakfast News*, and had been editor of *Newsnight* and *That's Life*. He had not long arrived in BBC Television News, having been drafted in to redesign and to refresh the *Six O'Clock News*. Just before my arrival, he had been made head of TV News. Unsupported by Broadcasting House, Ron had mounted a powerful, convincing and detailed defence against Norman Tebbit's attack on the BBC's Libyan bombing coverage.

Ron was apprehensive and guarded with me, but I quickly realised that he was the biggest, most talented and most decent person around. We were not of the same journalistic tradition, but we had a similar appreciation of good programme-making skills and we shared pronounced convictions about accuracy, fairness and impartiality. Ron, like me, was hostile to the cynics and to the excesses of Lime Grove, and he had already taken on some of the most conservative and entrenched elements in the newsroom in relaunching the *Six O'Clock News*. I felt Ron could be the bridge from the old world to a new journalistic era at the BBC. He would be the symbol of continuity, attracting the best talents of the old order. Ron agreed – nervously – to be my deputy, to run the News and Current Affairs directorate day by day, while I provided strategic direction.

I resolved to fill the other key slots on the team from both inside and outside the BBC, and – in defiance of BBC tradition – by direct appointment, without formal interview boards. I was certain we had to skip a generation or two to fill the lead management positions. I talked to some able and respected outsiders, like Liz Forgan and Stewart Purvis, but I couldn't lure them away from their rapid ascents at Channel 4 and ITN. Two young BBC editors caught my eye: Tony Hall, thirty-six, one of Ron's stable of trusties, a cool, precise Merseysider who had cut his teeth on *Newsnight*; and Jenny Abramsky, the bouncy, confident, plain-talking forty-year-old fireball who ran the *Today* programme. Ron and I appointed them to run all the journalism in TV and Radio respectively, a huge promotion for them both. The incumbent in TV Current Affairs, Peter Pagnamenta, was a conscientious executive, who had made some fine documentaries as a producer himself, but I judged he had neither the appetite nor the conviction to manage what needed to be done at Lime Grove, so I approached Samir Shah to come over from LWT to run TV Current Affairs as Tony Hall's deputy.

For the final member of the core team, I set out to find a managing editor: I searched for a print journalist with executive experience who could manage all the BBC's journalists, leading the recruitment of a new corps of specialist reporters, and raise the BBC's journalistic sights. I hit the phone and talked to a number of people I respected. The same name came up again and again: Ian Hargreaves, the coming person at the *Financial Times*. He was thirty-six years old and the *FT*'s features editor. He had previously been the paper's transport correspondent, its social policy editor and its New York bureau chief. Ian turned out to be a lean, wiry, austere Lancastrian, born in Burnley, who wore steel specs and had close-cropped hair, with a sombre, puritan manner punctured by shafts of wry, sardonic wit. He looked like a young, radical university lecturer: he wore a tweed jacket and cords and carried his papers around in what looked like a battered and tattered old school satchel. In fact, he had been a schoolteacher and a community worker on a drugs project before coming into journalism. He was very serious about how he lived his life, holidaying with his children, for instance, in Belfast or Gdansk. He was a beguiling mix of the idealistic and the hard headed. He had a complete absence of vanity, a burning honesty and transparent goodness; but he was also as acute a journalist as I ever met in the UK, with a deep grasp of the whole range of issues across the span of politics, foreign and social affairs, and the economy. He was also powerfully intuitive: over the next few years I would witness Ian on many occasions take just a few pieces of a mosaic – the clues, for instance, offered over lunch with a politician – and use them to create a convincing hypothesis of what the full picture might look like. He was a true sceptic, but never a cynic. Ian had doubts about coming to the BBC, but agreed to take the risk. Over the next few years, he worked untiringly to bring sharpness, revelation and relevance to all the BBC's news journalism. He was the key signing.

I warned the Governors in the summer of 1987 that we had a young and talented top team, but that we faced formidable problems, and that there would be blood on the wall. The next few years for the leadership group would indeed prove gruesome, as we fought battle after battle with the forces of resistance among BBC journalists, and with the rest of the BBC.

When most of the key appointments were announced, I did the rounds of the BBC's main centres of journalism with the core team. At Lime Grove, where their leader Peter Pagnamenta had been deposed, we faced a studio full of hundreds of hostile and aggressive journalists and technicians who could see only threat and no advantage to the changes announced.

The first significant obstacle I encountered was over money. I had accepted the job from Michael Checkland with no knowledge of the financial position of BBC News and Current Affairs. I soon shared with him my discovery that the journalism had been starved of resources by Network Television. I estimated the considerable sums

needed to recruit specialists, to open overseas bureaux and to start
new programmes. He listened but was non-committal. This made
Ron particularly edgy. In the end, I would get most of the money I
asked for, but it would be spread over three years, not one. This
delay brought about the first difficulties between Michael Checkland
and me.

We had enough money, however, for Ian Hargreaves to set out
on a vast recruitment and deployment exercise which would affect
the face of BBC journalism for a decade or more – giving a new
lease of life to neglected BBC stars, promoting and placing the best
of the young internal candidates, searching out able journalists
and specialists from print and broadcast media outside. Our
biggest catch was the brilliant, edgy Polly Toynbee, a real authority, who joined from the *Guardian* as social affairs editor, to lead a
team including Niall Dickson, who came from a specialist health
journal. We vastly expanded the number of financial journalists.
Daniel Jeffreys from Cazenove – and later Peter Jay – became the
BBC's economics and business editor. John Cole, an outstanding
political journalist, remained as political editor, but we beefed up
the team behind him. Denis Murray, a reporter of superb judgement, became Ireland correspondent. The commanding John
Simpson was the obvious choice for foreign affairs editor. In all, we
appointed eighty specialist journalists, a vast injection of knowledge and capability. Ian brought in, or brought on, Martin Bashir,
Martha Kearney, Nisha Pillai, Jeremy Vine, Huw Edwards,
Richard Quest, Evan Davies, Phil Bassett, Fergal Keane, Matt
Frei, Jeremy Bowen, Kim Catcheside, George Alagiah, Bridget
Kendall, Stephen Milligan, Ed Stourton and many more. Over the
next few years, we opened television news bureaux all over the
world, including Paris, Brussels, Bonn, Tokyo, Beijing, Moscow
and Washington. Eventually, we would have the most extensive
foreign news-gathering capability of any broadcaster in the world,
far outweighing CNN or any of the US networks or European
broadcasters.

Tony Hall and Jenny Abramsky marshalled the young lions to edit a new generation of news programmes. The take-over of the thirty-year-olds was described by one executive involved as 'a most violent act', and prompted a flock of early retirements. Twenty-nine-year-old Mark Thompson was appointed from *Newsnight* to fashion an intelligent, significant *Nine O'Clock News*, a prime show-case for our new corps of specialists. His core team were Mark Damazer and Richard Sambrook (who later became the BBC's news chief). This was the key moment of change for BBC News. Mark Thompson and his team created news on the BBC in its modern form, in the process amazing a deeply sceptical newsroom with their decisions – for instance, in their first months, devoting twelve minutes to the Chancellor's autumn statement, at the time a revolutionary idea. Mark Thompson's new *Nine O'Clock News* thrilled me. We had made our first great leap forward. In this same period many other bright young leaders of the future were placed in key executive positions, including Mark Byford, Roger Mosey and Rod Liddle. A new generation was now in charge.

The BBC's radio journalism was in much better shape than tele-vision's, but it benefited none the less from Jenny Abramsky's spirited dynamism. She moved on from the newsroom a cardiganed generation who had waited for news to be brought to them, and she introduced young blood which was proactive, energetic and ques-tioning about news. Radio news writing became less literary and academic, and more journalistic. Jenny sharpened the sequences: the *Today* programme in particular went from strength to strength, becoming ever more essential listening for the politically interested classes. James Naughtie was brought in to present *World at One*.

All these changes produced immediate improvements in the BBC's journalism but attracted difficulties in their wake: an older generation of powerful editors and generalist reporters was being sidelined and became truculent; the strong, conservative, green-eyeshade tendency in the newsrooms – who viewed news as a commodity – continued to deride notions of a more challenging

news agenda; the new, young appointees had not yet gained mus-
cularity and earned respect; the latest reporter recruits, particularly
the specialists, were seen as broadcasting and hard-news innocents;
Lime Grove was seething because it had been taken over not just by
me but by the old enemy – BBC News. Every day, a steady drip –
and sometimes a stream – of hostile and mendacious stories would
appear in the newspapers, reflecting the malcontents' concerns,
ridiculing our efforts, and increasingly focusing on me as the prime
architect of the changes. I was labelled Pol Pot by the self-exiled
Brian Wenham, my arrival as Year Zero, my stewardship as a Reign
of Terror. I was – the propaganda ran – exercising unprecedented
control, centralising the BBC's editorial grip dangerously. In the
media, our changes were described as 'a bitter struggle'. I was 'The
most feared man in TV'. I was introducing 'Stalinisation'. Even my
alma mater, *World in Action*, entered the fray in due course, alleging
that the BBC was being 'tamed'.

The bloodiest battle for the news group was with Network
Television. When I arrived at the BBC, Michael Grade was due to
succeed his mentor Bill Cotton as Managing Director, Television,
when Cotton retired the following year. I had long admired Bill for
his role in creating intelligent and popular entertainment for prime
time on BBC1. But he was also the most aggressive, self-confident
and independent-minded of the BBC's barons. When I had worked
with him to prepare Michael Grade for his interview for the director-generalship, I had been struck by Bill's contempt for the centre
of the BBC, for the executives at 'the other end of the motorway'.
(Westway joined Broadcasting House in the centre of London,
which housed the Director-General and the corporate centre, with
the BBC's Television Centre, the studios in west London where
Television executives had their offices.) Bill bridled at the centre's
authority. He believed that Television was all that mattered to the
BBC, for it had the bulk of the money and the audience. Radio and
the Regions were the poor cousins. Television should be allowed to

get on with it, without interference. Bill's main focus was on ratings, and he had little interest in any area outside popular television. I uncovered a strong sense among the Governors and at the centre that Network Television had long ago broken adrift – that it had lost sight of the BBC's wider public purposes; that it had failed to champion BBC editorial values; that it was inflated and inefficient; that even the simple things were not well managed. When a hurricane hit Britain in the autumn of 1987, the BBC fell off the air, unable to offer proper coverage, with no standby power, the victim of Television's failure to institute and test effective disaster and emergency procedures.

Bill Cotton certainly had had no vision for television journalism when it was under his control. He had lacked the expertise or the capability to grip the editorial issues when successive tremors had jarred the BBC. He had starved News of resources, and he resented Michael Checkland awarding them to us now at the expense, as he saw it, of peak-time television. Michael Grade's strongest instinct was to champion the concerns and interests of the people and groups around him, and it was inevitable that he would be influenced by his boss and mentor Bill, an old family friend from the same show-business tradition.

Michael had been warm and friendly to me on arrival. He wrote to me on my first day to say: 'I'm so looking forward to renewing our working association. It worked before – it'll work again. You know you have my complete support.' Michael Grade was the only person, other than Checkland and Hussey, whom I consulted about the changes I had made in News and Current Affairs. I felt his resentment, however, when the Chairman brought me into discussion at Governors' meetings on Television matters, or when I made observations to him privately about manifest shortcomings in BBC Television, or when I took charge of the BBC in the first summer – chairing the Board of Management, for instance – when Michael Checkland was on holiday. Grade didn't respond enthusiastically when I shared with him my aim to extend the *Nine O'Clock News* to thirty minutes (from twenty-five) and to have a fixed start-time for *Newsnight* at 10.30 p.m. The programme was currently floating all over the schedule, often starting well after 11 p.m., and as a result had little impact. However, I remained loyal to Michael as a former close colleague and friend: when Jeremy Isaacs attacked him for his focus on ratings in the summer of 1987 at the Edinburgh Festival, I rose to his defence, but Jeremy was adamant, writing to me to say: 'the BBC must stand for programme values other than those which Michael Grade espouses'.

The tensions between Michael and me, and between Television and the centre, finally erupted when the controllerships of BBC1 and BBC2 fell vacant: Michael Grade was stepping up from BBC1, and Graeme McDonald was about to retire from BBC2. Michael mentioned to me that Ron Neil – newly appointed as my deputy and lynchpin – was his favoured candidate for BBC1. I was surprised he would even consider Ron. Sorting out the journalism was the BBC's key priority, I suggested. News was experiencing a very bumpy ride and Ron was vital to the project. Ron shouldn't be taken away. Michael was non-committal, but Bill Cotton later raised the issue of Ron becoming Controller of BBC1 with Michael Checkland, who also ruled it out, supporting my argument. I mentioned to Checkland that I was expecting to participate in the appointment process for the controllerships of BBC1 and BBC2, in line with our agreement that I would be involved in key strategic decisions across the board. I saw him flinch, and sensed he didn't relish raising the matter with Bill Cotton. In the event, Bill and Michael protested vehemently and made my attendance an issue of principle. Simultaneously, I discovered that – despite the Director-General's ruling – Cotton and Grade were continuing to put Ron under pressure to desert the post he had only just taken up and to become Controller of BBC1. As the reforms in News gathered momentum, I was under assault on all sides. I felt isolated. I believed that Michael Grade, an old friend, should be helping me, not undermining me and adding to my problems by trying to steal away my key support. I was resentful and miserable, but stood my ground: for me, too, a seat on the board had become an issue of principle. Michael Checkland went silent on me.

One Monday in mid-October, Patricia Hodgson was uncharacteristically despondent. 'It's the same old story,' she said, 'the centre refusing to take on Network Television.' Checkland had been busy introducing five-year plans, and all of Network Television's declared plans were about resource and efficiency problems: there was no mention of programme or editorial issues. Patricia talked of leaving: 'The plan's not tackling Television's central problems. The Chairman says it's rubbish.'

Michael Checkland called me in to announce that it would cause too much trouble if I were on the board for the controllerships. I felt the rug being pulled from under me. I protested vigorously and later wrote to him:

> There is an issue here for the BBC as well as for me: as you
> know, I consider the BBC's problems go far beyond its
> difficulties with news and current affairs and the need to live
> within its means. Unless the BBC is given a strong editorial
> lead from the top, with the centre leading a vigorous debate
> about editorial strategy and laying down firm policy on
> standards across the whole range of programmes, I do not
> believe that its fundamental ills will be cured. The BBC
> needs more policy and less politics. It has been a federation
> of baronies for too long.

Relations between Checkland and me became tense. It was plain that Checkland did not see me as a partner. I was just one of the many plates he wanted to keep spinning. In early November he and I had a showdown: the News and Current Affairs directorate was being obstructed by the other directorates at every turn. In Checkland's latest absence on holiday, I had had to deal with a string of minor difficulties which had again demonstrated that the

Television directorate was acting unilaterally. I urged Michael Checkland to take hold of the BBC.

The next day he told me that he didn't accept my analysis, but that I would be on the board: we had to be partners. When they heard the news, Bill Cotton and Michael Grade went to see Checkland. They would not sit on the board if I were there. Checkland asked me to volunteer to stand down. I refused. Events moved fast. Patricia worked her wiles in the background. Hussey and Barnett entered the fray and ruled I must sit on the board. Bill and Michael Grade then demanded a meeting with Checkland and myself. High noon was in the Director-General's office. Bill was splenetic: he was rude and aggressive, suggesting strangely – since Michael Grade's commissioning and scheduling experience prior to the BBC was exactly the same as mine – that running the ITV schedule at the weekend was no qualification for appointing a BBC Controller! Michael Grade then made an emotional plea to me to withdraw. In all the circumstances – Television's continuing obstructionism, their unsympathetic attempt to lure Ron, and after Bill's insulting diatribe – Michael's plea fell on deaf ears. I reminded him I had been invited to the BBC to take on a wider role than News and Current Affairs. If authority with his troops was his concern – as he suggested – then he should chair the board. I was not prepared to withdraw. I was stonily resolute.

The appointment board when it happened was an intense affair. We interviewed all the candidates, including Alan Yentob, Jonathan Powell and Jim Moir. I had long been impressed with the hilarious Falstaffian Moir – both for his track record in entertainment and for his good character and judgement. I had tried to lure Jim to ITV, but he was a BBC loyalist and couldn't be bribed. Alan Yentob had been the BBC's eye-catching and innovative head of arts, who – unusually for a BBC executive – had engaged with the wider world, including with his fellow broadcasters beyond the BBC. Both Alan and Jim were outstanding in interview. Interestingly, Alan, unprompted, put forward the notion that *Newsnight* should have a fixed slot at 10.30 p.m. Jonathan Powell, head of drama, performed less well, and I had doubts about his track record: he had made some excellent programmes, but his pedigree was very patchy.

When the interviews were over and the discussion began about who should be appointed, Michael Grade immediately declared that none of the candidates was appointable to BBC1, and that only Jonathan Powell was right for BBC2. I was genuinely surprised by his judgement about Jonathan. I saw what was coming a mile off but argued for Jim Moir for BBC1 and Alan Yentob for BBC2. I believed, and said, that they were both outstanding candidates. Michael was dismissive of both Alan and Jim, possibly for effect. Then he made a big emotional pitch. Nothing was more important to the BBC than BBC1: Ron had to be released from News and Current Affairs to run it.

A chasm had opened up between two old friends. It was clear from the finality of Michael's tone and manner that if the choice went against him he would leave. Hussey was the key player. He had to make a choice between Michael and me, and he came down on my side: he said Ron couldn't be released, but that Michael should choose his own team. After some tense minutes of rearguard action, Michael plumped for Jonathan Powell as Controller of BBC1 and the previously unappointable Alan Yentob for BBC2. And that was that. On the following Monday evening, Jane and I were hosting a dinner at Broadcasting House for Neil and Glenys Kinnock and assorted guests from inside and outside the BBC when a note was passed to me to call Michael Checkland. I slipped out to hear the news that Grade had jumped ship to become Chief Executive of Channel 4. Jeremy Isaacs had apparently wept when he heard the news. And those who had worked closely with Michael in BBC Television felt betrayed by his premature departure. One of his closest aides – and no ally of mine – phoned me to say: 'I'm a mug. Michael Grade has no centre. He's just a shell. I saw that when he arrived – but I forgot.' One of the warrior

Governors, hardened by battles of the 1980s said: 'Good! Now we can get the Television service under control!'

I did not enjoy falling out with Michael Grade, for I had been genuinely fond of him. I knew from close observation, and from succeeding him at LWT, that he was weak creatively, managerially and strategically; but I had admired his quick-witted enterprise; I had enjoyed his wise-cracking; and I had been grateful for his unqualified support at LWT. We had shared a common trauma – Cyril Bennett's death. I had comforted him in New York when his grandmother died, and I had been touched by his vulnerability. I wrote to him immediately:

> Dear Michael
>   I hope it's what you want. I'm distressed by the outcome, and hurt by what has been said and alleged. I remain very fond of you, and I hate the idea of all this festering. We should have talked long ago, but better now than not at all. Could we meet?
>   Yours,
>   John

I received no reply. Six weeks later, I wrote again: 'There's been a lot of hurt but we need to come to terms with it all sometime. May I come and see you?' Michael responded bitterly:

> I'm sad it's come to this after all these years, but that was your choice. No point in meeting up really. You made your feelings pretty clear by your actions; more lack of feelings, I should have said. Of course we'll bump into one another socially and you can rely on me to maintain the public mask. Let's remember the good times. Among those things I shall always be grateful to you for is that you were the key player in me moving here. Where I am blissfully happy.

I responded:

> We see things differently. The key moment for me was early
> in the saga when you insisted I should not be on the Board.
> That was a real shock. It was an overt attack on the job I'd
> been invited to the BBC to do. And there had been no
> warning. Or at least there had been – in the papers – but I
> had not heeded the evidence. Later, I was told you and Bill
> said you would not sit on the Board if I did. Later still was
> your divisive and destabilising refusal to accept the DG's
> ruling on Ron. By the time we met in Mike's office – if that's
> what you mean by your reference to 'feelings' – I 'felt'
> markedly threatened. In addition, there were Bill's insults.
> The 'plea' was months too late. Why I was – even am – keen
> to meet, was to try to understand why you felt able to treat
> an old and loyal friend in this way. I needed help and a
> welcome and not what I got.
> John

Michael and I often encountered each other over the years, but we
never did discuss our differences. A woman Michael had been close
to told me: 'Michael never forgives those he feels have betrayed
him. He will never forgive you.'

There was an odd and inexplicable postscript. I heard from
Michael on just one occasion. In my second year at the BBC I gave
a lecture at the Royal Television Society called 'Decent Media'. It
set out my vision of the value of good journalism to democracy,
and my views on what a progressive framework of media law
should be – and it planted the BBC's News flag on the high ground
of ambition and integrity. Out of the blue, Michael wrote to me to
say:

> I've just read Decent Media (on my way back from the US).
> Congratulations, just what I knew you would bring to BBC

journalism. Where you lead, others will HAVE to follow – I
hope.

    Yours

       Michael

Shortly after Michael Grade departed, I had lunch with William
Rees-Mogg, who had been Vice-Chairman of the BBC in the troubled mid-1980s. He was self-critical. He lamented the Governors'
inability in his time to grip the institution. They had failed to intervene at decisive moments. Michael Grade's appointment had tipped
the balance towards ratings and away from public service. They
had lost the high ground. The cynical Wenham had been promoted
out of Television and into Radio to make way for Grade, and the
able and serious-minded Dick Francis had been ousted from Radio
to create a slot for Wenham. Grade's appointment had tipped the
whole balance of the institution the wrong way.

The next battleground with the Television service after Grade's departure was over a fixed start-time for *Newsnight* – the only news or current
affairs programme on British television to jump all over the schedules
on successive nights. Bill Cotton opposed the move, commissioning
reams of advocacy from Michael Grade's former aide Peter Ibbotson.
Peter attempted to show that placing *Newsnight* at 10.30 p.m. would
reduce BBC2's audiences and flexibility. George Carey, an old Lime
Grove and *Newsnight* alumnus, was press-ganged by Network
Television into opposing a fixed slot for his former colleagues.

    Michael Checkland had worked for Bill Cotton in Network
Television, and was most uneasy deciding against him – but, to
Checkland's great credit, he did. He ruled that *Newsnight* would
have a fixed start-time. An announcement would be made in due
course. A BBC wag once remarked: 'Good: the decision has been
made. Now the debate can start!' And that is exactly what happened: an even fiercer effort was now launched to reverse the
decision, both behind the scenes and in the media. The *Financial*

Times ran a front-page story describing the tensions at a senior level between Network Television and News and Current Affairs. Bill Cotton's seething anger was boiling over into the public prints. The morning the story appeared, there was a press conference to launch a new corporate initiative. I saw Michael Checkland beforehand and demanded that he should put a stop to the uncertainty and announce the *Newsnight* move publicly at the conference. Again bravely, he did – to Bill Cotton's lasting fury. The editor of *Newsnight* wrote to me to say: 'The news has given morale here a terrific boost. After eight years, no one really believed it would be done. You and the Director-General ought to have badges made saying "We deliver".'

Gorbachev reached an historic agreement with Reagan in 1987 to reduce the stockpile of nuclear weapons in both the US and the Soviet Union for the first time. The treaty was due to be signed while the *Six O'Clock News* was on air but was delayed. Ron Neil ordered the *News* to continue, displacing the BBC's regional programmes. The deal was finally signed a few minutes past seven, delaying the start of a BBC comedy. After the broadcast, Ron, pleased with his evening's work, walked down the corridor, on the sixth floor at the Television Centre, where the BBC executive offices are located. Jonathan Powell, Controller of BBC1, suddenly burst through the swing doors by the lift. He had kicked them open, cracking the glass. He rushed over to big, burly Ron – in the words of an observer – 'screaming like a maniac'. 'That was crap, shit, an abuse of airtime!' Powell shouted. Ron backed up against the wall. Powell put his face inches from Ron's, screeching invective. True to character, Ron remained calm and composed: 'Come and talk in my office,' he said. 'Fuck off. Why should I?' was Powell's response.

The incident depressed an already despondent Ron, troubled by dramas on all sides. He had discussed his situation with his wife Isabel: he was not inclined to stay at the BBC. Network Television continued to fight every inch of the way any threat to its authority, resources or airtime. Moreover, there were problems aplenty within

News itself. But Ron – a decent, loyal old trouper – was prevailed on by me and his colleagues to stay.

I felt pretty miserable and exhausted myself. Chairman Hussey, alert to my sagging spirits, gave me an impromptu lunch at his usual haunt, Claridge's. With ebullient cheerfulness, enthusiastically quaffing his favourite tipple, a glass of champagne, he declared the BBC to be 'A sick place where no one has a grip!' He was buoyed by and not the least disheartened by the overt resistance to my reforms. There would be no gain without pain, he suggested. It would be evident, he thought, to the world at large that at last something was happening at the BBC. Confirmation of his judgement came within days. Brian Griffiths, the economist and influential head of Mrs Thatcher's policy unit, wrote to me to say: 'the success of your policy can be clearly judged by the ferocity of the media towards you . . . I admire your courage.'

Michael Checkland finally backed off what had been his original affirmed intention to extend my direct-line authority to all sensitive factual programmes made by Network Television. I was perplexed that he should make such a decision when the universal view at the centre was that the Television service did not have the will or the skill to handle legally or editorially testing programmes. I accused him of not being straightforward, of having made promises he had not delivered. 'I changed my mind,' he said. 'We've done a lot. I can't always deliver. Cheer up!'

Despite our difficulties, there was much I admired in Michael Checkland, a plain, no-nonsense Brummie. Mike was not self-important. He lived modestly, disliked ostentation, maintained his Methodist beliefs, and was married to a kindly, dedicated primary school teacher, with whom he went away at weekends to stay in unpretentious B&Bs. As grammar school boys from ordinary backgrounds who went to Oxford, he and I had many shared perspectives and common values. But while he wanted to improve the BBC, and we both wanted to travel in the same direction, he was much less inclined than I was to upset the applecart.

Mike suddenly announced that he wanted Paul Fox – currently the Managing Director of Yorkshire Television – to replace Bill Cotton, and that he had held discussions with Paul. What did I think? I was fond of Paul from my days in ITV: he really was a solid, unflappable, all-rounder of sound judgement. But, at sixty-two, he was a consolidator when what Network TV desperately needed was a reformer. 'We can't open up a second front,' Mike argued. 'News has to settle down first.' The Chairman was uneasy that I was not on-side, and sought to reassure me, and he sent Joel Barnett, the Vice-Chairman, to sweet-talk me. Joel confided that he and the Chairman had grave reservations about the way Mike was handling the problems with Network Television, but they had to proceed by stealth. When Paul Fox's appointment was announced, Patricia reported the response of Brian Griffiths from Number 10: 'Why ever have you done it? After the Prime Minister visited Yorkshire TV she said: "I never want to see that man again!"'

Network Television's reach for independence continued under Paul Fox. I had appointed John Wilson as the BBC's Controller of Editorial Policy. John was a wise old head who had justly earned enormous respect – as head of Radio's journalism – for his sage editorial judgement. He was commissioned to draft a comprehensive, coherent set of guidelines covering every kind of editorial issue that every kind of programme-maker faces. He discharged this task with great distinction, writing in pithy, elegant and persuasive terms. The guidelines were designed around some key principles: they asserted the value of freedom of expression; but they also set out the need to be sensitive to the interests of those who appear in or who are directly affected by BBC programmes; and the need to take account of the mood and convictions of the viewers and listeners who receive them. They affirmed the BBC's commitment to accuracy, fairness and impartiality; to straight dealing, to privacy, to the avoidance of stereotyping. They proclaimed the virtue and value of programmes that challenged established ideas and opinions with integrity.

The new guidelines were solemnly agreed line by line by the Governors. They were widely welcomed outside the BBC as a persuasive ethical statement. They would be applauded and emulated across the world. They defined clearly John Wilson's authority as their interpreter, and his standing as the key point of reference on sensitive editorial issues. The BBC at large acquiesced in rather than enthused over the new code. Network Television alone had bridled, especially at John Wilson's role. Paul Fox sent out a note about the guidelines to his senior colleagues in Network Television saying: 'the editorial decision to include or exclude, to transmit or not to transmit, will be taken within the Network Television Directorate'. John Wilson was most upset: he felt undermined, but Paul's diktat went unchallenged: Michael Checkland no longer had the appetite to battle with Network Television.

In the summer of 1988, I returned from holiday deeply despondent about the BBC. I had a long talk with Howell James, the BBC's new Director of Corporate Affairs. I complained to him about the stifling conservatism and inertia of the organisation, its civil service culture, its hostility to change. There were too few reformers to create a critical mass for change, I said. The consolidators were in the ascendancy.

We still faced huge difficulties within the News and Current Affairs directorate itself, not least at Lime Grove, where Samir Shah ran Television Current Affairs. Lime Grove had been a British film studio before it was bought by the BBC. Plonked unnaturally in a residential street in the Hammersmith/Shepherds Bush area of London, the centre was British broadcasting's Gormenghast – a labyrinthine building of bewildering complexity, run-down and ramshackle, unsuitable for modern programme-making, a festering rabbit-warren sheltering hidden cliques. It was a happy day for me, a few years later, when Lime Grove was bulldozed to the ground, and a centre for the homeless built in its place. Lime Grove's culture at its worst was cocky, world-weary and sneering. There was no sense at all among its key programme-makers that the world was a difficult place to understand.

Samir Shah, my old colleague from LWT, set out to build a new ethos of programme-making at Lime Grove. He started alone and friendless, but eventually gained allies through internal promotion and from outside recruitment. He introduced a serious programme of political analysis, *On the Record*, presented by Jonathan Dimbleby – a programme of wit and style as well as analytical bite; he refocused *The Money Programme*; he started up a specialist social affairs programme, *Public Eye*; and he introduced a foreign affairs programme, *Assignment*. Among the new generation of editors and producers brought in to work on these programmes was a welcome influx from LWT, including *Weekend World* alumni Glenwyn Benson and the three Davids – Aaronovitch, Jordan and Nissan.

Samir's main battleground was *Panorama*. Even the old guard was quick to confess that the programme had been out of control. It had been ruled for many years by larger-than-life reporters who had effectively seized power. Editorial management had been weak. Sometimes a reporter would commandeer a film crew and shoot a story but keep the subject-matter secret from the editor. The *Panorama* editor would not always see a script of the whole programme, and would not know what the commentary contained till the sound dub on the day of transmission. On legally difficult programmes, lawyers had sometimes been called in at the last minute, rather than weeks before. I watched a lot of *Panorama*s myself on appointment. Overall the choice of subject was off-beam: the programme was not systematically addressing the key stories of the time. Some programmes were soundly made, but many lacked rigour or coherence: they had not bottomed out the issue behind the story. And *Panorama* was often unfair: those under scrutiny were not given a proper chance to answer the charges. Some of these faults were down to the process. At both Granada and LWT, we had thought through the story before filming: that way you knew what to shoot and what to ask. I had first learnt this approach from

David Plowright at Granada when he grilled me, pulling apart my outline on my first ever *World in Action*. Many *Panorama*s bore the tell-tale signs of the real story emerging at a late stage on the road, and having to be rescued in the cutting room against the grain of the interview and of other material already shot. I used the phrase 'cutting-room journalism' to describe and to condemn this approach.

Samir set out to reconstruct the editorial team and to refashion the process of making *Panorama*. Some of the old hands were moved to other programmes. Two of the leading members of the Lime Grove fraternity handed us an opportunity on a plate: there was strong evidence that they had committed serious and demonstrable journalistic improprieties. I pounced. The personnel function at Lime Grove pleaded with me – to my astonishment – to give both a second chance. I suddenly realised that they too were part of the fraternity – the loose but powerful assemblage of maverick reporters and middle-managers who ruled Lime Grove by strength of personality – but I insisted. One reporter denied his culpability but both in the end went without a fuss.

Tim Gardam, an intensely bright thirty-one-year-old *Newsnight* alumnus, who had worked on *Timewatch* and the general election, was handed the poisoned chalice of the editorship, and set out to get a grip. It would be a long march, with many difficulties and reverses along the path. The problem was not just that we were asking people to work in new ways, but also a lack of trust. It was not hard to see why even the good journalists at Lime Grove should be suspicious. The Tories had continually attacked BBC journalism. Hussey had been appointed by Thatcher. Alasdair Milne had been fired above all because he was thought not to have had an editorial grip on Lime Grove. Hussey had appointed Checkland and myself. No matter that at both Granada and LWT I had been associated with a sturdy investigative tradition, and that my own journalism there had repeatedly put the established order under tough scrutiny, I was none the less viewed with wariness by the *Panorama* school, who feared I had been imposed from the outside to neuter the BBC's journalism.

I was labouring with a related problem of my own: I had a set of Governors who had lost confidence in the BBC's ability to manage difficult issues, who were deeply suspicious of the reliability of BBC journalism. My own objective was to enable sound, well-founded, challenging journalism to be made at the BBC – and to carry the Governors with me by persuading them that such programmes would be copper-bottomed editorially and legally. It would be a while before leading BBC journalists would appreciate my motives, and I got off to a sticky start with someone who would become one of my favourite people – John Ware, a true journalist, fair-minded and sceptical, in no one's camp, with no axe to grind, who had impressed me at my first tense encounter with the *Panorama* team, where he had stood out: he had listened keenly, responded directly and unequivocally, and he had been very funny, making me laugh out loud.

John wanted to make a programme about the retired MI5 officer Peter Wright, who had published some astonishing allegations, including the claim that MI5 had plotted to destabilise the Wilson government. I held up filming because no written treatment was available, and this provoked a storm. A brilliant and important programme was eventually made, including an interview with Wright himself, which fatally undermined many of his own allegations; but there were further problems to overcome before the programme could be transmitted. Wright lived in Australia. The British government had instituted an action against Wright in the Australian courts. When Malcolm Turnbull, Wright's lawyer, realised how devastating to his client John Ware's interview with him was, he threatened us aggressively with legal action to stop us transmitting the interview. Our legal advice confirmed that, under the terms of our contract with Wright, Turnbull was on strong legal ground; but Turnbull had been arguing powerfully for Wright's right to publish his book in the courts on free-speech grounds. I calculated that

Turnbull would not want to find himself on the wrong side of the argument, to be seen in the court of public opinion trying to suppress his own client's interview. I decided, therefore, to take the risk and give the go-ahead to transmit. We never heard from Turnbull again. The incident helped me to begin to build a relationship with the BBC's most challenging journalists, and it taught me what a rock-solid reporter John Ware was.

Over the next few years, we put out a series of programmes on *Panorama* – many of them made by John Ware and by the impeccably impartial and translucently honest Peter Taylor – which exposed truths about Northern Ireland that the UK government wanted to keep hidden. A war in which terrorist groups commit horrible atrocities on civilians, the military and politicians themselves was testing territory for broadcasters. Mrs Thatcher's hostility to any broadcasting which seemed to aid the IRA's cause was well known. Her sensitivities were wholly understandable, for one of her closest political friends, Airey Neave, had been assassinated by the Provisionals, and she herself had almost been killed by the Brighton bomb. In 1988 Thames was crucified for the *Death on the Rock* programme about the SAS shootings of IRA members in Gibraltar. We were under enormous pressure to get right any programme we made about Northern Ireland.

Over the next years, BBC journalists bravely and expertly chronicled two different strands of story about Northern Ireland. They told the murky tale of the secret war waged by the UK security forces against terrorists in the 1970s and 1980s; and they aired the difficult and unwelcome notion that the IRA could not be defeated by military means, but needed to be drawn into a political process.

A *Panorama* in 1990 on the Ulster Defence Regiment (UDR) suggested that the regiment had colluded with Loyalist paramilitaries. This put the BBC's Northern Ireland Governor into a state of high indignation. To resolve the issue, I initiated and presided over a meeting between John Ware and two senior representatives of the UDR. John made his case carefully and persuasively, and they were unable to undermine his programme's argument in any way. We heard no more.

Another *Panorama* examined whether ambushes by the security forces were in effect part of a shoot-to-kill policy. A programme on British Army agent Brian Nelson revealed that a Force Research Unit had helped Loyalist paramilitaries to target and murder Provisionals. Our revelations provoked an inquiry. In yet another programme, the former British Army Commander of land forces, James Glover, aired his view that the IRA were intelligent activists, not mindless hooligans; that no military solution in Northern Ireland was possible; and that, in the long run, Irish unity was inevitable. We chronicled the difficult realities of Northern Ireland throughout the period with real distinction, culminating in Peter Taylor's remarkable and definitive trilogy – *The Provos*, *The Loyalists* and *The Brits*.

I had instituted a rigorous procedure for monitoring particularly sensitive programmes, modelled on the systems at Granada and LWT. John Wilson and I were to be notified before shooting began. BBC lawyers were to be consulted at every stage. I would see the programme seven days before transmission to allow time for any necessary changes. I would give the Governors plenty of warning: there would be no surprises. This system was much resented to begin with – but increasingly welcomed by the more serious journalists because they knew that when their programmes were eventually transmitted they had the full and unequivocal support of the BBC. Moreover, problems with the Governors on sensitive programmes all but disappeared. They began to believe the new team had a grip. We still had occasional prangs over the years, though, which continued to cause reverberations and mistrust.

I complained strongly about a *Panorama* on Rajiv Gandhi which I felt lacked rigour and fairness. Samir Shah, without my even knowing, delayed a *Panorama* on the economy made by Peter Jay just before the 1992 general election because he believed the programme was not politically balanced. It was uncomfortable for me to have two close supporters fall out. Without pressure of any kind, I delayed a *Panorama* on the Iraqi Supergun on the eve of British forces going to war against Iraq. The programme revealed the incompetence of UK government agencies in allowing valuable technologies to pass to Iraq. I judged we had to be especially sensitive to the feelings of the British people as war and loss of life loomed, and that our tale could wait till the war was over. That was a lonely and unpopular decision.

Loneliest of all was my decision to delay the *Panorama* on the SAS in 1988. This was a sensitive programme which suggested that the security forces were engaging in an undeclared war on the IRA. For the one and only time, the new system had broken down. When I was told about the programme, we were only days away from intended transmission. I had not forewarned the Governors. We had insufficient time to make any necessary changes. I angrily refused to countenance an early transmission. Ron pressed me. The programme was timed to coincide with the date of the inquest on the SAS shootings in Gibraltar. He assured me that everyone I trusted – including Ian Hargreaves and Samir Shah – had seen and approved the script. I relented and agreed to see the programme on the Saturday, when it was ready for viewing, just two days before transmission.

Unusually, I involved Michael Checkland in an editorial matter. I called and told the Director-General that there had been a cock-up, but that people I trusted had vetted the programme and that we should put the programme out anyway. We had not informed the Governors. In the circumstances I proposed the unusual step of our watching the programme together so that we could present a united front to the board, and subsequently underscore how seriously we had taken the issue. Checkland was understanding and agreed to drive up on Saturday morning from his home near the Sussex coast. I had no doubt at all that I would approve the programme, but, to my alarm, when I saw it I felt I could not. I told my colleagues, with deep regret, that the film was not clear or cogent enough; that it exposed ideas but didn't explore them. Checkland – who in fact had no strong views about the programme, one way or the other – supported my decision. My colleagues were horror-struck. The programme, amended to my satisfaction, was put out two weeks later.

There was much subsequent speculation about my reasons for insisting that the programme needed more work: it was suggested wrongly, for instance, that I did not want to risk inflaming the following week's Conservative Party conference. Neither then nor on any other occasion during my time at the BBC did I make – or was even asked to make – a programme decision for a political or institutional reason. Deciding to delay the *Panorama* on the SAS was a really low moment for me: I did not enjoy embarrassing my esteemed and hard-pressed colleagues – especially Ron, Ian and Samir. We were all bruised by the experience.

Mrs Thatcher's government was liberal on economic issues but not on free-speech ones, and this created a spate of difficulties during my time as Deputy Director-General.

Anne Sloman commissioned a serious *Analysis* for Radio 4 on the accountability of the Security Services. Former members of the Services contributed to the programmes. We sought formal advice from the secretary of the D-Notice Committee to vouchsafe that there was no breach of national security. Even so, the government demanded access to the programmes in advance of transmission. We refused. The government was not convinced by our assurance that national security would not be breached, and took heavy-handed action. The Treasury Solicitor was granted an injunction – on grounds of breach of confidentiality – suspending transmission. I attacked the government's action as 'draconian'. As part of the normal processes of the court, the government then had access to the disputed sequences. They withdrew the action and the programme was transmitted.

Tightening up the law after the Peter Wright affair, the government proposed an Official Secrets Bill out of the pages of Kafka.

The Bill was ingeniously drafted to close all doors and loopholes, and it flew in the face of natural justice and good sense. It made the unauthorised disclosure of certain categories of official information a crime, and removed both the burden of proof and the test of harm from the prosecution. The Bill also denied a public interest defence to a civil servant or a media organisation blowing the whistle – exposing iniquity, incompetence, mismanagement, lawbreaking or even treachery. Douglas Hurd, the affable, liberal Home Secretary, was put forward, with evident lack of relish, to make the government's case. The proposed Bill was vigorously opposed by me on behalf of the BBC and by all serious media organisations, but passed into law.

We had continuous difficulties with some cranky, cantankerous members of the House of Lords, who were obsessed with left-wing bias in the broadcast media. Two were Woodrow Wyatt and Ian Orr-Ewing, both former members of BBC staff. Woodrow Wyatt often called Mrs Thatcher early in the morning, before her private office was operating, to feed in his preoccupations. In our encounters, I humoured him as best I could. But he went a step too far to be tolerated: he wrote to the BBC in 1990 airing his obsession with the *Today* programme, and making an absurd series of demands. Wyatt wanted a curriculum vitae for every presenter and producer on the programme. He asked how each member of the *Today* team voted in the last election, how each intended to vote in the next, and what political parties they belonged to. We refused the information. He went on to mount an onslaught against *Today* in *The Times* to which I responded.

Wyatt and others in the Lords obsessed with impartiality (which was, in their case, code for left-wing bias) amended the Broadcasting Bill in 1990 to introduce rigid and stultifying obligations on broadcasters to achieve balance in a programme or series. Behind the scenes, they had Mrs Thatcher's personal support. Their proposals were impracticable, for impartiality is an approach rather than a formula. I spoke many times at meetings with their Lordships, many armed with fraying, yellowing, decades-old cuttings containing evidence of ancient *faux pas* by BBC producers and executives. I hope I convinced them I was sincere about impartiality – for I was a wholehearted believer in the principle – but I couldn't dissuade them from their course of action. In the event plans for an impartiality amendment put forward by the government foundered when Willie Whitelaw, who said he found the proposal profoundly disturbing and very upsetting, condemned it as unworkable. Whitelaw led Tory opposition in the Lords and forced the government into a limited retreat. The minister, David Mellor, then fashioned a compromise in which the regulator, not Parliament, would draw up an impartiality code. The determined ambition of the right-wingers had been defeated.

By far the most serious free-speech issue of the period was the so-called Sinn Fein ban, imposed by Mrs Thatcher after the horrendous bombing of a bus in Ballygawley, in which eight young army cadets were killed. The ban applied to all potential organisations linked with terrorism, but primarily affected Sinn Fein, whose voices, not faces, were barred in most circumstances. This was a low point for British democracy: it denied the UK citizenry the right to hear elected members of Sinn Fein, who, like it or not, were playing a growing part in the political process in Northern Ireland, and were already party to covert constitutional discussions with the British government. And it denied audiences the right to hear Sinn Fein cross-examined and subjected to scrutiny like other politicians.

For years thereafter, until the ban was lifted, we were subjected to the black comedy of Sinn Fein members being subtitled or voiced over with soundalikes. The most farcical example occurred in one of the most remarkable documentaries made during my time at the BBC – Peter Taylor's film shot inside the Maze prison, showing paramilitaries from both sides of the divide. Following the letter of the Home Office ban, John Wilson ruled that almost all the prisoners could be heard in their own voices because they were not speaking on behalf of paramilitary organisations. Exceptionally, we were *not* allowed to hear one of the prisoners complaining to the authorities about the poor quality of the sausage rolls in the canteen. He had to be subtitled because in making the complaint he was speaking on behalf of the IRA: he was the Provisional's *food* spokesman!

I took a vehement public stand against the ban when it was imposed, suggesting that it 'trespasses on the independence and editorial integrity of the BBC'. I continued to criticise it over the whole period it was in force – but it remained, for six years, an encouragement to repressive regimes all over the world, and an embarrassment to those who believed in Britain as a bastion of free speech and democratic values.

I had a number of spats over the years with the main political parties about the coverage of their affairs on the BBC. All the parties professionalised their approach to broadcasting following the ground-breaking work of my former LWT colleague Peter Mandelson when he reinvented political communication working for the Labour Party in the 1980s. The parties started operating less at executive level, and concentrated more on working reporters and editors – trying to persuade, cajole or bully them to adjust their lines from bulletin to bulletin. Working journalists soon became hardened to this process, and, knowing they would be supported, were well capable of taking care of themselves. Few complaints reached me. Occasionally, an anguished Cabinet minister would phone me in my office at some point in the early evening having been outraged by some item on the *Six O'Clock News*. I would listen politely, promise to investigate and then to write (which I would). Very rarely did I judge there was any justice to their grievance – though when I did, I would say so. Michael Howard wrote long, involved, lawyerly letters of complaint, which we would investigate thoroughly and to which we would respond at length. When Howard moved from the Department of Employment, a senior civil servant rang me up and said: 'I shouldn't say this – but the patience and care with which you dealt with Michael Howard was remarkable. I couldn't believe your forbearance!'

When a political party felt it was on the ropes, a high-level approach was usually made to me alleging systematic bias. Generally, though not always, this was the governing party. Over the years, I encountered successive Conservative Party Chairmen – Kenneth Baker, Chris Patten (flanked by a frowning and irascible aide, Shaun Woodward, ex-BBC, and subsequently Labour Party) and Brian Mawhinney (who at a party conference fluttered between rooms in his suite, lovingly serving his wife breakfast in bed in one room, then returning to chastise me about the BBC's current crimes over coffee in the next). Each Conservative Chairman in turn argued that the scale of the criticism of government policies aired on the BBC was unjust. None was heavy-handed. Chris Patten was a sheep in wolf's clothing: he had no relish whatsoever for the task of hard man. Nor did he have a sure touch. He railed unconvincingly against the BBC at a party conference, giving out a phone number that Tories should call to complain and so jam our switchboards, which they did. He raised the temperature so much it turned into a public row, forcing me to issue a statement saying: 'The BBC will not be bullied by any political party.'

All Tory Chairmen in private accepted my basic argument that governments enact policy, and therefore attract more day-to-day criticism than the Opposition. Sometimes there was point to their complaints, particularly when they suggested that BBC journalists were insufficiently rigorous in scrutinising and testing the Opposition's policies. And our journalists did on occasion let sectional interests affected by change get away with untested claims. Kenneth Baker – going in to bat with me after Nigel Lawson's resignation as Chancellor, and shortly before Mrs Thatcher's demise – was surprisingly generous about the improving quality and sophistication of the BBC's journalism, but said the government was being hectored. He was quick, however, to accept in argument that there really was a political crisis, and that the BBC's focus on Mrs Thatcher's difficulties was justified.

The Prime Minister's press secretary, Bernard Ingham, was scrupulous, always containing Mrs Thatcher, restricting his interventions to matters of fact, and to observations about the overall balance of debate. Alastair Campbell in opposition once overstepped the mark and wrote a public letter to the BBC demanding that Tony Blair's conference speech should be placed ahead of the O. J. Simpson trial verdict. I responded in public, labelling his fax 'crass and inappropriate' and proclaiming that 'The scale of attempts now being made to influence editorial decisions in advance of transmission is unacceptable', which it was. The calls abated. Peter Mandelson, as we became friends, mostly kept clear of complaining to me, reserving his interventions for my colleagues. Towards the end of my time, Peter was outed as a gay on *Newsnight* by a mischievous Matthew Parris. The BBC's guidelines protected individual privacy unless warranted by a public interest, so the doughty Anne Sloman, working in Editorial Policy, ruled – without reference of any kind to me – that other BBC programmes should not repeat the transgression. This brought wide protest, inside and outside the BBC, either from those who thought, wrongly, that Peter had been granted a special favour, or from those who did not regard respect for personal privacy as a principle worth maintaining. It was a sign of a shift in the public mood.

Only one politician ever threatened me in my thirteen years at the BBC. A senior member of a minority party said that his party's support for the BBC would be withdrawn on a critical broadcasting policy issue if a news complaint was not handled to his satisfaction. I told him his threat was deeply improper. I considered his complaint on its merits, but could not support it. He had been posturing: he never carried out his threat. I never believed he would.

My first years as the BBC's Deputy Director-General, presiding over the reform of the BBC's journalism, were the most unrelenting of my life thus far. I had battled on many fronts – against old Lime Grove, against green-eyeshaders in the newsroom, against bone-headed baronialism and obstructionism in the Television service, against an illiberal government – all under the eye of a hostile press. I had experienced deviousness, lack of steadfastness, and dishon-ourable behaviour, and it was debilitating. Machiavelli had written acutely and famously about the perils awaiting the reformer:

> There is nothing more difficult to take in hand, nor perilous
> to conduct, or more uncertain in its success than the
> introduction of a new order of things, because the innovator
> has for enemies all those who have done well under the old
> conditions and lukewarm defenders in those who may do
> well in the new.

Not a day would go by in this period without at least one – and generally many – hostile stories in the press focused on me. I once sat next to a man on a plane to Glasgow who painstakingly read an edition of *Private Eye* from cover to cover which I knew contained six separate stories about me. I was tempted to say, 'Boo!' At this stage of my career at the BBC, there were still some print journalists who appreciated the reasons for and the value of reform, and wrote intelligently about what was happening in the BBC. But, over-whelmingly, the stories about me were either wholly untrue, or half true, or true about another person, or score-settling, or simple bitch-iness. It took a while to get used to being denounced continually. In a long period in public life, I watched other victims of this process become obsessive and laid low by it. Some never recovered psycho-logically. I survived demonisation by learning not to care on my own account, growing a thicker skin, fighting on my own ground, not my enemy's, moving forward and not presenting a sitting target, realising that the pain may sting, but it quickly passes.

Being demonised increased my determination to see the reforms through. I had given up a happy slot at LWT and significant wealth.

Having made that sacrifice, I could not possibly walk away from a cause in which I passionately believed. My family upbringing, my schooling, all emphasised that you saw a job through. At the end of the journey, the BBC's journalism would be transformed. The beneficiaries would be ordinary people – our viewers and listeners. On occasions, not often, I cursed my lot, but I never wavered.

In my early years at the BBC, even in periods of particular difficulty, those working with me almost always found me cheerful. My meetings with colleagues were punctuated by laughter and often hilarity. But when I moved away from the inner group and dealt with people I knew were hostile, I increasingly put up my guard. I became defensive. My manner was invariably solemn, businesslike and earnest.

Throughout these difficult years my family and close friends gave me counsel and comfort. Jane and I would escape with a loyal group to exotic weekends in Berlin or Barcelona or some other beguiling destination. After a particularly exhausting period, she and I flew to Galicia to crash out and recover at a remote inn, keeping our destination secret. We arrived late in the evening to encounter a bemused John Cole in reception, as surprised to see me as I was him. He was there to film for the *Holiday* programme! At two o'clock in the morning Jane and I were awakened by the BBC crew noisily unloading its equipment, having filmed a midnight firework display in Santiago de Compostela. There was no escaping the BBC. When I was under particularly heavy assault, Liz Forgan arranged a 'Hooray for John Birt dinner' attended by what she termed 'a chosen group of supporters, enthusiasts and greedy old lags'. Old colleagues from my time in ITV offered unwavering support and solidarity. Many phoned, took me to lunch, or wrote. Typical was Philip Whitehead, Labour MP and a broadcaster of great principle: 'Any irresolute fool can buy time and transient esteem. Your initial difficulties are a measure of courage not cowardice.' My main soulmates at work were Howell James and Patricia Hodgson. Howell, the BBC's Director of Corporate Affairs, had a background in media and advertising. He had been David Young's political adviser at the Department of Employment (and later went on to be John Major's at Number 10). Howell is one of the cheeriest, most ebullient of people. He bursts into a room beaming, and lifts your spirits with a series of lightning comic jabs. He is an acute, sympathetic observer of people and what motivates them; he is quick-thinking and smart, and he sees all the angles. At the darkest of times, a gossip with Howell would leave me howling with laughter, and ready to see the shenanigans around me as farce rather than tragedy.

Patricia Hodgson, the BBC's Director of Policy and Planning, was a brilliant reader of the dense, complex web of manoeuvre and intrigue that was each day's staple at the BBC. She could dissect a meeting like no one else, spotting plots, sniffing out positions. No one could progress a plan with more tactical skill. Her moves were so complicated it was often impossible to identify the real ploy behind them. Patricia completed my education, and ended my innocence. Working with her, I learnt to spot tactics and to read the signs of off-stage lobbying. And though by temperament I liked to move forward forthrightly, in a straight line, and though I was incapable of changing my nature fundamentally, under Patricia's virtuoso tutelage I began to be more calculating and to acquire new skills. Patricia and I had little in common culturally – she was High Church and High Tory; she never revealed all her cards; she never gave anyone her absolute loyalty; she and I never became blood siblings – but, for most if not all my time at the BBC, she and I were allies: we fought on the same side for the same goal of a high-ground, high-standards BBC dedicated to public service.

The most vital support for me during the darkest days of the reform process in BBC News came from Chairman Marmaduke Hussey. When opposition seemed universal, when victory appeared unimaginable, and when faint-hearts among his own Governors blanched at the impact of the reforms they themselves had demanded, Hussey stood solid as a rock.

What I found most difficult to bear in this period was the impact of controversy on my family: they found it distressing to stand by helplessly and witness a son, a husband or a father vilified and portrayed in terms that to them seemed outrageously unjust, and I felt guilty to have been the agent of their distress. I was enraged when members of my family became direct victims, as each was at some point. One incident was particularly upsetting. After a year at the BBC, and after the main organisational and operational changes had been made in News, I took a further step back and elevated Ron to the position of Director of News and Current Affairs, still maintaining overall control myself. After I had made the announcement, Jane and I went off to Ascot for the afternoon as David Hatch's guests. (Ron told me later that Brian Wenham – still active and obsessed with the BBC, even in exile – phoned Ron's office every ten minutes to get the background to the appointment. Ron refused to take the call.) Leaving Ascot racecourse at the end of a pleasant afternoon's racing, I spied the *Evening Standard* headline 'BBC Shakes Up TV Chiefs'. 'Whoever can that be?' I observed to Jane. We bought a paper. It was me. The news reforms had failed, I read. I was out.

I was much amused by this typically baseless story until we reached home to find a tearful Eliza awaiting us. She was sixteen, and in the middle of her GCSEs, at home alone revising. During the afternoon, she had been doorstepped three times by two reporters from a national newspaper. Each time they called, they became more aggressive: 'Your father's in trouble. We need to speak to him. We know he's there.' When Eliza said I wasn't, they said: 'You're lying.' Being called a liar by two hostile adults had really upset her. They called again soon after. I confronted them. Normally I find it easy to remain calm and to control my feelings even in the most trying circumstances, but on that occasion I could barely contain my rage. I berated them for hounding a young person, and ordered them off my front step. They slunk away.

All of my colleagues in BBC News and Current Affairs were affected personally at some point by the hostility to the reforms. Ron

Neil was often deeply unhappy, stretched by old and new loyalties, his powerful sense of propriety affronted by unedifying conduct and backbiting on all sides. And Samir Shah's changes at Lime Grove had prompted a continuous stream of contempt, ridicule and vilification aimed at him personally. Once Samir had his bank and credit card statements stolen, and sent to *Private Eye*, who returned them to him, unpublished. Samir faced all this with pluck, cheerfulness and resilience, never wavering, a true hero.

Ian Hargreaves too had some low moments. He had exceeded all my expectations, recruiting brilliantly and raising the BBC's journalistic sights. He was as widely admired for his reasonableness, rationality and probity as for his journalistic skill, but he fell prey to rivalries within the News team, who resisted his writ. I was in part at fault for not pinning down his responsibilities with sufficient precision at the beginning. From time to time, Ian considered returning to the more peaceful world of print, once telling me he loathed his job. I pressed him to stay and increased his responsibilities. When the Managing Director of Regional Broadcasting retired in 1989, Ron succeeded him. (With Mark Byford, Ron would soon transform the look and expertise of the BBC's regional news, an area of chronic BBC weakness, as national news had been.) Ian succeeded Ron to the top job in News, until he left to become deputy editor of the *Financial Times* (and later editor of the *Independent*).

All of our jobs seemed pretty thankless at times. Not only were we assailed on all sides but the work was backbreaking. At the peak of the reforms, many of the key people were working eighty to a hundred hours a week, and were exhausted too.

Gradually we emerged into the light as the News and Current Affairs directorate became conspicuously more successful. We were helped on our way by an extraordinary news agenda, which demonstrated the massive new capability of the BBC's journalism. Most news broadcasters around the world had been pulling back while we had expanded. Alone among international news organisations, in

May 1989 we had a full team in Beijing covering the first Sino-Soviet summit for thirty years. So when the demonstrations – and later the massacre – occurred in Tiananmen Square, we not only had the footage, we had commentators of quality there who were able to offer real insight, including John Simpson, Brian Hanrahan, Kate Adie and Brian Barron. BBC News rose triumphantly to the occasion again when the Berlin Wall was pulled down. We reported the old Soviet Union crumbling from the inside. Douglas Hurd, the Foreign Secretary, wrote to say that the BBC's coverage of the storming of the Russian Parliament was a 'tour de force'. John Simpson produced a compelling and detailed investigation for *Panorama* on the dramatic fall of Romania's President Nicolae Ceausescu. We covered Lockerbie and the death of the Ayatollah with consummate skill. When Nigel Lawson resigned, we had the economic and political know-how to explain why, in a *Nine O'Clock News* of devastating power and acumen, edited by Mark Damazer. The night Geoffrey Howe resigned, the audience for the *Nine O'Clock News* was double that of *News at Ten*. Polly Toynbee commanded the social affairs field with extraordinary authority. When the Conservatives' health reforms ran into opposition, Polly brought confidence, insight and a sure touch to our coverage.

Nigel Ryan – ex-editor of ITN, ex-Vice-President of NBC News – wrote at the end of 1990:

> Birt stuck to his guns, ended the archaic separation of BBC
> News and Current Affairs. His insistence on rigorous
> research and a co-ordinated editorial approach appears to
> have ended the anarchy bedevilling the old Corporation.
> The results are there to see: a vastly improved BBC News . . .
> The BBC has not only opted for quality: it is winning the
> evening audience. Birt has confounded his critics.

The good-natured David Hatch wrote to me: 'Last year I worried you were not enjoying the BBC . . . [now] you seem relaxed, you laugh, you grin, infectiously. I think you're enjoying it, and I'm so pleased about that.'

Even the long war over *Panorama* showed signs of ending. Three successive and brilliant editors – Tim Gardam, Mark Thompson and Glenwyn Benson – brought grip, focus and journalistic brilliance. Testing issues were addressed without difficulty: in 1989 John Ware famously investigated Lady Porter, Westminster Council Leader and friend of Mrs Thatcher, showing that millions of pounds of ratepayers' money had been used in an attempt to boost the Tory vote in the local elections. A leading QC advised us he would happily defend the programme in any action Lady Porter took; but there was a risk, and – if we lost – it would cost the BBC three or four million pounds (and all our jobs, we thought). I gave the go-ahead. The programme resulted in an investigation by the Westminster District Auditor, which became the longest-running inquiry into local government corruption in history. We took on Robert Maxwell in 1991, exposing his dishonesty, demonstrating how he had manipulated his own share price. Maxwell threatened and menaced *Panorama* editor Mark Thompson right up to transmission. Again we involved a QC throughout, who helped us construct a programme we could defend in court. Counsel advised, none the less, that there was a high risk. We took it. A few weeks later Maxwell fell into the sea and drowned as the world closed in on him.

Few news stories, however, demonstrated the BBC's new virtuosity as a news and current affairs organisation as much as the dramatic, spellbinding events which led to the downfall of Mrs Thatcher herself. Just two weeks before her resignation in 1990, I had held a lunch at the BBC for her to meet the top managers and journalists in News. (We had had a dress rehearsal with exactly the same menu at a lunch for Tony Blair the previous week!) The lunch with Mrs Thatcher was chiefly marked by a quarrel between John Cole and Peter Jay, both of whom let their slips show – Peter earning the Prime Minister's warm approval for an attack on the Foreign

Office and the European Commission, John Cole her fury for suggesting that young people wanted the single currency. Mrs Thatcher
could barely contain herself: for a moment she looked as if she
would lean across the table and handbag the angry Ulsterman. At
one point Peter Jay, annoyed by a remark John Cole had made, spat
at him: 'Kindergarten economics!' Cole looked furious. On the way
down with me in the lift, Mrs Thatcher said: 'You can always tell
those old socialists. It's the way they ask the questions!'

Robert Runcie, the Archbishop of Canterbury – who had been at
university with Mrs Thatcher – shared his views on her with us at
another BBC lunch at about the same time. He observed with force
and fluency: 'Mrs Thatcher's values are Judeo not Christian. She
quotes her father's sermons at me. She doesn't like the wet vicar at
Chequers. She's trying to control appointments in the Church. The
Church will disestablish if need be.' When Mrs Thatcher resigned,
Andrew Turnbull, her principal private secretary, gave her – as a
parting gift from her private office – a short-wave radio and
explained: 'You can remain angry with the BBC all over the world!'

I went to see Mrs Thatcher shortly after her resignation in her
splendid new home in Chester Square to ask her to record her
memoirs for the BBC. (The result was Denys Blakeway's remarkable
The Downing Street Years.) She was full of energy and spirit, and I was
among the first to hear – it had not yet been reported – that she was
already on John Major's case, disapproving of the actions of the
new Prime Minister on a wide front. In particular, he was spending
too much. Her candour made John Whittingdale, her political secretary, squirm awkwardly. She waved him away impatiently: 'Don't
worry. John's trusted!' She carried on. Nigel Lawson's problems
were 'Vanity, vanity, vanity!' She was worried that no one had yet
emerged on the right; Portillo was the man, but it was too early. She
was delighted Nigel and Geoffrey had not got jobs. Theirs was
treachery of a high order!

I stayed with Mrs Thatcher in her drawing room talking into the
late afternoon. Occasionally she would look at her watch, become

slightly agitated, and ask: 'Wherever can Denis be?' Eventually there was a commotion downstairs. She jumped up and hurried away to return with her beloved and a gang of businessmen with whom he had had a very long lunch. She fussed over them all like a mother hen, sat them down, got them drinks, then quizzed them intently about their business, getting to the nub of their current commercial issues with lightning speed, showing a real hunger to understand and to learn. They were the worse for wear, but most impressed by her overpowering interest. When I finally left, far later than intended, she fussed over me but made me promise I would tell Jane that she had not kept me!

After we transmitted her memoirs, I gave a dinner for Lady Thatcher at Broadcasting House in 1993, to which I invited her most loyal supporters, and the senior civil servants who had closely served her, including Tim Bell, Gordon Reece, Harvey Thomas, Woodrow Wyatt, Peter Lilley, Robin Butler, Charles Powell and Andrew Turnbull. I wanted to signal to the right that the BBC was not in any camp, that they now had a stake in an organisation that – for much of the 1980s – they had reviled, and whose overthrow they had dreamt about. Mrs Thatcher made a moving speech in reply to mine – speaking from the heart, without notes, without stridency, but with sadness, telling her loyalists how proud she was of her achievements. It was all too clear that she wished she could have carried on.

After the dinner, Mrs Thatcher introduced Jane to Denis, saying: 'She is to John Birt as you are to me.' Denis responded: 'As everyone knows, I've got nothing between the ears, but I adore the old girl and there isn't anything I wouldn't do for her!' Mrs Thatcher took hold of both Jane's hands, and looked her intently in the eye: 'Look after John. He is under nearly as hostile an attack from his enemies as I was!'

Mrs Thatcher and I were in opposite camps on many issues – I was a social liberal, she a social authoritarian. But it was impossible not to admire her life-force, her fire, her determination to fight against bitter opposition and entrenched interests, against the odds. She was a grammar-school girl from a humble background, not a toff. She was a product of the meritocracy who despised the old establishment. She left Britain in a far healthier state than she had found it in the dark, miserable days of 1979. She put us on the road to conquering inflation; she privatised the nationalised industries; she reduced the power of the trade unions; she restored our economy to strength after decades of weakness; she made Britain more competitive, enterprising and self-reliant. She released our national and – though she didn't intend it – our creative and cultural energies too. Margaret Thatcher was a great reforming Prime Minister. In our series she had said: 'The Prime Minister should be intimidating. There's not much point being a weak, floppy thing in a chair.' That she never was!

In the early 1990s, I had lunch with the Chairman. We agreed we were through the woods, that we had achieved much. I told him how grateful I was for his courage and steadfast support. I also told him I was frustrated with Mike's conservatism, and could not imagine remaining Deputy Director-General for very long. The Chairman said he didn't know whether Mike would want to extend his contract, or whether the Board of Governors would agree to that. He made me promise I would alert him well in advance if I became determined to go.

Conservative backbenchers, who had queued up in the 1980s to deliver ferocious broadsides against the BBC, began to mellow as our commitment to good intelligent journalism and to high editorial standards became clear. When the Iraqis invaded Kuwait in August 1990 – and a Gulf War involving British forces became inevitable – I worked hard with John Wilson to define the special considerations that attach to journalism at time of war, mindful of the hostile criticism the BBC had faced during the Falklands. The BBC had to be trusted as a source of accurate and reliable information. We also had to be sensitive to national feeling, to the anguish of families of

aircrews and soldiers in the field, and to issues of national security –
we couldn't give away information helpful to the forces British
troops would be fighting. To settle an issue that had been controversial at the time of the Falklands War, we ruled that BBC
journalists could use both 'British troops' and 'our troops' when
referring to British forces. We made clear that we would report the
truth about the war, however uncomfortable; and that we would
carry a range of opinion, including those opposed to armed action.
With trepidation, John Wilson and I went to speak to fifty members
of the Conservative Backbench Media Committee to explain our
approach to the coming conflict, mindful that a similar group had
famously torn Alasdair Milne and his Chairman George Howard to
shreds in the 1980s. Thirty MPs spoke and asked questions. There
was overwhelming support for our guidelines. Moreover, again and
again, Conservative backbenchers went out of their way to praise
the quality and standards of the BBC's journalism. John Wilson
and I rubbed our eyes in disbelief.

It took the allied forces many months to ready themselves for
war, so BBC News had plenty of time to prepare and to make its
dispositions. This would be the first conflict of the satellite age. We
planned to cover it from every aspect, military and diplomatic.
The main problem was getting our people into Saudi Arabia, the
principal centre of operation. The Saudis listened to our pleas,
right up to the King, but ignored them. When John Major went to
visit British troops in Saudi, we conspired with Downing Street to
attach as many of our journalists to his coat-tails as possible, with
a nod and a wink that once they were there they would stay put.
Just hours before the allied forces started their attack in January
1991, Charles Powell, the Prime Minister's private secretary, called
me at home with a heavy hint that our correspondents in Baghdad
would soon be in a danger zone. There was no prospect, however,
of our people on the ground agreeing to evacuate. John Simpson
simply refused to budge from the Iraqi capital and reported the
conflict from the other side – a first in war reporting, which only

someone of John's stature and integrity could have pulled off so flawlessly.

The BBC had an exceptional war. Scores of BBC correspondents in the field performed superbly – old hands like Martin Bell, Brian Barron and Kate Adie showing their class, and newer recruits also displaying their expertise, like Mark Laity's commanding overview of the battleground. A dispatch from Jeremy Bowen caused much controversy. He reported that a building in Amiriya hit by a missile that killed hundreds had contained civilians, though it had been described by the allies as a bunker. In the new atmosphere of trust and confidence in its journalism, however, everyone in the BBC stood unwaveringly behind him.

The Gulf War was the coming of age of continuous news. By the early 1990s, the BBC was massively out-pointing ITN on the home front, but in the US and internationally CNN was proving its ascendancy with a round-the-clock service which reported news as it happened, not just at the next bulletin. When the Gulf War started in 1991, Paul Fox helpfully cleared the daytime television schedule for a continuous news service. And we ran a similar operation on Radio 4's long-wave frequency, despite the deep misgivings of BBC Radio's management, who were fearful that they would lose in perpetuity one of their two Radio 4 frequencies to another service. The Gulf War changed perceptions within the BBC about continuous news. Thereafter, we knew we had to offer non-stop news on both television and radio if we were to flourish in the future as a news organisation.

Just a day or so after the war was over, I flew to the Gulf with a small group of editors on Defence Secretary Tom King's flight to say thank-you to our front-line correspondents. We flew into Kuwait City in a Hercules through a vision of Hades, descending through black smoke from burning oil wells so dense that it blotted out the light. Occasionally the clouds parted to reveal great fires burning below, high flames shooting up towards us. In Bahrain, we met the war-exhausted pilots, looking more like boys than men, who had flown the hazardous low-level bombing missions. I attended, in the desert, under camouflage netting, the first debriefing by the British battlefield commanders for the Secretary of State. I flew low in a helicopter with General Peter de la Billière over a strangely empty Kuwait City, littered with charred vehicles and scarred by smouldering buildings. We swept over a desert landscape strewn with burnt-out Iraqi tanks, mile after mile of devastation. We wheeled around the astonishing, stomach-churning sight of ten miles of tangled, melted-down, nose-to-tail vehicles trapped on a motorway at the Mitla Pass which had been trying to escape back to Iraq. I met British soldiers and officers, and detected no triumphalism; they talked as if they were just professionals with a job to do. Only one showed anger and that was directed at Saddam Hussein for exposing his ill-prepared and defenceless forces to such needless destruction.

During my thirteen years at the BBC, News and Current Affairs went from strength to strength. It moved out of its many shabby premises into a modern, purpose-built, technically advanced complex at Television Centre. It became the founding tenant at Westminster's Millbank. It built a network of twenty-six international bureaux. Bringing financial discipline to News proved harder than I had anticipated, but it came eventually. The monasticism of BBC News ended: it routinely reached out and invited the world in to meet and talk to its editorial teams and decision-makers. A new brand identity was created. Tony Hall succeeded Ian Hargreaves, and pressed for the news agenda to become ever more serious and significant. The BBC became the main provider in the UK of serious investigative journalism, as the form withered elsewhere. BBC News facilitated the national debate with total conviction. Tony Hall oversaw, against both internal and external opposition, the successful introduction of continuous news on radio, television and the Internet – Radio 5 Live, News 24 and BBC News Online, which became the Internet's most comprehensive and insightful news service and took the world by storm. BBC News took over responsibility for World Service News and for BBC World, the global news satellite channel.

ITN – once a fine and professional news organisation – was weakened for want of support, funding and direction from a declining and unstrategic ITV. BBC News became the dominant news force in the UK, with a 70 per cent share of all broadcast news consumption. Around the world – across TV, Radio and Online – BBC News out-pointed CNN, becoming the world's leading news provider, reaching an estimated three hundred million people each week by the time I left the BBC. BBC News became the greatest centre of journalistic power and expertise in broadcasting anywhere in the world. For the small band who struggled to this summit, it had been a hard, bitter ascent; but the view from the top was glorious.

13

Producer Choice

As it became clear that BBC News was on the road to success, another item rose to the top of the BBC's agenda in the early 1990s: the Corporation's efficiency. Anyone looking at the BBC, even from the outside, could see it was a flabby and wasteful organisation. That was by no means unique in either the public or the private sector in Britain at the time, but things were changing. Mrs Thatcher had exposed the private sector to greater competition, and she had privatised the old nationalised industries – airlines, gas, coal, steel and telecommunications. Each in turn lost its subsidy, faced up to competition and massively reduced its costs, thus demonstrating how inefficient each had been when part of the state sector. A similar process was already under way in broadcasting: the ITV companies, aware they would soon face competitive bids for their franchises, had finally addressed their over-manning, outdated practices and inflated costs.

In the late 1980s Mrs Thatcher had fired a first shot across the

BBC's bows: she had linked its licence fee to the retail price index, effectively freezing the organisation's income for the first time in its history. The government's process for settling the role, form and funding of the BBC for the next period of its history would soon begin, for the BBC's Charter was up for renewal in 1996. Mrs Thatcher's beady eye was upon us: it was plain that the BBC would be the next comfy, cosy British institution in line for reform, and that the Prime Minister would relish taking the axe to an organisation employing legions of those most conservative and resistant of pressure groups – the British professional and creative classes. The tragic lesson of ITV was that, if you did not reform yourself, the government would step in and do it for you, perhaps badly. The BBC had to be able to offer not only a compelling vision of its purpose but a convincing account of how it would become more efficient and effective.

Hussey saw this keenly. He was not analytical, but he was smart. He did not understand the whys or wherefores, but he drew from his own day-to-day experiences of the BBC, and began to focus obsessively on staff numbers. The BBC's information systems were so poor that we shall never know with precision how many people worked in the organisation at that time, but it was probably in excess of thirty thousand. Hussey began to hound Michael Checkland to reduce these numbers, and seemed to enjoy the sport, for he was a natural stirrer and trouble-maker. The issue was raised over and over again at board meetings either by Hussey or by a Governor acting as his surrogate. Increasingly, it became clear that Hussey had Checkland in his sights, that he believed Mike would consider penny-packet reform, but would not grip the organisation.

Checkland had his own agenda, and it was legitimate. BBC staff turnover in many areas in the late 1980s had become unsustainably high – in some units, more than 40 per cent of staff were being lost each year – and it wasn't hard to see why: in almost every area, BBC pay was well below market levels. It was not surprising, therefore, that the unions were restive over pay. There had been a difficult negotiation in the summer of 1989 which had resulted in a series of strikes – for example, for a few hours starting at 5 p.m. in the afternoon, stoppages which had caused maximum disruption with minimal loss of income. Many on the Board of Management had been very irritated with Mike's handling of the 1989 dispute. A number of 'final' offers were made. We were asked to put all our weight behind each proposition, only to find it changed. I was among those who were infuriated by our inability to define and to hold a line we thought reasonable. Management looked weak, and lost credibility. Mike had a genuine feeling for staff, and he hated confronting them. He felt low and looked pale and shaken. Hussey had been highly critical of his vacillation, and was acutely aware that we had appeared timid in the eyes of government.

After the dispute was settled, Checkland acted: he initiated an exercise, called Funding the Future, to attack waste and inefficiency and to release funds to invest in market levels of pay in the BBC. In due course, BBC pay was indeed raised closer to market levels, and we were able to recruit and to retain people of talent and ability, one of Checkland's most important legacies. While applauding Mike's objective, I had been frustrated, however, by the way the exercise had been conducted, for there had been no attempt to identify the scale of the BBC's inefficiency, and the reasons for it. Rather, a group of people had set out on a quick search for obvious and easily unearthable money.

No one was a greater master of the quick hunt for funds than Checkland himself. A few years earlier, before he became Director-General, Mike had successfully attacked the machine – with a small guerrilla working party – to release resources for his predecessor Milne. Mike and his team had assaulted the BBC from the top down, in the sinisterly named Black Spot exercise, generally focusing on support services, and had come away with a pile of cash. Mike had a better understanding of the rickety Heath Robinson machine that was the BBC than anyone, for he was in effect – and had been for years – the leader of the bureaucrats who allocated resources to programme-makers across the organisation. This was a freemasonry – the real, secret management of the Corporation. I would often find Mike whispering conspiratorially on the phone to other members of this brotherhood when I entered his office. Mike was like an ancient, loving mechanic devoted to a clanging, hissing, outdated steam engine, keeping it going with a splash of oil, a bang of the hammer, a twist of the wrench.

The Funding the Future group reported in early 1990 and made some modest and sketchy recommendations. They identified two big ideas: first, they proposed the abandonment of the major buildings Checkland had himself planned – one a modern radio centre at White City, the second a single centre for my scattered BBC News and Current Affairs directorate, a key element of the package waved in front of me by Checkland to persuade me to join the BBC in the first place. Ian Hargreaves, the Director of News and Current Affairs, and I and others had laboured to bring the plan to fruition. Architects' plans were in place. The first sod was about to be cut. I knew Checkland was committed to a proper home for News. I was confident that the Governors would support me – as they had been steadfast in aid of all my News plans – and that they would reject the group's recommendation.

The night before the board meeting arranged to discuss the proposals, I had a crackly call from Hussey on his archaic car phone. He explained his position to me on the report's main proposals, saying about the News building: 'We will refer it back for savings.' I took this to mean the building would go ahead, but that we would be asked to deliver it at a lower cost – an acceptable compromise.

The meeting the following day turned without warning into a mass ambush. Close colleagues like Paul Fox and David Hatch urged abandonment of the News centre. More surprisingly, normally supportive and stalwart Governors like P. D. James and Curtis Keeble joined in. Ian Hargreaves was furious and mildly threatening. I was more emotional in my own plea to retain the News centre than I had ever been at a BBC meeting before or would be after. I regretted my display immediately, but the betrayals made me so angry I couldn't help myself. The senior group in BBC News had struggled so hard together. This was a cruel reward. The Governors pulled back: the proposal was referred for further consideration. I walked out of the meeting in a black fury. I saw the Chairman the next day. He was irritated too: 'You were an arse. Everyone thought you were going to resign. Hargreaves was a fool to threaten. I explained to you it would be referred back.' I protested that that was implausible: the whole drive of opinion at the meeting had been for abandonment. I reminded him what key Governors had said. Preposterously, he denied my account. When I persisted, he said, in character: 'It doesn't matter what they think – I'm the Chairman! Don't worry. You'll get your bloody building. I'll see to that.' Michael Checkland was very supportive: he had been irritated by the committee's recommendation and continued to believe in the value of the building. The incident brought us momentarily closer together than at any other time.

The second big idea in the Funding the Future recommendations would set in train a course of events that would have an historic impact on the BBC. Following a recommendation by the Peacock Committee, Mrs Thatcher's government had insisted that the BBC, like ITV, should commission 25 per cent of its television programmes from the independent sector. The BBC had fiercely resisted the proposal (wrongly, in my view) but had had to accept force majeure – that it was Mrs Thatcher's will, and that it would happen. When the quota for independents was to be introduced, in the early 1990s, the BBC would be making only 75 per cent of its own programmes, and would have considerable excess capacity. The Funding the Future group made an obvious recommendation: that the BBC should cut its television resource base – excess studios, outside broadcast vehicles, videotape-editing and so on, and the surplus staff who provided those services. The group had estimated the financial prize, but oddly had made no detailed suggestions at all about how the excess capacity should be cut. There were a fair number of loose ends of this kind in the report that needed tying up, and it was serendipity that Checkland asked me to turn this particular recommendation into a practical plan. My task would take me into the very heart of Michael Checkland's labyrinth.

To help me I had a core of people who would prove central to my life over the next ten years: Will Wyatt, a senior television executive, one-time factual-programme-maker, wise, cool and open-minded; John Smith, a sharp, funny, fast-talking accountant, newly arrived at the BBC from British Rail; Mark Oliver, the BBC's first strategist, quiet, shy, analytically brilliant; and Clare Riley, the cheerful, energetic, determined former programme-maker who administered the project. We were helped by Peter Hazell, a senior economist from Coopers and Lybrand, and a team of accountants he assembled. A number of other BBC executives were attached to the group – essentially some of the bureaucrats currently in charge of the machine.

Like explorers, we set out into the innards, the interstices and the secret byways of the BBC. We wanted to understand the BBC's television resource base, under the management not just of Network Television in London, but of Regional Broadcasting – scattered across the whole of the UK. We took evidence and sought opinion from inside and outside the BBC. Greg Dyke fed me an analysis of the scale of savings made in the cutbacks at LWT. John Harvey-Jones, the former ICI executive who had worked with the BBC while making the *Troubleshooter* series, entered the debate publicly by attacking the Corporation for denying choice to its producers – telling them, for instance, which camera or studio or editing crews they had to work with.

Our inquiries took many months, for, although the BBC was an organisation that spent around two billion pounds each year, there was little hard information about its basic business. It produced accounts for management and Governors, for example, only quarterly, with half a page of figures, and a single page of text. Its accountancy systems were medieval. We found almost no data about the demand for facilities or the utilisation of plant or people, so we used the Coopers team to collect raw data from scratch. We discovered that the demand from BBC programme-makers for facilities varied considerably across the day, the week and the year. We analysed the total capacity across the BBC, and we were astonished to discover eventually that even at the annual peak of demand the BBC had a vast excess of facilities. We found the BBC could cover Wimbledon, the World Cup and a world war, and still have unused facilities to spare.

A picture emerged of a form of imperialism, of every regional commander in every part of the BBC acquiring a full fleet of facilities, whatever the need – the broadcasting equivalent of having your own dedicated aircraft carrier, battleships, cruisers and destroyers. We uncovered expensively refurbished, over-engineered studios that were used for just a few hours a week, and many studios that were used for only 10 or 20 per cent of the time. The BBC owned churches, motor-vehicle maintenance workshops, fully staffed MOT testing centres. Some of the smaller regional centres had capacity they could never conceivably use, awaiting a vast order for programming that could never come. In one region, a huge studio had been built, but lay empty, in case recordings might be made with the local orchestra.

Staff utilisation was low, too. Some BBC technicians, for instance, would be idle for weeks awaiting work. We identified that we had between 25 and 50 per cent more staff than were needed in some areas. We uncovered a vast overhead of many thousands of support staff, their costs not charged to any programme-related activity. Throughout the BBC, staff and facilities had accreted for years, relentlessly expanding without challenge in an era when the income from the licence fee had grown and grown. Most BBC staff and managers were highly skilled and dedicated to excellent craft and technical standards, and to public service. As we later tightened up, however, we discovered some were corrupt and committing fraud, operating undetected for years amid this uncosted anarchy, undisciplined by market competition or effective controls.

Astride this slack and slovenly system were the BBC's bureaucrats, allocating resources to programmes, effectively controlling
two-thirds of the BBC's spend. Many of these bureaucrats were
personally benevolent, committed to solving programme-makers'
problems, reaching into their secret caches of cash to oil their way
when necessary. Michael Checkland had been one of the most helpful when he had worked in Television. Ron Neil always told the
story of going to Checkland's office with some black and white pictures of a shabby newsroom to make a case for refurbishment.
Checkland, without looking up, had said: 'Three million pounds
and not a penny more!'

Every BBC activity was funded directly from the centre. Facilities,
overheads and support services were not charged to particular programmes, so no one had the slightest idea how much it cost to make
programmes, or even to provide individual facilities. Accounts
everywhere were rudimentary. At 1990 values, we found one major
BBC department had a turnover of £250 million without a single
accountant on its staff. The system had emerged over the span of
the BBC's history. No one person could be blamed for it. It was
bigger than any individual, impossible to fight. But the BBC's way
of doing business was evidently wasting the public's money on a
mammoth scale. Every part of the organisation was putting its own
interest before the public's. I was offended and appalled.

My group began to consider its recommendations. Our analysis
had revealed a startling fact – that over 80 per cent of the BBC's
programmes were being made in London and the south-east. The
BBC was indeed a metropolitan, London-focused institution. One
of the world's greatest production departments – the BBC's Natural
History Unit – had started and flourished in Bristol, but this was
exceptional. Few other major programme units had taken root out
of London, so it was hardly surprising that little use was made of
the often state-of-the-art facilities around the country. As a northerner, I felt particularly strongly that the BBC should draw more of

its creative strength from outside the capital. We recommended an increase in production in the national and English regions, and we proposed moving production departments out of London to facilitate this. In the event, there were many months of haggling and many variations ahead of us before it was finally agreed that BBC Religion and Janet Street-Porter's Youth and Entertainment Features department would move to Manchester. We identified or created other centres of excellence around the country. Over the next few years, the balance of BBC production would fundamentally shift away from London.

My study group had identified the huge surplus capacity long built into the system, and the further excess capacity that a 25 per cent independent quota would leave us with. We then recommended a substantial cut, and which facilities we should lose. This was painful, for studios were iconic, whether utilised or not. I decided to recommend the closure of studios in Birmingham, Manchester and the south-east while increasing production outside London with location-based programmes.

More fundamentally, I wanted to sweep away the command economy that had produced such boundless waste and to introduce a system which would ensure the BBC would not only become efficient but remain so. We decided to recommend that the BBC should introduce Producer Choice, the biggest organisational shift in its history. The Controllers of the television networks and other services would control the full cost of their schedules. They would be free to buy their programmes at market prices from the independent sector or from BBC production departments, who in turn would have the freedom to buy their facilities from inside or outside the BBC. Overheads and facilities would be charged to the programmes and units using them. Both programme-makers and facilities departments would face the full blast of market pressure. To sell their services and to survive, they would need to achieve competitive levels of efficiency, and to charge market prices. (We would later discover that BBC programmes

and facilities – pre-Producer Choice – were 30 to 40 per cent more
costly than the market.) Producer Choice would not only promote
efficiency, it would bring creative liberation – more choice for programme-makers about whom they worked with, and more
freedom to spend their budgets.

We knew our approach would appeal to a Conservative government desperate to see the BBC reformed. We wanted, though, to sell
Producer Choice to the Opposition as well, who would one day
return to government. Peter Mandelson had left his job as Labour's
Director of Communication when he was selected to stand for
Hartlepool, and was filling in time waiting for the general election
by working for Denis Stevenson's consultancy SRU. In the autumn
of 1990, Patricia Hodgson recruited Peter to advise us, and he
examined our proposals from a Labour perspective. He advised the
BBC that an incoming Labour government would not defend inefficiency or wasteful union practices, but we had to make clear how
our proposals would bring benefits to viewers and listeners; and we
needed to turn the BBC into an organisation that valued, trained
and developed the staff who stayed. Peter's appointment to advise us
provoked a storm. A letter was drafted for Michael Checkland to
send justifying our action. Checkland refused to sign it and asked
Patricia to send it instead. She responded angrily: 'I'm fed up with
being employed as the statutory Tory. NO!'

As I worked with my group in the spring of 1991 on our final radical recommendations, our deliberations became a matter of intense
interest internally and played increasingly into institutional politics.
All the key players – Hussey, Barnett, Checkland and I – were
roughly a year away from the ends of our contracts. Hussey and
Barnett, I knew, were desperate to stay on for a second term. When
he had offered me the deputy director-generalship, Checkland had
said he was minded to serve only one term; but he had gone silent
on the issue, and I began to receive intelligence that he had changed
his mind, that he too wanted an extension. It was also becoming
plain, though it was never firmly stated, that Hussey – now openly

disaffected with Mike – would prefer me to be Director-General. It wasn't clear, though, that he could carry his board.

Whether or not Hussey's term was to be extended was in the gift of Kenneth Baker, the Home Secretary. Baker made plain, in public and in private, that BBC reform was high on the government's agenda. Hussey intensified the pressure on Checkland to produce results on staff numbers and reform at every turn. 'This is do-or-die,' he said on one occasion; 'we need proof we can sort ourselves out.' It was increasingly obvious that Hussey felt *he* needed to offer proof if *he* were to be extended. 'Staff numbers' became a mantra. Hussey particularly castigated the lack of reform in the Television service. The contract of Paul Fox, Television's Managing Director, was also up for renewal, and Mike Checkland was keen for him to stay on. Hussey, however, was adamantly opposed. The Chairman told me on two occasions that the Governors wanted me to take over Network Television when Paul had gone. Each time I rejected the notion. On the second occasion, Hussey looked distraught. 'If the board want a new managing director to report to me, fine,' I said, but I wasn't going to leave the centre for an operational job.

I urged that Will Wyatt should be put in charge of BBC Television instead, for, working with him at close quarters on the resources study, I had come to hold him in high regard: he was cultured and intelligent, with a fine track record in serious programmes, and impeccable editorial judgement. If he were appointed, I believed, the pendulum would swing back towards public service and away from the ratings emphasis of the Cotton–Grade era. Will was also an original and independent thinker, not prey to the knee-jerk notions of the media hot-house. He was managerially adept, and hard-headed rather than soft-hearted on the efficiency agenda. Will – I argued to the Chairman on each occasion that he raised the issue with me – was the best choice for Managing Director, Television.

At the same time, I made it clear to Hussey that I would not stay at the BBC if Checkland were granted a second term of office: I wasn't interested in being Mike's deputy for ten years. He was a gradualist; the BBC needed radical solutions. If I wasn't going to be Director-General, I would find other work. As these discussions came to a climax, Michael Green asked to see me. Carlton was bidding for the London weekday franchise: was I interested in becoming the Chief Executive? A generous reward and share scheme was proposed. I was torn: it was a good offer if I were going to leave the BBC, but, if I went, I would jeopardise for ever the prospect of becoming the BBC's Director-General. I told Michael Green I couldn't make an early decision.

The Network Television saga rumbled on. The Chairman reported that Checkland had become reconciled to Paul Fox leaving. Mike was now proposing Howard Stringer as Paul's successor – the capable, likeable Welshman who had had a brilliant television career in the US. The Chairman proposed a variant: Will should have responsibility for the television channels and production, and he and a resource head would separately report directly to me. I thought the proposed structure was unwieldy and probably unworkable, but I told Hussey I would reluctantly accept it as an interim arrangement. I didn't, however, change my position on the director-generalship. The Chairman went in to bat with his idea. Then, without any forewarning, without any vacancy being announced and without even an interview, Will Wyatt was summoned, to his surprise and bewilderment, to be told he would be the new Managing Director of Television. I was relieved and thrilled, even more so that the Chairman had been unable to deliver the proposal we had discussed. I doubted, however, that he would be able to deliver the director-generalship to me. I pondered the Carlton job afresh, and told Hussey what I was thinking. He went white and became visibly panicky. I began to surmise that I was a necessary part of Hussey's pitch to Home Secretary Baker. Renew me – Hussey was arguing – and reform will continue, but he needed me on the ticket to make that promise credible. I knew from intelligence that the Conservatives regarded me – after my success in News – as sound on reform; and I also knew that Checkland had not impressed Baker. Hussey summoned me to a formal meeting with himself and his Vice-Chairman, Joel Barnett: 'If we get renewed, and we may not,' Hussey told me, 'we *guarantee* we will seek to appoint you as Director-General, and extend Mike for only a short period.' Barnett confirmed his own commitment to the proposition. The Chairman added: 'Mike's extension will be months, not years.' It would be a modest sop to his supporters. They emphasised they couldn't guarantee success, but they would try. 'Then I'll give it a go,' I said. That was the last conversation on the subject I had with either of them.

The Chairman and Vice-Chairman *were* renewed – Hussey for an unprecedented five years, Barnett for two. This put the pair of them in a powerful position. Mike was stunned: he interrupted me during a meeting in Glasgow with the news, obviously shaken. There was some expectation within the BBC that Mike would be renewed immediately, but Hussey said and did nothing. He left Mike dangling, his authority undermined. At the annual conference of Governors and management at Lucknam Park in May 1991, the atmosphere was tense. The Chairman went out of his way at every turn to emphasise the BBC's difficulties, particularly in Network Television. So did Kenneth Baker, when he joined us all for dinner.

Hussey had invited Greg Dyke, by now LWT's Chief Executive, to speak to the conference. Greg explained how he had aggressively confronted the unions at LWT. Then he advised the BBC what it should do next:

> Introduce a real internal market for services. Reduce your facilities base to a level you can easily utilise. I know I'll offend many in this room, but they are only facilities. They are not the service . . . The BBC won't be left alone unless you change the culture of the organisation, and unless the world outside believes you've become a leaner and more efficient organisation!

I had had nothing to do with the invitation to Greg, nor with his speech, welcome though it was to me. But it was widely assumed I had, for those attending had heard all Greg's arguments before – in my mouth. In reality it was just another example of the LWT Mafia having a similar view of the world, but Greg's speech caused ill-feeling with Mike and his supporters, who assumed, wrongly, that it was part of a campaign by me for the director-generalship.

The culmination of the Television Resources study coincided with this increasingly nervy period of uncertainty over whether Checkland's contract would be extended. My group's recommendations were to be discussed at a board meeting in June. The Governors were due to dine alone the following week to settle the director-generalship. Events were coming to a head, but I was in difficulty over my recommendations. Oddly, there was no opposition to the introduction of Producer Choice, despite the radicalism of the concept, and the dramatic impact it would have on the BBC. To his credit, Mike Checkland – who would never have proposed Producer Choice himself – pronounced it inevitable. It was, he said, the way the world was going, and he supported its introduction while definitely understanding its implications. Others, less clever, did not understand. They couldn't conceive of anything other than the command economy they had always known. To them Producer Choice was an abstraction, and they didn't resist it because it would be just another complication in the Heath Robinson machine. Somehow, if it were introduced, they would find a way round it. They always had before.

Other proposals of mine, however, were problematic. The *casus belli* was the planned closure of regional studios. As our recommendations were due to be finalised, Mike – I was told – nobbled many of my committee members, and pressed them to withdraw their support for the recommendation on closures. Finally, Mike tried to dislodge me directly. He didn't want the BBC, he told me, to be unsettled by regional closures. He warned me: 'If you proceed, that's the end of the News building.' I was outraged by what seemed

to be blackmail: 'The new News building has no connection whatsoever with these issues,' I responded. Mike didn't reply. I refused to
budge.

Mike's pressure on my colleagues worked: they would no longer
support some of the recommendations we had framed. I had to
draft a minority report. I was furious. I had worked on the study for
the best part of nine months. The rigour of the analysis was flaw-
less. The case was compelling. The scale of waste we had uncovered
was a scandal. In such circumstances, the fierce, dogged side of my
nature came into play: I became unyielding. Reluctant to compromise, but understanding what was at stake, I turned for personal
advice to Terry Burns, my close friend, by then permanent secretary
at the Treasury. I went to see him at his home, explaining that I
feared certain Governors might fight shy of some of the proposals.
'Don't drive at a brick wall, drive round it,' Terry advised. 'You
have won the big prize [Producer Choice]. Don't make them swallow now what they'll have to swallow later.' Howell James, Director
of Corporate Affairs, and by now a good friend, also urged me not
to appear obdurate. Much was at stake.

I took my friends' advice. I presented my report to the Governors
with a flexibility I could not have managed a few days before. I
advocated radical action, but I gave the faint-hearted an easy exit
route, accepting that perception – the iconic importance of studios – had to be weighed in the balance with the savings. (I
emphasised though, the cost of *not* making all the cuts.) The
Chairman and some Governors were four-square behind the full
unadulterated proposal – they wanted all the studio cuts; but some
of the Governors who had most banged the table about efficiency
were among the first to baulk at real action, fearful of the opposition studio cuts would provoke. I didn't rise to the bait: Terry and
Howell had prepared me well. I appeared open and understanding
while seething inside at the Governors' faint-heartedness. It was
duly agreed that Producer Choice and most of the cuts would go
ahead. The most sensitive closures would be delayed to see how the

facilities fared under the new market disciplines. The minutes of the meeting on Producer Choice went through four separate drafts before they could be agreed.

The Governors met alone over dinner the following Monday evening. While they dined Jane and I were the guests of Marjorie Wallace – Chief Executive of the charity SANE – at another tale of bloody intrigue, *Macbeth*, at the open-air theatre in Regent's Park. Hussey had been scrupulous and had not discussed the succession with me since the formal meeting with himself and Joel Barnett. But my intelligence was that he was quietly confident he would deliver his plan – that I would soon be Director-General. In the event, it was more difficult than he had anticipated. He started with half the board on side, a few opposed, and a middle group whose position was not clear (fence-sitting was a consummate skill of many BBC Governors). Hussey felt badly betrayed by one of his colleagues, whose vote he thought he'd been promised, but who seemed to have switched sides. It became a long evening. When Jane and I returned home from the theatre, they were still battling away, and there was no news. I went to bed and slept soundly. The Governors finally fought their way to a compromise in the early hours: Mike would serve for another eighteen months; I would succeed him as Director-General in the spring of 1993. I was awoken the next morning at 7 a.m. by a call from Howell to be told I was to be the next Director-General of the BBC. A triumphant Hussey had called Howell in the early hours, flushed with his success at the marathon dinner, but saying: 'It was stickier than I thought!'

I was to assume the precious mantle – the premier job in British broadcasting – indeed I was to lead the world's greatest cultural institution. I was thrilled, but not immediately jubilant, for I had been put into power by a coup, led by Hussey, designed to overthrow for the first time the established interests and power structures of the BBC. I also knew that the gradualists and the massive forces of inertia within the BBC would be hostile to my appointment.

Moreover, I had to mark time for eighteen months and to endure an uncomfortable handover with Michael Checkland. I had no doubt there would be many battles ahead, that we were far from the end of what would be a very long war. It was hard to feel joyous.

Later that morning, I was in the middle of a routine meeting with Tony Hall when Katie came in with a note asking me to go up to see the Chairman. Hussey was sitting bolt upright in his chair, stiff and solemn, looking moved and serious. He started to speak as I walked through the door, well before I could sit down. There was no flim-flam: 'You and Mike have behaved impeccably during a difficult period. The Governors want you to be the next Director-General. You will assume office in 1993.'

'Thank you, Chairman. I'm most grateful, and especially to you. The transition will be difficult, but I'll make it work.' I paused, mindful of my difficulties over studio closures: 'I have only one question, Chairman: you and I want change. The Governors sub-scribe to the objectives, but do they have the will to bring them about?' Hussey hesitated, then said quietly: 'I think they do.'

I went straight to see John McCormick, the BBC's gentle, hon-ourable Secretary, whose loyalties had been pulled in every direction by these events. At last I felt moved: I talked to him about the honour I felt, the responsibility I would have, my wonder that I could have made this incredible journey from Bootle to the high peaks of the BBC.

Minutes later I went to Mike's ten o'clock routine meeting with key staff. It was a taut occasion. Mike looked drained, but attended to the business chattily. He nodded to me at the end. I stayed behind. Everyone else fled nervously. 'Yes?' Mike said. 'Sorry. I thought you nodded for me to stay?' 'I'm thinking,' he responded blackly. I walked away in silence.

Half an hour later, he called me in: 'The Chairman is pressing me to stay. Do you want me to?' 'It won't be easy,' I responded, 'but I will try to make it work if you do. The problem will come if you don't allow me a role in decisions which take effect after you're

gone.' Mike spat back: 'If I stay I won't be a lame-duck DG.' Shortly
after, he walked unannounced into my office. 'I've decided to stay,'
he declared, and walked straight out again, before I could respond.

John Tusa, head of the World Service, reacted furiously to the
news of my appointment, demanding to see the Chairman, protesting that he had not been give a chance to apply.

In the evening a small group of old friends joined Jane and me,
JJ and Eliza, at home for a celebratory drink – including Terry
Burns, Nick and Gilly Elliott, Barry Cox and Katie, Peter
Mandelson, Greg Dyke and Sue, Polly Toynbee and Peter Jenkins,
Jonathan and Phillida Gili, Andrew Turnbull and Howell James.
The next day at the morning meeting there was a small toy duck on
Mike's desk. 'A friend gave me a present. As you see, it's not lame,'
he said with a defiant smile. I received warm, enthusiastic and
relieved letters of congratulation from some BBC colleagues, but
many were muted, no doubt torn between Mike and me. I received,
though, sackloads of correspondence from former ITV colleagues,
old friends and acquaintances. The letter that gave me the greatest
pleasure was from B. B. Cooper, my old and revered maths
teacher – writing to me in inimitable style from retirement in
Birmingham – bursting with pride in his old St Mary's pupil.

At the next meeting of the Board of Management, Checkland
began aggressively. 'I won't be a titular DG,' he declared, and
ignored me for the rest of the meeting. This made my colleagues
nervous and me gloomy. Patricia Hodgson said afterwards: 'He has
to go.' Eight days after my appointment, Mike abandoned my cherished News and Current Affairs building.

David Elstein, giving that year's McTaggart lecture at the
Edinburgh Television Festival, soon set out my challenge:

> The first two jobs John Birt has undertaken for the BBC –
> merging news and current affairs, getting onside with the
> politicians – are simply the essential preliminaries to the
> streamlining that will be required . . . If there is a rational

course of action that will secure the BBC's future, he is the
likeliest person to find it. Nobody yet in broadcasting has
built a career out of under-estimating John Birt!

During the long eighteen-month wait to become Director-General,
I set out – in David's words – to 'streamline' the BBC, to implement
Producer Choice. I was critically aided in the task by Michael Starks,
a BBC long-timer with the sort of take-no-prisoners qualities that
were in woefully short supply in the organisation. Starks had the
energy, the relentlessness and the cleverness to drive the biggest
project in the BBC's history. Sleepy old departments, directly
funded, with inadequate financial systems and no management
information had to be transformed into business units. They had to
be organised to produce a service of quality and to sell it at a price
a buyer was willing to pay. Every unit had to learn to manage every
aspect of its business.

There was no blueprint to which we could turn. None of the privatised nationalised industries had been as radical as we intended to
be. The reforms within ITV had been on a far smaller scale. We
had to begin by sorting our records, which were a shambles. There
was no adequate register of the BBC's capital assets. In addition, we
had literally hundreds of different accountancy systems across the
BBC, many of them unnecessarily bespoke and created at great
expense. How could we unify our systems, and have smooth and
speedy transactions between units when buying and selling began?
Did we have enough accountancy skill? I was soon advised by
Coopers and Lybrand that our financial capabilities were inadequate, at every level, with few exceptions. John Smith, who had
worked with me on the group that designed Producer Choice, was
the prime exception. Did our managers have the skills and compe-
tencies? Manifestly not: most BBC department heads regarded
themselves as team leaders, not managers. Many behaved like shop
stewards representing the interests of their people, not the wider
BBC. At best, they were administrators. Nor were most born to be

traders. Could they adapt? Some would flounder and leave, wholly unable to adjust; but many could and did acquire new skills for a new world, and prospered.

As the implementation process gathered momentum, it became clear that some of the barons of the old order plainly did not believe a new day would dawn. In some cases, it was a failure of imagination. The most bone-headed of the dinosaurs dragged their feet, believing – with diehard optimism – that they would be able to circumvent the new systems and to continue to operate the levers in secret as before. I wrestled with this obstructionist tendency in meeting after meeting for much of the implementation process.

How long would it take to introduce new IT systems, to retrain managers on an enormous scale, to make the huge changes necessary in almost every business unit before they were fit to trade? We were advised by Coopers and Lybrand that in an organisation of around thirty thousand people the task was mammoth, that we should take thirty months over it. The political imperative dictated that we had only eighteen months. It was clear to Hussey, Patricia, Howell and myself that we had to introduce Producer Choice in April 1993 – at the beginning of the BBC's financial and budgetary year – if we were to affect the Charter Review process with firm evidence, and not just a promise, that the BBC was really and truly on the path to efficiency, to offering the licence-payer value for money. It would be a race against time.

Over eighteen months, thousands of complex problems were addressed, new systems designed and introduced, an immense programme of training and mentoring launched. Margaret Salmon, the quiet, steely Yorkshirewoman brought into the BBC from Burton's as Director of Personnel, took a cool look at our central overheads and cut 1250 staff. A major redundancy programme was launched, on generous terms, so that every unit – in theory – would be lean and fit when trading began.

The unions resisted Producer Choice at every turn. The sweeping nature of the changes alarmed staff who had been used to a

BBC which traditionally moved at a snail's pace. They complained to their programme-making colleagues, who understandably supported them. David Attenborough protested: 'The BBC is being gravely eroded, the morale of its staff seriously damaged, and the very things that gave it its unique stature and strength destroyed.' David's virtuoso series of programmes for the BBC over the following decade – *The Private Life of Plants, The Life of Birds, The Blue Planet* – would offer compelling evidence to the contrary, but in 1992 he caught the general air of trepidation. In the summer, Michael Grade intervened in the debate. His timing was perfect. The BBC was in a high state of uncertainty; we were in the middle of the long handover between Checkland and myself; there was real nervousness about the imminent introduction of Producer Choice. Grade gave the McTaggart lecture at the Edinburgh Television Festival, the television industry's biggest platform, the annual gathering of all its clans. Michael's lecture was an act of vengeance, directed against Hussey and Checkland as well as me, carefully and skilfully drafted, playing on fear, designed to appeal to every programme-maker's prejudices, to every staff member's hostility to change. Grade made the case for the status quo, for no change, for a populist BBC. His lecture was vindictive, overstated, without dispassion. And he concluded:

> My nightmare is as follows: the BBC continues on its present course and dismembers itself in return for a licence fee renewal. Governments naturally hate putting up prices and continue to press for more cuts in return. The result is that the licence fee will become a dwindling asset, and this great institution become marginalised. All the human misery resulting from all the cuts becomes a sacrifice in vain. It must not be allowed to happen.

History would prove Grade wrong in every respect, but in 1992 his hysteria played well in the hall. The temperature rose, and it would stay hot for a long time. Hussey counter-attacked on the day, describing Grade as a 'Bourbon in red braces'. Jane and I were touring New Mexico when the lecture was delivered, and our holiday was interrupted by a journalist from the *Sunday Times* who tracked me down, with great ingenuity, for a comment. Number 10 let us know that they regarded Grade's speech as 'morally disgraceful – and only what was to be expected from the old-style television establishment'. Reforming the BBC plainly meant war. We had certainly taken the harder path.

The final death knell for the old order, which Michael Grade defended, came around the time he gave his lecture. The inadequate, creaking financial systems in Network Television produced the disaster that had always threatened. When the BBC's auditors, Coopers and Lybrand, conducted their normal annual audit of the accounts at the end of the 1991–2 financial year, they discovered that Network Television had overspent against budget by over a hundred million pounds. (The extent of the overspend was mitigated after the year had ended, but before the accounts were published, by collecting debts and other actions.) No one had known about or noticed the overspend. It had arisen because there was no meaningful forecast in Network Television of future spending, including contractually agreed items like sports rights, and because there was no effective control of the timetable of Network Television production. Without rudimentary financial procedures in place, spend had run ahead of budget. The root cause of Television's scandalous lack of control was not a few, insufficiently skilled or capable financial souls who happened to be working in Television Centre at the beginning of the 1990s, but generations of BBC Television executives who had brought no discipline or grip. Years of intense effort would be needed when I succeeded Michael Checkland – with new financial leadership, new systems and a vast influx of skilled outside recruits from the finance sector – before the BBC's financial operation would become sophisticated and reliable. In the short term, though, there was a silver lining:

the shame of the overspend reconciled more people within the BBC to the radically different future of Producer Choice.

It became clear that even if I had accepted the long handover to Michael Checkland, Hussey had not. The Chairman was still aiming to make life difficult for Mike, hoping he would go early. When that didn't work, the ever resourceful Hussey primed his contacts to see if Mike could be lured away with a fancy job offer. But Mike would stay – as I always believed he would – till the end, or at least to within a few weeks of the end. A little before the date of his intended departure, this normally equable, unflappable and generally unvengeful man finally snapped and let his feelings show. Questioned by Jon Snow at a public conference, he first described the length of the handover as 'ludicrous'. Then he said: 'It's a mistake to have a Chairman for ten years . . . when you're leading the BBC into the next century at the age of seventy-three, it is bizarre.' Checkland delivered his coup de grâce against Hussey: 'When we talk about FM, I want to be talking about Frequency Modulation not fuzzy kind of monsters!'

Michael Checkland's BBC was a huge step forward on Alasdair Milne's. I admired him for his plain, unfussy good sense. He brought calm and stability after the chaos of the Milne years. He was modest and unaffected, and ended the BBC's reputation for arrogance. We differed because Mike didn't want to make the good ship BBC sail faster than it wanted, and I believed the institution was at grave risk if it did not.

Producer Choice took effect in April 1993, a few months after I became Director-General. On that day, for the first time in its history, the BBC became a trading institution, and ceased to be a command economy. The change, to everyone's relief, went incredibly smoothly. It was an extraordinary achievement – though we didn't get everything right, and over the years modifications and simplifications had to be made. We started with too many business units. It took many managers a while to identify the optimum way of charging for some facilities and services, and in some areas there were too many small transactions – which irritated producers – when bulk purchase arrangements would have been more effective. We had a particular difficulty with some services – for example, library research – that had always been free to programme-makers and valued by them. When the true cost of providing these services was revealed by Producer Choice, and they had to be paid for, programme-makers jibbed at the price and – without stopping to think – blamed Producer Choice as if it were responsible for the high charges, rather than simply a system which had finally revealed the true and sometimes enormous cost of the services they had previously consumed for free.

There were unforeseen difficulties: it took a while for the large buying departments to learn that they needed proper long-term relations with their suppliers, sharing problems, and dealing with them together, if both sides were to be happy with the results. Problems emerged too when BBC programme-makers changed their behaviour following the introduction of Producer Choice. Some producers, although not many, went outside the BBC for their facilities, much as we had anticipated. More importantly, now that they held their own budgets, and now that facilities were no longer free but paid for, BBC producers used their new discretion to spend less on facilities – and more on other items, like the script – and they took more care to use facilities efficiently. As a result, there was even less demand for facilities than we had forecast, and more redundancies were needed. In practice, voluntary redundancy schemes meant that in some highly skilled areas where we had to shed staff we lost the more talented people – those our programme-makers most wanted to work with – and this was a great loss to the organisation.

The main sadness of Producer Choice was that in an organisation where staff had had a cradle-to-grave expectation of security, and a loyal commitment to the cause of the BBC, over ten thousand staff would be made redundant or transfer out during the 1990s, the first contraction in the BBC's history. Most BBC facilities staff would never get over the introduction of Producer Choice, and it would be raised at every staff meeting I attended for years. Producer Choice meant that forever after BBC staff – and those who departed – would see me as the demon agent of brutal change. Many would forever, and understandably, focus on the impact of Producer Choice on them personally – because it obliged them to work harder, or took away their security, or lost them their job. In any institution this would have caused resentment. In a creative institution, their hostility was vocally and widely expressed, and obscured the immense and historic gains Producer Choice heralded. For, despite the teething troubles, Producer Choice fulfilled – indeed surpassed – all our hopes. It enabled us to win a myriad of insights into our ways of operating that had previously eluded us; to learn, for the first time in our seventy-year history, how we spent our money; to begin spending it infinitely more effectively for the benefit of our licence-payers. Because of Producer Choice, our spend on programmes grew in the 1990s even though our licence income was pegged. By the end of the decade, Producer Choice meant that on average the cost of each BBC programme had *halved* in real terms. In every genre, the cost of our programmes dropped below the independent sector's. Over the 1990s, not thousands or millions but many *billions* of pounds were released from funding wastefulness and over-capacity and reinvested in programmes. The BBC had been even more bloated than any of us had appreciated. Whole new services were introduced, funded by Producer Choice. More money and lower unit costs meant that hundreds of thousands of hours of programmes were made that without Producer Choice would never have seen the light of day.

By the end of the 1990s, the balance of the BBC's workforce had changed fundamentally: there were far more programme-makers and journalists in the BBC and – despite oft-stated claims to the contrary – far fewer managers, support and facilities staff. The new system helped create a cohort of managers, much younger than their predecessors, who were confident, skilled in business methods and, in sharp contrast to previous generations, ready to be called to account, to take responsibility and not to blame it on the system.

Producer Choice also brought a new creative impetus to the BBC's networks, as commissioners and programme-makers exploited their new-found freedom and extra resources. Producer Choice signalled the end of real bureaucracy at the BBC – old-style command and control. It brought the biggest devolution of power and decision-making in the organisation's history. It changed the BBC's culture fundamentally – for ever and for the better – bringing transparency, rigour and accountability where obscurity, opaqueness and muddle had been the rule.

For most of its existence, the BBC had expanded on a tidal wave of revenue growth. Mrs Thatcher had put a stop to that. Producer Choice finally persuaded Britain's politicians that the BBC *had* become more efficient. Thereafter, they knew that any extra money for the Corporation would not disappear into thin air, but would be used to fund extra programmes. In the ensuing years, this new trust resulted in substantial additional funds for the BBC, enabling the organisation to grow and to embrace new broadcasting technologies and opportunities.

Producer Choice was the single most decisive change for the better during my time at the BBC, the long overdue and necessary proof that the BBC could sort itself out, that it could put its own affairs in order. But, by itself, Producer Choice would not be enough to see off the threat from Mrs Thatcher and her powerful cohort of supporters to change fundamentally the nature and role of the BBC when our Charter came up for renewal.

14

The Battle for the BBC

When I joined the BBC in 1987, it was not clear how and in what form the organisation would survive, for skirmishes and battles between the Corporation and the Conservatives had continued for years. During the 1980s, the drive for change in broadcasting had come from a powerful axis of Nigel Lawson, Nicholas Ridley, David Young and the Number 10 policy head Brian Griffiths. I had witnessed this threatening but clever and energetic band close-up at the infamous Downing Street Seminar, chaired by Mrs Thatcher, that I had attended in 1987 soon after joining the BBC. These men wanted to use market forces to blast open British broadcasting. They were attracted to a light-touch regulatory model, along the lines of the Australian and American systems, with minimal public service obligations on commercial broadcasters. They wanted greater competition to drive efficiency and to stamp out wasteful union practices. And they were ambitious to extract for the Exchequer the full value of the spectrum that broadcasters used for free.

The marketeers and their fellow travellers on the back benches also harboured radical thoughts about the BBC. Some were attracted to privatisation or to funding the BBC with advertising. Others wanted a rump BBC, with a £40 licence fee, pruned back to BBC2, Radio 3 and Radio 4. As far as I know, none of these groups ever developed a detailed blueprint for a radically different BBC, but there was a constant swirl of debate around the need for a fundamental root-and-branch reform of the organisation. Ranged against the reformers on all the broadcasting issues was the benevolent wing of the Conservative Party – enlightened paternalists like Willie Whitelaw, Douglas Hurd and David Mellor – who placed a far higher premium on public service and tradition. Both groups competed for Mrs Thatcher's support and – though her first instinct was with the free marketeers – she was not wholly in either camp, and she was always wary of taking on Willie Whitelaw.

Mrs Thatcher chaired a Cabinet sub-committee, which circled around these broadcasting issues endlessly. She would frequently open the meeting with the same fierce peroration with which she had begun on the previous occasion – often railing against the BBC – and Douglas Hurd or someone would say: 'But we settled that issue at the previous meeting, Prime Minister.' 'We did *not* settle it!' she would explode, and they would start again.

The first material Conservative assault on the BBC, in 1986, before I arrived, had been at the hands of the Peacock Committee, led by the earnest Scottish free-market economist; but the attempt backfired, for Peacock did not recommend advertising on the BBC, as had been expected. Rather, the free marketeers were handed a different prize: the tendering of the ITV franchises to the highest bidder, subject only to a modest quality hurdle. But, as events would prove, their interest in the BBC would not be easily deflected.

As the Corporation had come under increased scrutiny in the Thatcher era, it had withdrawn into its keep, viewing the Thatcher government and its radical ideas with disdain, as beyond the liberal pale. For her part, Mrs Thatcher had regarded Alasdair Milne as an arrogant public school toff, presiding over an unmanaged, out-of-control institution. Tory backbenchers were also viscerally hostile to the BBC, and for good measure the Murdoch press joined in to batter the Corporation, to ridicule it and to demand sweeping reform, most notably in a series of leaders in *The Times*.

Hussey's appointment as Chairman brought a brief lull in the hostilities. The BBC's critics could see immediately that this cheerful bluff old soldier shared their root prejudices. Michael Checkland was viewed at the beginning as brisk and businesslike, a bright, unaffected new broom. I was perceived to be bringing order to anarchy in News. But it was clear to me when I arrived at the BBC that the organisation was ill equipped and ill prepared to do battle with the Tory titans, at the peak of their power and self-confidence – for I soon discovered that the BBC had remarkably little knowledge about itself, or its position in the wider world, or what the newly emerging future of cable and satellite might hold. It also lacked the most basic insights into the broadcasting market place. Nor was there any repository of expertise for dealing with government on issues of policy. In short, the BBC had no corporate brain, no capacity to articulate and communicate a vision of its own future. I soon proposed to Michael Checkland, and he agreed, that we should put the capable Patricia Hodgson in charge of a unit, reporting to me, with responsibility for the BBC's corporate strategy, for dealing with government and regulators, and for formulating and monitoring compliance with editorial and other policy. Thus was BBC Policy and Planning born, the most powerful capability of its kind anywhere in European broadcasting. Patricia forged a powerful team: she was a great talent-spotter and brought into her unit over the years wave after wave of the best and the brightest from the strategy and policy worlds, driving her people hard, building up capability and knowledge. She and I were agreed that, if you had the best-considered plan, you were likely to win. And Patricia and I began to develop a plan for everything.

She and I would fight side by side and with great success on many fields in my thirteen years at the BBC, putting the organisation ahead

of the game again and again; but our early years together were difficult for Patricia, for Michael Checkland did not share my
enthusiasm for Policy and Planning, and downgraded its importance. Patricia often fumed with frustration, and considered
leaving – but she stayed and proved an invaluable companion as we
steered the BBC together through and out of the tempestuous
waters of the Thatcher era.

The challenges came thick and fast. I had not served out my first
twelve months at the BBC before Brian Griffiths, Mrs Thatcher's
policy chief, was confiding to me over dinner at L'Escargot that the
Prime Minister feared that 'The BBC's revolution is skin deep.' She
trusted the intentions of Hussey, Checkland and Birt; but she
doubted that Checkland had the compulsion and the confidence to
see a revolution through. The Lady was not yet convinced.

In 1988, under pressure from the DTI, the Home Office
announced that it was considering a madcap scheme – that BBC2
and Channel 4 would be removed from terrestrial transmitters and
transferred to the BSB satellite, once satellite had achieved 50 per
cent household penetration, thus depriving half of the population at
a stroke of receiving BBC2 and Channel 4. David Young explained
his reasoning to Hussey: 'There isn't enough terrestrial frequency for
advertising.' We managed to kick the idea into touch.

In the same year Douglas Hurd, as Home Secretary, launched a
White Paper on broadcasting, *Competition, Choice and Quality*. I had
intelligence from a government insider that Hurd, Kenneth Baker
and Geoffrey Howe had restrained Margaret Thatcher and Nigel
Lawson from announcing in the White Paper that the licence fee
would end in 1996, to be replaced by subscription. The key argument used by the BBC's friends in government to oppose this action
had been that we were beginning to sort ourselves out. Reforming
BBC News showed we meant business, they said. We had provided
just enough ammunition to stave off a deadly danger, for subscription was a lethal threat to the BBC. The BBC's public purposes were
inextricably bound up with its public funding via the licence fee.

Changing the nature of its source of funding would change the BBC itself. Subscription funding would put the BBC into the commercial arena, following commercial imperatives. We had drawn Mrs Thatcher's sting just in time, but not for ever.

Hurd's White Paper ushered in the cable and satellite age, embracing more choice for audiences. It imposed independent production on the established broadcasters, and endorsed Peacock's proposals for tendering ITV franchises. But the threat to the licence fee had been suspended, not removed. Looking over his shoulder at his Prime Minister, Hurd declared: 'I do not think the licence fee can be regarded as immortal.' New funding solutions for the BBC, including subscription, would be considered for the new Charter, after 1996. 'The Government looks forward to the eventual replacement of the licence fee,' the White Paper declared. In the meantime, the real value of the licence fee would be frozen. This in itself was a huge shock to the BBC's system, for the organisation had hitherto enjoyed ever rising revenues, funding costs, like pay and rights, that rose faster than inflation, in line with the rest of the industry and the wider economy. Holding the value of the licence fee constant put greater cost pressure on the BBC than any other major part of the public sector. However severe the financial blow, though, the BBC had had a lucky escape: we had lived to fight another day. Hurd's manoeuvrings had ensured that the final decisive battle for the BBC in the era of Conservative dominance would take place in the early 1990s, when the next Royal Charter would be settled.

I set out to lead the BBC out of its keep, to build bridges between the Corporation and every section of society – even to reach out to our enemies. We began by opening our doors, by engaging, by starting a dialogue. We held dinners in honour of every leading politician from the main parties. We invited a jolly mix of BBC insiders to these to provide glamour, wit and interest. From academia, industry and the arts, we called in outsiders of power and influence. And from politics we invited friends and associates of the

guest in question. We entertained at the Cup Final, Wimbledon
and the Proms. Every Christmas we held parties in the Council
Chamber, full of leading players from the BBC, from politics and
from every walk of life. We took our ideas right into the heart of the
political parties, and to every major interest group, explaining ourselves and what we were trying to do. We made sure that all the
senior civil servants in Whitehall knew what we were about. We said
we understood we had to change and had the determination to do
so. Gradually, over many years, we shed the BBC's old image: the
charge of arrogance ceased to be made, and slowly we began to
appear like a lively, confident, open, outgoing institution. The BBC
finally began to lose its anonymity.

In our working dealings with Government, Opposition and other
major institutions, we set out to be forthcoming, to be candid about
our difficulties and intentions, to be straightforward, straight-dealing
and undefensive. The temperature dropped slowly. The BBC still
occasionally provoked bile and vitriol, but less often.

We set out to signal that the new BBC would not resist or be dis-
dainful of competition. We invited ITV executives to BBC occasions
for the first time. When Sky started in February 1989, I attended the
launch and went on afterwards to their studios on an industrial
estate in Osterley Park – a far cry from the totemic premises that
had characterised British broadcasting hitherto. My attendance held
powerful symbolism. Rupert Murdoch and his Chief Executive
Andrew Neil were surprised but pleased to see me. In media interviews on the night, I warmly welcomed Sky to the broadcast family.
We had no illusions, though, about the momentum Murdoch was
building. I had in effect joined the BBC at the very end of the terrestrial age. Our TV channels were about to experience a
competitive onslaught. Soon we would lose our seventy-year
monopoly of national radio.

Mrs Thatcher invited Hussey, Barnett, Checkland and myself to a
dinner at Number 10 in February 1989. She was relaxed, cordial and

good humoured. She accepted that the BBC was changing, but she still felt that 'There's too much rubbish! You've no business putting on *Dallas*, *Dynasty* and horror films!' She had noticed the films while channel-hopping late at night. She queried whether we were clear about our purpose. Most emphatically, she focused over and over again on the iniquity of what she termed 'the compulsory levy', for she could not bring herself to call it a licence fee.

At the dinner Hussey was in jovial-old-buffer mode, excited to be there, talking too much. He and Barnett dominated the BBC's side of the discussion, freely offering views about broadcasting issues, occasionally skating on thin ice as they trespassed into areas of which they had little grasp. Mrs Thatcher plainly had his measure. There was little room for Checkland to speak. I said even less, intervening only a few times – briefly and diplomatically – to rescue some point. The next day, one of Mrs Thatcher's aides called, to my bemusement and amusement, to tell me that she had stayed behind after the dinner for a whisky and a gossip and that Mrs Thatcher had said: 'When Hussey's term ends, we should make John Birt Chairman of the BBC!'

Our problems with Mrs Thatcher had not gone away, but they were less intense. And her easier demeanour gave our friends more confidence: two months later I shared a platform with Douglas Hurd and sat back with pleasure as I heard him explaining – in a new emphasis – the difficulties of replacing the licence fee with subscription.

Attacks, though, still came from other quarters. In 1989, our fledgling competitor Sky flexed its muscles when Rupert Murdoch lambasted the established broadcasting order from a pulpit at the Edinburgh Television Festival. Murdoch said UK broadcasting was run by an elite that made dull programmes; that we were obsessed by class and the past; that we were cowed by government; that by contrast US TV offered a cornucopia of choice. Neither I nor anyone else, to our shame, found the right words on the night to contradict him. I counter-attacked the following day, however,

declaring his portraits of British and American TV to be carica-
tures. I suggested that no other television system in the world
succeeded better than the UK's in serving all needs, tastes and interests. None had done better justice to every strand of opinion, or was
readier to expose wrongdoing or to test the policies of government.
But there was always scope for extra choice, and we welcomed Sky.

Within a few months, the BBC's critics at the heart of government were in retreat. The free-market wing lost its most ferocious
and able advocate when Nigel Lawson resigned after falling out
with Mrs Thatcher. David Young had already moved on. The Prime
Minister herself was severely weakened, but radical ideas still held
sway in the party. In the reshuffle following Lawson's departure,
Douglas Hurd was made Foreign Secretary, John Major Chancellor.
David Mellor was pulled back into the Home Office, where he had
worked before, to steer the Broadcasting Bill through Parliament for
the new Home Secretary, David Waddington. This was the Bill that
would introduce the tendering of ITV franchises, following
Peacock's recommendations. I had privately lobbied the Home
Office against the proposal, and I had attacked tendering publicly
for its likely impact on the quality and range of ITV's programming.

Mellor himself had little sympathy for the notion. Though only
forty, he was already an unusually confident and experienced minister, having served in government for eight years. He was also
deeply disgruntled with Mrs Thatcher, and had become truculent,
insubordinate and devil-may-care, ready to do his job his way or not
at all. Setting out single-handedly and without authority to improve
the Bill, he introduced a far higher quality hurdle, and the safeguard
that a contract could be awarded to a lower bidder if the programme promise was of exceptional quality. He bulldozed these
changes through, tilting the balance towards quality. Home
Secretary David Waddington bravely covered Mellor's flank, supporting the changes before a politically weakened though still feisty
Mrs Thatcher – who was none the less unreconciled to Mellor's bold
buccaneering. One weekend I was called at home by a civil servant

in her private office at Number 10, who had been charged with finding out what on earth Mellor was up to. I was the wrong person to ask: I was applauding his surprise manoeuvrings from the sidelines and said I wasn't able to help.

David Mellor's amendments to the legislation stopped ITV turning overnight into an out-and-out commercial network, but he still could not prevent a material shift in the centre of gravity of the system. Within a few years, ITV would be dominated by three new-comers – Gerry Robinson, Michael Green and Clive Hollick – with no prior experience of broadcasting or programmes. The old, difficult, curmudgeonly ITV leadership had been unstrategic, conservative and resistant to change; but they had had first-hand experience of, and a commitment to, programmes, and had created a fine and powerful creative tradition which now would move into gradual decline. The ousting of my old mentor David Plowright from Granada less than two years later would be the defining event in this sad transition.

The Tory right may have been in retreat, but it had not gone away and it could still bite. In February 1990, Norman Tebbit described the BBC as that 'insufferable, smug, sanctimonious, naïve, guilt-ridden, wet, pink orthodoxy of that sunset home of third-rate minds of that third-rate decade, the Sixties!'

In May, Mrs Thatcher asked me to a lunch at Chequers for South Africa's President de Klerk. I drew up behind Murdoch, who was driving himself and his wife at the time, Anna. Mrs Thatcher greeted me warmly and introduced me to the South African Foreign Secretary: 'This is the man who's *trying* to make the BBC a professional organisation. He's succeeding quite well. But I still hear of occasions when he does not!' She turned to me with a mischievous twinkle: 'Is that fair?'

Over lunch, Charles Powell demonstrated his invariably good judgement and prescience. He gave an optimistic assessment of the talks about the future of South Africa and predicted confidently: 'de Klerk and Mandela [who had just been released] will work together and push it through.' (Charles Powell was not the only person of good judgement in Mrs Thatcher's circle: a few days later, the independently minded Bernard Ingham, in no one's pocket, said to me: 'The Labour Party is doomed until it gets to the Blair generation!') As we mingled after the Chequers lunch, Cecil Parkinson teased Anna Murdoch: 'You'd better succeed as a novelist as your husband's losing so much money on Sky!' Mrs Murdoch nodded in vigorous and unamused agreement.

There was a hostile motion about the BBC at the Conservative Party conference in October 1990, encouraged by party Chairman Kenneth Baker to please the crowd. As the relevant minister, David Mellor had to give the response from the platform, but he refused to please. Rather, he defended the BBC, and left the stage to only muted applause. The Conservative backbencher John Wheeler, a shrewd judge of his party, told me at this time that the licence fee remained in the balance, but that it might yet survive. Even weakened, the Tories remained at heart a zealous, reforming and determined party.

Just before the conference opened, the BBC had been dealt a blow. For the further encouragement of reform, 3 per cent was knocked off the value of the licence fee. This was in the same week that I began to lead the Television Resources Study, which would lead to major cuts in BBC capacity and to the decision to introduce Producer Choice. The following month Geoffrey Howe resigned, precipitating a crisis and, within weeks, Mrs Thatcher's resignation. John Major became the new Prime Minister, Kenneth Baker Home Secretary. An election was due within eighteen months. We had to be ready for either a Conservative or Labour government with our case for the renewal of the BBC's Charter.

Michael Checkland proposed that he and I should steer the Charter process, and that Howell James and Patricia Hodgson should drive it. The management consultants, McKinsey and Co., were brought in to help us build our case. The young Matthew

With Robin Butler on the Milford Track, New Zealand, 1998

With Chris Smith in mid-Wales, 1999

Friday football with Greg Dyke, 1999

Marmaduke Hussey, BBC Chairman when I became the twelfth Director-General in 1992. Our relationship was to sour (BBC)

With Michael Checkland at Broadcasting House, 1987. Despite our differences, there was much I admired in this plain, no-nonsense man

With some of the Board of Management in 1987. From left to right: Michael Grade, Bill Cotton, Michael Checkland and David Hutch

Ron Neil (seated, left) and me with our news team, including Jenny Abramsky, Ian Hargreaves (standing, centre), and Tony Hall and Samir Shah (standing, right) in 1988

At the Proms with John Major, 1995. Joanna Trollope is directly behind us (Press Association)

Receiving an Emmy from David Frost in New York, 1995

Above The BBC's top team in 1999: (seated, left to right) John Smith, Colin Browne, Will Wyatt, Margaret Salmon, Tony Hall, Patricia Hodgson. (Standing, left to right) Mark Byford, Ron Neil, Rod Lynch, Rupert Gavin

Right Key staff in 1999: (from left to right) Sonia Cooper, Clare Riley and Katie Kay

Among the best BBC programmes of the 1990s were *The Human Body*, *Pride and Prejudice*, *Absolutely Fabulous*, the *Panorama* interview with Princess Diana, *The Royle Family* and *Teletubbies*

Goodbye party in January 2000 at Television Centre with, top to bottom: Alan Yentob; Norman Blackwell (left) and Nick Lovegrove; Penny Cobham and David Mellor; Virginia Bottomley; Patricia Hodgson; with Jane, leaving the BBC for the last time as Director-General, 2000

At Buckingham Palace to be knighted, with Jane, and Ida and Leo Birt, 1998

Outside 20 Forthlin Road in Liverpool, Paul McCartney's family home, which I persuaded the National Trust to acquire (National Trust)

Jane with Sulayman, JJ (left) and Fozia (right); Adam and Eliza, 2002

Bannister – who had put the BBC's London radio station, GLR, on the creative map – was made the project manager. Checkland sensibly wanted to open up the debate about the BBC's future right across the organisation – in true Maoist fashion, to let a thousand flowers bloom. Fifteen task forces were set up containing the best and the brightest of the BBC's young, the corporation's most challenging minds, each group examining a particular role of the BBC – as cultural patron, as technological innovator, as information provider and so on. There was no route map. The task forces would explore the terrain. Then we would work out what to do next. Our bright young things charged all over the BBC, turning over every stone, airing every prejudice, trampling on every cherished notion. In the process, Tim Gardam, the live-wire from *Panorama* – later Director of Programmes at Channel 4 – famously accused the ancient cultural warrior from Radio 3, John Drummond, of being 'tainted by experience'.

A few months after we began the Charter Review process, I was appointed Director-General, though still with eighteen months to go before I was due to take office. Checkland remained involved, but increasingly I took the reins, conspiring regularly with Howell and Patricia. I struck a close bond with Nick Lovegrove and Norman Blackwell, the able, experienced and skilful consultants from McKinsey. And I started private, off-the-record discussions with Home Secretary Kenneth Baker.

The new Prime Minister John Major and I had a natural affinity. We were almost of the same age, both grammar school boys from striving families that had known hard times. I had first encountered John Major in 1987 – when he was still Chief Secretary – when I had had to intervene at a BBC party to rescue him. A drunken BBC current affairs producer had cast aside the impartiality and political independence required of a member of BBC staff and was outrageously abusing him and the Conservative government, castigating Major for all their evil works. Major had graciously accepted my apology, and, far from alleging that this was behaviour to be expected of the BBC, suggested the opposite. Subsequently, I arranged tickets for him and his family to attend the Last Night of the Proms, and, in April 1990, Jane and I held a dinner for him and Norma at Broadcasting House – by which point he was Chancellor. It was easy to form a bond with the gentle, music-loving Norma, who, over the following years, often wrote to me for help in tracking down Radio 3 programmes or TV concerts she had missed. Jane was well used to sitting next to leading politicians for an evening, but she judged John Major most unusual, for he had listened, enquired, was keen to understand her, and had encouraged dialogue. He had also demonstrated an acute understanding of the reforms in progress at the BBC, and was aware of the price I had paid for driving them. After the dinner, Jane declared that John Major was an unusually sensitive man, and predicted he would go far!

Shortly after he became Prime Minister, a backbench MP lobbed a softball to him at Question Time about BBC reporting of the Iraqi conflict, offering him a chance to give the BBC a ritual bashing. He answered, as Mrs Thatcher would never have done: 'I believe what the BBC are doing, in what has already been some remarkable reporting, is trying to keep proper balance.' For John Major the BBC – alongside cricket, thatched cottages and warm beer – was part of the Britain he most enjoyed. A few weeks into office, he came to lunch in the same room where Mrs Thatcher had almost handbagged John Cole just two months before. At the end of the Thatcher visit, I had stood on the pavement outside Broadcasting House with her for five minutes, chewing over the conversation at lunch. Unnoticed by her, a silent crowd gathered – but they kept a respectful distance. When, weeks later, I started talking to John Major in exactly the same spot, an admiring throng quickly crowded right up to their new, approachable premier. He chatted to them warmly, signing autographs. But John Major still presided over Mrs Thatcher's legacy. The forces at work within the Conservative Party did not change, even if power tilted towards the moderate wing. At an early dinner, the new Home Secretary,

Kenneth Baker, soon told me: 'You know, the BBC still has no friends!' Baker complained about our inefficiency. I gave him a private briefing about Producer Choice – still not yet introduced – explaining just how radical an impact it would have. Behind his beaming, Brylcreemed exterior, Kenneth Baker was a learned and erudite man – but he was also a man for schemes. He judged, he told me, that the BBC needed not only to transform its efficiency but to slim down, to rid itself of local radio and Radio 1 and 2, to consider advertising at the margin, late night on BBC1 and BBC2, to generate the extra revenues he was sure we would need. I listened and asked questions and tried to draw him out.

Within the BBC, the task forces were examining everything the organisation was doing, and what more we should do. I was troubled. The process was producing some interesting proposals, but we were in danger of complacently asserting the value of the status quo, and assuming the benefits of expansionism, as if they were self-evident. No strong, over-arching principles were emerging for piloting the BBC into a new world. I myself had firm convictions about a BBC guided by creativity, decent values, seriousness of purpose, and a commitment to being a modern, efficient organisation; but I too had not yet defined a set of principles we could set our compass by. I was brought to my senses by a single conversation with the eccentric but acute and brilliant David Cox, my old colleague from LWT who had inherited the mantle of *Weekend World*. David asked to see me, and spoke firmly and bluntly. ITV had lost control of its future, he said, because it had failed to see the challenge of Thatcherism and to frame its own response to it. Unless the BBC could provide a convincing and compelling answer to the question 'Why, in a world of proliferating TV and radio networks, do we need a BBC *at all*?' we would not win the Charter debate and maintain control of our destiny. There and then he challenged me to provide a justification for our huge public funding.

Thanks to David Cox, and to his friendly but forceful candour, I began there and then the journey that would lead to the proposition

we finally set out in *Extending Choice* – the document which would
define the BBC's shape, role and purposes for the next period of its
history, which would enable us to win the argument with the main
parties and with the public at large for the continuation of a strong
BBC in the new age of broadcasting, and which would effectively
become my personal manifesto. David elicited from me, and helped
me develop, a first response to his question, and I went on to batten
down the argument with Howell James and Patricia Hodgson.

The role of the BBC in an age of multiple television and radio
services would be to do those things that the market would not, or
which would be ever more at risk in a rapidly expanding and
inevitably more competitive broadcasting market. Public funding
could be justified only if we were different and distinctive. The BBC
would protect, sustain and nurture Britain's unique national culture,
husbanding our art, heritage and traditions. We would create space
for Britain's greatest talents – whether writers, directors, actors,
comedians, musicians, composers or artists – to produce innovative
and challenging work, to give expression to a unique British voice.
The BBC would safeguard the quality of Britain's national debate,
providing serious coverage of events of significance at home and
abroad, of the trends that really shaped people's lives, reporting
them with an unmatched pool of journalists of authority and
expertise. And we would maintain and develop a set of programmes
that would allow the nation's politicians, commentators and the
electorate at large to dissect and to debate the questions of the day.
We would expand the horizons of every individual, offering a comprehensive series of programmes that would take them to the
frontiers of understanding about the natural world, science and history, or introduce them to great accomplishment in the arts. In all
our programmes, we would aspire to the highest quality and standards – to excellence of thought, language and craft, and to high
ethical standards. We would be British broadcasting's benchmark. In
short, the BBC would extend choice. We would be a cherished and
invaluable complement to the world of commercial broadcasting.

And such a vision was possible only with public funding. Any other form of financing would change our programme purposes and produce a BBC indistinguishable from commercial broadcasters.

The BBC – we declared in *Extending Choice* – would not only provide a unique programme service, it would also be at least as lean and efficient as the market place, embrace modern management ideas, be open, transparent and accountable as never before, responsive, attuned to the needs of our licence-payers.

I suggested to my colleagues that we needed to argue for our Charter from first principles and from a position of some humility, that we should not appear to presume we had a God-given right to eternal existence. There was some discomfort among the task forces and the senior management group with these ideas. Some wanted a more assertive and demanding proposition. Could we not simply fight on our record? Surely the Tories would not dare take us on? I urged them to look at what had happened to ITV. We could be savaged by subtle as well as blatant means. We should do only what we thought was right, and what would carry wide support, but we did need to respond to the legitimate questions that were being asked of us. We should not take anything for granted.

Others were uncomfortable with the high-ground vision for the BBC's programmes in *Extending Choice*. Did this mean we would turn our back on popular programming? No: every household paid a licence fee; every household must watch or listen to BBC programmes for significant amounts of time each week; but our licence-payers needed to feel that the BBC offered them a unique mix of programmes they could not in the round find elsewhere. The BBC would embrace every programme genre – comedy and quizzes as well as drama and documentary; but we couldn't just be ITV plus. The BBC's programmes needed always to strive to be distinctive, to move the genre on, to innovate, to make demands of the audience, not to pander to it. Nick Lovegrove of McKinsey – who had brought an outsider's rigour to challenging, refining and helping shape our emerging thinking – began formally drafting

Extending Choice in New York while making arrangements for his wedding.

I tried out the headline ideas on Neil Kinnock. The general election was imminent: he might well be the next Prime Minister. It was impossible not to like this well-meaning man, brimful of energy and ideas. Neil had shown extraordinary vision and determination in leading the Labour Party away from the brink – away from the regressive, interventionist, anti-market politics framed by Labour militants in the early 1980s. But, as yet, I did not feel personally that Labour had journeyed far enough. When we met and talked, Neil was as enthusiastic and supportive of the BBC as ever, embracing the aspirational programme vision in *Extending Choice* and firmly endorsing the principle of a better-managed, more efficient and more accountable BBC. Neil was bursting with ideas of what he could do for the BBC if he became Prime Minister: he would secure long-term funding for us, a higher licence fee, a firm place for us in the British film industry. He joked: 'Sky won't prosper if we make them take down all their dishes!'

On 11 December 1991 John Major returned to London from the Netherlands, where he had negotiated special terms for the UK in the Maastricht Treaty. The Prime Minister came straight to my Christmas party at Broadcasting House, flushed with success, exuding elation and triumph, mixing in and staying till the end. That evening a modest, unaffected and mild-mannered John Major, a year into his premiership, was fêted by the British creative community, most of whom were on the left. And the powerful symbolism of a Conservative Prime Minister turning up for the first time in memory at a BBC Christmas party was lost on no one.

John Major won the election in April 1992 with a narrow majority, and – in a stroke of great good fortune for the BBC – appointed David Mellor to the Cabinet in the new post of Secretary of State for National Heritage, putting him in charge of broadcasting. Mellor and I met over a series of dinners at Green's Restaurant in St James's, just the two of us huddled over a table in a private booth.

At the first meeting, in April 1992, he set out his stall in a firm but friendly message. The BBC had to change, he said: 'The status quo is not an option.' It was a 'stupid decision' by Governors to have me hanging around in the wings for eighteen months to take over from Checkland; but if, as Director-General, I could define the BBC's purposes convincingly, if I could promise to overhaul the institution, if I could transform its efficiency, he felt for his part he could deliver the BBC whole, and avert any disastrous amputations. I told Mellor of Kenneth Baker's view that Radio 1, Radio 2 and local radio should be taken away from us because they duplicated what the market already provided. Mellor disagreed: he said that if we could refashion these services and make them distinctive, he believed he could win the argument in his party for us to retain them. I explained the radical transformation of the BBC's efficiency that would result from Producer Choice, and I laid out the programme proposition that would be at the heart of *Extending Choice*, our argument for Charter Renewal. Mellor endorsed the approach roundly.

He moved promptly and decisively to take advantage of his honeymoon period. Just a few weeks into his term of office, Mellor appeared on David Frost's Sunday-morning programme on TV-am and effectively cut short the decade-long debate within his party about the licence fee:

> All kinds of ideas have floated past my nose about alternative
> ways of funding the BBC. I don't want to stop anyone
> wafting a few across me again. But I'm absolutely clear about
> one thing and that is that the idea will have to be a very good
> one . . . because I've yet to find one that actually had the
> simplicity of the licence fee.

Events moved quickly after this remarkable statement. Three days later, I explained the *Extending Choice* principles to the Governors at our annual conference at Lucknam Park, and David Mellor appeared the following day to talk to both boards, setting out the challenge for the BBC with cheerful ferocity. In part Mellor was offering me covering fire against any faint-hearts among Governors or among the senior management team. He demanded a strong, intellectually robust proposition from the BBC, a statement of principle and belief, not one based on yesterday's notions. It must be rigorous and not defensive. Inefficiency must end. It would be tough to win the argument for the licence fee. The BBC must be 'for the council house dweller in Gateshead as well as for John Julius Norwich'. John Tusa – soon to retire – took Mellor to task and they tussled. Tusa argued, in defiance of our emerging proposition, that offering competition to commercial broadcasters was a sufficient justification for the BBC. Mellor was coruscating: 'That is not a load-bearing concept! It's not an argument! The BBC is funded by a tax. You've got to give a full justification why.'

Mellor went on at the conference to insist – and we acquiesced – that the publication of *Extending Choice*, intended for the summer, should be delayed until his own Green Paper on the BBC was ready for publication. (Mellor later told me privately that the Green Paper was a long way from being ready; that the early drafts he had inherited did contain proposals for privatising parts of the BBC, including Radios 1 and 2.)

In June I took a risk. I was a Visiting Fellow at Nuffield College, Oxford – a postgraduate centre specialising in political, economic and social policy. Jack Straw, Patricia Hewitt and Terry Burns were among the other Visiting Fellows. I gave a confidential seminar to Nuffield, unveiling in some depth my thinking about the BBC's future. I was nervous of the reception I would receive on the left. In the event the *Extending Choice* vision played well. The reactions of Jack Straw and Patricia Hewitt were especially heartening. A new concept of public service, hostile to old elites, seemed to be gaining ground across the political divide. I left elated, confident in the robustness of the BBC's proposition. After many years of bitter disputation, I felt there was a real prospect of peace at Westminster for the BBC.

At one of our dinners in July, Mellor was slightly less confident. He told me he faced difficulties with his colleagues. The back-benchers were rumbling. There was 'an overwhelming need' to demonstrate that the BBC meant business on efficiency. Sparing my blushes he told me I was the best argument for maintaining the BBC: my commitment to the programming high ground; my deter-mination to create a modern, efficient organisation was the clinching argument for him with his colleagues. I had credibility. It was hard, he said, to protect the Governors. They were felt to have had a poor record historically in keeping the BBC on course. We would need to redefine and focus their role if they were to survive. BBC1 did not seem to be a public service network: it was hard to defend and needed to be more distinctive. The argument for the BBC to retain the radio networks looked 'OK'; but Mellor jumped at my suggestion that the BBC should open up radio by introducing a voluntary quota of 10 per cent of independent radio production, saying that that would win the argument with his sceptical free-market colleagues for retaining BBC Radio whole.

Ten days later a bombshell burst: the story of David Mellor's relationship with Antonia de Sancha broke on the front pages, and I understood in a flash why our dinners had always started and finished early. I was distraught. I greatly liked and admired David. Moreover, I had become confident that our strong alliance would see the BBC through to a new Charter. I wrote him a letter of support. 'There's hardly anyone who will not want to see you win through. Maintain your dignity; hold your patience; the prob-lem will gradually go away.' I was wrong. John Major stood by David Mellor for almost two months, but the attrition was too great, and David finally resigned. I worked with many politicians over the years, from all parties, and generally successfully. David Mellor was a rarity: he combined conviction and ability. He was in politics to make the world a better place. He had fought coura-geously in the trenches for public service broadcasting, more so than any other politician of his generation. With his quick lawyer's mind, he dissected issues easily. He was a powerful and fluent advocate, energetic, bold and street-smart. David Mellor knew how the world worked and how to make the right thing happen. I would miss him.

In fact, David and I stayed in touch, and he helped the BBC behind the scenes. And he and I combined effectively one more time. We were on the same side along with Charles Powell in a knock-out football tournament at David Frost's sixtieth-birthday celebration. Our team reached the final. At full time, the scores were level. The golden goal in extra time would be the decider. David Mellor took a throw-in, aiming perfectly at me. I rose above the mass of teenagers and ancients and glanced the ball thrillingly past goalkeeper David Frost's outstretched hand into the far corner of the net!

I had a second bombshell the month after Mellor's resignation: Howell James was lured away by his old champion David Young to lucrative work at Cable and Wireless. Howell had become, and would remain, a close friend, but the loss of my most trusted adviser, of my best BBC companion – with his dash, exuberance and dazzling wit – left a great hole in my life. Howell stayed at Cable and Wireless for two years, before moving on to Number 10 to become John Major's political secretary.

Peter Brooke, the new Secretary of State, was a courteous, gentlemanly, old-school Tory who was altogether more formal and conventional than David Mellor. Brooke didn't want to plot at secret dinners, and I worked instead with the senior civil servants at the Department of National Heritage, who continued to report that the outcome for the BBC was uncertain. We worked together on a tighter definition of how the BBC could become more accountable. Many of the BBC's senior managers had a long-standing tribal hostility to Governors, and were attracted to any notion that distanced them from the BBC's affairs, preferably by their abolition. I disagreed, believing strongly that the Governors were the best safeguard of the BBC's role and independence; but I accepted that their remit needed closer definition. In the absence of such clarity, Governors continually trespassed on matters which were self-evidently the responsibility of management, or which were simply trivial.

So, for the first time in the BBC's history, we closely defined the Governors' role, identifying them as the custodians of the licence-payer's interest. Their job would be not to manage the organisation but to vouchsafe that BBC managers had the right strategy for meeting the public's long-term interest, and to check that management was achieving that strategy in every respect, making the right programmes, spending the licence fee efficiently, ensuring the BBC complied with editorial and other policies. Until the Hussey era, the Governors had performed lamentably in monitoring the BBC's efficiency. I undertook, when I became Director-General, to redesign the BBC's processes so that Governors could truly fulfil their function – which, working with the new Secretary, Michael Stevenson, I did.

During the autumn of 1992, I had intelligence that the young Turks at the Treasury had pressed at the last minute for the government's Green Paper to declare the BBC to be a publisher only, privatising its programme departments and facilities. The Treasury was briefed about Producer Choice – by now in the final stages of preparation – and withdrew its challenge.

Patricia and I shared our ever-being-refined draft of *Extending Choice* with the officials who were writing the government's Green Paper. The response was gratifying: they found it 'lucid and compelling'. The Green Paper, finally published in November 1992, was an elegant statement of the questions and challenges the BBC needed to address. Peter Brooke had followed the lines laid down by David Mellor. Two days later – sitting alongside a soon-to-depart Michael Checkland – I launched the BBC's response, *Extending Choice*, seen by all observers as addressing the very questions the Green Paper had just put. The collaboration between the government and the BBC was all too evident. The government had not committed itself definitively to all the terms of a new Charter, but it was plain to all that – after a decade of vicious debate about the BBC, of threats to terminate the licence fee, of proposals for tearing the organisation apart – the BBC now had a steady and secure future, albeit as a reformed institution. We still had to close the end-game, but we had manifestly piloted our way successfully through the stormy, rock-infested seas of the Thatcher era to the calmer waters of Majorism with a mixture of good fortune, instinct and skill. We had outflanked the hard-liners in the nick of time with our own ideas, actions and proposals, averting someone else's being imposed upon us. But everything we had planned would benefit our licence-payers. We were only going to do what we ought to do. And we had won the argument while maintaining our independence and carrying opinion across the parties. An organisation that in 1987 had largely been friendless had reached out and built significant bonds of trust.

It would be my job, however, as the BBC's twelfth Director-General, to deliver on all the promises we had made to secure our Charter – and that would prove to be an enormously difficult and dangerous path.

15

Modernising the BBC

During the long wait to be the twelfth Director-General of the BBC in 1992, I joined a group on a three-week trek in the Himalayas, climbing Annapurna in winter to around sixteen thousand feet. Up each day before dawn, we were sound asleep in our tents soon after sunset. As we tramped, we were surrounded by the overpowering splendour of the Himalayan wilderness, a towering jumble of sharp peaks on every side, their every detail crystal clear in the pure, cold air. All day we were either pulling ourselves up – or stopping ourselves hurtling down – steep, rough, rocky mountain tracks. There were no roads or cars, phones or modern conveniences. We showered under icy waterfalls. As we climbed higher, I found myself wading through deep snow, occasionally falling through the frozen crust. At the highest point, I was at the limits of my endurance. But I returned home leaner and fitter, with my soul purged of all the poison built up during my first years at the BBC, and with a dynamism, energy and sense of urgency that others noted and commented upon. I felt ready to take on the mantle of the top job in British broadcasting, and prepared to complete the task of bringing the BBC into the modern age.

From its earliest days, there had been a disjunction between the BBC and its senior management. BBC wags in the 1920s had poked fun at the stuffy bureaucracy. In the 1930s, *Ariel*, the BBC's in-house magazine, carried complaints from staff:

> The BBC machine is destroying the individuality of its men and women.

> Please give us a little more space . . . Letters will do something to dispel the curious idea current in some sections of the press that the BBC staff suffer . . . under the heel of dictatorship.

A staff member in 1936 proposed some questions for an examination paper for a proposed BBC management development course:

> Question 1: Consider the expansion of the Administration Division: how in your opinion could it be most expensively extended?

> Question 2: Disentangle the line of red tape running through the Corporation.

> Question 3: What is the place, if any, of broadcasting at the Corporation?

In 1942 BBC staff member George Orwell wrote:

> The thing that strikes me in the BBC . . . is not so much the ultimate futility of what we are doing, as the feeling of frustration, the impossibility of getting anything done, even a successful piece of scoundrelism. Our policy is so ill-defined,

the disorganisation so great, there are so many changes of
plan, the organisation is so over-staffed, that numbers of
people have almost nothing to do. I [am] just footling
around, doing imbecile things . . .

Malcolm Muggeridge described the BBC in the 1950s as an organisation that

came to pass silently, invisibly; like a coral reef, cells multi-
plying until it was a vast structure, a conglomeration of
studios, offices, cool passages along which many passed to
and fro; a society, with its laws and dossiers and revenue and
easily suppressed insurrection.

Sir Talbot Duckmanton, the Director-General of the BBC's sister
organisation in Australia, memorably described managing a public
service broadcaster as 'like pushing a mattress up a spiral staircase'.

The internationally renowned sociologist Tom Burns wrote of the
decline of the BBC's management in the early 1960s, suggesting that
it had 'faded into chronic diffidence and tentativeness', that its role
was 'subsidiary', and its approach 'hesitant, almost guilty'.

In the 1970s, however, the writer John McGrath lamented that 'The
BBC has altered its structure. Centralised control, elaborate
systems of command, supervision, check and review have
been introduced. And . . . the bully boys have moved in to stay.'

The BBC I joined had been a confederation of tribes – sometimes
warring, sometimes combining – loosely bound by a set of values,
but with no guiding brain or real central authority, clustering
around a set of powerful personalities, the BBC's chieftains, who
guarded their fiefdoms fiercely. The BBC I joined would have still

seemed familiar to Orwell. It looked in on itself, obsessed with its own politics, with no strategic faculty, no analytical capability, no depth of understanding about any aspect of its business. Over-populated by white males, the BBC was additionally weakened by a failure fully to appreciate and reflect the richness and diversity of wider society. It had failed to train its staff in the skills and compe-tencies common in the best modern corporations. And the BBC's financial, marketing and personnel functions were antiquated, a long way behind best practice in the private sector. The BBC was administered rather than managed.

What the BBC did have at its best – the reason I joined it – was deep creativity. It had led the world in developing broadcasting as an art form, as a medium of education and enlightenment. It had shel-tered some of Britain's best talents and given them space to produce work of often sublime quality and originality. But even here the anarchic nature of the organisation had meant that in some areas poor creative performance was being tolerated, rather than good work encouraged.

I used the long, difficult eighteen-month handover from Michael Checkland to work out how I could transform this leviathan.

First, I traversed the length and breadth of the BBC and sat and listened as staff and managers told me of their problems and of their hopes for the future. I talked to Colin Marshall and Iain Vallance about their experiences turning British Airways and BT respectively from ailing nationalised industries into modern cor-porations. Iain piquantly advised me: 'Don't be afraid to contemplate a lot of change. Organisations are extraordinarily resilient and resourceful. They can move twice as far and as fast as you think they can.' I worked with Margaret Salmon, the BBC's newly appointed personnel head, and Bob Nelson, who had helped manage BA's leadership and staff development pro-gramme, on a far-reaching programme of change. We set out to find the best advice possible, and soon identified that the American academic Warner Burke, a professor at the University of

Columbia, was the acknowledged authority. Warner's gentle, modest manner belied his stevedore build. He spent days with me in a country hotel helping me to appreciate that all organisations are unique, that you need to understand their complexities and particularities before you seek to change them, that culture, values, leadership, structures, processes and work practices are all part of the genetic construct of any organisation. Warner explained that every aspect affected the whole, that transformational change comes only when many levers are pulled simultaneously, and that change for the better comes only gradually, and with some difficulty, over many years. The experienced Warner would eventually describe the BBC from close association as 'The damnedest of cultures!'

Working with Margaret Salmon and with Nick Lovegrove and Norman Blackwell from McKinsey, I fashioned a plan. We would not only remain the most creative broadcaster in the world, we would become the best-managed public sector organisation. We would cast out the baronies, encourage collaboration between colleagues, settle issues on their merits, not in corners but out in the open and on the table, after a proper dissection of the evidence, with everyone involved and having their say. The senior management team would not only be straightforward with each other but with Governors too. We would hold nothing back.

David Hatch, when Managing Director of Radio, had once commented ruefully to me: 'When the lift at Broadcasting House goes wrong, the Chairman phones *me!*' David, like all the senior executives, was responsible for everything – the canteen and the cleaners as well as the programmes and the networks – and could focus wholeheartedly on nothing. The BBC would be restructured so that different managers could now concentrate on each of our key purposes: commissioning and scheduling networks to satisfy our audiences; making excellent programmes; providing facilities of quality; and effectively exploiting the commercial value of our programmes. The BBC would have a smaller centre focusing on strategy, performance and compliance; and we would devolve, outsource or rationalise the services which – at the point I became Director-General – employed many thousands of staff at the centre of the BBC.

Our aim was to raise the BBC's performance, collecting meaningful data about every aspect of its business, introducing comprehensive and measurable objectives and rigorously reviewing progress in meeting them. Pay would be linked to results, not to long service. We would develop our managers, sending some to the best American business schools (Michael Jackson, Mark Byford and others went to Wharton). Many would attend our own tailor-made MBA course (at the University of Bradford) in public sector management.

We would learn from the world's leading authorities. Over the next few years, we would work with Larry Selden, a cutting-edge thinker on finance from Columbia Business School in New York; Jean-Claude Larréché, Professor of Marketing at INSEAD in France; Professor Robert Kaplan of Harvard Business School, the authority on performance management; and Craig Fields, one of America's leading technologists. Each in turn would take me and my team to the frontier of ideas in his own sphere, to help us understand how the world's most effective organisations were succeeding, and to work out how we could materially raise the BBC's game.

Our plan was to create a meritocratic BBC with tighter recruitment processes, employing more women and staff from ethnic minorities. We would recruit from the private sector managers and people with the skills we lacked. We would design a programme of continuous staff communication and involvement.

I set out to recruit my top team. The BBC needed outside blood. I wanted a Deputy Director-General who could manage BBC World Service, oversee the new facilities division I intended to form and develop the BBC's commercial activities. I sounded out three people: Greg Dyke, still at LWT; Howard Davies, then at the Audit Commission; and Bob Phillis, Chief Executive of ITN. Greg and Howard were not ready for a move, but Bob was and accepted my offer. Liz Forgan, the jolly, principled, liberal but tough-minded programme head from Channel 4 agreed to run Radio after a series

of secret discussions at her north London flat. David Hatch, wise
head and generous spirit, close to retirement, became my adviser.
Rodney Baker-Bates, a posh Liverpudlian who had been Managing
Director of UK Banking at the Midland Bank, joined as Director of
Finance and IT to refashion our archaic finance function and information systems. Pamela Taylor from the BMA (and later Colin
Browne of BT) became Director of Corporate Affairs. A burly,
straight-talking Scot, Rod Lynch – a former Special Forces officer
and BA executive – came to take on probably the thorniest job,
managing the newly formed facilities division, BBC Resources. The
team was completed by the staunch redoubtables Will Wyatt (TV),
Ron Neil (Regions), Tony Hall (News), Patricia Hodgson (Policy
and Planning) and Margaret Salmon (Personnel).

Early in 1993 I announced the new structure and team for the
BBC. It was described by the *Daily Telegraph* as the 'most radical
shake-up at the BBC for 25 years'. Hussey sent me a bottle of his
favourite champagne and a warm note about my presentation to
BBC staff: 'That was a marvellous start – clear, comprehensive and
delivered with authority . . .'

In my second week as Director-General, I went away with my new
and lively top group to Amberley Castle in Sussex. We lifted the draw-
bridge and brainstormed – excited and uplifted by the challenge –
about how to build a better, non-baronial BBC. We left with our spirits
high, not really appreciating just how difficult our task would be. For
the next three years, we would be in a state of war, fighting on every
front. The battles of the first year were some of the worst.

As an executive, I had had no luck with money. When I succeeded
Michael Grade at LWT, I faced an immediate advertising downturn
and savage programme cutbacks. Michael Checkland's legacy was
no easier. During his tenure, the BBC had lived off past savings and
borrowings, spending over four years the best part of £400 million
more than it received in revenue. When I became Director-General,
the BBC had just moved into debt and was not far off its statutory

borrowing limit of £200 million. Moreover, we needed cash to fund
the transitional costs of Producer Choice – to be launched months
into my term of office. As a result, various colleagues wanted to
approach the government with a demand to raise our borrowing
limit. Hussey thought that would be bad politics. With the Charter
not yet settled, and our future still uncertain, he judged the para-
mount need was to show that the BBC could sort itself out, not ask
for help. I agreed. We decided to manage within our existing borrowing limits, an experience which would prove hair-raising.

Rodney Baker-Bates – our new pinstriped, fob-watched Finance
Director – paled when he got his feet under the desk and discovered
just how antediluvian the BBC's financial operations and systems
were. He found in particular that there were no effective systems for
precisely forecasting the BBC's forward cash needs. He set about
recruiting proven finance people from industry and the Square Mile,
and overhauling the systems. In the event, it took Rodney two more
years before basic financial disciplines were in place, and at least five
before the BBC's financial management (eventually under Rodney's
successor, John Smith) could reasonably claim to be world class.
But Rodney had to get a grip immediately on the BBC's cash spend,
heroically managing it day by day, monitoring the big cheques, at
one point watching borrowings reach £197 million – just £3 million
away from our statutory limit, the breach of which would have
been unlawful and critically embarrassing to the BBC. Gradually,
Rodney managed the BBC's debt away from the danger zone, often
bearing messages to his colleagues they'd rather not hear – because
it constrained their spending – but never shirking his lonely task.

Two months into our Herculean labours, a hurricane struck. At the
end of February 1993, the *Independent on Sunday* splashed the story
that I was employed not as a member of BBC staff, but via a
company, John Birt Productions Ltd. The accounts of my company
were lodged at Companies House, and extracts were featured in the
article. The newspaper alleged that being contracted through a com-

pany reduced my tax bill, and that I claimed personal expenditure on the company, like clothing, which could be offset against tax. A large picture of me in an elegant, freshly pressed suit adorned the front page. It would soon emerge that there was no material tax advantage to my being employed via a company; and, moreover, that neither I nor anyone else could offset personal clothing against tax. Nevertheless, Armanigate was born, and would result in the three most horrific weeks of my professional life.

The reasons for my personal employment arrangement were more cultural than financial, and went back twenty-five years – to the sixties – when I was first employed at Granada TV. Up-and-coming producers and directors at the time increasingly sought freelance rather than staff status, even those who were employed full time by Granada. Winning freelance status was a sign you had won your creative spurs, for you were no longer assigned to programmes without consultation (which is what had happened to me in my early years at Granada). Rather, each new contract term prompted a two-way discussion about what you would do next, and what you would be paid. The arrangement matched the mood of the times, for my generation bridled at the notion of being corporate pawns. We appreciated, of course, that freelance status meant you paid slightly less tax. And we also realised that the advantage of the device for Granada was that we – not they – were responsible for our pensions. But we were a generation that couldn't imagine growing old, so few of us instituted immediate arrangements to save for our old age. We needed accountants, though, to deal with the steady stream of forms that arrived from the Inland Revenue. Mine was the charming, untidy bohemian Michael Henshaw, a legend in the creative community, who had been introduced to me by John McGrath. (I had met John – Merseyside playwright, and one of the original writing team on *Z Cars* – when he came to see my naive Oxford film *The Little Donkey*, and had kindly taken me under his wing.)

Mike Henshaw in his own youth had worked for the Inland Revenue, but a friend from his hometown of Derby had introduced

him in the early sixties – in the CND era – to the smouldering café
society of the London left. Mike attended angry debates in the
Partisan Coffee Bar with Arnold Wesker, Iris Murdoch, the firebrand Paul Johnson and others. When Wesker founded Centre 42 to
encourage ordinary working people to participate in the arts, Mike
became his administrator. Frank Cousins, Jennie Lee and Doris
Lessing were on the board. They exhibited a Barbara Hepworth
statue alongside a great slab of coal hewn by miners. When Wesker
acquired the Round House in Chalk Farm for Centre 42, Robert
Maxwell became their Treasurer. Pink Floyd played an early gig;
Allen Ginsberg and Lawrence Ferlinghetti came to perform.

When Centre 42 eventually collapsed, Mike set up as an accountant and hauled a great galaxy of talent into his net, much of it
from the left. He had hundreds of clients, including Wesker, Tony
Garnett, Ken Loach, Ken Trodd, Ted Hughes, Tony Smith, Fay
Weldon, James McTaggart, Brian Wenham, Michael Palin, Simon
Gray and Ralph Steadman. I was flattered when Mike agreed to
take me on. Meeting him in his elegant office in Regent's Park, surrounded by first editions and the large canvases of his clients, was
always a pleasure: he was well informed, and took a real paternal
interest in your career. Filling in tax forms was way down his
agenda, something he took care of off-stage. Mike, however, could
be frustrating to deal with. Queries went unanswered, and his letters
were not always comprehensible to the lay person. In the end,
though, it all seemed to work fairly painlessly – Mike took away all
your forms, accounts and bills and dealt with the tax authorities
directly, occasionally demanding a large cheque for the taxman,
and a small one for himself.

In 1981, when I worked at LWT, Brian Tesler, the Managing
Director, advised me to set up a company as the vehicle for my own
pension scheme, which LWT paid into. (Many senior LWT executives adopted similar arrangements, which became widespread in
the industry.) When Michael Checkland invited me to the BBC he
didn't quibble for a moment about continuing LWT's practice of

contracting me through my company, and making a direct contribution to my private pension. The arrangement was never secret and was referred to openly during my early years at the BBC.

In the eighteen months between my appointment as Director-General and taking up office, a number of senior colleagues pressed me to move on to the BBC's staff when I became Director-General – Tony Jennings, the BBC's Legal Adviser, Ian Phillips, the Finance Director, and Michael Checkland himself. Theirs – as events would prove – was good advice; but I was at first reluctant to accept it, for I was generally attached to the arrangements which, in one form or another, I had worked under for twenty-five years, and I was fearful in particular that moving on to staff would undermine the value of my private pension. But I was worn down in the end and came to the reluctant view that in principle I should dismantle my arrangements and move on to staff.

Towards the end of 1992 I asked Mike Henshaw and my lawyer David Teacher to consider the implications of staff status – particularly the impact on my pension – and told Hussey of my change of view, which he welcomed. When Michael Checkland made his surprise Fuzzy Monsters attack on the Governors, and subsequently decided to leave the BBC months earlier than intended, I suddenly found myself having to advance my plans urgently, and to settle in a great rush the recruitment of my top team. I agreed with Margaret Salmon to set aside the discussions on my contract as Director-General – including staff status – until the flurry was over. At the beginning of February, the Governors' remuneration committee insisted on expediting the matter. A month later, when the *Independent on Sunday*'s story about my employment status first appeared, the issues were well on the way to resolution, but had not yet been finalised, and my old contractual status was still in force. I don't know if the newspaper stumbled across my publicly available company accounts by accident – as a journalist friend told me at the time – or was tipped off by someone who had been a party to the BBC discussions.

On the afternoon of the day the story appeared, I watched with a sinking feeling as reporters fanned out down the road in Wandsworth where we lived, knocking on doors, quizzing our neighbours – who remained loyal and refused to co-operate. The story played prominently in Monday morning's papers, with initial expressions of outrage, most prominently from the staff unions, who immediately called for my resignation. The main argument in the papers was that my reforms were having a punishing effect on BBC staff, and that it was monstrous that I was not even a member of staff myself. The story looked as if it might build, so I needed to nip it in the bud. Hussey was in Hong Kong, so I agreed with the Vice-Chairman, Joel Barnett, that I should cut through the issue and join the staff straight away. We would sort out the ancillary matters later. The decision was announced that day, but the story did not go away. A new line of attack emerged: it was alleged in the press that I was saving thirty thousand pounds each year in tax, and my colleagues told me that many staff were affronted by these revelations. We were only four weeks away from launching Producer Choice, and the new Resources directorate would soon have to make its own way in the world without direct support. Many staff were facing redundancy or uncertainty. They had already been nervous. The revelations about my employment status and my tax advantages made their feelings even more raw.

I found it hard to get the soundbite clarity I needed from Mike Henshaw to answer the detailed questions flooding into the BBC, which I was being pressed to answer. My lawyer, David Teacher, offered me excellent advice which would prove decisive: that I should turn for help to one of the big accountancy firms. He suggested Barrie Akin, a personal tax expert in Ernst and Young. Barrie, who would be my saviour, was sharp, fluent and clear thinking, and he and his team moved rapidly to take charge. He said Ernst and Young would write a report for me on my own affairs. Mike Henshaw gladly handed over all my tax papers, and the Ernst and Young team ferreted through them at lightning speed and quickly gave me the headlines: all my arrangements were lawful and proper and agreed with the Inland Revenue; but there was a sting in the tail – there was hardly any tax advantage to the arrangements I had had for years. Over the next days, Ernst and Young would audit my accounts and show that the benefit to me was a modest £810 per year – for at my level of income there was no material advantage to using a company to supply my services. Ernst and Young also established that Henshaw had included in my accounts at Companies House lots of information about my expenditure which did not need to be declared, as the statutory format required only limited disclosure. Moreover, much of the information Henshaw had provided was extraneous, irrelevant and misleading, for he had mixed up personal and business expenditure. Given the way my accounts had been presented, the *Independent on Sunday* could be forgiven for the base inaccuracy that would haunt the affair – and that no amount of subsequent briefing could dispel – that my Armani suits were tax deductible. They were not.

Failing to understand any of these nuances, the papers had grossly libelled me. Barrie and I saw one of the country's most illustrious QCs and he advised that the defamation was clear cut and that I would win substantial damages if I took legal action. I decided, however, that court cases settled long into the future would not resolve my current deepening crisis. I needed more urgent action.

On the following Monday, eight days after the first story – and aided by Pamela Taylor, Director of Corporate Affairs – I set out to respond to and deal with the issues. I expressed my sincere regret to my management colleagues for the storm I had created, and I asked for their advice and support. Understandably, they were reeling from a week of hostile staff and media reaction, and I encouraged them to question me about my financial affairs, which they did. They issued a statement after the meeting: 'Directors appreciated his openness, honesty and expression of regret and gave him their full support.' A member of the Board of Management wrote to me afterwards to say: 'Your board are absolutely unwaveringly behind you.' I sent a letter to the BBC's staff expressing my regret and apologising. On the same day, Ernst and Young issued their report on my tax affairs – demonstrating the modesty of my tax gain – and Barrie Akin patiently steered journalists through the maze of issues.

Hussey and Barnett released a statement: 'so much of what has been written has been misleading and unjust . . . John Birt is a man of integrity and conviction . . . an executive of great capacity and drive. He has our full and unqualified support.' The newspapers the following day were more calm and reasoned, especially those that had been briefed by Barrie Akin. But it was just a lull. We were in the eye of the hurricane.

On the day of our counter-attack, one of the Governors, Keith Oates, wrote a long, detailed and unsupportive letter to the Chairman, asking who had agreed my arrangements, outlining many technical questions he wanted answers to, and demanding an independent report. This was the first sign of a breach in the unity of the Governors. Oates had infuriated Hussey – never to be for-given – because he believed Oates had promised him his vote on the night I was appointed, only to discover he hadn't.

The following evening I was due to take the stage of the National Film Theatre for a long-planned interview with Jeremy Isaacs. It was my first public appearance since the story had broken and Jeremy gave me a hard time. The audience was certainly not uni-formly hostile, but a section – containing some BBC union activists – catcalled and commented loudly among themselves throughout the interview. Wilf Stevenson, the British Film Institute's Director, wrote afterwards to suggest: 'You gave as good as you got, and by the end had the audience on your side.' It certainly didn't feel that way. On the contrary, I formed the strong impression, for the first time, that no one wanted to hear my explanation. The fact that my arrangements were common in the industry, that they were widespread in the BBC, that they were designed chiefly as a pension vehicle, that they were lawful and agreed by the Inland Revenue, and that they brought me minimal tax advantage, cut no ice. The truth was that, at a time of great change and uncertainty, I had handed anyone opposed to me a stick with which to beat me, and they were taking their opportunity. And others were joining in simply for the sport. At the NFT event, I was warned that a large, lively crowd, including film crews and photographers, had assembled outside, and that I would have to run the gauntlet to get to my car. I peeked outside and didn't like the look of what appeared to be a lynch mob. I knew from experience that if I went outside the pictures on that evening's main news bulletins would be of me being jostled by a jeering, hostile crowd. I would appear a man under siege. As a film buff, I knew the complex layout of the NFT well. We were also right by LWT, and the adjacent streets were familiar territory. I made a spot decision, and motioned my colleagues to 'Tell Brian [my driver] on his carphone to meet me where I play football on Friday.' I darted down the back stairs, slipped unnoticed between the pillars of the South Bank's dark concrete jungle, and dashed through the shabby, empty streets of Waterloo to the deserted municipal centre which I visited each week to play five-a-side. Waiting for Brian in the shadow of a doorway, I felt hunted and truly downcast. He soon joined me, though with difficulty: the crowd had jostled his car and had tried to block his departure. He had felt threatened himself, but he was kindly and offered me every human support and sympathy on my way home.

Terry Burns had seen the *Nine O'Clock News* and rang me as soon as I got back for a council of war. It was clear to both of us that the drama was escalating. I knew instinctively that the media would now stake me out. (They did: from the next day there was a major media presence at my homes in London and Wales.) I didn't want the day-by-day iconography of a hounded individual to dominate the news – as had been the case with David Mellor and many others – so I moved immediately out of my Wandsworth home and lodged in secret with old friends Nick and Gilly Elliott in Putney, where I would stay, enjoying their sympathy, advice and hospitality for the next ten nights. (Jane was in America visiting her family, keeping in touch by phone.) I continued to work in my office, and to run the BBC, but more and more time was taken up with the intensifying crisis.

The press was in full cry and other matters were unearthed. Mike Henshaw turned out not to be qualified (though the people working for him doing the accounts were). Jane was revealed as the company secretary (she prepared all our accounts). The media were now engaged in a feeding frenzy, and in the increasingly hysterical atmosphere issues were inflated and all perspective lost. Most of the stories carried the implication that I was doing something untoward, that I was more worried about money than about the BBC. There was no sense at all that when I decided to leave LWT I had turned my back on high pay, share options and the prospect of huge wealth. The mob was on the rampage, and in no mood to think or to listen. Commentators began to write that it couldn't go on, that the uncertainty was damaging staff morale, indeed the institution itself. The frenzy reached a crescendo on the second Sunday. The *Observer*, among others, called for Hussey and Birt to go. Our heads were now being demanded.

Then, as I pondered for the first time how long the institution could take the media punishment, and how long I could survive, the wheel finally began to turn. Up to this point, my old friends and close colleagues had offered me generous succour and advice. They were worried but not deeply concerned. They assumed the storm would blow over. Suddenly, there was a spontaneous realisation that I was under threat. All at once, I had a flood of messages and letters of solidarity, all suggesting, and for a variety of motives – whether support for reform, or belief in me, or simply comradeship – that on no account should I resign. I had fighting advice by letter, telegram and phone, for instance, from fellow Scousers:

Laurie Taylor: 'Box on.'

Jimmy Tarbuck: 'Don't give in!'

Tony Booth: 'St Mary's boys don't quit. They stand and fight.'

John Freeman was one of hundreds of old friends and associates who wrote or contacted me over those few days: 'There is an army of those who have worked with you who know that you are the right man in the right job. Courage and strength!' A close BBC ally wrote:

> It is quite clear that your enemies and critics believed that if they toppled you, the whole reform effort at the BBC would be severely damaged. I think they were right, judging by some of the backsliding I have seen over the past two weeks . . .

Another group of staff in BBC News sent me a personal letter: 'We remember what it was that you inherited. We see the difference every day and we know that the process must be continued . . . Hang on in there!'

Tim Bell, the communications specialist who had advised both Mrs Thatcher and the BBC since Alasdair Milne's day, demanded to see me and urged me to fight. He waded in fiercely and energetically on my behalf with the press. Peter Mandelson put out a statement. James Callaghan sent a message urging me not to resign. David Mellor wrote a rousing article in the *Guardian*. Some of the BBC's most senior journalists – Robin Oakley, John Simpson, Polly Toynbee, Peter Jay, Martyn Lewis and Peter Sissons, wrote to *The Times*:

> Old axes are grinding, old scores are being settled in the attacks on the Director-General of the BBC . . . John Birt's real offence is to be the architect of the plan which is effecting radical change . . . What we are seeing here is a last-minute and underhand attempt to destroy it by destroying him.

A group from the creative industries – including Fay Weldon, Harry Enfield, Richard Eyre, Germaine Greer, Adrian Noble, David

Puttnam and Nicholas Serota – wrote to *The Times* urging me to stay.

Elspeth Howe and I had become close when we worked together on the successful Opportunity 2000 campaign to persuade public and private sector institutions across the UK to take gender equality seriously. I acquired in the process a high regard for Elspeth's delicacy, drive and determination. She wrote, with Margaret Jay, Peter Mandelson and Graham Mather: 'He is an experienced, dedicated and outstanding broadcaster, and the BBC needs him to implement the changes required if it is to survive and prosper.' I was most touched when my colleagues on the BBC's Board of Management took to the airwaves in numbers to defend me and wrote to *The Times* to say: 'John Birt is the best person to lead the BBC and he has our unanimous support.'

As the tide was turning, I had a small stroke of luck. The Board of Governors was due to discuss the affair for the first time, and Keith Oates looked like the Governor who would cause the most trouble. But someone had been leaking against him too. Oates was the Joint Managing Director of Marks and Spencer, and the *Daily Mail* unexpectedly revealed that the company paid some of his salary outside the UK. Oates' arrangements were legitimate. Although he was a UK resident for tax purposes, it later emerged that the Inland Revenue had agreed he was domiciled in Monaco. By chance, I was with Hussey in his office when Oates phoned in to discuss the *Daily Mail* story on him; and Hussey mischievously put the call on loudspeaker so that I could overhear the conversation. Oates complained that he was being doorstepped over his own tax affairs by reporters, and protested the iniquity and unfairness of it all. Hussey feigned deep sympathy with Oates on the telephone, but in reality was gleeful, pulling faces and winking at me as he offered his cod condolences.

Barrie Akin and I met the Governors together. They had received, I was told, a number of letters of support for me, including unsolicited character references from Jim Callaghan and Robert

Runcie, the former Archbishop of Canterbury. Barrie was confident, persuasive and authoritative. The arrangements I had with the
BBC, he told the Governors, were proper, lawful and agreed with
the Inland Revenue. He had examined the papers and could vouch
for my personal integrity. Keith Oates was subdued. It was clear that
the other Governors had hated, understandably enough, sixteen
days of distressing non-stop media coverage, and that they devoutly
wished I had not been employed via my company when I first joined
the BBC – but it was also plain from the exchanges that they understood I could not be condemned for signing a contract the BBC had
drawn up; or for tax arrangements agreed with the Revenue which
Ernst and Young was vouchsafing. They had no grounds whatsoever – even if they had wanted them – for demanding my
resignation. I left the meeting knowing I was going to survive, even
though there would be a further discussion in two days' time.

The following day, Will Wyatt told his senior management group
in Television that I had the clear, unambiguous support of the top
management team. He was aware of the deep upset about my
employment status, but he believed the attacks on me contained

> an element of vendetta and revenge. Some see no necessity
> for change in the BBC, and seem to take the view that if
> John Birt is destabilised, change won't happen. That's not an
> option. I understand the sadness of those who feel John Birt's
> tax arrangements had demonstrated a lack of understanding
> of BBC values. It has clearly been a bad mistake, but it was
> not the mistake of a bad man. John Birt is an outstanding
> leader and executive and is needed.

On the same day, something extraordinary happened: Barrie
Akin was phoned by a senior Inland Revenue official who said he
wanted to come over to Ernst and Young's offices to see Barrie.
This was highly unusual – Revenue officials did not normally leave
their citadels to visit accountancy firms. The Revenue executive

arrived. 'In five words, Mr Akin,' he said, 'we have lost the file.' He explained that, as Barrie Akin had himself proposed, the Inland Revenue had called for my tax files, lodged in Bristol, to be sent to London. The files went via a depot in Wolverhampton. There they were logged as arriving, then leaving, but they never reached the tax offices in London. The processes for transporting tax files were highly secure. The files did not carry my name on the outside. They were transported in a locked cage in a van. Every vehicle in the fleet, every warehouse, had been searched. Foul play was feared. The Revenue agreed to take immediate legal action to recover the files if their whereabouts were revealed. In the meantime, Barrie offered to share all of his and Henshaw's papers with the Revenue, which he did.

I was flabbergasted. Many years of experience as a journalist had persuaded me that cock-up rather than conspiracy is the most common explanation for suspicious events – but I was told the disappearance of such a file was unprecedented. I had been tipped off months before that a group of BBC expats and malcontents met regularly to plot against me. I had doubted this, but I couldn't explain either the initial *Independent on Sunday* story or the missing files.

Michael Grade, who had shown himself deadly and ruthless in his criticism in his McTaggart lecture, had been oddly subdued about my travails. On the morning of the final climactic Governors' meeting, however, Grade broke his silence: 'One feels so sorry for the staff. It must be very demoralising.' On the very same day that Grade offered his comment, it was finally revealed to me by BBC personnel staff that when I joined the BBC in 1987 my contract had been modelled on Michael Grade's and John Tusa's. Thus I had been one of three members of the Board of Management enjoying broadly the same employment arrangements. Grade's and Tusa's contracts had been instituted in the Milne era, which had not stopped Milne huffing and puffing about my difficulties during the crisis. In all – the Governors and Board of Management were informed that day – there were around twenty contracts like mine at a senior level in the BBC. The news about Michael Grade's contract leaked immediately but merited only a short paragraph in one or two papers.

On the day of the final Governors' meeting intended to settle the affair, some of my senior management colleagues – who had never been enamoured of Hussey – suggested privately that he should resign. I said I didn't think there was any fairness in that at all. At the meeting, the no-nonsense Brummie trade union leader Bill Jordan voiced the same point, and invited Hussey to consider his position, but Hussey refused to budge. And that was the end of the matter. The affair was over. Press interest quickly subsided. The experience had been wearing, and was an undoubted reverse at the very beginning of my term of office. And I'd brought it on myself: I had been duly warned, but I'd responded reluctantly; I had failed to act with dispatch. The affair had put a terrible burden on my colleagues, friends and family. It had rattled the BBC's staff. And it completed my demonisation, affecting forever my relations with the British press. But I survived – above all, with the help of my colleagues and friends – and was deeply relieved that I could complete the journey I had begun.

There were various postscripts to Armanigate. I soon received the standard letter routinely sent by the union to all new BBC staff:

> Dear John,
>   We congratulate you on your appointment to the staff of
> the BBC and wish you well in your job. If you are feeling a
> little apprehensive and on your own, don't worry. Your
> colleagues will quickly put you at your ease . . .

At BAFTA's glamorous annual prize-giving, soon after the affair had ended, Jane and I encountered Emma Thompson and Kenneth Branagh. Kenneth put a hand on my shoulder, looked deeply and sincerely into my eyes, and said: 'John, fuck 'em!' He paused: 'Fuck 'em! Fuck 'em! Fuck 'em!' He went on . . . and on, repeating the phrase over and over again – 'Fuck 'em! Fuck 'em! Fuck 'em!' – continuing when I thought he would stop, repeating the phrase thirty or forty times, rolling it on his tongue, changing the rhythm, raising the pitch, relishing the sound, like the great actor he is, building to a crescendo, then suddenly speaking softly, then finally and emphatically: 'Fuck 'em! Fuck 'em! FUCK 'EM!'

At the end of March, to celebrate Jane's fiftieth birthday, I organised a mystery tour for about sixty of our close friends and family – who had suffered with us, and supported us loyally. We boarded a coach at Streatham Common early one Saturday morning, stopping first at the go-kart track in Battersea. All morning we competed in heats, our friends driving to win. In an exciting and fiercely fought final the highly competitive Christopher Bland emerged the victor, with – to everyone's surprise – the laid-back Peter Mandelson a close second, and Ian Hargreaves third. Jane was the fastest woman. We ate McDonald's hamburgers for lunch while we drove to the Chilterns, and up a long drive to a house from which Cilla Black emerged to sing Jane 'Happy Birthday'. We stopped at Waddesdon Manor, where Jacob Rothschild gave us tea. As dusk fell, we arrived at Magdalen College, Oxford for a hauntingly beautiful evensong sung by the College's choristers, organised especially for Jane by Tony Smith, now Magdalen's Master. We dined in the senior common room at St Catherine's and returned home in the small hours tired but happy and thankful for friends.

The rumpus over my tax status brought huge recognition on the UK's front pages to the inspired Italian designer Giorgio Armani. Years later, just before I left the BBC, Jane and I visited him with Howell James at his Milan palazzo. Armani had hundreds of designers working for him, and he observed that his British designers were among the most imaginative, constantly challenging conventions, but often unruly and undisciplined. 'Mr Armani,' I responded, 'I have thousands of such British creatives working for me!'

My missing tax file finally turned up four years later in circumstances which intensified the mystery of its disappearance. In 1997 a BBC World Service production department was moving from Bush House in the widespread changes following the controversial restructuring I had announced the previous year. The office was dismantled, and all the files placed in tea-chests for the move. At the end of the day, a 'farewell to Bush House' party was held during which a World Service executive noticed a file on the top of one of the chests different in colour from all the rest. Investigating, he discovered my long-lost tax file, which he handed immediately to his Managing Director, who passed it to Margaret Salmon, the BBC's Director of Personnel, who handed it over to the Inland Revenue. I don't know – and may never know – how my personal tax file, which was transported in conditions of high security, ended up in a BBC programme department.

The affair over, we all got back to the happier business of running the BBC. Early in my term of office, I launched a programme strategy review, to be led by two of our brightest creative lights, Liz Forgan and Alan Yentob. They stimulated a deep discussion in every area of the BBC about how the organisation should serve every kind of audience. They identified how key audiences – like children – had changed, and how our programming was failing to keep pace with them. They pointed to audience needs – like leisure – that the BBC had served patchily. They looked at the range and quality of our programme-making in every area. They established how we could reach out more effectively to attract and to develop talent. For the first time, we began to think seriously about serving our audiences not at the expense of, but with, high-quality, innovative programmes. Alan and Liz brought about a major cultural shift in the BBC.

BBC1 was looking tired and listless when I assumed office: the channel had failed to reinvent itself after the halcyon days of *Dr Who*, *The Two Ronnies* and *All Creatures Great and Small*. The final

straw had been when Jonathan Powell, the Controller, had commissioned *Eldorado*, the soap opera set in an expatriate community in
Spain. The team involved had a fine pedigree: Verity Lambert, the
producer, had introduced some of ITV's most striking successes, like
Rock Follies; but when the series came on air it was an instant disaster: it felt synthetic and two-dimensional; the characters had no
depth; the production standards were unacceptable.

Jonathan Powell left for a job at Carlton just before I assumed
office. Will Wyatt and I were united in believing Alan Yentob should
succeed Powell as Controller, BBC1. For many, Alan was not the
obvious choice: he had been a brilliant, innovative Controller of
BBC2 who had brought the network into the modern world, but his
background was in the arts, his strength recognising and backing
talent at the edge. Could he adapt to BBC1? Alan was a wonderful
companion: a good talker – sharp, witty, alert, attentive; a supreme
networker always up on the gossip; a superb creative entrepreneur
famously comfortable in the company of 'Orson' and 'Salman' and
other cultural icons. He was equally famous for putting off a decision till he was comfortable with it, in the meantime chewing it
over with a glittering galaxy of media panjandrums. But Will and I
believed the bull-point was that Alan's decisions when made were
invariably right, that his programme judgements were excellent,
that – most importantly of all – as Will put it: 'Alan hated crap.' He
didn't make cynical commissioning decisions. He always acknowledged and never defended failure. He was the right person, we
judged, to bring weight and quality to BBC1.

One of Alan's first acts as Controller was to abandon *Eldorado*, a
decision I greeted with deep relief. He and his successors – Michael
Jackson and Peter Salmon – went on adventurously and rapidly in the
1990s to redefine the centre of gravity of BBC1. They touched a
national nerve with makeover leisure series like *Changing Rooms* and
Ground Force. Pioneering with lightweight cameras and small crews,
Alan brought the docusoap to the main channel, with entertaining
series like *Hotel* and *Driving School*, making Maureen Rees a star for her

sublimely poor driving. Alan's innovations were widely copied. He showcased major documentaries like Peter Taylor's magnum opus on Ireland, and Michael Palin's gentle worldwide journeys. He brought *French & Saunders*, Harry Enfield, Ben Elton and *Absolutely Fabulous* to BBC1. Over the following years, he and his successors refreshed the comedy form with contemporary insight, bringing *Vicar of Dibley*, *Men Behaving Badly*, *Thin Blue Line* and *The Royle Family* to the BBC's main channel. Victor Meldrew spoke for grumpy, frustrated busy-bodies everywhere in *One Foot in the Grave*, which became a classic. Popular quality drama was re-established with series like *Ballykissangel*, *Jonathan Creek* and *Hamish MacBeth*. As Controller, BBC2, Alan had helped to reinvent the classic serial with *Middlemarch*. For BBC1, he commissioned the talismanic drama series of the 1990s, *Pride and Prejudice*. Roddy Doyle's *Family* and Jimmy McGovern's *The Lakes* brought grit to the BBC's main channel. It began to look as if BBC1, with a high-quality schedule, would eventually overtake ITV.

On Alan's recommendation, the shy Michael Jackson took over BBC2. Michael, from Macclesfield, was a media studies graduate, who had a deep historical and theoretical understanding of television, allied with a canny, open-minded intuition about how best to move the medium on. The ferociously bright Mark Thompson later succeeded Michael. Alan, Michael and Mark in succession made BBC2 the most outstanding UK television channel of the 1990s. And, under David Docherty, the commissioning and scheduling function in BBC Television became professionalised, informed, sharp and considered, a centre of true expertise. It was commonly suggested that the rigours and burdens imposed by Producer Choice and the modernisation of the BBC undermined programme quality, but in fact creativity flowered at the BBC in the 1990s as never before, and the leadership group, whatever the other pressures on us, never stopped thinking and talking programmes. And, as the massive savings from Producer Choice came through, they were invested in more programmes and in programmes of greater ambition in every genre.

The exceptional talents we were able to cast in channel controller jobs in the period were matched by outstanding leadership in the production areas. Jana Bennett, for instance, in BBC Science, was the guiding force behind programmes of remarkable editorial and technological virtuosity like *The Human Body*, *Earth Story* and *Walking with Dinosaurs*. Alastair Fothergill raised the ambition of the BBC's natural history programming with the *Private Life of Plants*, *Life of Birds* and *Life in the Freezer*. BBC Television pioneered in comedy, as never before in its history, with Steve Coogan's *Alan Partridge*, Armando Iannucci's dazzlingly inventive *Saturday Night Armistice*, the laddish genius of Frank Skinner and David Baddiel in *Fantasy Football League*, the bizarre surrealism of *League of Gentlemen*, the light Brit-Asian wit of *Goodness Gracious Me*, the wickedly funny, paranoid confrontations of Ruby Wax, the quirky eccentricity of *The Fast Show*.

Later in the decade, Tinky Winky, Dipsy, Laa-Laa and Po took the whole world by storm, the novelty and charm of the *Teletubbies* inspiring, delighting and capturing the imagination of children of every age, everywhere.

One of the greatest achievements of the period was the unmatched chronicling of contemporary history week by week in Laurence Rees's *Timewatch*, and in series like Brian Lapping's remarkable *The Death of Yugoslavia*, *The Second Russian Revolution* and *Poisoned Chalice* – the story of Britain and Europe. Simon Schama's *History of Britain* – Will's baby – which told the story of the nation with verve, imagination and sublime insight, was launched in the period. *Video Diaries*, championed by Jeremy Gibson, empowered people to tell their own stories and let us hear the raw, unmediated, unadulterated voice of Britain. We brought a fresh eye and contemporary production skills to the great novels of English literature, with powerful series like *Martin Chuzzlewit*, *Our Mutual Friend* and *Vanity Fair*, the latter adapted with verve, bite and his usual sure touch by Andrew Davies. Simon Curtis's *Performance* captured classic theatre thrillingly for television. We advanced the drama form with mould-breaking series like Tony Garnett's *This Life* and *The Cops*, challenging drama production conventions, cutting through the clichés of the increasingly tired peak-time dramas on the main channels. Peter Flannery's *Our Friends in the North* piloted a group of friends with profound insight through our recent political history, and Tony Marchant's *Holding On* brought contemporary London to life searingly.

As in every period, we had magnificent failures, for example *Gormenghast*, and less magnificent failures, like *Rhodes* and *Nostromo* – and we commissioned our share of the mundane. We struggled to find intelligent entertainment for the main channel in the early evening, and never had as many peak-time drama and situation-comedy successes as we wanted. The National Lottery programme attracted large audiences, but we never quite succeeded in giving it a public service patina. But BBC Television as a whole scaled the creative peaks in the 1990s, dominating the prize-givings at home and abroad, delivering on the promise we had made in *Extending Choice* to provide high-quality, innovative programmes that the market would not. Towards the end of 1994 I turned up uninvited to Network Television's weekly review of programmes. BBC Television that year had won more of the key international prizes – in the Prix Italia and the International Emmys – than any broad-caster ever. In the previous few days I had watched *Harry Enfield, Measure for Measure, Ruby Wax, Seaforth, Martin Chuzzlewit, Absolutely Fabulous, Knowing Me, Knowing You* and a brilliant education cam-paign encouraging viewers to learn French. Will Wyatt deserved the congratulations I offered, the magnum of champagne I pre-sented to him and the prolonged ovation he received from his top team. Will presided over, and Alan Yentob was the most important creative force in, a period as golden as any in the history of BBC Television.

One shameless perk of being the BBC's Director-General was to enjoy meals cooked by the BBC's many excellent star chefs. The

unspoilt, food-loving, proselytising Delia Smith had had a profound
impact on attitudes to food in Britain. One night she cooked dinner
for Jane and me, David and Debbie Owen and her husband
Michael at her flat in Docklands, standing in her kitchen as we sat at
the table, bubbling with enthusiasm about the delicious meal she
was preparing. My top team's Christmas lunch was cooked over
the years by many of the BBC's star chefs – once, memorably, by the
Two Fat Ladies, who lounged at our table into the late afternoon,
drinking and smoking and haranguing us without fear.

BBC Radio was in altogether better shape than BBC Television
when I became Director-General. Programme standards were generally high. The creation of Radios 1 to 4 in 1967 by Frank Gillard
and others had shrewdly segmented the audience. The BBC had the
best frequencies, and, incredibly, had not faced competition from
national commercial networks until 1992. David Hatch, Managing
Director since the late 1980s, loved radio with a deep passion and
bustled busily down the corridors and through the studios of
Broadcasting House every workday from early in the morning,
handing out plaudits or kindly but pithy admonishments. David
was an astute, straight-dealing and utterly committed champion of
the medium. When he became my adviser in 1993, he offered me
wise, canny, candid counsel – usually in the form of a witty, beauti-
fully composed, handwritten note pushed under my door – on how
my colleagues and the wider BBC were responding to the punishing
programme of modernisation I had instituted.

    As the new Managing Director of Radio, the challenge for Liz
Forgan was one faced by all mature media: to change and to develop
the radio networks in step with their audiences, not to drift behind
them. This problem was most acute at Radio 1, which had grown
old with its start-up audiences from the late 1960s and 1970s. Radio
1 was still playing Electric Light Orchestra and the Rolling Stones
when I became Director-General, and the average age of its listeners was over thirty. Radio 1, I felt strongly, was letting down the

younger audience. The DJs, I observed, were on average 'older than the Prime Minister, the Archbishop of Canterbury and the Director-General of the BBC!' Harry Enfield and Paul Whitehouse had mercilessly lampooned two ancient, patronising, sexist DJs, Smashie and Nicie, steering too close to reality for Radio 1's comfort. The station was at risk of being privatised: many politicians believed it was barely distinguishable from commercial radio, and that the network did not justify public funding. Liz Forgan and I appointed Matthew Bannister to run the network. As an innovative head of GLR, the BBC's local radio station in London, Matthew had proved good at spotting and developing talent, and, as the manager of the *Extending Choice* project, had proved sound on public service principles.

Matthew embarked on a famously audacious, difficult and painful path of reform at Radio 1. DJs and staff, well dug in, sensed that change was in the air, and were nervy. A troubled Dave Lee Travis walked out, precipitating emergency action before Matthew had fully fashioned his new plans. The result was a hesitant and improvised start, but over the next few years Matthew would triumph. He overhauled the network, focusing on the younger audience, and created a distinctive service proposition. He introduced a new slate of DJs, including the brilliant, exuberant, mischievous Chris Evans; and he promoted the witty motormouth Danny Baker, the erudite John Peel and the lively, aware Andy Kershaw to peak slots. He created opportunities for niche music, uncovered and championed Brit Pop (recording sessions with Oasis before they had commercial releases). He scheduled serious music documentaries, played Chris Morris's extraordinary Blue Jam late night, and marketed the station cannily.

At the beginning of this radical process, overall listening declined rapidly as we lost most of Radio 1's older listeners, and Matthew, as a result, was subjected to an intense and prolonged period of vilification which he bore stoically. Some Governors were nervous that the audience would keep on falling for ever, but Liz Forgan was a feisty, unyielding champion of Matthew's strategy. So was I, inviting all the DJs and the key staff of the beleaguered station into my office in a defiant show of support for Matthew and his plans. Everyone held their nerve until the audience finally stabilised at a respectable twelve million listeners, and Radio 1 began to attract a substantial proportion of the younger listeners it had lost decades previously. It also cast off the Smashie and Nicie tag and attained real street cred. Eventually it was recognised that the courageous Matthew was responsible for a glittering creative success.

Many younger MPs listened to Radio 1, including Tony Blair, a Simon Bates fan, who needed to be persuaded by Matthew that the Labour Party was not the only British institution in need of modernisation. One of the keenest Radio 1 fans among MPs was Thatcher loyalist John Whittingdale, who contacted Matthew at the peak of his travails to say: 'Don't let them get you down. If you had not lost audience, I wouldn't have believed you had been radical enough to justify Radio 1 as part of the BBC.' Matthew had not only reclaimed the young for the BBC, he had averted the station's privatisation.

Liz Forgan worked with Tony Hall and Jenny Abramsky to rescue the BBC from a hole we dug for ourselves over a continuous news service on radio. When the Gulf War broke out, BBC News had mounted a highly applauded continuous news service on Radio 4's second, long-wave frequency, following which there was a widespread sense that the BBC had to offer a permanent service of continuous news both on TV and Radio. The US experience had demonstrated that in news emergencies America switched to CNN and didn't hang around for the networks' evening bulletins. As a result, CNN had become America's premier news provider, and the BBC needed to learn from this lesson. The *Extending Choice* task forces had recommended that we should act. Michael Checkland, with my support, announced that we would offer a continuous news service on Radio 4's long-wave frequency. The government had ruled that broadcasting Radio 4 and other networks on two frequencies was wasteful, so in addition the decision protected us from losing the second wavelength.

The Radio 4 audience erupted in protest, for many listeners believed that the move would stop them receiving their beloved Radio 4. BBC engineers had insisted that almost every home in the country could receive Radio 4 FM, but that turned out to be on tall aerials on the back of BBC Engineering Land Rovers, not old transistor radios on top of the fridge. We faced questions in Parliament, letters by the thousand, and demonstrations outside Broadcasting House. In my office one afternoon I heard the politest of activist chants:

'What do we want?'

'Radio 4!'

'Where do we want it?'

'Long wave!'

'What do we say?'

'Please!'

The Governors themselves revolted and demanded a rethink. Liz, Tony and Jenny reinvented the notion of continuous news as Radio 5 Live – and I accepted their recommendation. The old Radio 5 was an improvised and disjointed collection of refugee services from other BBC networks – sport, education, children's programming and adult contemporary rock. Some of the programmes were successful in their own terms, but the network had no creative or audience focus. Radio 5 Live in its place introduced a service of intelligent news and sport for a younger audience and was confident and coherent – and welcomed – from the outset, soon becoming an established part of the radio landscape.

When Matthew Bannister eventually succeeded Liz Forgan to the leadership of BBC Network Radio, three key strategic challenges in Radio remained. The first was to stop Radio 2 growing old and dying with its audience. Radio 2's barrel-shaped Controller Jim Moir – former head of TV entertainment – was one of the most delightful people in the BBC. He combined good creative and savvy management judgement with a public service commitment, astute powers of observation, a knowing look, a delicious sense of humour and superb boom-boom delivery. Jim's job was to steer Radio 2 through the difficult transition from Frankie Vaughan and Alma Cogan to the Beatles and the Stones, and in the process woo back to the BBC some of the older audiences lost by Radio 1's repositioning. Jim pulled off the trick gradually, stealthily and with great accomplishment, introducing new DJs like Steve Wright and Jonathan Ross, shedding Radio 2's fusty, fifties image, and boosting audiences. His was one of the great successes of the period.

The second challenge was Radio 4 – a treasure-trove of intelligent news, information and wit, revered by its ultra-loyal, diehard audience, who had a long tradition of resisting even modest programme change. Will Wyatt, Matthew and I appointed the steely, focused James Boyle to succeed Michael Green as Controller when Michael retired. James had won infamy in Scotland with a fundamental and controversial but highly successful reform of BBC Radio Scotland during which he had been dubbed 'MacBirt' by the Scottish media. I had greatly admired what James had done, and his bravery in seeing it through. When we appointed James, and knowing his reputation, I said to him, and to Will and Matthew: 'Radio 4 is not a problem for the BBC. It's not like Radio 1. What changes we need to make, we can make gradually. We don't need to open another battlefront in Radio!' I was persuaded that Radio 4's schedule needed refashioning to take account of modern working patterns, to schedule programmes when contemporary audiences were available to listen, and not least to recognise that more women were at work and fewer at home. In addition, some programmes were tired, and some Radio 4 drama was too theatrical and old-fashioned for a generation reared on quality films and challenging TV drama. But we were not under any pressure, and we could make these changes over two or three years. James and Matthew were, if anything, more naturally zealous than I, but they were under the aegis of Will Wyatt – the safest pair of hands around. I was reassured.

Six months later I had a surprise: James Boyle unveiled his new plans at a meeting of the Board of Management. No papers were distributed in advance, and James showed us his new schedule on a projected slide. He proposed radical change, including shortening *The World at One* and moving *The Archers*. His arguments were impeccable. He had considered incremental change but decided against it on two grounds: every move of a Radio 4 programme – like the shift of *Woman's Hour* to the morning – provoked a row. It was better to have one almighty row rather than a succession of lesser explosions. Moreover, it was hard to make the changes incrementally. A move in any one part of the schedule inevitably had a knock-on effect, and more mayhem was caused by a succession of measures than by a single move. One change James proposed was to abandon *Yesterday in Parliament* – appreciated by MPs but roundly rejected by the audience in the half-hour before 9 a.m. – and to replace it at other times in the schedule with other programmes about Parliament.

As James, Matthew and Will talked, my mind churned: they were proposing change on a scale I had not asked of them, but the mood had shifted in the BBC by this point in 1997. The senior team was buoyant, self-confident and imbued with a can-do spirit. My colleagues warmed to James's radicalism. I made a snap decision. I deeply trusted and admired all three of my colleagues. I had my doubts about the proposals; I wished – as would normally have been the case – that I had had forewarning and some time to consider them; but such clear-sighted daring, I concluded, deserved support. In hindsight, I should have held them back, and reiterated the original brief, but I did not: I supported them without qualification. So did the Governors. On the move of *Yesterday in Parliament*, one said: 'It's the Berlin Wall. Tear it down!'

James conducted an impeccable programme of communication about the changes, but in the process alarmed Radio 4 listeners, producers and other key interests. He commissioned a large number of new programmes and drove a hard bargain on

price. The conservative radio production community, unused to
such tough-mindedness, reeled. Audience resistance intensified
when the new schedule was launched. Even those programmes
which would eventually be recognised as excellent were not immediately widely welcomed by many. Too many new programmes –
particularly in comedy and entertainment – had been commissioned
at the same time, and some were weak. As the general furore grew,
Speaker Betty Boothroyd led a revolt in Westminster against the
moves affecting *Yesterday in Parliament*. (Later, a compromise was brilliantly engineered by Jenny Abramsky, maintaining the programme
at greater length, but only on long wave.) James's bold new schedule
survived the months of disgruntlement. The programmes became
stronger. Some of his commissions – including John Peel's outstanding *Home Truths*, *Front Row* and *Broadcasting House* – would
become new favourites. Radio 4 drama became notably more contemporary. One play, Lee Hall's *Spoonface Steinberg*, was as moving
and powerful as any drama on TV or radio during my time as
Director-General. The storm eventually abated. Radio 4 remained
a marvel and a treasure-trove.

Radio 3, the third challenge, had an astonishingly high budget for
its small audience. I was comfortable with this mismatch because we
were supporting live music and BBC orchestras, investing in British
music, and encouraging new composition – and the glorious fruits of
this policy had been evident for decades. Helping to sustain a
vibrant part of British culture in this way was an important justification for the BBC. Successive Radio 3 Controllers had all been
brilliant impresarios. The Proms, in particular, quickened the pulse
each year, offering delicious musical confections and virtuoso thrills.

I was less comfortable, however, with the tone and ethos of Radio
3. Historically, the network had carried a Keep Out sign and had
been welcoming only to musicologists. It was like a stuffy private
club, out of tune with a meritocratic modern Britain, in which love
of serious music was growing, as the extraordinary success of
Classic FM – with many times Radio 3's audience – demonstrated.

Radio 3's defenders in the 1980s had acted like old cultural buf-
faloes, snorting and charging at any invader threatening change.
Controllers Nicholas Kenyon and later Roger Wright worked
valiantly to build a bridge to new audiences while maintaining the
cultural and intellectual authority and integrity of the station – but
the bridge was never quite completed in my time as Director-
General.

The gruff and forthright Rod Lynch, Managing Director of
Resources, faced the biggest challenge of anyone on my team. Rod
amalgamated into one division every kind of production and support staff from what had previously been the entirely separate
divisions of Television, Radio, the Regions and News. Rod found
himself with twelve thousand staff, hundreds of independently managed, independent-minded units, and hundreds of millions of
pounds' worth of studios, facilities and buildings. He employed, for
instance, all the BBC's camera operators, sound technicians, studio
operatives, designers, engineers, canteen and security staff. The
analysis conducted when we designed Producer Choice had shown
that the BBC had far more people and facilities than it needed. We
had already shed some, but we knew that Rod would have to shed
more. Resources staff, however, were already grieving and in shock,
for they had previously been part of Television or one of the other
divisions, their activities directly funded. They had led protected,
easy and generally satisfying lives. Now they were bracing themselves for the fierce and unaccustomed forces of the market, for
they had to *sell* their services to their former colleagues, and in competition with the independent facilities sector. The tradition within
the BBC's engineering and facilities arms had long been that *they*
would determine the nature of the service their programme colleagues needed. Henceforth, their clientele, BBC producers – and
not they – would decide what was required. This transition would
prove impossible for some Resources managers and staff, and
difficult and lengthy for many.

There was an additional problem: BBC Resources needed to introduce basic business planning for the first time, to understand how much their activities cost, and to price their services – and yet they had inherited a multiplicity of weak and differently designed financial systems, which needed a fundamental overhaul. For Rod Lynch and his team, it would be a marathon. Over the next few years, new ways of working and new conditions of service were introduced, and the staff of BBC Resources was nearly halved, to 6400 – all of which was achieved, to our surprise, without major industrial action. The first reason for this was that the workforce never united around a single proposition. And the BBC unions were not strong: the main union – BECTU – was fighting for its own survival, and had had no moral support from a Tory government and little from a modernising Labour Opposition. Moreover, the BBC's redundancy and early-retirement packages were generous. The peak of union resistance when it came was over new conditions of service designed to modernise our pay structures. A series of short stoppages was called and, when they threatened to escalate and to become seriously disruptive, the management team decided to draw a line. I wrote a letter to all BBC staff:

Many licence payers working in other industries, and some who are not in work at all . . . will see resistance to proposals that apply widely in British industry as demonstrating that the BBC's unions, and some of its staff, are out of touch . . . Though the principles underlying our proposals never were and never will be negotiable, we were ready – over many days of discussions – to refine the detail in the light of proper staff concern expressed through the unions. These discussions were fruitful; they produced a final, rounded proposition; and they are at an end. No further discussions will take place at corporate level . . . If there is any further industrial action we shall invoke formal procedures.

This last point was code – widely understood – for declaring that anyone taking further industrial action faced dismissal. My letter produced an angry response, but the industrial action ended and new working conditions were agreed.

In BBC Resources Rod Lynch was battling on other fronts, not least attempting to create a customer service ethic in the directorate. It was proving arduous. And although Resources won 90 per cent of BBC business and immediately attracted tens of millions of pounds of outside custom, many business units struggled to adjust to the new realities and to break even – and it was some years before BBC Resources finally moved into profit. But Rod's heroic, unsung labours – reducing over-capacity and promoting efficiency – produced a dividend of hundreds of millions of pounds a year in savings which was reinvested in extra programmes, in better pay and in sports rights. Rod's reward for making life better for the licence-payer was to become the target of an orchestrated hate campaign. His phone was tapped, his private life exposed, and an ugly and anonymously edited samizdat magazine targeted at him was circulated in his department.

The introduction of Producer Choice and the modernisation drive were a great shock to BBC staff, who had existed in a steady state for decades. In a world without e-mail, plans for communicating with them did not initially work well. All major announcements were broadcast live on the internal system. *Ariel*, the staff paper, would carry full accounts of every change. Special briefing documentation would be cascaded down to managers and staff. But we soon realised that our middle managers were not doing what we asked of them – to meet routinely and regularly with all their teams, and to interpret what BBC-wide policies meant for their particular group. Managers had traditionally never 'owned' BBC-wide plans or policies, ruling their fiefdoms as *they* saw fit. Moreover, many feared they had neither the skill nor the knowledge to deal face to face with the testing and hostile questioning of their staff, so they were nervous about convening meetings.

Borrowing a device British Airways had used, we decided to introduce daily workshops in BBC offices in Marylebone High Street in London, which – over the next few years – twenty-three thousand BBC staff attended. Each day, a hundred staff drawn from every part of the BBC would spend a morning and an after-noon learning about, and debating, the BBC's challenges, and the strategies for meeting them. At the end of the day, two members of the Board of Management – one of them often me – would face an hour of questions, and stay for a drink afterwards. As a result, the top team had a daily insight into the way the debate in the BBC was moving. At the beginning, the sessions were generally tense, antag-onistic and truculent, and I would often respond pugnaciously, pulling no punches. Sometimes, though, they were sad, hesitant and quizzical. Many BBC staff had been drawn to the organisation not only because it offered satisfying work but because it promised a secure and unpressured environment. They realised they were living in a Britain where nearly every organisation – whether in the public or in the private sector – was also experiencing profound change, but it was only human to hope it would not happen to them. They felt disconnected, and it was not difficult to sympathise with their situation however unavoidable it was. When we began the workshops, few staff had considered the position of the BBC over-all, understandably focusing on their day-to-day work. But, over the months, the organisation moved – the challenges were better understood. Increasingly, the dialogue was about effective imple-mentation rather than the objectives themselves. Around six months in, the management team occasionally began to receive applause at the end of the hour of grilling.

We introduced a whole battery of additional communication measures. The senior management team ran seminars, for instance, in the Council Chamber for the creative community – top writers, presenters, producers and performers. We knew these big beasts

enjoyed moaning to anyone who would listen – a dinner-party companion, a visiting politician, any journalist who phoned them up. We
employed some of the greatest talents in the land, but many were
egocentric, uninterested in the BBC's wider problems, obsessed only
with the comfort of the particular creative space they themselves
inhabited. We would explain the big picture, listen to their complaints and try to address those that were justified. My senior team
and I were determinedly patient: we became inured to adverse criticism, never responding with the wicked thought that sometimes
silently crossed our minds – that these were the carping whinges of
the precious and protected, and that any hundred licence-payers
plucked at random from the real world beyond Broadcasting House
and the BBC's Television Centre would have given the poor luvvies
short shrift.

Ben Elton came to one session and soon stood up. I feared we
were about to be the target of one of Ben's devastating comedy
onslaughts, but he turned his back on the management team, and
took out his ire on the audience, expressing brilliantly and with great
comic and rhetorical force what we secretly thought, poking fun at
their preciousness, their failure to appreciate how privileged they
were, pointing out just how much their lives and working conditions
contrasted with most people's. Afterwards Ben wrote to me at length
to let off steam: 'Have you ever heard such self-serving whinge-
ing? . . . how you and Will kept your tempers is beyond me . . .!' He
ended generously: 'thank you for ensuring that there still is a BBC'.

We introduced regular surveys of BBC staff opinion in the 1990s,
conducted independently by an experienced specialist organisation
and on the same basis as a number of other large institutions. It was
commonly observed in the press – as it had been when I first arrived
at the BBC following the crises in the mid-1980s – that staff morale
had never been so low, and that we faced an exodus of talent. The
evidence for this was the barrage of staff criticism to which the
press was continuously exposed. The natural complainers were not
afraid to grumble, mostly anonymously, but hard evidence told a

subtly different story. Staff were remaining at the BBC, not leaving. Turnover was well below the average for large institutions, and well below the position in the BBC in the late 1980s. Our survey showed that staff believed in the BBC and were proud of and satisfied with their work. They were not, however, happy with the way the BBC was managed. This was not new: a staff survey conducted in the World Service a few years before I came to office revealed precisely the same picture. Moreover, staff opinion was not in general out of line with other large organisations, not least those undergoing change. Over the years, as we worked away at our mammoth task, our surveys told us that staff were gaining a deeper understanding of the reasons for change, and that morale was beginning to show significant improvement, reaching a high-water mark in 1997. Morale at the centre – and among the top two hundred managers – was high, as it was with new young recruits, who were often scathing about their moaning elders. Morale was lower among the BBC's middle-aged male managers, among Resource staff (suffering the most painful change), and among news journalists – natural serial complainers (and the group most available to other media).

For many BBC staff, though, and especially the persistent com-plainers, I would be seen for ever as the person who had blasted their world apart – and though many would silently welcome the new freedoms and opportunities, the opening up of the BBC that the changes had brought, some would forever treat me with trepi-dation, fear or hostility.

My daughter Eliza once went clubbing in London with a girl-friend from Cambridge. Her friend found herself dancing with a dishy young man who turned out to be a BBC stage-hand. The two girls wound him up and encouraged him to talk, not revealing Eliza's identity: 'Yeh, the BBC used to be a right cushy number until that bloke John Birt took over!' he revealed.

In 1993, as the reforms began to bite and public debate about the modernisation process grew, we faced an increasingly hostile press, chiefly focused on me. For some BBC old-timers, I was a foreign body they still wanted to see expelled from the organisation. Mark Tully, our revered Delhi correspondent, whom I had visited the year before, mounted a surprise attack in July at a conference of radio programme-makers in Birmingham. Tully started softly. He found me 'sympathetic and understanding', 'warm, relaxed and friendly, quite the opposite of the impression I had been given'. Then: 'As someone who has worked for the Corporation for nearly thirty years, I don't think he understands what the BBC was, or indeed what it should become.' He proceeded systematically to oppose not only the reforms themselves, but even the notion that any significant change was necessary. He was a justifiably popular figure, and his speech was well received and reported as a sensation. I was due to speak from the very same platform on the following day. I bashed back. I singled out 'old BBC soldiers, sniping with their muskets, still telling nostalgic tales of the golden days when no one bothered much about management, when all was creativity and romance . . . They say all the BBC has to do to ward off political predators is to make good programmes . . . They are ostriches if they really believe that!'

I had a surprise at the end of my speech: I received a long, warm ovation, just like Tully's the day before. I concluded that the audience sympathised with us both. They understood why an old soldier wanted to hold on to his world; they understood too why that world had to change and sympathised with my lot as the main agent of that change. I would note such ambivalence again and again in the years ahead. Jeremy Isaacs sent me a note: 'That was an excellent speech yesterday, a leader's speech . . . your people and your policies will win through.'

In August, Dennis Potter – at his peak, a writer of great emotional power – took to the stage at what was becoming for the BBC the troublesome Edinburgh Television Festival. As Michael Grade had done the previous year, Potter dipped his pen in venom and aimed savage, hysterical abuse at me and my works:

The small minority who are the political right – before its wholly ideological transformation into the type of venal, wet-mouthed radicalism which can even assert without a hint of shame that 'there is no such thing as society' – before these people had yet launched their poison arrows . . . we have in the fullness of such darkness been sent unto us a Director-General who bares his chest to receive such arrows, a Saint Sebastian eager for their punishing stings . . . My impression was that there is now a one-way system of communication, and that the signals being sent down the narrowed track were so laden with costive, blurb and bubble driven didacticism that they were more than half perceived as emanating in a squeak of static from someone or, rather some*thing*, alien and hostile. And you cannot make a pair of croak-voiced Daleks appear benevolent even if you dress one of them in an Armani suit and call the other Marmaduke.

We bounced back quickly. Will Wyatt immediately issued a response: 'I make no apologies for seeking a BBC that is well run. The beneficiaries are the programmes and the public. Pennies don't rain down from heaven in broadcasting.' When I was interviewed by Kirsty Wark at the Festival the following day, she asked me if I regretted leaving behind the riches of LWT for the treacherous waters of the BBC. Suddenly spying Greg Dyke – now mighty rich from his LWT share options – in the front row of the audience, I asked: 'Which would you prefer, Greg, seven million pounds or national vilification?' A wave of friendly laughter and sympathy from the audience washed over me.

The next day, the Festival debated the motion 'The BBC is in danger of destroying itself from within.' Steve Morrison from Granada and Roger Bolton supported the motion and Bob Phillis and Mark Thompson opposed it. The debate took place in front of about five hundred of the most vocal producers and creative talents in the industry. Steve Morrison lectured the BBC patronisingly on how to manage. Roger Bolton was more convincing as the BBC's loyal but saddened friend. Bob Phillis for the Corporation responded with bonhomie, energy and conviction, Mark Thompson with wit and a compelling case for our creative credentials:

> I would argue that creative leadership, programme leadership – the leadership that matters to the BBC more than anything else – is stronger today than it's been for years . . . There's a buzz in the air, a sense that we're entering a period of intense programme renewal.

David Aaronovitch, from BBC Current Affairs, LWT alumnus and inventor of *On the Record*, delivered decisive support from the audience, demolishing with humour a key proposition of Steve Morrison – who had denounced Producer Choice on the ground that it had cost £125 to acquire a black tie for a BBC presenter. David fought back:

> The producer was told that you had to have somebody take half a day off to take a taxi and go to the place where the black tie was, pick it up, and all that would cost 125 quid. And this was an example of the ludicrousness of Producer Choice. But hold on a second. What happened before Producer Choice? Well, of course, a person took half a day off, went in a taxi, picked up the tie, and brought it back. The only difference was that you never knew that's how much it cost you! What Producer Choice allowed you to do was to find out that a ludicrous thing was going on and stop it!

David brought the house down, and turned the argument. John Woodward – the steady, astute leader of the Independent Producers' Association – also spoke up in support of the BBC:

> If you had asked delegates two years ago what we'd be debating in Edinburgh in 1993 . . . it would have been: is the

BBC actually going to survive? The truth is Producer Choice
is an integral part of a strategy . . . to keep the BBC and its
public service objectives in place.

We had expected to lose the debate, but to our relief, when the vote
was taken, the anti-BBC motion was overwhelmingly defeated.
Potter's vitriol had not proved persuasive. The industry was more
considered than we had thought.

Soon after Edinburgh, Prime Minister John Major and I compared notes. He had his own problems with a fractious and
disunited party and a small Parliamentary majority. He and I laugh-
ingly agreed that England manager Graham Taylor – after a dismal
series of results – was top of the national vilification league; the
Prime Minister second; and me third.

The top team continued the fight-back: Alan Yentob and Liz
Forgan went into bat in September. Liz:

> [We are] now in an acute phase of re-examining every single
> bit of procedure and overhead in the BBC, shaking it upside
> down and causing a lot of grief and a lot of redundancies
> and a lot of very tough thinking. This has been dedicated to
> one end, and that is to eliminate absolutely every piece of
> expenditure that we don't have to spend on things other than
> making programmes.

Alan:

> Whether you approve of this system or not, there has to be
> change . . . it may be uncomfortable, and knowing what we
> used to spend on things may be uncomfortable – but on the
> other hand without it we will have no future.

I was impressed by the fighting power, the willingness to do battle,
the confidence and resilience of my top team. We were under

assault, but anyone seeing us together would not have found us downcast. Our discussions were comradely, spirited and lively, open and frank, full of good jokes and laughter.

Peter Brooke, David Mellor's successor as Secretary of State, lent us his support:

> if the BBC had not made – and does not continue to make – changes, the future of the licence fee in the short term, and of the BBC itself in the longer term, might need to be considered from a very different perspective. We might . . . find ourselves contemplating, rather sadly, the demise of a dinosaur . . . The bureaucratic monolith that remained intact from the war might have survived in Jurassic Park, but it would have no chance in the real world.

The *Sun* waded in: 'Hard luck, luvvies. Welcome to the real world. John Birt's daunting task is to drag the BBC into the Nineties . . . If he fails he'll get the sack and there'll probably be no BBC.' The *Sun*'s support wasn't typical. However much we were winning the debate in hand-to-hand fighting, and where it mattered, the papers were ceaselessly reporting the continuing opposition of many BBC staff to the reforms.

In 1993 I attended a seminar at Chevening organised by Sir Robin Butler, the Cabinet secretary, who had become a friend. He invited six senior permanent secretaries and six outsiders – mostly chairmen or chief executives of top British companies. As a group, we let our hair down, making true confessions, sharing our problems and approaches, with a business school professor as our convenor. Before the conference the professor had asked us all to fill in a questionnaire with hundreds of questions to which there was no obviously 'right' answer: 'Would you rather sail on a lake or on a sea?' Or: 'At a party, do you prefer talking to one person for a long time or to many people for a short time?' After the final session on the second day, he handed each of us a chart. We were supposed to take our charts back to our rooms for study – but each of us had a large, elaborate star drawn on the cover which immediately caught the eye. We soon noticed that each delegate's star had a different shape, and gathered round curiously. 'It identifies your key characteristics,' the professor explained. Someone observed that, while most of the stars were wildly different, three were very similar – that of Terry Burns, my good friend, who was by this time permanent secretary of the Treasury; that of David Gilmour, head of the Foreign Office; and mine. Each of us had a star with a strikingly sharp spike, far longer than anyone else's. 'What does it mean?' we asked. 'It means that the three of you are very determined to see through a course of action; that you are really *ruthless* in pursuit of a goal!' the professor explained to laughter, noting that public sector managers seemed, on this evidence, to be tougher than the private sector's. Terry's spike was one notch longer than David's or mine, at the very end of the scale. 'He is the most ruthless of you all!' declared the professor. The civil servants among us were most tickled, pleased to have their prejudices about the Treasury scientifically confirmed. 'But at least I only got nine out of ten,' Terry responded defensively. 'Nine is the highest score you can get!' the professor shot back.

By 1994 the Charter process had long been settled in principle, but as the final details were being hammered out I had a meeting in the Cabinet Room at Downing Street with John Major, who took me aback with his generosity. He listened patiently as I explained what the BBC was trying to do to become more creative, efficient, effective and accountable. Then he responded: 'I know a great deal about what's been happening. I consider it an *astonishing* achievement. The BBC was facing decline. It is now making a remarkable recovery. I congratulate you!' He and I went on to talk for nearly an hour and a half. The Prime Minister seemed tired and gloomy – not surprising given his tiny majority, a hostile press and a party bitterly divided over the single issue of Europe, with a sizeable faction not afraid to cause him trouble. He ruminated about the importance of the BBC. He wanted *Blue Peter*, not cartoons, for Britain's children. *The Antiques Roadshow* touched the heart of Britain. The BBC must maintain its quality and have the financial capacity to do so. We discussed the funding need. He went on to despair about the growth of satellite and its impact on Britain: we were being flooded with lowest-common-denominator material; satellite was promoting a culture of violence. Why did the BBC have to collaborate with Sky on sport, the Prime Minister asked? I explained that Sky's subscription funding had priced us out of most live sport, and recorded rights were all we could generally afford.

At this point he asked his civil servants to leave and we were left alone in the Cabinet Room together. Not for the first or last time, he let his hair down with me. Others told me he felt comfortable with me because I wasn't a toff, and he was sensitive to people he felt looked down on him. He railed against Murdoch, and his power, against the unfairness of the press, particularly the Tory press, and his difficulties over policy. It was impossible to spend time in John Major's company without feeling he was a really decent, well-motivated man with good instincts who had been unlucky in his moment of power. (In an unsung act, he would later veto, against the advice of colleagues, the privatisation of Channel 4.)

At the end of the session, we turned back to the BBC. Hussey had been a good Chairman, I told Major – arguably the first in the BBC's history who had not been seen off by the institution. I hoped the next Chairman would be as resolute.

In the summer, at the invitation of producer Sue Birtwhistle, I went to see *Pride and Prejudice* being shot in Wiltshire, and stayed for lunch with the cast. The assurance and self-confidence of the whole team was tangible. It was to be a good summer: in July the government's White Paper on the future of the BBC was finally published, giving us all that we could have wished for. Peter Brooke told Parliament: 'What has been said about the BBC, and within the BBC, over the past two or three years has demonstrated that a

major revolution has been taking place in the corporation.' Years of
hard and grinding work had paid off. Somewhat to my surprise, the
following day I had my best press ever at the BBC, dominating the
front pages:

VICTORY FOR BIRT'S BBC REVOLUTION
(*Guardian*)

BIRT'S BBC IS GIVEN ITS REWARD
(*Independent*)

A TRIUMPH FOR BIRT AFTER TWO YEARS OF
SNIPING AND REFORMS
(*Daily Mail*)

By convincing Ministers that the BBC is serious about
efficiency and value for money, he has ended a decade-
long battle between the corporation and the Tory Party.

BIRT TRIUMPHS IN BATTLE OF THE BBC
(*The Times*)

He has overcome every obstacle and come out on top . . . For
Mr Birt, the White Paper vindicates years of job cuts and
re-organisation . . . Mr Birt won everything for which he had
campaigned during six turbulent years.

I had done nothing whatsoever directly to prompt such coverage,
and could not have anticipated it, given my generally adverse press,
but these plaudits created a significant problem for the very first time
between myself and my Chairman, Duke Hussey. My sources told
me that Hussey was bitterly angry that I – and not he – had been
handed the credit for delivering the BBC whole and intact at the
end of the marathon Charter process. Not only did Hussey not feature in the headlines, he was nowhere mentioned in the stories that
accompanied them. There was justice in his resentment. One of my

colleagues said of Hussey: 'He sees two or three things really clearly: the rest is a fog.' Hussey would not have had the slightest idea himself how to reform the BBC's journalism, or how to turn the BBC into a modern and efficient organisation. But he was cunning, a good networker and gossip who picked up scuttlebutt and what the critics and wiseacres were saying; and he could be effective at spotting the small signs that showed that something big was wrong. His intuition told him I would sort out the BBC; he had supported me wholeheartedly. He was definitely on the team and deserved much more credit than he got. But the day I stole the headlines was the moment when our relationship began to deteriorate – for Duke Hussey was a vain and egocentric man, and his pride had been hurt.

Jane organised a surprise party for my fiftieth birthday in 1994 in the form of a pantomime based on the story of my life. Andy Mayer – my old *Nice Time* co-conspirator – wrote the script as a series of sketches chronicling the main chapters of my life, the parts acted by friends. Ben Elton did the warm-up, David Frost was the narrator. Howell James, who as a child actor had appeared in *Goodbye Mr Chips*, played me as an infant tidying the drawer, and as a schoolboy in a St Mary's uniform that Laurie Taylor had purloined. Laurie himself played a chilling Christian Brother, as to the manner born. Mick Sadler, comedy supremo from my Oxford days, took the part of me as a grown-up menace to society. Gus Macdonald, Barry Cox, Nick Elliott, Greg Dyke, Peter Mandelson, Cilla Black and Nick Lovegrove all played supporting parts. Terry Burns and Peter Jay appeared trying to teach me economics. Germaine Greer sang. JJ played my dad. Ron, our builder, played the music. Richard Eyre, from the National Theatre, held up cue cards. The audience was divided into pro- and anti-Birtists and issued with whistles and blowers. Journalists in the audience like Polly Toynbee, Ian Hargreaves and Simon Jenkins wore reptile masks. Robin Butler, Colette Bowe and Lucy Lambton were the cheerleaders for my supporters. The antis held up placards: 'Birt, Birt, Birt. Out, Out, Out.' 'Dirty Birty hides under Maggie's skirty.' The pros: 'More Internal Markets please. We can't get enough.' 'John's our man with the masterplan.' Early in the proceedings, Christopher Bland was put in a cage with a bullwhip, and the audience was threatened that Christopher would be unleashed if they didn't behave. He snarled and rattled his cage and cracked his whip at them. Afterwards we ate scouse and drank Manhattan cocktails. Peter Jay made a sweet speech of tribute. Everyone gave my mother an ovation. A group gathered round Tony Blair, keen to meet the coming man. I had a lovely evening, surrounded by family and friends, enjoying the wit, style and brio of British public life at its best.

I needed my friends, for the following year, 1995, was distressing. The savings were coming through. We were making more programmes, and had almost eradicated the long months of repeats in the spring and summer. Network Television had met budget, its managers insisted, for the first time in twenty years. But the work for me and my team was exhausting, and we were coming into our third year of it. The task of reforming a large, complex organisation split into hundreds of activities, with complicated interrelationships, was vast. We were having to rethink, to redesign, every aspect of how the corporation functioned, revising archaic, outdated systems and ways of working, inventing from scratch where there was no system. We tackled a huge array of issues from programme failure to a new technology backbone to equal opportunity to unprofitable commercial subsidiaries. As the new systems came on stream, we had much better information, which normally meant we identified fresh problems to tackle.

Day in, day out, we laboured. A simple, modest change could take months to achieve. Each day would normally bring ten or so intense meetings, from nine in the morning to seven or eight at night, most dealing with a matter of real substance and importance. An enormous amount of off-stage work would normally accompany each meeting, with a paper prepared in advance to focus the discussion and analyse the decision to be made. Katie Kay marshalled all of my time, helped by the unendingly cheerful Sonia Cooper. Clare Riley, who had been on the Producer Choice project team, worked all hours and tirelessly for much of my time as Director-General as my chief of staff, driving every activity with which I was involved, progress-chasing, making sure the right work was done on time. I would read papers all day Sunday, on most evenings late into the night, and from the moment I was picked up each morning by my driver, Brian. My colleagues had to work just as hard.

In truth I was pressing them and the organisation relentlessly and remorselessly, urging every part of the BBC to tackle a great stack of problems of every kind that had piled up over decades. Under such intense pressure, many managers and staff, under-standably, craved a return to laissez-faire. But I had never been able to tolerate disorder or manifest weakness and I was impatient to turn the lumbering, dysfunctional giant of the BBC into something more adept, agile and fleet-footed. I was certainly driven, better sometimes at identifying problems than applauding success – and, for at least some of my colleagues, I was over-zealous. The whole team was on occasions worn down by the punishing pace, by work which was rewarding in the long but not in the short term, and not always much fun. We were all of us caught up in a just but gruelling cause, as in a war. I felt sad that I should be their leader in a period of such adversity, and moved and impressed that for almost all of the time we stood shoulder to shoulder.

Other difficulties outside our control also pressed upon us. Rodney, our Director of Finance, had on arrival put his foot sharply on the brake to control the rate we spent cash, and thus stop us exceeding our borrowing limit. In 1993 Secretary of State Peter Brooke had added to our problems by requiring us to reduce our considerable borrowings to zero. Controlling our cash more tightly put significant extra strain on the system and forced us to revisit our long-term schedule for making programmes. Some series were delayed, bringing protests.

After my relationship with Hussey started to sour over the Charter announcement, he had taken to lecturing me about staff morale. He heard grumbles – as I did – wherever he went in the BBC, but in all the circumstances I found his concerns a bit rich. No one had pressed me harder than Hussey to reduce staff numbers, to make the BBC more efficient. We had embarked on a process which would in the end shed many thousands of staff in an organisation which, historically, had only ever known expansion. We had introduced much tougher, more rigorous discipline to a previously chaotic Corporation. We were slowing down our programme-making to reduce our borrowings. We could hardly be surprised if the staff weren't exactly happy, but we were making progress – as the daily staff meetings, and the surveys showed – in instilling some realism in the BBC. We had averted significant industrial action. Our programmes and services were manifestly improving. What we were achieving was little short of miraculous. But Hussey would not hold back from criticising. Indeed, he opened up new lines of attack. With a new Charter secured, I had begun work on the implication of the new digital technologies, which I sensed would have a revolutionary impact on broadcasting. Hussey nagged me to abandon the work, saying I should give the BBC a rest for a few years, but I persevered. He began pressing me to ease up on my colleagues and on my plans in general.

In truth, with the Charter won, Hussey had no goal, and he was indulging his pronounced appetite for mischief. He was more of a nineteenth- than a twentieth-century man, more colonial administrator than modern manager, and he distrusted analysis, preferring to live on his wits and instincts. He had no taste at all for the drive to modernise the BBC. Moreover, he had sustained terrible injuries in the war and had endured pain without complaint ever after, but now it seemed to be wearing him down. He was looking far older than his seventy-one years. When I had first met and worked with him, his plotting, backbiting and egocentricity had been tempered by his cheerful good humour, his jolly, crackling laugh and his spirit for a fight. By 1995 he was invariably cantankerous, cranky and obsessive, and his company was hard to bear. He and I spent little time together. The awful burden of supporting this once successful but now crumbling relationship fell on the BBC's young Secretary, Michael Stevenson, a one-time Radio 3 and TV current affairs producer, still only in his thirties. Michael had a fine mind, extraordinary resilience and firmness of purpose and sagacity beyond his years. More than anyone, he would hold the BBC together in the difficult period ahead.

Hussey started to inflate the importance of the kind of tricky editorial issues which, in the BBC, were as inevitable as bad weather: a permanent secretary protested about secret filming in government offices; *Panorama* scheduled an interview with John Major just before local elections in Scotland which the Scottish courts interdicted; Labour organised its historic conference to drop Clause 4 just before local elections and the Tories protested that the BBC planned to televise it.

At the 1995 annual spring conference of the Governors and senior management, Hussey orchestrated huge dramas, taking the Governors out of the joint session to meet alone, trying to find ways of forcing me to slow down or halt the modernisation process. Michael Stevenson sought to broker a deal between Hussey and myself. I was furious and refused to consider any proposal: Hussey in my view was not making a serious point – he was simply creating trouble. Michael Stevenson thought I sailed very close to the wind, but Hussey didn't persevere. Rather, he chose another battleground in his increasingly personal campaign to reduce my power and to re-establish his own: the battle was over a project termed Stage 6.

Michael Checkland's vision had been to bring together all the BBC's journalists not just under a single management, but on a single site. The original intention had been to build a stand-alone News centre. When Checkland abandoned this plan, the fallback was to site the journalists in a low-cost extension to Television Centre. The process had already taken a frustrating eight years.

Tony Hall, the head of News, was due to bring the final detailed implementation plan to both boards in the summer of 1995. The case was strong: rationalisation would bring substantial savings, and Tony would have his command under one roof for the first time. Even more important, bringing Radio and TV together meant that specialist teams could be shared, and more efficient and effective dispositions made in the field.

The journalists all worked for Tony Hall, but, to my regret and distress, Liz Forgan – Radio's head – decided to oppose the move. BBC Radio had resisted the formation of a united News directorate in 1987, and had an understandable but sentimental attachment to journalists working for their networks operating out of Radio's heartland, Broadcasting House – and this despite the fact that the Radio newsroom there was one of the worst of many slums in the BBC, and as far away from being fit-for-purpose as could be imagined. Liz made her case with charm and care but she could not sway me or her colleagues on the Board of Management. Once a decision was made, we would normally assume collective responsibility for it when it went before the Governors. Unusually, Liz would not agree to that, and insisted on arguing her case to the Governors, and taking myself and her colleagues head on.

A crisis was brewing. I soon learnt that Hussey – who had accepted the case for a single News centre from the day I had joined the BBC – had reversed his position and would now join Liz in her fight. For eight years, Hussey had been effective in getting his board to unite behind him, so my immediate supposition was that he was likely to succeed on this occasion too – but he did not, for Michael Stevenson ensured that all the Governors understood the case and the implications of turning it down. A group of experienced Governors had become an increasingly important force on the board: Lord Nicholas Gordon-Lennox, an ex-ambassador; Sir David Scholey, a City chieftain; Bill Jordan, the union leader; Gwyn Jones, a successful Welsh entrepreneur; and Sir Kenneth Bloomfield, ex-civil servant head of the Northern Ireland Office. They didn't vote as a bloc as they didn't always agree, but they were rational, independent and in no one's pocket – neither mine nor the Chairman's. At the critical board meeting in August 1995, Liz made her case reasonably and eloquently for keeping the radio journalists in the bosom of Broadcasting House, but it wasn't accepted. Hussey supported her, and some Governors sat on the fence. But those who declared themselves voted for Stage 6 to go ahead. One Governor said afterwards: 'The world has moved on. The BBC has to change. The case was very strong. The time for sentiment and nostalgia is over.'

Hussey was distraught. He had taken me on and lost. I was as surprised as he evidently was. Liz – to no one's surprise, but to everyone's regret, including mine – decided that she could not stay on at the BBC. She was not an easy colleague but I was really sorry to lose her. She had tackled with energy and finesse some critical problems in Radio; she had been a passionate, articulate and prin-cipled defender of the BBC's highest ideals on the Board of Management; and she had been a tough, funny colleague, sturdy in a crisis. When I was knighted in 1998, the message that pleased me most was from Liz: 'For saving the BBC it's a modest reward. Congratulations.'

The Governors, or at least a steel core, had kept the BBC on course: the modernisation process would continue – but from that point Hussey's and my relationship broke down irretrievably. He resented me deeply. For my part, I had worked hard to take him with me on the path of reform; I had held nothing back from him; but he had forfeited my trust. As he became increasingly tormented and dis-tressed, he cast a gloom over the whole of the centre of the BBC, his irascibility and irrational behaviour depressing those with whom he came into contact. The prospect of another year before his term ended seemed unendurable. Life outside the BBC had never seemed more attractive, and for the first time as Director-General I con-templated leaving.

As the Hussey crisis gathered momentum, something happened which would have seemed a preposterous plot point in a bad novel: on 31 October 1995 Tony Hall told me that Diana, Princess of Wales had agreed to give an interview to Martin Bashir of *Panorama*. The interview would be conducted on Guy Fawkes Day. It would be her first and only major interview, and it would plunge the BBC into crisis.

Bashir had been investigating for *Panorama* the murky and mysterious business of how information about the private lives of both Princess Diana and Prince Charles had been uncovered, including the interception of private phone calls. He talked to people in Diana's circle, including her brother Earl Spencer, and eventually to Diana herself, who was obsessed with a perpetual and invasive scrutiny she felt unable to combat or to escape. She told Bashir she was followed wherever she went, the media constantly tipped off about her whereabouts. She suspected some of her staff were agents working for others, whether for Prince Charles's household or for a major newspaper group. One of her intimates showed Bashir the junction box from which Diana believed her phone calls were intercepted. Bashir told us he had been introduced to a former member of the intelligence services who claimed that Diana's private apartments in Kensington Palace were bugged. *Panorama* was unable to obtain corroboration of any of these allegations, so no programme based on them could be mounted. But exploring Diana's concerns with her and her circle helped Bashir to establish a relationship of trust with Diana. She began to talk to him about the wider issues which consumed her – her marriage to Prince Charles and her relationship with the Royal Family. Eventually Bashir proposed, and Diana agreed to, a *Panorama* interview.

Princess Diana placed no restrictions on her appearance, but she did impose one condition: she and she alone must inform the Queen about the programme, after it had been recorded, and after Her Majesty had returned from a state visit to New Zealand, but seven days before transmission. Secrecy must be maintained till Diana had told the Queen; there could be no leak. Diana did not stipulate that the interview should be kept secret from Hussey, but she offered her judgement that if Hussey were told the interview would never happen, that it would be stopped. She had good reason for thinking this, for Diana knew her man and Hussey's loyalties were clear and understandable. His spouse – the striking, characterful and strong-willed Lady Susan – was a long-standing lady-in-waiting to the Queen and Her Majesty's closest intimate. Hussey himself was an ultra-monarchist. I knew from years of chatting to him that he revered the institution like no other. Hussey had an older toff's disdain for many politicians, particularly the younger crop on both front benches, but he was a devoted supporter of Prince Charles and he took the Prince's side unquestioningly as the dispute between Charles and Diana became ever more public. Hussey's emotions, unlike mine, were intensely engaged by these matters. On a number of occasions he had spoken to me poisonously about Diana's character, as had others in the Charles camp. I knew Hussey would be outraged by Diana breaking ranks and speaking out. (After the event, Hussey would say: 'I don't think the BBC should have got itself into a position involving the private problems of the Royal Family. That's not what the BBC is about.')

Tony Hall and I discussed the issues raised by the interview – first together, then with a small core group who were in on the secret: Tim Gardam, head of current affairs, Richard Ayre, the BBC's editorial policy adviser, and Steve Hewlett, editor of *Panorama*. Was an interview justifiable? We had no illusions that Diana speaking out would create a sensation, but we could see no reason not to proceed: Charles himself had spoken to Jonathan Dimbleby about his private relationships, and if Diana wanted to put her own point of view that was surely her right. We talked long and hard, though, about issues of taste. We knew there would be a furore over the interview, and that it would raise powerful emotions. The acid test, I stipulated, was that the British people, as a whole, when they saw the completed programme, should be comfortable with it, that they should feel the BBC had behaved appropriately, that while the tone could be journalistic and questioning, the interview should be dignified and not intrusive, that we should be mindful of the sensitivities of the many in the audience who revere the Royal Family.

'Will you tell Hussey in advance about the interview?' Tim Gardam asked me at the end of the meeting. 'Leave that to me,' I replied, and didn't expand further.

Alone I wrestled with the issue Tim had raised, but not for long. My relationship with Hussey had deteriorated to the point where we had not spoken informally for many months. The situation at the top of the BBC was already highly combustible. My judgement was that Hussey would explode when he was told about the interview. If he were told before it was recorded, in his current emotional state, the outcome was unpredictable. Any move by Hussey, whether direct or indirect, to subvert the interview in advance would create a real constitutional crisis within the BBC and beyond. Moreover, I reasoned that telling Hussey would put him in an impossible personal position. If, against my expectation, he *did* sit on the information until after the interview was recorded, and until Princess Diana had told the Queen, after the event Hussey would be seen by his wife and by the Royal Household to have been complicit in Diana's betrayal – a betrayal which I knew would be greeted in the Palace with a mix of fear and outrage, because for some there – if not all – Diana was seen as the enemy.

I decided that waiting to tell Hussey at the same time the Queen was informed was the best of the unappealing options – and I made that decision alone, painfully aware of the implications for me personally. I told Jane that I thought it was very likely that I would lose my job because of it – for I well understood that in any normal circumstances the Director-General would have informed and sought counsel from the Chairman on such a sensitive matter as soon as it emerged. I had one strong if not clinching argument in my favour: I would be alerting the Chairman, indeed the world, about the interview seven days in advance of transmission. Hussey had often declared – mindful of the farrago in the 1980s when the Governors had attempted to ban the broadcast of the *Real Lives* programme featuring Martin McGuinness – that the Governors would never preview a programme before transmission, that their judgement about any programme would always come *after* the event. He and his board had a week to reverse that policy if they chose to. Denying them foreknowledge of the interview did not take away their right to act as they wanted.

The interview was recorded at Kensington Palace in conditions of strict secrecy. I was immediately given a full report of its contents but I asked not to see the interview until it had been edited to Tony Hall's satisfaction. The programme was assembled away from the BBC under tight security at a hotel in Eastbourne. Princess Diana was due to put her call in to the Palace early on the morning of 14 November. Hussey would be told at the same time by the intrepid intermediary Michael Stevenson, who, for his own protection, was brought into the circle of knowledge only at the last minute. The media would be informed a few hours later.

I took a daring and unconventional decision. On the Sunday before the announcement, I briefed a third party in strict confidence about the fact of the interview, and gave him an outline account of its content. I asked him – likewise in strict confidence – to brief the Royal Household the following day immediately the Queen was told. My purpose was to avoid an overreaction before transmission based on fear and ignorance. I wanted the Palace to understand that Princess Diana's interview was powerful but dignified and restrained.

Hussey *was* furious when told of the interview, and indignant he had not been informed earlier. When the news was released, it caused a sensation. When I saw the interview myself I didn't ask for any changes. I was impressed by the Princess's judgement and composure. She told the story of her time as a member of the Royal Family openly and compellingly but loyally. She was generous of spirit and not recriminatory or vindictive. Bashir had handled the interview well. Stories of Hussey's unhappiness soon reached the press, however, and were front-page news. When they were picked up by BBC News in a way not to his liking, Hussey ordered Colin Browne to order Tony Hall to order media reporter Torin Douglas to carry in full a statement from the Governors. The calm, unflappable Colin ignored the direction.

Ultra-Royalist forces were outraged that the BBC had given Diana a platform at all. It was put to me by several traditionally minded members of the House of Lords that my first duty was to the Queen and that I should have stopped the interview taking place. I had the chilling sense that a few centuries earlier my head would literally have rolled for the crime committed. A group of MPs and peers demanded that the BBC's Royal Charter be revoked. A *Telegraph* leader on the Friday before transmission said:

> It is very nice for the BBC to get its scoop and flog it around the world for vast sums, but does that make it right to act as it has done and betray the trust of the monarch who gives it the Charter and her officials who deal with the corporation honourably?

The mood was sombre at a Governors' meeting that had long been scheduled in the week before transmission. Some of the more conservative members were distinctly edgy, one asking me: 'Why spend money on such a programme?' Another fumed that we had breached a protocol with the Palace. But there was no substantive discussion: they were keeping their powder dry till they had seen the programme. Some of my closest friends and natural supporters told me that I had been wrong not to inform Hussey in advance, and were not much persuaded when I told them why I hadn't.

On the night the interview with Diana was broadcast, the streets of Britain were largely deserted. Twenty-three million people watched the programme. I was out of the country to receive an unexpected honour. Whatever their reception in the UK, the success of the BBC's reforms was increasingly noted abroad and an endless parade of visitors journeyed from every corner of the globe to see what they could learn from us. I was in New York to receive an Emmy, presented to me by David Frost, for my 'successful leadership of the BBC during a testing period in its history'. On the very same day that I basked in the warm applause of the world's media chiefs, an article by William Rees-Mogg, friend and country neighbour of Hussey, appeared in *The Times*: '. . . John Birt will have to apologise for his conduct, or he will have to go . . .' At JFK Airport on my way back to London the following morning I bumped into playwright David Hare and Richard Eyre – who had just been appointed a BBC Governor. Both were deeply tickled by the affair, enjoying the establishment's tribulations, much amused by Hussey's predicament.

The *Panorama* interview with Princess Diana was shown, almost simultaneously, over much of the world, and went on to dominate the news agenda in the UK for weeks. The thought in some quarters, prior to transmission, that in some way the interview was illegitimate all but evaporated the moment it was shown: Princess Diana's conviction, fluency and charm carried too much force to be denied. That did not inhibit Nicholas Soames, however, a Prince Charles loyalist, from implying in a *Newsnight* discussion on the night of the broadcast that the Princess was mentally unstable.

In the following days, the Palace seemed to be in a state of shock. From the moment the interview had first been mooted, I had been clear that it would adversely affect relations between the Palace and the BBC, which had historically been strong. The BBC took its role of chronicling major national events and institutions seriously, whether the Trooping of the Colour or the Queen's Jubilee. We had made substantial documentaries about the Royal Family. I had regularly met Robert Fellowes and Robin Janvrin, two of the most senior members of the Household, to discuss current issues, and I had become fond of them both. They were sensitive, decent, loyal servants of the Queen; they had exquisite courtesy and old-fashioned good manners; and they had thought hard about the place of the monarchy in contemporary Britain. We had often reflected together on the similarity of the issues facing both the BBC and the monarchy – the need to maintain the unchanging, long-lasting values of the institution while reinterpreting them so that they resonated with a modern, diverse Britain. I sympathised with the problems Fellowes and Janvrin had – of working not with a corporation which could in theory be changed but with a family with mortal needs and frailties, its membership fixed.

I knew from the beginning that Fellowes and Janvrin would be hurt by the fact of the interview. BBC programmes involving access to the Royal Family were normally painstakingly negotiated. The *Panorama* interview had by-passed these normal channels, in effect treating the monarchy like other institutions. I was sorry to hurt such good people, but we were not only recognising the need to report the breakdown of the marriage of the heir to the throne and of the future head of the Church of England, we were also recognising a shift in realities in a more democratic age: whatever the BBC had done in the past, its prime duty now was to its licence-payers. In effect, the Diana interview marked the end of the BBC's institutional reverence – though not its respect – for the monarchy.

I discussed some of these issues at an early, pained meeting with Robert Fellowes. Under pressure of argument I said to Robert: 'Modern institutions in the end have to operate as the public would wish – and we did. And they have no choice any longer but to be completely transparent. There are no long-lasting secrets at the BBC.' Pressed on why I hadn't alerted them to the interview earlier I had to say: 'It was Diana's right to tell, not ours.'

In the immediate aftermath of the interview, all the focus was on what Diana had said, but Hussey was at work and he had set out to oust me. He convened several meetings of the Governors without asking me to attend, as would have been normal. In the first, I was told, he tried to establish whether there was any appetite for condemning the programme, but he made no headway on that issue. In the second, he focused on the more promising matter that I had mishandled the setting up of the interview. Following this meeting, a stinging rebuke was drafted which he wanted all the Governors to endorse. He calculated, I was told, that its receipt would oblige me to resign. Most Governors thought I should have told Hussey about the interview in advance, and they felt a real sympathy for his confusion of loyalties – but they also understood *why* I hadn't informed him. They appreciated that the circumstances were unique, and they didn't want me to resign. Some Governors refused point blank to sign Hussey's tract. Gwyn Jones, the Governor for Wales, was particularly adamant that he would not put his signature to a note of condemnation.

The detail of these events as they unfolded was known only to the Governors and to myself, but as they were approaching their climax I had a long-planned social encounter with an intimate of Prince Charles, who surprised me by a thorough knowledge of events under way at the BBC. Someone had been briefing the Palace.

Michael Cocks, the BBC's Vice-Chairman, became the man of the hour. Lord Cocks was the lugubrious, taciturn former Labour Chief Whip in the first half of the 1980s who had been deselected by militants and hated the far left. In fact, he was a passionate social-ist, above all determined to help those who couldn't help themselves. He was also a cricket-lover, a stamp-collector and an incorruptible chapel-goer who came to the BBC by bus, having turned down the car and driver Hussey had offered him. Michael Cocks had no pre-tensions: he made no effort to understand broadcasting and he said little at meetings. He could be eccentric: in a roomful of people he would often go to a window and stand looking out for half an hour, muttering under his breath. Out of sorts once at a BBC conference, Cocks escaped to play snooker alone with another Governor, Nicky Gordon-Lennox. As the game progressed, Cocks drummed his fin-gers and hummed tunelessly as he often did, but said nothing. After ten minutes, he suddenly said: 'You know what, Nicky?'

'What, Cocksy?'

'I don't give a fuck about any of this!'

Fired by the experience of his deselection at the hand of Labour activists, however, Cocks did care about pressure groups. He would research them in the House of Lords library, visit their offices to sniff them out, and denounce them at BBC board meetings. He had astonishing dirt on individuals from – to me – undisclosed sources, which he would sometimes confide to me in an over-loud whisper in the middle of board meetings.

For some reason that I never understood, Cocks supported me from the day of his arrival at the BBC. At our very first meeting, he dubbed me 'Boss' and called me that ever after. He was not hostile to Dukey, but he always supported me when I needed help. He told his wife Valerie: 'The man's bloody good. The BBC couldn't get better!' When Hussey came after me over the Diana interview, he told Valerie: 'Hussey wants to fire Birt: I've told him he can't do it.' Cocks worked with the adroit Michael Stevenson to steady the situation.

As Hussey's manoeuvring against me intensified, Cocks's call to arms to some of his fellow Governors was typical: 'Come on, we've got to save that nice old fucker from himself.' Cocks articulated to his colleagues that, even though I was not a generally popular Director-General, the BBC would side with me and rally to my support if the Governors acted against me for facilitating a bold and revealing piece of broadcast journalism. And Cocks thought the Governors would be bound to lose any such battle for hearts and minds within the institution, for he too was mindful of the lesson of *Real Lives*. He sought a face-saving device for Hussey: it was proposed that a group of Governors would see me to discuss the Diana interview, and put the issue behind us.

Christmas intervened: as we broke for the holidays one of my colleagues close to the Governors wrote to sum up the point we had reached:

The Board of Management have suddenly seen that for all the difficulties of the autumn you remain firmly in charge. From the mood of the Board [of Governors] meeting [your

colleagues] realise that the core of the Board will not support
a move to embarrass you, and conclude that the Chairman is
isolated . . . Most [Governors] believe you should not have
embarrassed the Board . . . but see it as flowing from a break
at the top which they hold the Chairman fractionally more
responsible for than the DG.

Before my meeting with the group of Governors could be
arranged, I learnt through friends in government that relief was at
hand. National Heritage Secretary Virginia Bottomley – always
most sensitive to human issues – had concluded that my relationship
with Hussey was going nowhere. Her personal reading was that our
relationship had begun as paternal, but had become strained as I
ploughed my own furrow. She saw I felt oppressed and claustrophobic, and decided the matter needed to be brought to a
conclusion. She talked confidentially and gently to Hussey, and suggested that his work was done, that this was a good time to move on,
and he was persuaded.

The date for the meeting with the three Governors – Nicky
Gordon-Lennox, Bill Jordan and Michael Cocks – was set. By
chance it was put in the diary the very day before Hussey's retirement would be announced. I knew this, but the Governors I was
seeing did not. At the meeting, the Governors were more anguished
than condemnatory. Michael Cocks set the tone by saying the interview had been in the public interest and he now hoped the matter
could be laid to rest. Bill Jordan said the programme was excellent
but I must see it as part of my duty to keep Governors informed.
Nicky Gordon-Lennox was tougher: not telling the Chairman had
been an error of judgement, but my reasons for not doing so were
accepted. Their remarks were brief. I responded at length. Of
course I had an obligation to keep Governors informed, I said. I
believed no Director-General had ever done more to share with
the board the real issues and decisions facing the BBC, nor had been
more willing to be candid with them about sensitive and difficult

operational matters. I had kept nothing from them for nine years. I completely rejected the notion that I had made an error of judgement. The circumstances were unique. In those circumstances, I had made the right judgement.

Within minutes of the meeting starting, the three Governors cut straight to the central issue: what had gone wrong in the relationship between myself and the Chairman? They were surprised when I told them that Hussey and I had not spoken – except at board meetings – for around a year. I did my best to explain why the relationship had deteriorated, and the price the BBC was paying: some issues were festering, the reform process stalling, because Hussey had placed them out of bounds. What could we all do, they asked, to get the relationship back on the rails during Hussey's last twelve months? I knew his departure would be announced on the morrow, but I had no choice but to go through a long and uncomfortable charade exploring with them a plan of action. They proposed to help me by instituting regular discussions with a hard core of the board so that all the issues would surface and the BBC could stay on course. They left the meeting with their tails up, indignant, distinctly sympathetic to my position, resolved to see Hussey straight away and in a clear mood to remonstrate with him. They marched next door to Hussey's office. Before they could even sit down, Hussey told them, 'You'd better read this,' and handed them the statement about his resignation that was to be released the following day. The group was confounded.

While I had been meeting with the Governors, Colin Browne, the BBC's Director of Corporate Affairs, had taken a call from the *Daily Telegraph*. They had it from the highest source, they told Colin, that the Director-General had been severely censured by Governors. The *Telegraph* had been briefed about the outcome of a meeting which was still in progress. 'That's news to me. I'll come back to you,' Colin responded.

Colin talked to Hussey, who couldn't confirm the story. 'It wasn't me,' he protested, 'I wouldn't talk to the press.' Colin phoned back to deny the story. 'That's strange,' said the *Telegraph* journalist, 'Hussey just rang Charles Moore [the *Telegraph*'s editor] to tell him so!' The *Telegraph*'s story was untrue and uncorroborated but this didn't inhibit the paper from running a front-page story the next day: 'John Birt has been given a dressing down by governors . . . Mr Birt accepted that a mistake had been made.'

Just before the announcement that Hussey was to leave early was made public, I decided to phone and offer an olive branch. It was our first private conversation for a great while. I swallowed hard and paid tribute to him. I said that, whatever our recent differences, I recognised his invaluable role in getting the BBC back on the straight and narrow. He was bitter and ungracious. He had no emollient words to offer in return: 'Because I was going, and I knew I was, I had to bring out those differences,' he said.

The news that Hussey was to depart spread like wildfire. An announcement was made right across the organisation by a BBC News journalist on an internal loudspeaker system. Stumbling, the journalist said that Marmaduke Hussey, the *Director-General* of the BBC, was leaving. He immediately corrected his error. Hussey was on the phone to me straight away, splenetic: 'I want that person fired within ten minutes!' he demanded. I refused point blank to do anything about it, asserting that the punishment he proposed bore no relation to the crime. He slammed the phone down.

Then I learnt that Hussey was to hold an impromptu drinks party that evening in his office. Patricia Hodgson and Margaret Salmon came to drag me up. I was reluctant. 'Bloody well go up there!' Margaret ordered. I went grudgingly. We all sat around drinking champagne while Hussey ruminated and held forth. He had hated the way BBC old-timers like Brian Wenham, John Tusa and Mark Tully had attacked the current BBC, in the process damaging the institution. As we quaffed his champagne, Hussey repeated over and over again: '*I'm* not going to spit on the deck.' We had not yet read the *Telegraph*.

The Diana interview would reverberate for a long while to come.

Four months after transmission, in March 1996, Will Wyatt was
called to a meeting at the Palace with Robert Fellowes and Charles
Anson to be told that they had been considering for some time,
well before the Diana interview, taking away responsibility from the
BBC for the Queen's Christmas message and inviting ITN to produce it instead for the next three years. They had now decided to do
this. Will responded that the move would be seen as: 'The Royal
Household doesn't get mad, it gets even!'

Eighteen months later, I was woken at four o'clock on a Sunday
morning by Tony Hall with the shocking news that Princess Diana
had been in a car crash in Paris and was probably dead. The following days were editorially the most testing during my time at the
BBC. I drove straight to Television Centre, as did Will Wyatt and
legions of BBC editors and journalists. BBC News 24 did not yet
exist, so it took a while for the world's biggest broadcast news operation to get up to speed. I nominated Tony Hall to take the lead in
steering the whole of the BBC's response to the momentous news.
He chaired a group of the BBC's senior editorial figures who met
regularly throughout the day. Tony was impressively commanding –
calm and careful but swift in making a series of difficult programme
and operational decisions. I watched and listened to our output
continuously throughout the day and – with Will – contributed to
Tony's discussions, occasionally touching the tiller. The challenge we
all identified for the BBC that day was to gauge and to represent the
full measure of the nation's horror and loss. It was soon clear that
almost everyone was overwhelmed by the death of Diana: there
was a spontaneous outpouring of grief, and it was growing. The
BBC's task was not only to report events as they unwound but to
reflect those feelings, to meet the needs of the nation without
indulging them. On that day I was awed by the good judgement of
the BBC's news and programme teams operating across Britain.
    As the week progressed, the BBC continued to read the mood of
the country well as Kensington Palace became a place of pilgrimage,

surrounded by acres of flowers. I visited Kensington Gardens myself and saw the power Diana had to move every kind of Briton, of every age and background, men as well as women. The Palace that week did not read the mood well. The original intention had been for Diana's body to be sent to a public mortuary rather than to lie in state in a royal chapel. The Queen, Prince Charles and Diana's sons remained at Balmoral, silent and apart, remote from the grieving masses and their mother's body. The Queen was due to return to London by train only on the morning of the funeral, and to return to Balmoral the same day. The initial short funeral route was chosen, I was told, to facilitate her departure.

In the middle of the week the press turned ugly, demanding a more emotional response from the Royal Family, and they responded swiftly, returning to London. Diana's boys met the crowds, and the Queen gave an effective broadcast to the nation. A looming crisis for the monarchy was averted. The BBC had had a trying and challenging week helping the nation to mourn but had risen to the occasion well.

No senior BBC managers were invited to the funeral service but normal relations between the BBC and the Palace were eventually restored. Years later, the responsibility for the Queen's Christmas message reverted to the BBC. When I left the Corporation, I had a private audience with the Queen at Buckingham Palace. We had a long, friendly and convivial chat about the state of the BBC and other issues – she is an easy and relaxed conversationalist. But we did not touch on the difficulties over the Diana interview.

Who would be the new BBC Chairman after Hussey? I learnt that Virginia had first pondered Douglas Hurd as Chairman. Even as a pensée, though, this was vetoed by John Major as too political an appointment. Virginia eventually concluded that the BBC needed a Chairman from the fast lane – someone who was competent in finance and business, who was comfortable with strategy and who was at ease on the global stage.

The BBC had always needed a Chairman who was robust enough to protect its independence and to withstand the storms that, history showed, routinely rocked the institution. Now the BBC needed in addition a Chairman in a contemporary mould, at ease with change; someone who actually knew what a modern organisation looked like and who would not be daunted by the revolutionary challenge ahead that digital technology would bring. I was told that the government was considering a shortlist of two, both of whom fitted the bill: Christopher Bland, ex-LWT, forceful, independent, skilled in business, and Christopher Hogg, whom I also knew and admired as a calm, authoritative, tough-minded Chairman of Reuters, and Chairman and Chief Executive of Courtaulds. Both Christophers were exceptionally strong candidates. The main downside of Bland – in the government's mind – was that he and I would be too close, having been colleagues at LWT, and having remained friends. Virginia was also worried that the Labour Party would bridle at Bland's Conservative connections, but she knew he had many Labour friends and admirers, not least Robert Winston who had seen Bland in action chairing an NHS Trust. Virginia – more public spirited than party political animal – wanted, close to an election, a candidate who would command wide support. Both candidates were sounded out. Christopher Hogg's other commitments didn't allow him the time to take on the BBC, so Christopher Bland became the only candidate.

The day before Bland's appointment was to be announced, Virginia Bottomley telephoned to ask me to do all I could to get the Labour leadership to accept it. Tony Blair was en route back from Singapore and Jonathan Powell arranged for me to speak to him as soon as he landed. In the meantime, Virginia Bottomley's office rang back to say that Jack Cunningham – Labour's Heritage spokesman – had reacted badly to the embargoed news of Christopher's appointment. Cunningham was reported to have dubbed it the Conservative government's 'most Thatcherite appointment yet'.

Tony Blair called me as soon as he landed, his normal brisk and businesslike self. He came straight to the point, with no small-talk: 'Do you think Bland's the right man for the job?' I explained why I thought he was. 'He's a Tory: will he be impartial?' Tony demanded. I explained that, though Christopher had indeed been active in Conservative politics when young, he had been an impartial Vice-Chairman of the Independent Broadcasting Authority, and Chairman of LWT; that he had worked successfully and had friendships with people from a wide variety of political backgrounds; and that I was certain of his ability to hold the ring fairly between the parties. Tony was decisive. He would need to talk to his colleagues – but subject to that, he told me, Labour would not oppose the appointment. When the news was announced later that day, there were only mild grumblings from the Labour benches. I had not shared with any of my BBC colleagues the manoeuvrings over Hussey and Bland. On the day of the Bland announcement Patricia Hodgson looked me firmly in the eye and said: 'Well done. The whole autumn's been devoted to a power struggle. I'm glad it's all over.'

Jane and I took the Blands to dinner at the Ivy that night to celebrate. Over the next few days the media examined Christopher's appointment from every possible perspective. At the weekend he remarked: 'Tell me it gets less and the skin thicker!'

16

Finishing the Job

Christopher Bland's arrival as Chairman of the BBC in April 1996 marked the beginning of my happiest period at the institution. The fruits of years of reform were now evident. My first and greatest passion was programmes, intensified through all the wonderfully creative years at Granada, LWT and now the BBC, and I took keen pride and pleasure in the inspirational work we were producing. We had appointed a powerful team to the key channel and production positions, and they were triumphing. We were embarrassingly dominant at the annual BAFTA and Sony awards. We were winning more international prizes than at any time in our history. Despite massive new competition, 95 per cent of licence-payers were still consuming BBC services for a significant period of time each week, and we were stubbornly holding on to 45 per cent of all viewing and listening in the UK. Alan Yentob's ambitious, public-service-inspired BBC1 was maintaining share while ITV was rapidly losing it. BBC News was confident, forging ahead comfortably on every front, and was now dominant, with a massive 70 per cent share of all broadcast news consumption.

Ron Neil had raised the game of the BBC's journalism and programme-making in the nations and regions beyond all recognition. The top few hundred managers in the BBC were increasingly young, can-do, skilled and flourishing. Our own MBA scheme and other advanced management programmes had begun to have a significant impact. Where once the BBC had been administered, now it was managed, and it was being managed by far fewer people. During my first term as Director-General, the proportion of programme-makers and journalists in the BBC rose from under a third to a half of all staff. Meanwhile, managers and facilities and support personnel reduced in number. BBC staff were calmer and more strategically aware, if not yet reconciled to the scale and intensity of change. And at long last we had a grip on our finances. We had paid back our borrowings and we had money in the bank. The really critical challenges of the previous nine years – creating a powerful BBC News, introducing Producer Choice, winning the Charter – had all been accomplished. We had broken the back of – if not yet completed – the modernisation process. I faced two major additional challenges: identifying exactly how the BBC should respond to the looming digital revolution, and finding the substantial funding necessary if the organisation was not to be left out of that revolution.

The appointment of Christopher Bland restored my sagging morale after the black days with Hussey. The new Chairman took me to dinner at the Oak Room after he had conducted his initial appraisal of the state of the institution. He was touchingly flattering: 'I am impressed by the thoughtfulness of your BBC. You must stay for a second term,' he said. I would be happy to lead the Corporation into the new millennium, I responded, and we agreed I would do four more years. Christopher and I discussed the BBC's challenges. It was refreshing to be deliberating over the tasks ahead with a modern and experienced Chairman, unafraid of change, comfortable with contemporary management ideas. During my second term as Director-General, Christopher would prove far-sighted, decisive and sturdy in supporting a raft of initiatives to make the BBC fit for the future. He didn't offer me or anyone else an easy ride, though, for friendship never inhibited Christopher from vigorously scrutinising everything I proposed, and stating his reservations boldly.

The BBC took a while to get used to Christopher's blunt, forceful style, particularly his fellow Governors. Hussey had cunningly courted his colleagues, involving them in his machinations. Christopher by contrast never wooed members of the board, or plotted with them, dealing with issues straightforwardly on their merits, as I had also strived to do. He chaired meetings briskly, and reprimanded Governors as well as managers for being long-winded or for drifting away from the point. Christopher drove us on, and sharpened our decision-making, but the Governors didn't much appreciate his abrasiveness.

He and his Vice-Chairman, Michael Cocks, immediately got off on the wrong foot – and never shifted on to the right one. Cocks took against his new Chairman even before they had met. Christopher's appointment, unsurprisingly, attracted much media interest, and Lord Cocks decided he was a publicity-seeker – unfairly, for he was not – and measured with a ruler the hundreds of column inches that Christopher had attracted. Cocks confronted a bemused Bland with the precise statistic at their first encounter – over lunch at the House of Lords – and again in front of his embarrassed colleagues at an early meeting of the Governors. He and Christopher never really made up, though they muddled along well enough, and I maintained good relations with them both.

Christopher's wit, straight-dealing and enthusiasm for programmes, however, soon won over most of my management team. The new Chairman brought a welcome feistiness to our affairs. When attacked, I was restrained in punching back. By contrast, Christopher was a biffer and a basher. One-time Olympic fencer that he was, he never let a jab go unanswered, and always gave at least as good as he got. One among many examples was Christopher's letter to *The Times* in response to an article about a speech by Michael Grade attacking the BBC: 'She [the writer of the article] is wrong to distinguish Michael Grade's ritual attack on the BBC from the remainder of his interminable speech: it was just as boring as the rest.'

In his first few months, Christopher and I debated a proposal for carrying the restructuring of the organisation one stage further. Any strategic issue like this would normally have been on the table and chewed over and agreed by my senior management colleagues – but restructuring was the exception, for what I had in mind would affect many of them individually and significantly, and they would have found it hard to remain objective about the issues. Instead, it was Christopher who first subjected my detailed thinking to robust and rigorous scrutiny and helped me to refine a proposal. The centrepiece of the plan was the final separation of the running of the networks from programme-making within the BBC, bringing a single-minded focus on the one hand to serving our licence-payers, and on the other to the making of excellent, innovative programmes – at one and the same time finally breaking up the BBC's ancient baronies and power structures. The Governors agreed to the proposal and it was announced, as expected, to much controversy.

The least controversy was around BBC Broadcast, which, under Will Wyatt, would run the networks and stations – all television, radio and online services, at national, regional and local level. Ron Neil would separately manage BBC Production, bringing together all the programme-making departments in television and radio outside news – drama, entertainment, factual, sport. The BBC would now have a smaller, more compact team at the helm, highly focused on what most mattered. Creating BBC Broadcast to pay more attention to our licence-payers in particular was a decisive and historic shift for an organisation which had generally directed its energies inward.

We set out to learn more about our audiences than ever before. We divided our licence-payers into the Hundred Tribes of Britain – for example, young children, or twenty-five- to thirty-four-year-old women, or Muslims, or Scots, or older married couples, or sports-lovers. We found out about every group's passions, interests and concerns, what media they consumed, what they thought of the BBC. We had some nasty surprises. For example, in cable and satel-lite homes we were losing the children's audience to commercial channels focused exclusively on engaging them, unable to compete with the brief time slots devoted to children's programming on our main channels. The BBC, we realised, was at risk of losing a gen-eration. Other groups, particularly young people, did watch or listen to the BBC, but didn't value us. 'We like Radio 1 and Alan Partridge,' they would tell us, 'but we think the BBC is a fusty old organisation.' Other sections of the audience – particularly the older, more prosperous and better-educated groups – esteemed the BBC highly.

Our work on the Hundred Tribes of Britain deepened our under-standing of audience need, and influenced our commissioning. And we decided to create channels and other services offering a distinc-tive public service alternative for children. Martin Lambie-Nairn, who, long ago, had designed the *Weekend World* titles, reappeared in my life again to help us connect better with our audiences. He redesigned the BBC's brand identity, reinventing the logo in the clean, classic style of Eric Gill, introducing the inspiring floating globe to BBC1, and giving a new feel to every BBC service. Martin's work created a coherent, contemporary visual look for the whole BBC, giving us a fresh, vibrant identity and underscoring the wider modernisation process. We began to run promotional films, aimed at every kind of audience, to boost the appreciation of the BBC as a provider of wonderful programmes. 'Perfect Day' – the unique collaboration of singers and musicians, including Lou Reed, Bono, David Bowie, Lesley Garrett, Elton John and Tom Jones, in a recording of Reed's haunting song – won widespread accolades.

Our seventy-fifth-birthday campaign carried moving plaudits by Gorbachev, Billy Connolly, Whoopi Goldberg and the Dalai Lama. Marketing – led by Colin Browne, Sue Farr and Jane Frost – became a widely recognised discipline for the first time across the BBC. Professor Jean-Claude Larréché from INSEAD brought rigour to our marketing thinking. By the end of the decade, we would be named corporate brand of the year by the Marketing Society and British brand of the century by *Marketing Magazine*.

One unwelcome sign of the BBC's success was the loss of Michael Jackson in 1997, when he was lured from BBC Television to run Channel 4. Since my days at LWT, he and I and Alan Yentob had discussed programmes intensively whenever we met, so I was specially touched by his valedictory tribute to me: 'You are truly one of the great creative figures in British television history.'

The restructuring brought Ron Neil in BBC Production a difficult inheritance, for he had to rationalise scores of production units across the whole organisation, fashioning, for instance, one science department into a single centre of excellence where previously there were three. Ron inherited some of the world's best programme-makers, but he also had to tackle creative underperformance in some areas which had been masked under the old system by outside commissioning. BBC2, we identified, had been buying 40 per cent of its programmes from outside the BBC. Some of our commissioners had been working around creative weakness within the BBC – particularly in entertainment – rather than confronting it, which Ron now had to do. In addition he had to rationalise the overhead, to cut previously concealed over-capacity, and to introduce the more efficient and empowering digital production technologies. Yet again, the caring, sensitive, conscientious Ron faced a daunting, thankless challenge. BBC in-house programme-makers had been historically accustomed to working without competition, and in many cases to supplying channel Controllers with programmes determined by the producers themselves. They were also used to often untaxing performance regimes and to relaxed working conditions in a slack financial environment. Many resented the greater authority in the new system of the network Controllers in radio and television and were anguished by the businesslike negotiations over price. The intense focus on audiences, channel performance and creativity in our new structure, however, did bring enormous benefits, as our newly empowered controllers drove the BBC to fresh heights of innovation and ambition in every sphere. It was a while though, even with Will and Ron working together harmoniously, before we were able to create an embryonic sense of partnership between BBC Broadcast and BBC Production – encouraging the two divisions to work together, to mutual benefit, to solve common problems. Eventually, Ron and his successor, Matthew Bannister, would arrest and reverse BBC Production's long-term decline.

The restructuring of the BBC provoked the greatest controversy in World Service, which I had first resolved to reform when I trekked up Annapurna in the winter months of 1992. I ate in the communal mess-tent just after sunset each evening and – with the temperature rapidly dropping to previously unexperienced icy depths – I soon returned to my own tent and snuggled into my down sleeping-bag for warmth. For three weeks, deep in the Himalayas, my only contact with the outside world, my only media experience, was BBC World Service. I had always taken a short-wave radio with me on overseas trips and dipped briefly into the World Service for news. But now I listened to it in my tent for hours at a time, and was dismayed by what I heard – for this was a broadcasting service preserved in aspic, speaking with the plummy tones of a Britain that scarcely existed any longer. As a network, it lacked all coherence, its presentation was outdated, its programming a mish-mash. A dry, erudite, academic treatise on world religion would be followed by a tacky, mindless pop show presented by an ancient refugee from Radio 1. The network had little wit, humour or comedy. It failed completely to put on show the exciting, distinctive, diverse culture of contemporary Britain. World Service news was sober and authoritative but dull, and didn't belong to the emerging world of CNN and continuous news networks.

BBC World Service in English neither inhabited the creative frontier nor seemed to have any sense of its audience, and I was reminded of this over subsequent years whenever I encountered the new elites in my travels abroad – like the savvy young gang responsible for turning Singapore into an advanced digital city. They were in a world apart from BBC World Service's imagined audience. Research later underlined my first-hand experience: listeners, we identified, found the World Service's English-language network dull, old-fashioned and out of touch. The network *did* have a bedrock of appeal – to retired expats, or to insomniac small-'c' conservative politicians of all parties listening overnight with nostalgia to a service with resonances of a bygone age. I was altogether more impressed with the forty-plus language services that emanated from Bush House, produced by inspiring cells of committed people representing nations and groups from across the globe – a kaleidoscope of colours and creeds, lively and vibrant, genuine centres of expertise and knowledge.

John Tusa had been the Managing Director, World Service, when I arrived at the BBC. He had been bizarrely catapulted into the job by Governors after a career as a working journalist, and without significant management experience. On an early all-day visit to Bush House, I had discovered him – as Michael Checkland jokingly predicted I would – sitting at 8.30 a.m. in his office reading *The Times* and listening to Radio 3. At 5.30 p.m. I returned to find him in exactly the same position reading another newspaper. But Tusa was popular in Bush House: he led from the front, attacking the Foreign Office over low funding, proclaiming the virtues and brilliance of the Service to one and all. Within the BBC, Tusa had positioned Bush House as an autonomous, semi-detached state, dealing directly with the FCO, its funders in government, and claiming the freedom to choose whether to embrace or to discard wider BBC policies.

Michael Checkland had tolerated this. High up on Annapurna I resolved to bring BBC World Service into the BBC fold, to modernise the programming and the organisation.

Bob Phillis began that process in 1992 when I appointed him to succeed Tusa, tailoring World Service in English to the needs and availability of listeners in different regions and time zones. There was progress, but Bob was working against the entrenched attitudes of many of his executive team, and the World Service remained a state within a state. When I was contemplating the restructuring of the BBC in 1996, the separation of commissioning and production into different divisions, I decided to bite the bullet and to draw BBC World Service wholeheartedly into the new BBC-wide structure. There was no better, no more comprehensive news provider in the world than BBC News, and the World Service would commission its news from them. Likewise, it would buy its programmes from the excellent BBC Radio production departments and purchase its facilities from BBC Resources. There would be a rise in quality as well as a major efficiency gain as departments were merged and overheads reduced. Efficiency savings would be particularly welcome to a service whose income from a Conservative government was dropping markedly – by 8 per cent in the year of the changes alone.

I had no illusions that drawing the World Service into the heartland of the BBC would be seen as a highly aggressive act. On becoming Director-General, I had signalled that network commissioning and production would one day be split. That change was regarded inside the rest of the BBC as inevitable, and I had had many informal conversations with senior colleagues about its broad implications. By the time I announced the separation in 1996, it was accepted – if not enthused over – across the BBC. I also realised, however, that Bush House would have assumed without a second thought that I would not dare invade the citadel and envelop them in the wider changes, and I knew there would be an almighty row when I confounded that assumption. I could have simply parked the

World Service as an issue, but it would have been on my conscience if I had. I was later much criticised for not inaugurating a period of consultation with the World Service before applying the restructuring to them. I would be accused, with some justice, of ambushing Bush. But I made a deliberate decision *not* to consult, for I was not naive: the result of any such consultation would have been ferocious, obdurate, territorial resistance – after which it would have been highly unlikely that the reorganisation would have proceeded. I was going to have a battle anyway: I wanted it to be on ground of my choosing – namely *after* the decision had been announced as one part of BBC-wide change.

The day before the restructuring was to be made public, Christopher Bland and I visited Virginia Bottomley at the Heritage Department to brief her on our plans. We also asked to see Malcolm Rifkind, the Foreign Secretary. He was out of the country, so we saw instead Sir John Coles, the lead FCO official, and briefed him thoroughly. I knew Coles far less well than other senior Whitehall officials, an inevitable consequence of the FCO's and World Service's historical insistence on managing the relationship themselves, and cutting out the centre of the BBC. Coles was uncomfortable, but we were well within our constitutional rights to make the changes, as he understood, for the business of managing the World Service was formally for the BBC, independent of government. We were certainly acting outside established convention, though, for we were moving the furniture in a previously untouched room.

By lunchtime on the day of the announcement in June 1996, John Tusa was already on the radio talking as if he were the World Service's leader in exile, denouncing the plan in vituperative terms, stoking up feeling, marking the beginning of a long campaign of bitter resistance. In the following days, he described the plans as a 'mission to destroy' and as an 'act of bureaucratic vandalism'. He wrote in similar terms to Christopher Bland, who responded that Tusa's views were 'quite simply absurd'. Protest mounted. Hundreds of World Service staff demonstrated publicly. Wreaths were attached to the front of Bush House. Commentators fulminated. I was summoned before the House of Commons Foreign Affairs Select Committee on two separate occasions to be keel-hauled, to be accused of acting like a 'Tsar', and to be pressed to back down, but I was unyielding. Robin Cook, the Shadow Foreign Secretary, phoned my office – but, finding me out, spoke to Katie and left a dictated message demanding that the changes be put on hold. Cook threatened that if they were not they would be reversed when Labour came to power. The *Guardian* began a months-long campaign against the changes with daily articles. Hundreds of eminent, uninformed folk from the ranks of serial protesters signed ritual letters of dissent, offering knee-jerk support for the status quo, effectively arguing for the World Service to be preserved in its aspic for ever.

The scale of opposition, however, rattled the Governors and obliged the Foreign Office to be seen to be doing something. The hero of the hour was Caroline Thomson – the sunny, progressive, open-minded number two at the World Service – who had not long arrived at the BBC from Channel 4. Caroline set out to get everyone off the hook. With nervous MPs and peers – and with the FCO itself – she pursued the same line: the changes were right, but those concerned should press for safeguards. The quality of news and programmes should be monitored after the changes. When efficiency savings came through, they should ensure that Bush House was the beneficiary. The FCO duly convened a working party of officials, BBC executives and outsiders, a move welcomed on all sides. Sarah Hogg – fresh from Number 10 as John Major's policy head – was one of the outsiders, and carried the baton for reform. Michael Stevenson looked after the BBC's interests on the committee. When the Working Party reported, three months later, the safeguards were all agreed – in effect the programme of reform had been endorsed. The changes went ahead as planned, and the protest fizzled out. My gamble had succeeded.

It would take a long time before World Service managers and staff were reconciled to the changes, but a few green shoots soon sprouted. Some in Bush House, for instance, were generous enough to acknowledge an immediate and substantive improvement in service, as were some in News, and programme staff began slowly to appreciate the career benefits of being part of BBC Production's far larger departments.

When Labour came to power in 1997, no attempt was made to reverse the changes. Instead Robin Cook, the new Foreign Secretary, kept his distance: in nearly three years I met him only once – a rushed, unsatisfactory encounter lasting only twenty minutes. The Labour government did, however, reverse the long decline in World Service funding – but no thanks to the FCO, which failed to champion BBC World Service's cause. When the time came to submit budgets to the Treasury, we discovered that the FCO had discarded the BBC's claim and was not pressing it. We outflanked them, appealing directly and successfully to Number 10, and the World Service's budget was duly increased. Soon after, the FCO tried to transfer responsibility for their difficult charge at Bush House to the Department of Culture, Media and Sport. A leading official at the FCO was blunt with me in private about their motivation: the BBC was an extremely effective lobbyist, he asserted. He knew we would argue again in the future for substantial rises in funding to enable the World Service to offer sophisticated services on the Internet. The official calculated, he told me candidly, that the BBC would win this argument for more funds and that our gain would be at the expense of the Foreign Office's own budget. But his arguments didn't find favour within Whitehall and the Foreign Office was obliged to retain custody of its troublesome, unwanted progeny.

Sam Younger, a Bush long-timer, had succeeded Bob Phillis as head of the World Service. Sam had been caught uncomfortably between the centre of the BBC and his staff when the restructuring happened. When he left, in 1998, to become Director-General of the British Red Cross, Mark Byford was appointed in his place. Mark was a muscular moderniser, a great bear of a Yorkshireman, bursting with vitality, optimism and good cheer, and a devout Catholic dedicated to public service. As Director of Regional Broadcasting he had shown himself to be both a charismatic leader and an effective manager who could make difficult things happen. Under Mark, BBC World Service finally made the great leap forward. The Labour government did eventually inject substantial new funds, and the reforms did produce major efficiency savings, which were ploughed into extra programmes. Mark embraced the Internet wholeheartedly, modernised the content and sound of the English-language service, introduced a second stream of continuous news and focused energetically on understanding audiences and meeting their needs. BBC World Service finally became a service of which we could be truly proud.

In 1996 Jane was diagnosed with breast cancer, and had chemotherapy and radiotherapy at the Marsden. Throughout the many months of this tense, troubling, punishing treatment, she was buoyed by family and friends rallying around, offering stalwart moral and practical support, making clear what a rock she was in all our lives, valued for her great gifts of love and friendship, for her spirit, humour and sense of fun. At the end of the treatment, we held a party to celebrate and Jane triumphantly hollered at full pitch an old Native American chant passed down through generations of her family. She made a full recovery and flourishes.

The Governors had been alarmed by the falling out between Hussey and myself. Now many had the opposite concern: they were fearful that the new Chairman, Christopher Bland, and I were too close. There were minor rebellions. One took me back four decades to the prejudices and attitudes of my Catholic childhood.

The Central Religious Advisory Committee (CRAC), composed of representatives of all the established faiths in the UK, advises broadcasters on religious matters. It is one of the oldest bodies in broadcasting and, historically, the chairmanship of CRAC had always been held by an Anglican diocesan bishop. In 1997 a new chair was due to be appointed, and religious programming executives in the BBC and ITV conceived of a modest and unremarkable reform – that after seventy years it was time for disestablishment, for ending the Church of England's hold on CRAC's chairmanship. They proposed that the next appointee should be a Roman Catholic bishop. Christopher Bland was consulted before the proposal was put to Governors. 'I'm a Northern Ireland Prod, and if it's OK with me, it should be OK with them!' was his pithy response. But it wasn't. One Governor objected, at a session attended only by myself and other Governors. Looking nervously at me – for I was seen as a Catholic, even if I no longer practised – the Governor uttered the immortal words: 'I've got nothing against Catholics – some of my best friends are Catholic – but we have an established Church in this country, and this is not a position we should give up.' To my surprise, other Governors joined in to blackball the appointment, and the board was split right down the middle, creating an impasse to which the Church of England was eventually alerted. Over months, a very British compromise was fashioned behind the scenes. The Anglicans would hold on to the lead slot, but a new post of vicechairman would be created, and a Catholic would fill it, who would, in due course, succeed to the chairmanship. One more piece of discrimination against Catholics was ended.

In the second half of the 1990s, there were still occasional tensions, as there often had been in the past, around BBC1, the pull between the public purposes of the BBC on the one hand, and the channel Controller's inevitable instinct on the other to compete hard and to maximise audiences, allied with the difficulty of asserting high editorial values in a looser age. Overall the channel's mix remained bold and innovative, but I was unhappy at the lack of distinctiveness of some of its programming. *The Vanessa Show*, a daytime series, was a warning sign. It had tabloid values, and stumbled badly when it emerged that some guests were fake. I intervened, strongly asserting our public service ideals. I also became concerned by the creeping marginalisation in the BBC1 schedule of arts, religion and current affairs programming, like *Omnibus* and *Question Time*, which I asked to be reversed. I opposed plans to extend the number of episodes of drama serials in peak time, and the move of the *Nine O'Clock News* – the BBC's vital public service commitment at the heart of peak time.

Sport was an issue that increasingly taxed us. Competition from subscription-funded broadcasters, especially Sky, was driving up the price of sport far faster than our income. As a matter of arithmetic, we could not follow the trend or one day sport would crowd out every other programme on the BBC. We substantially raised our spend, but set a limit, which was hard on our dedicated sports teams. Christopher and I were both sports lovers, but we concurred that the ultimate justification for the licence fee was to provide programming which the market would not, or which was at risk, and we simply could not justify spending huge sums on live sport that the market was only too eager to provide. ITV joined in the general hysteria, and overpaid for rights, well beyond sport's commercial worth. We focused instead, with some success, on persuading the government that the great national and international events should be available live on at least one of the main terrestrial channels for the whole nation to see, and on ensuring that those licence-payers who were unable to afford premium sports channels – and to see live sport – could at least watch recorded sport on the BBC.

In the late 1990s, having done their time, various of my colleagues moved to other jobs. Bob Phillis became Chief Executive of the Guardian Media Group; Rupert Gavin, a powerful signing from BT, replaced him as Chief Executive, Worldwide. Rodney Baker-Bates went off to the Prudential and John Smith, a key collaborator on Producer Choice, took over as Director of Finance; Rod Lynch went back to the airline business; and Margaret Salmon, my main partner in crime on the organisational reform of the BBC, became Chief Executive, Resources in his place. In my latter years as Director-General, I had the most accomplished set of colleagues I had ever worked with. The BBC's upper echelons were full of skilled, talented, capable people, a glittering array of ability in every domain. If in the early 1990s only the centre of the BBC had acquired a brain, now every part of the organisation was knowledgeable and thoughtful. There are inevitable tensions in every workplace, and there were in ours, but my team was increasingly collaborative, ready to join forces in the BBC's interest, not their own. They were developing their own well-considered strategies, and driving widespread change. They were leading their own capable, skilled, talented teams. Young, able people across the BBC were moving up faster. Accomplished outsiders in every field were queuing up to join the BBC in huge numbers at every level. New systems, processes and ways of working were bedding down. The whole organisation felt confident – as if it was on the move, naturally, without being pushed. When I visited a local radio station, for example, I was no longer asked for money by a man in charge, but was given a devastatingly impressive account of its position and forward thinking, often by a woman.

Together, my team and I drove forward the remainder of the modernisation agenda. The BBC had commissioned only one distinguished building in its history – Broadcasting House, a modern Art Deco masterpiece – at the summit of the institution's self-confidence in the 1920s. Orwell and Muggeridge would still have felt at home inside Broadcasting House in the 1990s, with its warren of offices, its Rubik's cube complexity, its long, dark, windowless corridors. The BBC's major building expansion had been in the 1960s and 1970s. Right across Britain our staff worked in ugly, cramped, scruffy, untidy buildings and workspaces, wholly unfit for their purpose. We knew it would take a decade or more to change but John Smith, Margaret Salmon and I looked at best practice around the

world in workplace design and fashioned a plan to collaborate with
the private sector to modernise every BBC building; to create an
airy, pleasant, civilised, technologically advanced work environment.
We began at Broadcasting House, restoring the public spaces to
their original beauty, tearing down the corridors and creating open
areas with glass-walled conference rooms and glass-fronted cubicles
for private working. I moved out of the Director-General's oak-
panelled hideaway – first occupied by John Reith – and into an
open-plan area alongside the new lean, corporate centre responsible
for BBC strategy, policy, compliance, finance, marketing and communication, human resources and technology. Only two hundred
people now provided direction to the BBC where once there had
been thousands.

However, we never entirely brought BBC Resources – our facilities division – to stability. Rod Lynch had bravely cut the cost base
and reduced the massive losses that the division had effectively been
making before Producer Choice. But BBC Resources had no real
growth potential, for there was substantial over-capacity in the
whole British facilities sector, and market demand was weak. I came
to the conclusion, with some of my colleagues, that the best prospect
for the BBC, and for the wider industry, would be to sell the component parts of Resources to other facilities groups in the industry,
or to merge them into joint ventures, allowing industry rationalisation and creating independent facilities companies with real growth
prospects. But this proved a touchy subject for the Governors – sensitive to trade union and staff concern – and it was clear to me that
this was one BBC reform too far: I would not be able to sell BBC
Resources.

We worked further to improve the BBC's accountability. The
Governors introduced and enforced a new fair trading regime,
independently audited, to underpin an obsessive determination on
our part that not a penny of licence funding should be used to
subsidise any of the BBC's commercial activities. We introduced
a Programme Complaints Unit, unpopular within the BBC, for

rigorously examining serious complaints from those affected by BBC programmes, with a right of appeal to the Governors. We were already offering a candid appraisal of our performance in our annual report – again not popular within the BBC – but now we set out to listen more methodically to our licence-payers, and to expose ourselves to informed scrutiny. We organised public meetings on particular BBC services – for example, Radio 1 – bringing together the station's decision-makers with their audiences. Expert independent panels routinely audited BBC performance in discrete programme areas and reported direct to the Governors. The Governors regularly held conferences where BBC executives had to give a public account of themselves on key current issues and hear alternative views.

We had to account to Parliament and to the media too. In my early years at the BBC, the politicians had been in the driving seat, pressing reform on the organisation, albeit according to an agenda with which we largely concurred. But as the reforms bit, and we became ever clearer about our strategic purpose, and transformed ourselves into an ever more modern and effective organisation, we grew in confidence, and we – rather than the politicians – began to set the pace. Christopher Bland helped that process. He was robust and independent minded, assertive about the BBC's strengths, and withering about the ill-conceived notions of anyone opposing us. When he and I appeared together, for example before Gerald Kaufman's Select Committee, we seemed to have an answer for everything, and while some politicians found us compelling and convincing, I was told, others considered that we came over as know-alls.

Christopher took a little while to learn how to frame politic rather than blunt, pithy, uncompromisingly direct answers to the Committee's questions. In advance of one of our first appearances together before Kaufman, we had, unusually, identified one question which we did not want to be asked – because there was no answer we wanted to give. I cursed inwardly when the question came up, and straightaway Christopher turned to me to answer. I set off on a long, elaborate and – I thought – ingenious journey of evasion, dulling the interest of most Committee members, but bringing a frown of frustration to the member who had asked the question. I could feel Christopher to my left squirming with irritation. The moment I finished he whispered to me over-loudly: 'You didn't answer the bloody question!' 'I wasn't trying to answer the bloody question!' I whispered back.

Our many appearances before Gerald Kaufman's Select Committee were in general dispiriting. I respected some of the members – John Maxton was thoughtful, and Joe Ashton was passionate and informed about the adverse impact of the licence fee on the poor. But, overwhelmingly, my impression of the Committee was not of democracy in action, of a public institution being rightly held to account, of an informed Parliamentary commission digging deep on behalf of the citizenry on the issues that really mattered – but rather of petty point-scoring; of preening vanity; of cheap headline-seeking. Kaufman himself was a puzzle: a Labour man of deliberate precision and icy confidence, he was convinced that the BBC should be privatised or taken over by BT. I found his reasoning unfathomable.

My period as Director-General in the 1990s coincided with seismic cultural shifts. The 1960s were marked not only by exuberance and self-expression but by generosity of spirit. The 1970s and 1980s were grim, but the notion of public service remained powerful. In the 1990s for whatever mix of reasons – whether stability after decades of upheaval and disorder, or wide and growing prosperity, or ever fiercer competition – we entered an era where style, laddishness, celebrity and cynicism triumphed over substance, where cruelty, whether in drama or humour, became the hallmark of much of popular culture. The prevailing values of a Catholic childhood – compassion, concern for others – came to seem outdated. The highest ideals of the BBC were under constant assault. I felt out of sorts with my times.

I was also caught on the wrong side of another set of arguments. In the 1990s the age-old tension between art and science, between anarchy and rigour, erupted as a rebellion against the developing management culture that Mrs Thatcher's revolution had encouraged in both the public and private sectors. In reality, Britain was just catching up on a set of ideas – management science – that had emerged since the war, chiefly from the US business schools. Britain's failure to apply these notions in earlier decades was one factor behind our relative economic decline. As a scientist by education who had forged a successful career in the creative industries, I thought the tension between creativity and rigour was entirely reconcilable. Bringing greater discipline to the anarchic BBC had demonstrably improved the scale and intensity of our creativity. But there was no persuading the average arts critic, front-line journalist or newsroom inhabitant – nervously defiant of their own distant hierarchies – of the virtues of modern management. One of the vices of the science was the dense and opaque jargon its practitioners often used, and it proved an easy target for lazy, closed minds.

In the print media in the 1990s, the *Sun* had prospered with sharp, sensational, funny, often vulgar and aggressively opinionated journalism. The approach spread quickly, first enveloping the other tabloids, then the broadsheets, which in their turn became progressively more angled in their reporting towards personality, power manoeuvrings and sensation. Serious, substantial, analytical journalism about the weighty forces that were changing the world went into sharp decline. Comment displaced evidence. Journalism increasingly became a game, not a noble, professional, ethical discipline.

The great Harry Evans – one-time editor of the path-finding *Sunday Times* – had been a strong influence on me when I worked on *World in Action* in the 1960s and *Weekend World* in the 1970s. Harry lived and worked in New York in the 1990s, but visited me in my office in Broadcasting House towards the end of my term as

Director-General. We lamented together the lack of quality of the British press, especially striking for anyone who has access to the serious, solemn and solid US broadsheets. I told Harry that he had defined the ideal of aspiring journalists in my youth, but that – in a roomful of young BBC editors and reporters I had met the previous day – the demand had been to take the BBC away from the high ground and into tabloid territory.

When I began work in broadcasting, a tiny handful of media journalists – like Peter Fiddick and Rod Allen – worked conscientiously to chronicle the cultural, political, social and industrial dimensions of broadcasting. In my early years at the Corporation, at least some coverage of BBC issues had been serious and balanced, but by the mid- to late 1990s a legion of journalists reported broadcasting as little more than a racy part of the national soap opera. I had no appetite for this game. Others did – leaking and briefing to curry favour; playing cheeky chappie like the media pack themselves; offering pungent, adversarial quotes to grab a headline. But I was squeamish and found the process distasteful. By the second part of the 1990s, the transformation of the BBC, audited and chronicled in searching independent reports, admired by fellow broadcasters the world over, heralded and emulated by other major organisations, was neither understood nor reported. Rather, a decade of tough, controversial reform, and my reluctance to play by the new media rules, guaranteed me an unvaryingly bad press.

The BBC subscribed to a media monitoring service which measured the amount of positive and negative coverage it received, and adjusted the results according to the number of people estimated to have read the stories. Some months my personal negatives ran into the billions! How did I feel about my bad press? No one ever reads anything untrue or unfair about themselves without wincing, and occasionally a period of hostile press would bring me low. Being demonised certainly made me more defensive and suspicious when dealing with the world, and I resented having to engage with people whose view of me had been informed only by my media coverage.

The protesting cry after a social encounter with a stranger, 'You are not at all like your media image,' became monotonous. But like a boxer or a soldier in combat I became used to the punches and to the bullets flying, if not quite oblivious to them. My skin hardened and thickened. The pressure of work distracted me. But probably the most significant impact of the bad press I received was to increase my stubborn determination to see my task through to the end.

My emotions were, however, engaged fully when my family paid the price: sometimes I had to make special trips to reassure my mum and dad after a particularly bad spate. Jane bore our tribulations bravely but abhorred the injustice of it. My son JJ converted to Islam and married Fozia, a delightful, lively D.Phil. student from a Leicester family originally from India; but JJ and Fozia were soon subjected to a major newspaper investigation, during which JJ was tricked on the phone into revealing his recent history and whereabouts by someone falsely claiming to be from the Department of Social Security in Newcastle. My daughter Eliza – who worked in advertising after Cambridge – married Adam, a wry, laconic, generous-natured lawyer; and they faced some light but hostile attention. At such times I felt a deep sense of guilt that my work, and my determination to continue with it, had placed such a burden on my family. And my guilt was exacerbated by their unqualified, defiant, loving support of me through every storm.

Why did the modernisation process steam ahead in the BBC in the 1990s, despite media and staff opposition? Because the generation of people in power – whether BBC Governors, senior civil servants, politicians or business leaders – had lived through the 1970s and 1980s, understood how desperately British institutions needed fundamental reform and, by and large, supported those charged with delivering it. The reformers talked to one another, and learnt from each other's experience. I compared notes over the years with Elizabeth Esteve-Coll at the V&A, and Mary Allen at Covent Garden. I spoke to Stella Rimington's team at MI5 and

Bob Ayling's at British Airways at key strategy conferences. Colin Marshall, Iain Vallance and other business leaders shared their insights with my senior managers. Occasionally, some of those in the vanguard of reform would share their misery too!

Tony Blair came to power in 1997. The Britain that I had been born into and that he inherited had changed fundamentally. It was less stratified and hierarchical, more tolerant and diverse, its institutions more open and accountable. It was a country as vital and vibrant as any on earth, its citizens leading freer, richer, more satisfying lives. But there was still work to be done. The British crisis of the 1970s was still playing out: we had successfully conquered inflation, and restored the health of the British economy, but at the price of creating a disaffected, under-educated, dependent class; and at the cost of chronic under-investment in the public services. Shortly after the election, Jane and I spent a recuperative week in Italy, the first few days in Florence with our friend Howell James, who had been John Major's political secretary. One night over dinner, Howell told us the unabridged story of the four weeks of the election campaign from inside the Major camp in a breezy and compulsive three-hour monologue. Jane and I then joined Carla Powell and Peter Mandelson on the Mediterranean to walk the Cinque Terra, Italy's spectacular coastal footpath.

Another night over dinner in a seaside restaurant, I asked Peter to tell us how the election was won, expecting to hear the mirror image of Howell's story. 'The election was won by the time it was called,' Peter said calmly, adding, in true *Weekend World* style, 'The journey began in 1985.' For the whole of that evening he held us enthralled as he described the key events and landmarks on New Labour's long odyssey to power. Peter made no great claims about his own part in that success. He was exceedingly generous to others. But it was impossible for his listeners not to conclude that he had been a far-sighted and flinty prophet, and a key architect of Labour's recovery from its desperate position in the early 1980s.

Jane and I had known Tony Blair and Cherie through Katie Kay and Barry Cox since the early 1980s. I had had no sympathy for Labour policy in its dark years, and I had admired Mrs Thatcher's and John Major's drive to nurse an ailing Britain back to health. But Tony Blair was a politician who – in alliance with Gordon Brown and Peter Mandelson – had fearlessly embraced the value of markets and wealth creation and sound money, yet at the same time wholeheartedly valued effective public services too, run for the benefit of the citizenry and not for those who worked in them. This mix of ideas chimed with my own. Moreover, I had always liked Tony personally. He was decent, sensitive and unusually modest and self-effacing for a politician, the last in his circle to appreciate his own appeal. Once or twice over the years he had turned to me for personal guidance, and his humility was striking. Both he and Peter spoke admiringly of Gordon Brown's policy grip and political nous. It has often been suggested that Peter betrayed Gordon and eased Tony's path to power. From my experience, this was certainly not the case, for I witnessed at first hand Peter's deep distress at the time of John Smith's death. Admire as he did both the other members of the triumvirate that had invented New Labour, Peter couldn't bear to choose between Tony Blair and Gordon Brown. Tony was simply raised to office by general acclaim and Peter accepted the inevitability of that.

Though I was friendly with both Peter and Tony, I held no animosity for Gordon, and was never caught in the tribal hostilities between their followers that would sometimes occur. I did have one odd experience, however, of the internecine warfare. Geoffrey Robinson – Gordon's supporter and Treasury minister – asked to see me in his suite at the Labour Party conference in Brighton in 1997. Geoffrey spoke with a plain, open, friendly manner, but his message was strangely menacing: I was part of a cabal, he said, composed of Tony Blair, Peter Mandelson, Terry Burns – the permanent secretary of the Treasury with whom Robinson was having difficulties – Robin Butler and Robert Fellowes. I needed to

understand, Robinson said, that Tony had promised to stand down
after eight years and to pass the baton to Gordon. I should realise
that Gordon was the future. I protested, truthfully, that I was indeed
friendly with all the people on his list, but that we were certainly not
a freemasonry, and that we didn't plot. I don't think Geoffrey
believed me.

A few months after the election which swept Tony Blair to power,
I visited John Major in his Westminster office to persuade him – successfully – to record his memoirs for the BBC. My heart went out to
the former Prime Minister, who was still mourning the loss of an
election, and looked gaunt, frail and bruised. He told me he knew in
advance he'd lose. 'I inherited a lousy pack of cards,' he said. He
had taken over an economy of which Margaret Thatcher had lost
control, a party divided on Europe – and still, in part, loyal to
Thatcher – and a country still disgruntled about the poll tax. That
day John Major aroused my paternal feelings, but he would soon
bounce back and begin to enjoy life again. His party, on the other
hand, like Labour in the early 1990s, departed for the wilderness,
narrowing their obsessions, isolating, as Mrs Thatcher had never
done, their liberal wing.

At a state dinner for President Clinton at Number 10 not long
before the election, I had realised to my surprise that John Major
expected to lose the contest. Tony and Cherie Blair attended –
their first visit to Downing Street. At drinks before the banquet,
John Major grabbed Cherie and myself to introduce us to the
President. While we waited for a suitable moment to interrupt, the
Prime Minister started briefing Cherie in detail on the accommodation at Number 10. And even as I began chatting to the President
my ears burnt as I heard John Major explaining to the attentive
Cherie in his most courteous and gentlemanly fashion how the
rooms of the Prime Minister's flat could be reconformed for a
larger family.

When Tony Blair was in opposition he often popped by my
office – after appearing on a radio programme at Broadcasting

House – to say hello to me and Katie and to stop for a chat. He was naturally sympathetic to the modernisation process at the BBC. Not all of his party were, and many of my long-time opponents held out hope that Labour would find a way of reversing the BBC reforms. Old Labour still bellyached in the background, and after the election the new Secretary of State – the shy, awkward Chris Smith – couldn't bring himself either to warmly support or roundly condemn a decade of reform in the Corporation. Instead, he threw hints to the gallery, dropping remarks that the unions and the luvvies were pleased to hear, that echoed their concerns.

The BBC had prepared for the moment: we had continued to take the Labour Party seriously when most other organisations had ignored it, patiently explaining everything we had done, always aiming to persuade Labour of the value of change. And for many in New Labour, the reformed BBC was a model of a modern, well-run, efficient world-beater, devoted to public purposes. One totemic indicator of the new balance of power within the governing party was the indecently young and baby-faced but brilliant and tough-minded James Purnell, who had left the BBC immediately after the election to work at Number 10. As head of performance management at the BBC, James had been one of my key aides. By temperament an arch-moderniser, intensely committed to reform, and hard headed about the need for delivery, at Number 10 James took over the broadcasting portfolio, liaising between the Prime Minister and Chris Smith and other relevant departments. His appointment was a sign of the new political realities: Old Labour would continue to grumble, but the process of modernising the BBC would not be stopped in its tracks: it would continue to the end of my term.

By the time I left, I was able reasonably to claim not only that the BBC was the world's most creative and trusted broadcaster, but that we were now also the most effectively managed public sector institution in the UK. The dinosaurs and the bone-headed bureaucrats had long departed. For everyone who remained, life was tougher.

Staff everywhere had to work harder, their performance keenly measured, and they were obliged to account for how they spent the public's money. But we were also successful, strategic, rational, rigorous, agile and accountable. We were fit for a new world. Orwell's BBC was no more.

17

The Digital Journey

When broadcasting first began in the early part of the twenti-eth century, the new medium used analogue technology, which transmitted information as waves, like ripples on a pond. Analogue remained the dominant technology throughout my career and right up to the end of the century. It had changed the world, but its limitations had also become clear: analogue allowed only a hand-ful of radio and television networks, and for the consumer it meant that broadcasting offered restricted choice and a largely passive experience.

In the 1990s broadcasting faced its own industrial revolution, which would turn our world upside down. It became clear that – after a century – analogue would give way to digital technology, which transmitted information encoded as a stream of digits. Digital had fundamentally different capabilities. It offered the prospect of an abundance of channels and thus an end to scarcity; better pic-ture and sound quality; the facility to order programmes on demand; the opportunity for consumers to interact, participate or track down information of their choosing; the ability to hold one's own massive archive, in the home; and increasing mobility, with access to video and audio on the move.

Understanding what was at stake with digital – and adjusting and adapting – took the BBC the major part of the 1990s, my period as Director-General. The BBC ended up better positioned for a new century, for the new digital era, than any other established broadcaster in the world. But this was not a smooth and easy experience: it was a voyage into the unknown, propelled by curiosity, instinct, enterprise and luck. It was a journey marked by disasters narrowly averted, by intrigue, and by bad decisions as well as good ones. It was a journey which would bring me and the BBC into direct contact with the leviathans of both the old and the new media industries.

For twenty-five years after I left university, my background in science had had barely any impact on my work, but in the 1990s it helped me to appreciate early on the significance of new technology. My favourite teacher at school, the brilliantly gifted and endearing B. B. Cooper – who taught me maths and further maths in the sixth form – had been ahead of his time. He had made his unlikely Liverpool lads do research projects and lecture the science sixth on their findings. In 1962 he set me the task of explaining the difference between analogue and digital technology, how computers worked, and the nature of the binary language they used. Thirty years later, I had long forgotten the detail, but I retained enough understanding to grapple with the functionality of the new technologies – what you could do with them – even if I could no longer grasp their internalities.

I had also been helped by the insights of others. In the 1970s Peter Jay alerted me to the boundless possibilities of fibre-optic cable. In the late 1980s I had spent time at the MIT Media Lab, run by Nicholas Negroponte, an early blue-skies visionary of the digital

world. Thus I had gained a broad feel for the transformational possibilities of new technology, but I had no precise sense about when
it would all happen. Nor could I yet see the implications for the
BBC. In the early 1990s, as we battled to introduce Producer Choice
and to modernise the organisation, a lurking apprehension about
the revolutionary nature of digital remained in the back of my
mind. Even as we celebrated the winning of a new Charter,
Margaret Salmon – the BBC's sage, widely experienced Director of
Personnel – remarked to me: 'Any modern, well-run institution
worth its salt has a ten-year perspective.' She clarified how, in order
to flourish, an organisation should project into the future all the
forces in play – economic, social, cultural, political or technological – and try to understand their potential long-term impact. With
that in mind, it should be attempting to develop a vision of what the
organisation wanted to be in ten years' time, and to devise a plan for
achieving this.

Margaret's observation had a profound impact on me. It chimed
with my feeling that all we were doing – difficult though it was – was
dragging a highly creative but bad-tempered and antiquated institution into the present day. So no sooner had we ended one process
than we began another: to consider the BBC's long-term strategy –
and in particular to get to grips with digital. Some of my colleagues
groaned. Hussey protested that I should give the place a rest. In particular he argued that I should ignore technological change. He
kept repeating that he had warned Rupert Murdoch at *The Times* in
the early 1980s against focusing on new technology. He had been
proved right then. He claimed he would be proved right again.

Our deeper insights into the new technology did not come all at
once. We knew digital would enable us to provide more channels
and to offer vibrant widescreen pictures of far higher quality. Digital
radio would allow us to introduce more services to fill the gaps not
covered by Radios 1 to 5. We had an embryonic vision of the power
of interactivity for learning. But the first critical understanding we
gained in the early 1990s was that the BBC was about to lose what

it had taken for granted for forty years – automatic access to licence-payers each time they switched on their televisions.

The BBC, along with ITV and Channel 4, had historically controlled the television gateway into the home via terrestrial transmitters. Analogue cable and satellite had already started to introduce limited competition; but within a decade, we realised, digital satellite, digital cable and digital terrestrial broadcasting would bring unparalleled competition and multiple pathways into the home. The BBC simply could not afford its own satellite, cable and telecommunications systems. It was inevitable that others would soon control the gateway into the home, the price to reach viewers, the position of channels on the household dial. And no one was in a better position to dominate this new world than Rupert Murdoch, whose bold move into analogue satellite had put him in pole position for a leap forward into digital. Rupert Murdoch would begin to loom ever larger in the life of the BBC.

The other early insight we had was that Brussels would increasingly encroach on the life of the BBC, as the new powers of the European Commission (EC) to regulate competition and state subsidy began to take effect. Since the 1970s I had been an instinctive Europhobe, nervous of Britain ceding economic and political independence, and I had bridled in the 1990s as more and more Brussels-related business appeared on BBC agendas. But I soon recognised the importance of coming to terms with – and taking advantage of – the new power of Brussels. My chief companion on the tricky path towards an uncertain digital future would be the BBC's formidable and fearsomely driven Director of Policy and Planning, Patricia Hodgson, whose finest hour this journey would be.

Patricia and I identified early on a key but simple principle, and we held to it: as our licence-payers made the switch to digital, they would choose different means – satellite, cable, terrestrial and eventually telecom – and the BBC had to be waiting for them when they did so. The BBC had to transmit its services on all the different means by which our licence-payers would receive them. This meant in part supping with the devil – Rupert Murdoch – who would control digital satellite because of his ability to migrate his subscriber base from analogue, and because of his powerful stranglehold over movies and live sport. Many of our BBC colleagues were uncomfortable with our all-platforms strategy – though Hussey, and later Bland, fully supported the realpolitik. My former colleagues in ITV lobbied us hard against our plans. They had a visceral fear of someone from outside the club, and were nervous of the significant commercial competition Murdoch would bring for the first time to ITV. We should support our fellow club members, they pleaded, and not deal with the enemy. We should put all our eggs into the basket of Digital Terrestrial Television (DTT), and keep the BBC off Sky.

The virtue of DTT was that it could be received through an existing aerial and didn't require a dish disfiguring your home. On the other hand, DTT had limited capacity and offered less choice – only tens of channels by contrast with the hundreds or thousands possible for cable or satellite. DTT might appeal to conservative viewers, perplexed by a digital cornucopia, but most households – we anticipated – would want the far fuller choice that satellite and cable offered. We believed that the BBC couldn't, Canute-like, try to hold back the digital tide, and so we rejected ITV's pleas. (ITV would stick to its guns, making the first of many catastrophic strategic errors in the 1990s, finally limping on to Sky Digital only in 2002, having in the interim lost significant audience share.)

Despite our reservations, however, we did want DTT to work. The leadership of cable was weak (it had developed no significant services of its own) and DTT was an important counterweight to Murdoch, diminishing his likely dominance. We set out to improve DTT's chances. In October 1995 I wrote to Virginia Bottomley identifying DTT as 'a high-risk venture' but proposing measures to make it viable, including a single set-top box for all the different digital distribution systems. But the industry was in no mood for collaboration. The Secretary of State continued to press the case for

DTT, holding a sumptuous dinner at Hampton Court for all the moguls to promote the cause. It was clear that night that no one in ITV had done their homework. They wanted to colonise digital terrestrial, not to understand it. Michael Green of Carlton strutted his stuff and said he was up for it. Subsequently, at the launch of ITV's digital distribution system (OnDigital) he said: 'We will be the mass television platform . . . Every single television household will be watching digital terrestrial television at some point in the future. It's only a question of when.' Michael Green's hubris would eventually prove disastrous for his company. The BBC committed to provide services on DTT; but – unlike ITV – we would not bet the bank on a single system. We had asked Virginia Bottomley to award us the most technically choice channels on DTT, and she phoned in December 1995 to tell me she had granted them.

Our next major challenge was to press for a regulatory regime which would constrain Murdoch and others from abusing their new monopoly positions over the gateways. We were not optimistic that we could achieve this with the British government, though we would try. Margaret Thatcher had allowed Murdoch's holdings to grow until he owned a substantial chunk of the national print media. John Major, on the other hand, was deeply hostile to Murdoch, whose papers had been merciless at his expense. He believed that Murdoch had done enormous damage to the UK, and he contemplated radical legislation on media ownership. In 1993 Major had asked me to submit some confidential analysis and a proposal, which I did, urging strict limits on ownership by sector. A Green Paper was published in 1995, but no action taken. Major's colleagues were disunited: I was told that some – like Heseltine – saw Murdoch as an entrepreneur to be supported rather than held back, a good bet for Britain; others – like Peter Lilley – didn't want the press to be constrained on libertarian grounds; still others were simply fearful of the consequences for them as individuals if they took on Murdoch head to head. I talked to one Cabinet minister in this period who was about to have breakfast with him the following day to discuss media ownership, and who was visibly quaking at the prospect.

John and Norma Major came to a dinner at the BBC in July 1995 and Jane and I had a long conversation with them about Murdoch's potential digital dominance. The Prime Minister's interest was sharply engaged. I subsequently learnt that he pressed his colleagues in the following months to do everything possible to promote competition with Murdoch. I didn't doubt John Major's bona fides on the Murdoch question, but I had no illusion about the political obstacles he faced. Nor did we expect the Labour Party to commit harakiri as it positioned itself for the run-up to the 1997 election – and it didn't, Tony Blair famously and successfully taking his arguments right into the lions' den at a conference in Australia of Murdoch and his executive teams.

Murdoch's main ally in government was the DTI – historically unsympathetic to public service broadcasting; unwilling to take any action which would hamper a major industrial player; and anxious not to deny him all the fruits of his first-mover advantage. Brussels was debating a cross-European directive which would define the regulatory regime for digital broadcasting in each member state. Commission officials were standing back, unwilling to impose regulation on the industry, hoping for an industry-led solution to emerge. BSkyB was making the running. Britain, represented by the DTI, was the most hard-line of any member state, opposing tight regulation to control the gatekeepers. The BBC needed to press its case.

Bob Phillis, Patricia and I had already visited a number of Commissioners. The supremely confident free-market German Commissioner Martin Bangemann had not drawn breath when we met him, so passionate was he in his hostility to public service broadcasting, which he regarded as being in one of only two camps: either elitist or a commercial masquerade. (Eventually, we managed to win Bangemann over to a grudging admiration for the BBC's considered, coherent commitment to public service.) Another

Commissioner that Bob, Patricia and I visited in Brussels had descended into incomprehensible, heavily accented Euro-babble for an hour, making it impossible to understand a word he said. At the end of the meeting, he escorted us to the lift. The moment the door closed, we all collapsed in helpless fits of giggles – to the astonishment of Matteo Maggiore, the BBC's serious, conscientious Brussels lobbyist. Our paroxysms continued for a full five minutes.

Colin Browne, our Director of Corporate Affairs, Patricia and I determined that it was time to take Brussels by storm, to mount a BBC assault on Europe's heartland. In March 1995 we took over to Europe the *Antiques Roadshow* and other programmes; put on a concert with one of our orchestras; organised a series of meetings and seminars; held a large party in the Hôtel de Ville; and mounted a splendid dinner at which I was to speak and to lay out our case. A sparkling array of Euro-stars – Commissioners, Director-Generals, MEPs and the President of the European Parliament – had accepted our invitation, but, to our regret, not the leading Eurocrat Jacques Santer, the President of the Commission, who had sent his apologies. Moments after we had summoned our hundreds of guests from drinks to dinner, the lofty Jacques Santer entered the room with an entourage. He was coming to the dinner after all! A panic-stricken but quick-thinking Dinah Garrett, the BBC's hospitality head, pushed me in front of Santer to block his path while she rushed off to change, at lightning speed, the carefully considered placements. Dinah placed the President at my right hand, and bumped another guest to a far-flung table.

That night we began the process of conditioning the Eurocrats to think of the BBC as a European institution of which they could be proud; as a broadcasting organisation which reported Europe seriously; as a far-sighted institution which would help Europe to pioneer in the digital age. We wanted the EC to understand how revolutionary and important the coming change was, and that, if Europe's unique national cultures were to be safeguarded and nourished, it was vital to regulate the gateway and to maintain the role of public service broadcasting in the new era. This was the first of my many outings as a digital proselytiser.

Our Brussels week was a great success: over the next years, the BBC could always rely on a warm welcome and a keen hearing in Brussels. We were perceived as industry leaders, as digital innovators, as an organisation worth listening to. I visited Brussels a few times each year, generally dining when I was there with – and being briefed by – one or both of the British Commissioners, Leon Brittan and Neil Kinnock. I struck up a particularly good relationship with the impressive Mario Monti – the courteous, clever, civilised Italian Commissioner, whom we convinced in 1996 to exclude public service broadcasting from the media ownership rules he was contemplating. I instituted an annual meeting of the Director-Generals of Europe's main public service broadcasters in France, Germany, Italy and Spain and mustered them to lobby the EC hard to a common agenda.

The BBC was not alone in arguing for an effective digital directive from Brussels, but we led the charge, and we succeeded, despite strong opposition from Murdoch's lobbyists. The result was a huge and historic advance – an EC directive in autumn 1995 which obliged Murdoch and other gatekeepers to offer access to audiences on 'fair, reasonable and non-discriminatory terms'. It was not all we wanted, but it was enough – and we had luck: OFTEL was the regulator in the UK that would interpret the new Brussels directive. Its head was Don Cruickshank, a cool-thinking, hard-edged, fearless Scot. Patricia and I met him and it was clear he was sympathetic to the BBC's cause. The EC directive handed him a weapon, and it looked as if he would use it.

The negotiations between the BBC and BSkyB about access to digital satellite stretched over the best part of eighteen months, the wily Dominic Morris leading for the BBC. We started miles apart on price. Sam Chisholm – Murdoch's abrasive, square-built chief in the UK – declared he had us over a barrel, as we had openly proclaimed our all-platforms policy. But Dominic told him our policy was 'Not at any price'. Relations between the BBC and BSkyB became tense. Murdoch wrote a long letter of complaint to Christopher Bland in November 1996 about the BBC's attempts to influence the regulators. As time dragged on I met privately with Mark Booth, Chisholm's successor, so that we could offer mutual reassurance that both sides really did want a deal, that the impasse could be broken. I told Booth the BBC was not playing games: we wanted in, but at the right price. It was clear that Booth also wanted the BBC to be part of Sky Digital's launch. Booth remarked that 'ITV is dying,' and I agreed.

There was a further hiccup in relations with Sky when a bad-tempered Murdoch appeared at an EC conference in Birmingham in April 1998 to make a speech setting out Sky's own bona fides as a Euro-institution, and attacking the BBC. Murdoch ridiculed an observation I had made in a speech at the same conference that the poor would be disadvantaged in a media world where more and more television would be paid for, that a 'digital divide' could emerge. Murdoch complained that he couldn't hear himself over the noise of grinding axes. He protested that no one challenged the power of the BBC, or complained about our dominance. Presumably miffed by losing the regulatory fight in Brussels, Murdoch criticised the number of advisers and lobbyists thrown into the battle, claiming there was an army of 'over a hundred in the BBC alone'. It was the formidable wiles of Patricia Hodgson and Colin Browne – and a small number of aides in Brussels like David Levy and Chris Bryant – that were responsible for our effectiveness, not the sheer weight of numbers; but Murdoch's jibe created a mythology about Patricia's empire which would endure and grow: she would eventually be accused over and over again of having three hundred storm troopers involved in strategy, when the true number was around ten.

The government was mildly embarrassed when, after Murdoch's Birmingham speech, Robin Cook and Chris Smith were captured on camera, courtier-like, fawning at Murdoch's feet. The papers billed Murdoch's speech as an attack on the BBC. He called me from Los Angeles a few days later, no doubt prodded by nervousness at Sky about what the BBC's reaction to his speech had been. 'I hope you are not upset by the reports,' Murdoch said, 'we do want a deal.' 'It won't affect our calculation of our self-interest,' I responded.

The impasse between the BBC and Sky was finally broken when Patricia alerted Don Cruickshank informally that the BBC was about to make a complaint to the regulator against BSkyB under the new code. Cruickshank immediately alerted Sky to the potentially dire consequences for them if OFTEL had to intervene, and as a result determine their whole rate card not just for the BBC but for all their customers. A deal was quickly done at a fraction – one-seventh – of Sky's original asking price, a very good deal indeed for the BBC. Sky also agreed to reverse its original intention and place BBC1 and BBC2 as the first two channels on its electronic pro-gramme guide. We didn't win everything we wanted in the negotiations: the rest of our channels were scattered across Sky's guide and the BBC's overall digital proposition was hard to find; but thanks to the European Union, to Cruickshank and to Patricia Hodgson, we had won a far better position than we had once feared.

On the day in 1998 that we finally signed the deal with Sky, I arrived home in Wales for the weekend to be told by Jane that Murdoch had phoned. I called him back, and was entertained by the strains of 'The Blue Danube' on the line as I waited for him to take the call. 'Thanks for signing,' he said. 'I know you were under pressure not to on every side.' I demurred: 'We didn't do it to help Sky. We signed only because it was in the BBC's interest to do so.' 'Still,' Murdoch responded, 'someone else might have buckled under the pressure. Thanks.'

Sky Digital was much delayed but was finally launched in October 1998, its success quickly demonstrating the wisdom of the BBC's all-platforms strategy: in its first year, Sky won a resounding 85 per cent of the digital TV market, compared with 15 per cent for ITV's OnDigital.

At the outset, the BBC's digital channel proposition was quite limited – though we would refine it later as our marketing drive, our Hundred Tribes work on the audience, and our understanding of the digital world developed. The concept of one of our new digital channels – BBC Choice – was born more of frustration than of original thought: it would be the spillover channel, the channel that let our existing networks breathe. Viewers would switch to BBC Choice to watch an *Omnibus* about Jane Austen after watching *Pride and Prejudice* on BBC1; it had the space to show sporting events at length, or to devote time to the Proms. A second new channel, BBC Knowledge, would show education and factual programmes. We had insufficient money to make the new channels substantial, even though Virginia Bottomley had given us a modest increase in the licence fee to help out. I had concluded, however, that the BBC needed to inhabit the new digital space from the very beginning, and that we could argue later for additional funds. A third network, BBC Parliament, would show gavel-to-gavel coverage of the Commons. Finally, BBC News 24 would be launched, meeting a declared aim of the BBC since *Extending Choice* was published in the early 1990s, and achieving a strong personal ambition of my own.

BBC News 24 had been ready to launch for some time, but had been held back by the postponement of Sky Digital. Sky was highly antagonistic to the idea of the BBC offering twenty-four-hour news, seeing the service as a direct competitor to Sky News, and unwarranted. Frustrated by the delay, we sought permission in 1997 from Secretary of State Chris Smith – which we were obliged to do under the terms of our Charter – to launch News 24 first on ana-logue cable. Sky was furious. We were entering their own backyard, supplying BBC News 24 to cable operators for free, as part of our licence-funded proposition. Sky feared that as a result the cable operators would drop Sky News (which indeed some of them did, despite the BBC's opposition to their action). Department of

Culture, Media and Sport officials tipped us off that Sam Chisholm had been in to see Secretary of State Chris Smith and had ranted and railed against us for over an hour, that Smith was rattled by this, and that the decision might go against us. In the end, it did not: as would happen again, Chris Smith came through when it counted, however much he first equivocated.

Sky protested Smith's decision, then immediately lodged a complaint in Brussels to get News 24 closed down by the Commission. The complaint had to be adjudicated by Commissioner Karel Van Miert, a plain, solid, former Belgian trade union official with a natural sympathy for public service broadcasting, with whom I had already established a good working relationship. It would be another two years before the adjudication would be published, but long before that Van Miert made clear to me that the BBC had nothing to fear, and that the Commission would rule in our favour. One reason it was easy for Brussels to find for the BBC, Commission officials explained, was that, alone among broadcasters in Europe, we had gripped the key fair trading issues. We had convincingly separated out our publicly and commercially funded services, and we had a defined policy – underpinned by credible compliance and independent audit – to ensure that our commercial services were not subsidised in any way by the licence fee. Eventually Brussels would impose the BBC model on other European broadcasters.

BBC News 24 felt like my baby, but the network had an uncertain start. We had used the new digital technologies to create the most advanced news production environment in the world. Each of the systems we installed worked on its own, but problems arose when they interacted with each other. As a result, there were many embarrassing on-air slip-ups in News 24's early months which some of the world's best technologists – from inside and outside the BBC – struggled to resolve. In addition, we had a wholly new team of presenters and editors, many of them relatively untried, and some took time to find their feet. News 24 faced continuing hostility – from Sky, from Gerald Kaufman and, true to ancient BBC tradition, from other parts of the BBC, irritated by the resources that had been invested in the new service. But gradually Jenny Abramsky and her team won through, and the teething problems were resolved. News 24 soon became an important place to turn to for breaking news, and in time a vital part of the UK media landscape, a superb show-case for the world's most intelligent and powerful news machine.

At a late stage in the Charter discussions in the early 1990s, Michael Heseltine – back in government as John Major's deputy – had inter-vened in the BBC's affairs with a new agenda: he insisted that the BBC must more effectively use the burgeoning media environment to exploit its commercial assets at home and abroad. As a stimulus to us, he organised a seminar of British industrialists. We sat and lis-tened patiently and courteously – but through gritted teeth – to their uninformed advice. Bob Phillis had not long been in charge of the BBC's commercial arm, BBC Worldwide. We shared our embryonic thinking with Heseltine, but could give no clear answers on the long-term financial possibilities. 'Where's the beef?' he growled. Bob and I met with Patricia Hodgson in my hotel room in Blackpool during a party conference and – to head Heseltine off – agreed to accept a target to triple the commercial benefit to the BBC over the life of the new Charter. It was a tough challenge, for BBC Worldwide, like the rest of the organisation, lacked the infor-mation systems necessary to ascertain if a myriad of activities – selling BBC programmes across the globe, releasing videos, licensing merchandising, publishing books and magazines – was not just gen-erating income but was, activity by activity, making a profit. As a result, we could have no precise idea of future potential. When, years later, we did finally introduce proper financial disciplines to BBC Worldwide, we discovered that much activity was indeed loss-making. First Bob Phillis, then later Rupert Gavin, tackled these problems, boosted profitability and established BBC Worldwide as Europe's largest media exporter, the biggest outside America. By the time I left the BBC, our annual commercial turnover was nearly

£500 million and we were well on the way to meeting the impromptu target we had agreed with Heseltine.

At the heart of our commercial success in the 1990s were two joint ventures – with Flextech in the UK and with Discovery around the world. In the 1980s the BBC had made an unwitting error of historic proportion: new cable channels in the States – like Discovery and Arts and Entertainment – had become massive commercial successes, worth billions, largely on the back of purchased BBC programmes. The BBC had made money selling the programmes but had had no share of the massive capital value of the channels that we had helped to create. (The exception was UK Gold, a British cable channel which was a joint venture established by Michael Checkland.) We set out to remedy the BBC's strategic error and to create a family of commercial channels at home and abroad in which the BBC would have a stake.

Sky wanted to be our partner in creating new channels in the UK, but in preference we chose Flextech, part-owned by the US media conglomerate, TCI (Tele-Communications Inc.). In 1997 we agreed with Flextech to create a 'bouquet' of advertiser-supported channels for cable and satellite under the 'UK' brand to exploit the BBC's archive of drama, entertainment, documentary, arts and lifestyle programmes – the largest in the world. This was a good deal for the BBC. Flextech took all the risk and put up all the investment; the BBC was paid for the programmes shown, and we had a 50 per cent ownership stake in the channels. Eventually, four channels – UK Style, UK Horizons, Play UK and UK Arena – joined UK Gold and quickly gained high commercial value.

When I joined the BBC, we broadcast two television channels in the UK. By the time I left we were transmitting twelve in the UK, and an additional five around the world. Launching all our new digital services was the biggest implementation project in the BBC's history. It was driven by Patricia, helped by a dogged and worldly project manager, Charles Evans, whose previous job had been to mastermind the manufacture of the locomotives for the Channel Tunnel link. Our multiple launch established beyond doubt that the BBC's technologists had virtuoso digital skills, and led their field in the UK.

We chose Discovery as our lead global partner. Discovery was set up in 1985 by John Hendricks, a charismatic university administrator from Alabama, who had both a vision and the drive to see it through. His dream – of serious factual programmes for American audiences which would engage and entertain – was not exactly the same as the BBC's, but it was a close relation. Discovery executives were serious-minded yet impressively sharp on the business side: Hendricks's team had a deep grasp of the cable and satellite channel business in the States and around the world, and high-quality people in every department. It took Discovery and the BBC two years to finalise a joint venture of enormous complexity, and saint-like patience from John Hendricks and Judith McHale at Discovery to satisfy the needs of every part of a demanding and pernickety BBC. The legal agreement finalised in 1998 ran to so many volumes that it filled the Council Chamber, and took a whole morning to sign. But Discovery and the BBC did finally launch together two worldwide channels – Animal Planet and People and Arts – and, at long last, the BBC's very own network in the States, BBC America. Discovery took the investment risk, the BBC supplying the programmes and acquiring an ownership share. On the day the deal was signed, the BBC's holding in the Animal Planet channel in the States alone was already estimated to be worth $100 million. It was another good deal! Our relationship with Discovery would deepen. And when I left office, BBC America was already in eleven million homes in the US and climbing.

Our most hair-raising – yet most glorious – endeavour internationally was BBC World, our twenty-four-hour global channel, which provided news, like the World Service, with an international agenda. BBC World had been started by Michael Checkland and John Tusa under the auspices of the World Service. Mrs Thatcher had denied the venture any public money and the channel had struggled to pay its way commercially. Bob Phillis brought in new funds through a joint venture with Pearson, which also included a European entertainment channel, BBC Prime. CNN was well ahead of us in the race to build a global television news channel, although, thanks to the World Service's lead in radio, we still reached more people internationally with our news. Overall, CNN was snapping at our heels, however, with the iconoclastic Ted Turner defiantly supporting a loss-making international expansion of his news network.

The rivalry between the BBC and Ted Turner was friendly. It was impossible not to admire his buccaneering spirit and commitment. CNN was more respected by the BBC than any other news competitor, and vice versa. Turner was also a fellow traveller in other ways. Sitting next to me at a dinner in London, he protested the malign impact on broadcasting of Rupert Murdoch, and quizzed me about the BBC's experience of him. 'Call me any time,' he said, 'anywhere in the world. Anything you want me to say, I'll get straight on a plane. I'll do anything to help you fight that man.'

BBC World's path was strewn with misadventure. The channel was broadcast on the Star satellite into China and the Far East. The Chinese authorities were obsessive about the BBC's journalism, bridling at all reporting of opposition to their government. On a number of occasions, they had excluded or thrown out BBC journalists from China itself. (In later years, they would also jam our Internet news service.) In 1993 Rupert Murdoch bought the Star satellite which beamed BBC World and other networks into China. Speaking at the magnificent Banqueting Hall in Whitehall, a few months after he acquired Star, Murdoch waxed lyrical about the force for freedom the new broadcasting technologies represented:

> Advances in the technology of telecommunications have proved an unambiguous threat to totalitarian regimes everywhere . . . technology has been a key factor in the enormous spread of freedom that is the major distinguishing characteristic of recent years.

By the end of the year, however, it was clear that Murdoch was going to throw BBC World off the Star satellite service into China, which he was entitled to do under the contract. This was a catastrophic strategic, editorial and commercial reverse for the BBC. But in his typically straightforward way, Murdoch made no attempt to hide his true motive. He explained to the *New Yorker* why he had excluded us: 'The BBC was driving them [the Chinese] nuts . . . it wasn't worth it.' When I saw John Major in the Cabinet Room in March 1994, he was in a black fury over Murdoch's actions against BBC World, which – to my surprise – he had followed closely. He vigorously condemned Murdoch for giving in to a totalitarian regime.

BBC World struggled with other powerful governments. We had negotiated a deal to broadcast into Saudi Arabia via the Orbit satellite, and to include within BBC World a news segment in Arabic. A large corps of Arab journalists was established at BBC Television Centre in Shepherds Bush to provide the service. Our deal with our Arab partners guaranteed the BBC's editorial independence, but in the event, when we ran into difficulty, this agreement proved to be no protection. When we covered stories, for instance, about the Saudi dissident Dr Mohammed al-Massari, a critic of the Saudi Royal Family, the service was sometimes blacked out without explanation.

A crisis which would prove terminal blew up over a *Panorama* on Saudi justice – due to be transmitted on BBC World. The offending programme contained strong evidence that the Saudi police were extracting confessions under torture, as a result of which innocent people had been convicted and beheaded. We were told that if we transmitted the *Panorama* direct to Saudi Arabia BBC World would be taken off the Orbit satellite. The decision over whether or not to transmit came to me to take personally. It was painful though not difficult. If we proceeded, we would forfeit a substantial contribution to BBC World's operating costs, and scores of BBC Arab journalists would lose their jobs. If we caved in, on the other hand, we would be conceding the BBC's editorial independence. There was no choice: I was clear we had to transmit the programme, whatever the consequences. The BBC was in it for the long term. We would out-live the world's totalitarian regimes. Our independence was far too precious an asset to trade. As predicted, when the programme was shown, we were immediately thrown off the satellite. Money and jobs were indeed lost. And a major hole duly appeared in BBC World's income stream.

For BBC World it would be a long haul: the global news network would take many years to approach break-even. Some of my col-leagues thought that funding BBC World's operating losses from our commercial revenues was too high a price to pay. But I was res-olute we should, and I was supported unflinchingly in this by Christopher Bland and the board. Gradually, incrementally, BBC World grew, reaching 137 million homes worldwide by the end of the 1990s. Taken together with BBC World Service radio, and BBC Online News, by the end of the decade BBC News still reached more people internationally than CNN and, all in all, the BBC's burgeoning portfolio of global services was reaching an estimated 360 million people each week – behind MTV's global reach, for instance, but none the less the biggest audience of any of the world's comprehensive news- and programme-providers. At the end of the 1990s, the BBC remained the world's best-known broadcast brand, a showcase around the globe for British talent and the first choice for trusted and authoritative news – indeed, the world's most accom-plished all-round broadcaster.

The BBC's emergence as one of the world's most successful Internet players too was haphazard. BBC Education were early pioneers when, at the beginning of the 1990s, Internet services consisted of nothing more than wispy, indecipherable electronic pages jammed with print, containing no pictures, whether still or moving – in short, when the Internet seemed to have only limited appeal and applica-tion. All over the BBC, however, technologists and producers were

siphoning off modest funds from programme and other budgets
and experimenting, normally on the back of established programmes. Norman Blackwell of McKinsey was the first to raise the
Internet at a strategic level in the BBC when we began our ten-year
thinking, but it was low down on our list of concerns. Of all my
friends and colleagues, Terry Burns was the first to adopt the
Internet in his day-to-day life for e-mails and for information-gath-
ering, and to raise my awareness of the new medium's value.

In the mid-1990s the BBC developed a false view of the Internet.
We decided that it was really an extension of the magazine business
and that BBC Worldwide should take the lead in developing commercial applications. Again we had to find a partner, and we chose
ICL, owned by the Japanese electronics company Fujitsu. ICL
wanted to gain profile and experience – which they could exploit
commercially elsewhere – by developing Internet technology alongside the BBC as we fashioned new services for the Internet which
ICL would fully fund. The deal we agreed in 1996 was extremely
limited from ICL's perspective and very flexible and advantageous
from the BBC's. The term of the arrangement was just three years,
with no commitment thereafter, and ICL would have no stake in
any business created. The conception of the partnership with ICL
would prove brilliant for the BBC, and all credit for this was due to
Jeremy Mayhew – who had come to the BBC to work as an analyst
in Corporate Strategy after a period as Peter Lilley's special adviser.
Jeremy had been evangelical in asserting that neither the BBC nor
ICL really knew where the Internet was going, and that it would
therefore be madness for either party to tie itself down. Jeremy's perception – and his single-minded insistence on following it through –
would prove the BBC's salvation.

The moment of truth came in 1997 when Jeremy himself put forward a proposal for a BBC News Internet service at just the point
when web technology was developing rapidly and was suddenly
allowing clear print, attractive graphics and brilliant colour pictures. Moreover, video streaming would soon facilitate the first

moving news footage on the Internet. Jeremy's case for a BBC News service online assimilated these developments, and provided immediate and persuasive evidence of how attractive news on the Internet could be. But his proposal was for a commercial service, which would place advertisements in the BBC's heartland – news for UK audiences – in an environment analogous to broadcast TV news. Alarm bells rang immediately, and there and then I made a difficult decision – especially so given that it would gravely undermine Jeremy's far-sighted and conscientious work. I declared that BBC News Online could not be commercial, that it must be publicly funded. The very flexibility of the contract Jeremy had negotiated with ICL made that decision possible.

I immediately put my shoulder behind BBC News Online. Jenny Abramsky was the executive in charge, while the editor was Bob Eggington – a dedicated, driven, no-nonsense BBC News journalist who went on to create what was by common consent the most comprehensive, effective and admired online news service in the world.

I now understood that the Internet would be significant. BBC News Online was off the launch pad; but the BBC did not yet have a comprehensive all-embracing strategy for the new medium. In 1994 and 1995 I had spent time in the US, Hong Kong and Japan immersing myself in new technology, understanding many of the new digital applications. I visited – inter alia – Time Warner, Oracle, Sun Microsystems, Videostream, Hong Kong Telecom, Sony; but the Internet was still not at the top of anyone's agenda, and the penny had not generally dropped, least of all with me.

The breakthrough came when I visited California and Seattle in July 1997 with a thoughtful, alert and companionable young BBC corporate analyst called Jamie Reeve. Jamie, through friends in the States, had been monitoring the burgeoning world of Internet start-ups. He shared his insights with me, and opened my eyes. Much of the innovation centred on Los Angeles, San Francisco, Silicon Valley and Seattle, all of which we visited on our trip. Many of the companies that welcomed us and briefed us that week – like CitySearch, C-Net, @Home, GeoCities, Netscape, Web TV – would, within two years, be capitalised together at tens of billions of dollars: GeoCities was bought by Yahoo for $5.7 billion; @Home by Excite for $6.7 billion; and Netscape by AOL for $4.2 billion. But in 1997 the companies that Jamie and I visited were housed in scruffy warehouses off the beaten track, predominantly run and staffed by teams in their twenties and thirties, web pioneers who bowled me over with their energy and vision, their management know-how, their willingness to take risks. The stock market would soon react hysterically to their breakthroughs and grossly over-inflate the values of the companies these and other young entrepreneurs had built – but that would take nothing away from their foresight and audacity in creating an entirely new medium which changed the world.

By the time Jamie and I took off from LA to fly north to Seattle, I felt I had finally understood the true power of the Internet to gather together communities of interest, to serve individuals in those communities with tailored, focused, personalised information and services, and to enable interaction between individuals and within communities. Much of the BBC's Internet activity hitherto had been programme based. I now understood we needed an entirely different vision, and to design unique online services to meet particular needs. Flying north along the Pacific coastline, I said not a word to Jamie but worked flat out to commit my new insights and thinking to paper. A couple of hours later, as we taxied into the terminal at Seattle, I waved a sheaf of papers at Jamie and proclaimed gleefully: 'Here at long last is the BBC's Internet strategy!' And it was – duly refined by Jamie, who went on to help implement it.

I returned to London with all the zealousness of the convert. I could not immediately persuade all my colleagues to share my enthusiasm. There was an understandable reluctance to spend money on an untried service rather than on radio and television programmes. But gradually attitudes changed. I held a number of Internet parties in the Council Chamber for both devotees and sceptics across the BBC. We ordered pizzas and sushi on the Internet for instant delivery and consumption. The converts showed their fellow partygoers their favourite websites from around the world, and pointed out innovation and best practice across the web. We uncovered Internet zealots hidden away right across the organisation. Jonathan Drori, from BBC Education, was among the first to realise the amazing creative possibilities of the web. A brilliant technologist from our Research and Development arm, Brandon Butterworth, was so committed that he ran the technology supporting our embryonic online services from his own bedroom.

The mood within the BBC swung. Just in time we caught the wave and established BBC Online as the most comprehensive content website in Europe, arguably the most innovative and respected in the world, and a public service base camp for the new digital era. Once established, it grew at a dizzying rate, soon becoming the most visited content website in Europe. We quickly left most of our fellow broadcasters – in the UK and around the world – standing.

Jamie and I had ended our West Coast trip with a visit to Microsoft. At the end of a long day of meetings, we visited Bill Gates in his office. We had one piece of business to transact. Gates agreed to place BBC Online in a prominent position on the new Internet Explorer web browser. But the main purpose of the meeting was to swap views on where the new technologies were heading. I had encountered Gates previously at the World Economic Forum at Davos, but this was our first meaty discussion. Gates is an intense companion: he listens attentively; he responds crisply and to the point; he is a quietly witty and pleasant conversationalist; and he has so much surplus energy that he jiggles his leg up and down rapidly as he speaks, barely able to confine himself to a chair. Over the next few years I experienced more of him: he invited me to attend a small annual conference in Seattle of chief executives, mostly from the States, but with a sprinkling from around the world, to debate the impact on business of the new technologies.

On these visits I saw Bill Gates and Microsoft close up and he impressed me more than any other executive I ever met. He is intellectually curious and gifted, at ease with ideas, interested in science, informed about a wide range of developments, and quick to see the significance of a breakthrough – as he was in apprehending the software revolution in his early twenties. Gates is the driving creative force in his own company, comfortably leading software developments at the front line. He is a brilliant marketeer, not only understanding products but how to introduce them to the customer. Finally, he is an impressive chief executive: in Microsoft Gates has created an awesome, tightly run entity, with rigorous business processes, which scours the world for talent, incentivises it and ruthlessly moves out the weaker performers.

Meeting the cream of the US business community at Gates's conferences – people like Jack Welch and Warren Buffett – made me appreciate just how much more rigorous, ruthless and innovative US industry is than British or European. Many contributions from the chief executives attending were scintillating and gave me invaluable insights about best-business practice that I could apply on my return to the BBC.

The conference attendees dined one evening at Bill Gates's illustrious, newly built waterfront home, arriving by boat. We were shown around the house, which, as Gates explained to me at dinner, he had minutely specified before appointing an architect. Every part of his home had a purpose. On my first visit, I found myself in a large room with a wall-to-wall black floor, which turned out to be a rubber trampoline. Rupert Murdoch's young, spiky-haired, tattooed son Lachlan – by far the youngest conference delegate, and a News Corporation executive – entered with me. He and I bounced up and down together on the trampoline, something I had not done since childhood. Doing a forward somersault again for the first time in forty years, I felt like a naughty schoolboy.

The following year, Lachlan's dad Rupert turned up himself at the Gates get-together. He was newly married, slimmed down, made over, wearing fashionable, cashmere polo-necks, and more limber – walking out by himself each day for exercise. Rupert Murdoch was also more mellow. After one session, he and I were the only two who took the opportunity when offered to stay behind to look at all of Microsoft's new prototype technologies, which had been left on display for us. As we examined them, Murdoch remarked gloomily to me: 'Technology is scary!'

He and I had lunch alone together, sitting outside at a picnic table. We were poles apart in our attitudes and our values. Sky and the BBC had been on opposite sides in the great battles over regulation in Brussels and Whitehall. The BBC had had difficult negotiations with Sky Digital that had gone to the wire. We had fought over News 24 and Star TV in China. A few months earlier I had been in the vanguard of arguing against Sky's attempt to buy Manchester United. Murdoch's newspapers had helped coarsen British culture and our political discourse. I had spent my life in broadcasting dedicated to the public service ethic. But Murdoch was straight dealing; his business sense was acute; his appreciation of the significance of new technology in the 1980s and 1990s had been visionary; and in Sky he had created the only effective, strategic broadcasting organisation in Britain besides the BBC. Murdoch's papers had savaged the BBC in the 1980s; but had noticeably eased off for a while in the early 1990s when I became Director-General. His was the only group broadly friendly to the BBC's reform process. At Murdoch's Banqueting Hall speech in 1993, one of his editors had said to me: 'The old man approves of what you're doing, turning round the BBC. He hasn't told his editors what to write, but we all know what he thinks. That's why you've had an easier ride from us.'

Murdoch and I didn't discuss any of these things – or indeed anything serious at all – as we sat in the warm Seattle sun eating our Microsoft canteen lunch. We just chatted gently: sharing an admiration for Yahoo; pondering when pay-per-view movies would make money; speculating how much households would eventually spend on pay television; enjoying a gossip about the rapidly changing business of which we were both a part.

By the latter part of the 1990s the BBC was in technological ferment. For decades, technology issues had hardly ever reached the top table. Now we appreciated that digital technology would affect everything we did. Rodney Baker-Bates had shown real foresight: he had built a powerful digital distribution network across the BBC – a digital motorway – to enable us to carry moving pictures and information online across the organisation, including to the desktop. We had been the first organisation in Britain to install Windows 95. Now we realised that the BBC must become a coherent, digital institution all the way from the licence-payer, through the gateway, to distribution, production and support services. But we needed help to steer this challenging course. After hunting far and wide we recruited an American, Craig Fields, as the BBC's Technology Adviser. Craig would become one of my favourite people. He was a wiry jack-in-the-box in his fifties, married to a senior CIA official. He had been one of America's leading defence scientists, director of a defence research agency, and Chairman of President Clinton's Defense Service Board. Craig was also one of the fathers of the Internet, and he gave me – when I left the BBC – a present I treasure and keep in my study. Mounted on a wooden block is a piece of history – a neatly sawn-off part of the original, technologically antediluvian Internet A server, from the very earliest days of the embryonic World Wide Web.

In the late 1990s Craig helped frame a plan to turn the BBC into a fully digital organisation. He recruited Philip Langsdale from Cable and Wireless as our Director of Technology to implement the plan – to forge information, telecom, broadcast, production and Internet technologies into a single seamless entity. Craig lived in Washington DC, but visited us monthly, burrowing into every part of the organisation – encouraging, counselling, mentoring, progress-chasing, then writing me lucid, achingly candid appraisals of where we were adrift from our plans. He dealt with everyone he encountered in the same coruscatingly honest way – but always won you over because he belonged to no camp, because he was so constructive and fair, and because he delivered his commentaries with verve and wit.

Technology demonstrations became a routine part of BBC executive life in this period. Before he left, Rodney had worked with the US company Informix to build the world's first convincing display of video-on-demand. Politicians and others travelled far to see it. Tony Blair came to the BBC in autumn 1996 for a private briefing and demonstration. Now we scoured the world for intelligence about technology breakthroughs, and always – when we could – made them tangible by showing the new developments to senior BBC managers. By the end of the 1990s, with the aid of BBC technologists like Ian Jenkins, we had as acute an understanding as any broadcast organisation in the world of what was happening on every relevant technological front. The BBC had a keen digital capability.

In the late 1990s, Ed Richards, the BBC's head of corporate strategy, led a far-ranging review of where the digital world was heading, over ten- or twenty-year horizons, building on our previously hard-won insights. The review was launched with all the BBC's senior managers at a conference at Hever Castle, and thereafter became known simply as 'Hever'. Ed propelled us far into the future with his Hever work, closely defining the possible shape of the total digital universe ahead, beyond the world of linear networks, in which consumers move seamlessly from TV to PC to radio to handheld mobile devices, a world in which consumers will interact and obtain services on demand and will use small, light storage devices with a near infinity of memory. In the Hever work we posited what the broadcast services in such a future might be, and their significance for the consumer and for the BBC. Ed Richards's work was the most creative, satisfying and daunting strategy exercise conducted during my time at the BBC. It helped us understand how the BBC could avoid becoming marginalised in the digital age, how it could continue to present a public service alternative. When the total digital future comes to pass – and the timing is highly uncertain even if the broad outcome is not – it will pose a substantial challenge for the BBC, but one which the organisation will be abundantly equipped to meet. In the shorter term, however, our digital acuity would bring an unexpected benefit: it would prove decisive in the final, climactic event of my director-generalship – the negotiation of a licence-fee settlement to take the BBC into the new millennium.

18

Holding the BBC Together

In 1998 the BBC was consumed by a battle different from any other I faced in my time, either with politicians on the outside, or with conservatism and inertia on the inside. It was a bitter battle to prevent the BBC being split apart by the fissiparous forces of devolution that had been unleashed by the incoming Labour government's plan to give Scotland its own Parliament and Wales its own Assembly.

Tensions within the BBC between London and Scotland had been growing for years. As a northerner and an ITV alumnus, I had felt more strongly than most that the Corporation had focused its energies too much on London, and that its radio and television networks had failed historically to reflect the extraordinary diversity of expression across the UK as a whole. As a result, I had driven a fundamental shift of money and production away from south-east England; and Ron Neil and Mark Byford in their turn had responded by transforming the quality of news and programme-making in the nations and English regions – a part of the BBC that had been distinctly sleepy in the 1980s. BBC Scotland had had more than its share of unreconstructed management, but when John McCormick – who had been the BBC's Secretary in the Checkland era – became Controller of BBC Scotland in 1992, he quickly connected us to the cultural renaissance increasingly manifest north of the border. *Mrs Brown*, *Hamish MacBeth*, *Tartan Shorts* (an Oscar winner) and a revitalised Radio Scotland were the result.

I visited Scotland regularly and observed – alongside cultural renewal – an increased flexing of political muscle. Voices in Scotland were demanding more resources, an increasing share of the licence fee, and more independence for BBC Scotland. The main driver of these demands – growing as the 1990s progressed, and surfacing regularly in the Scottish media – was the BBC's Broadcasting Council for Scotland, an essentially consultative body composed of the Scottish great and good, and chaired by the BBC's Governor for Scotland.

The Broadcasting Council would often spit. Shortly after I became Director-General I attended a bad-tempered dinner in Glasgow with the Council which ended abruptly when one of its members declared: 'We've just had an accountant [Checkland] as Director-General. Now we've got an engineer. When will we have someone *creative* running the BBC?' I thrived on argument, but I was never able to stomach outright discourtesy – so that was my last social encounter with the Scottish Council. I addressed them formally the next day in a cold fury.

The climate of ideas in Scotland was different from that of England: market mechanisms, increasingly consensual south of the border, still aroused suspicion or hostility in Scotland. When Producer Choice was introduced, and cuts were planned in our staff and facilities in Glasgow – as they had been right across the BBC – the Scottish Broadcasting Council continued to press me hard to conjure up more money for programmes, but vigorously resisted any cost-saving cuts in Scotland's inefficient resource base to fund them.

When the new Charter was being finalised in the mid-1990s, the Council made a late push behind the scenes to increase their powers, to seize control of local and network programmes, and to wrest budgets away from the centre of the BBC. Michael Stevenson and I countered this move, working hard and successfully with Whitehall officials to clarify and codify the Broadcasting Council's powers – but not at the expense of the unitary nature of the BBC. When I went up to Glasgow around this time to make a speech, a severe cleric, asked to say grace before the meal, intoned mournfully: 'May the good Lord protect us from whatever John Birt is about to mete out to the people of Scotland.' (Unprepared for the fractious mood of the occasion, and lacking the agility to adjust my prepared, written text on the hoof, I proceeded to make the worst speech of my life.)

In 1995 the Prime Minister, John Major, agreed to give an interview to *Panorama*, an important coup for the programme. It was timed just before local elections in Scotland and England. Though the subject-matter was national and international, the prominence of the interview raised the issue of fairness to other parties so close to an election. This was not an unusual problem. In the previous twelve months there had been seventeen weeks during which one kind of election or another had been pending. Normal politics couldn't stop at such times, but News and other programme-makers did need to consider the electoral implications of individual programmes and the overall balance of views during the period. BBC News executives had addressed the particular issues of fairness raised by the Major interview, and they had identified opportunities to talk to the other parties – although in hindsight with insufficient boldness.

I heard about the interview only a few days before it was due to be broadcast. I expressed my unease, but, caught between the devil of Scotland and the deep blue sea of banning a rare, long interview with the Prime Minister, I allowed the interview to proceed. When news of it was released, there was an immediate clamour in

Scotland to abandon the programme. On the day of the intended broadcast, to our astonishment, the Scottish High Court granted an unprecedented interdict banning transmission in Scotland to representatives of the Labour and Liberal Democrat parties. We appealed and lost. The BBC should have been more sensitive to Scottish feeling; we could and should have gripped the issue more decisively; but legal precedent over seventy years had previously established that constitutionally it was for the Governors not the courts to rule on matters of judgement like political impartiality. The forced withdrawal of the Major interview by the High Court in Edinburgh was a resounding victory for Scotland over London, and Scottish opinion rejoiced.

John Smith had pledged the Labour Party to devolution, a commitment that after his death was maintained by Tony Blair. In advance of Labour coming to power, the BBC lobbied to ensure that broadcasting was not devolved to the newly planned constitutional bodies in Edinburgh and Cardiff, and that the BBC was not in the process broken up. A few days after the election was won, Jane and I were invited to a private party in honour of Tony and Cherie Blair, and we sat by Derry Irvine, who was to supervise Labour's devolution plans. I was reassured to discover that Derry and I saw eye to eye on the issue.

In 1998, with a new Scottish Parliament in sight, there was a ferocious battle royal over a proposal from the BBC in Glasgow to opt out of the *Six O'Clock News* and to produce in its place an integrated international and local news programme from a Scottish perspective. I was deeply resistant to the proposal. It could have dire consequences for the BBC, and unintended consequences for the United Kingdom. I readily recognised the obvious – that our programmes in Scotland needed to be enhanced to deal with the fresh situation following a new constitutional settlement, and that the new political realities in Scotland ought to be reported fully on our UK-wide news – but I was convinced that, once Scotland opted out of the *Six*, Wales – which in my experience always used its political weight to follow Scotland's lead – would soon follow. Northern Ireland would be close behind. Once the *Six* was conceded there would be no argument for resisting the takeover of the *One* and the *Nine* as well. Within a few years there would be no UK-wide news on the BBC. I calculated that this domino effect would continue, with a momentum of its own, until eventually the BBC itself was either turned into a weak, federal institution – each part going its own way – or was broken up, with an English Broadcasting Corporation headquartered in London. The EBC would be a lesser force than the BBC – with reduced revenues, and with its status as the world's most successful cultural institution much diminished. Moreover, in Scotland, Wales and Northern Ireland, low-funded sister institutions would be broadcasting in place of the BBC, with a fraction of the impact the Corporation currently had in those nations. Surveys registered only a modest appetite for such change among the Scottish people themselves, but it was clear, none the less, that Scotland's opinion leaders would fight to opt out of BBC News.

As devolution loomed as a reality and the emotional temperature rose, BBC executives in Glasgow, the Broadcasting Council, the Scottish media and even Scottish civil servants all began to support the case for an independent *Six*. Norman Drummond, the Scottish Governor – cleric, former head teacher and rugby blue – led the charge. I resolved to ensure that this potent alliance was not joined by all the main political parties in Scotland, in particular the powerful cohort of Scottish Labour politicians – Gordon Brown, Robin Cook, Derry Irvine, Donald Dewar and Alastair Darling.

I wrote to, and then went to see, the new Prime Minister Tony Blair. I expounded not just from the BBC's perspective but from the nation's. I argued that we were one of the few institutions which bound Britain together. BBC News was iconic. Opting out of the *Six* would be a powerful symbol of Scotland moving away from UK-wide institutions. Scottish viewers would be deprived of the breadth of UK-wide and international news that formed the common knowledge underpinning a UK-wide democratic system. The end of a single, common experience of UK news would, moreover, encourage separatist tendencies. The BBC should of course respond to the considered, settled will of the British people. If the Scots one day chose independence, that was their right – and the BBC, like everyone else, would have to accept the consequences. But, I argued, we should follow constitutional change; it was not our role to lead it. Blair was quick, as ever, to grasp the case. 'Let's fight,' he said.

Blair agreed that Peter Mandelson, the Minister without Portfolio, would marshal Labour's forces. Peter worked with Michael Stevenson on a plan of action. When Mandelson moved to the DTI, Michael continued to work with James Purnell from Number 10. In the bitter battles of the following twelve months, Labour held the line. Gordon Brown, for instance, wrote a series of carefully argued, high-ground articles for the Scottish papers advocating the virtues of the union from Scotland's perspective. We feared at the BBC that Donald Dewar, the Scottish Secretary of State, widely seen as father of the Scottish nation, might break ranks – but he refused repeatedly to be drawn into the argument, making only one guarded, elliptical comment, which appeared to disparage the notion of a Scottish-focused news:

> I am not saying, not for a moment, that devolved broad-
> casting would necessarily mean Kailyard programming, if
> I can put it like that. But I am saying that it is not self-evident
> that separating out a Scottish BBC would be for the best.

'Kailyard' was a reference to a nineteenth-century school of Scottish writing which offered a parochial and sentimental view of Scottish small-town life.

I also went to see the new Conservative leader, William Hague, but fared less well. We had an amiable and engaging conversation. Unsurprisingly for a McKinsey alumnus, Hague first pressed me for an account of the BBC's digital plans, demonstrating a real appetite for detail. He heard me out on Scotland and readily supported the case, as Blair had done. Hague, however, was less optimistic than Blair of success with his own colleagues in Scotland. His lack of hope turned out to be justified: David McLetchie, the Scottish Tory Party leader, soon joined the alliance for an independent Scottish *Six*. For the most part, though, Scottish politicians at Westminster held the line, and were at odds with their brethren at home. David Steel allowed his opposition to a Scottish opt-out to become known; and I received well-argued letters of support from the two leading Scottish Tories – Malcolm Rifkind and Ian Lang – which I was able to use to buttress my case with the Governors at the crucial moment.

At an early discussion of the issue in the spring of 1998, many English Governors had expressed an outspoken, visceral opposition to the idea of a Scottish *Six*, and initially I was optimistic that the board would reject the proposal. But as the debate intensified, and the pressure was on, new Governors joined the board who had no strong convictions on the issue. From experience I knew that no one liked saying no to the Scots, and doubts about victory began to enter my mind. Chris Graham – Michael Stevenson's cool, composed successor as BBC Secretary – managed the machinations of the next six months with mandarin skill. Christopher Bland did not declare his own hand. Indeed, after several years in the job, he was trying hard by this point to shake off his early reputation as a railroader and to forge consensus among his fellow Governors. Christopher was fearful that if the Scots lost the argument he might preside over the mass resignations of the BBC Governor, the Controller and the Broadcasting Council of Scotland – a prospect he did not relish.

Bland pressed compromise on me. I looked with my colleagues at ever more ingenious ways of refashioning the BBC's national and local news hour at six. I promised a major programme of education – and new processes – to ensure that the BBC's programme-makers and

news decision-takers would be more alert to Scottish sensitivities, but
I refused to compromise on the basic principle of one national news
for the whole of the UK. As a consequence, Christopher and I had
our only harsh words of our time together at the BBC. He chided me
for carrying out the wishes of the London politicians. I denied vigorously that we were dancing to their tune – I protested that I was acting
only in the long-term interests of the BBC.

The debate in Scotland reached fever pitch in the autumn of
1998 – arguably the high-water mark of Scottish nationalism. The
BBC's Controller in Scotland, John McCormick – a decent, pas-
sionate public servant, naturally loyal both to Scotland and to the
BBC – was caught in a terrible, anguishing vice. The quiet, dignified
Mark Leishman, the Secretary in Scotland – who bore an uncanny
resemblance to his grandfather Lord Reith, the BBC's founding
Director-General – worked tirelessly to keep everyone on board the
BBC ship. Will Wyatt, Tony Hall, Mark Byford and Michael
Stevenson went up to Glasgow to face the music at the Broadcasting
Council, and to put London's case. They were lambasted and plastered like guilty men all over the Scottish papers. In November, I
went with the Governors and the Executive Committee to Glasgow
for a meeting billed as a chance for the Governors to 'listen' to the
Council. For two hours Bland and his colleagues were exposed to an
incessant tirade of bile, vitriol and abuse – the most excruciating
meeting of its kind I ever attended. Despite this onslaught, the
resolve of the Governors just about held. The steelier remained
steely. Barbara Young, the Scottish Vice-Chairman, equivocated
but eventually decided to oppose the Scottish *Six*. The centre
ground on the board refused to jump either way.

The Governors met finally to decide the issue in early December.
At the meeting, I argued strongly that our surveys of opinion
demonstrated beyond a doubt that while some Scots did want
change only a minority wanted to opt out of the network news.
Christopher finally came down in support of management's proposal. Emotions ran high, but in the event only one person – from

the Broadcasting Council – was lost overboard through resignation when the decision against the Scottish *Six* was finally announced.

This painful episode had an ultimately benign outcome. In 1999, when devolution finally became a reality in Scotland and Wales, no organisation was better prepared to serve both the nations and the UK as a whole than the BBC. Meanwhile, the *British* Broadcasting Corporation lived to fight another day.

19

Happy Ending

M y last great ambition for the BBC was to place the institution on a sound financial footing once more.

The BBC's financial history is critical to any understanding of its true nature and achievements. From its formation in the 1920s to the middle of the 1980s, the BBC had ridden a tidal wave of money, growing inexorably each year throughout the period at a remarkable rate – on average about 4 per cent per annum. Driving this long-term growth were three great surges of revenue: at the beginning, in the early part of the century, the expansion of radio ownership; after the war, the introduction of a higher licence fee for the expanding new medium of television; and in the 1970s and 1980s huge growth on the back of a higher licence fee for colour. This flow of money had enabled the BBC to grow and to develop, always to do the next new thing, and never to have to prioritise. Yet it had also created an internal culture of supplicancy, an obsession with grabbing hold of funds through lobbying, persuasion and campaigning. It had further helped to create an inflated, wasteful organisation, with a mass of excess fat – for with the money rolling in no one ever had any strong or continuing incentive to promote efficiency or value for money. There was no culture within the BBC of facing up to difficult choices. Budgetary discipline scarcely existed.

The most momentous date in the BBC's financial history was 1985, during Mrs Thatcher's reign, from which point the value of the licence fee was frozen. For the next decade, the licence fee remained constant or was reduced in value. A tiny incremental growth in the number of licensed households in the period produced some modest additional revenue, but for over ten years the BBC's income was essentially flat. Most of the organisation's costs, however – like staff, talent and rights costs – were *rising* at least in line with general economic growth. So, if nothing else changed, a fixed income would quickly precipitate the BBC for the first time in its existence into decline. Savage cuts in programmes and services would be inevitable.

Mrs Thatcher had intended that freezing the licence fee would deliver a rude shock to the BBC's system, and oblige us not to cut services but to transform our efficiency. And her device would achieve that aim decisively – but it did not do so immediately, for Michael Checkland began his term of office with a huge cash surplus in the bank, some of it intended for capital projects – like a News building – which were abandoned. So, in the years after Mrs Thatcher administered her shock, the BBC postponed the evil day. First it used up its savings, then it borrowed, spending more on programmes each year than it was earning from the licence fee. But the borrowing could not continue, for we were limited by statute as well as by prudence. Whoever had become the BBC's Director-General in 1992 would have faced the same tough choices I did, choices that could be delayed no longer.

At first, when I explained our financial problems to managers and staff, they looked blankly back at me, not wanting to grapple with the grisly and unprecedented realities of our frozen income, wishing they would just disappear. But they would not, so we embarked on a long-term programme to sort ourselves out – reining back spending to eliminate our borrowings and to live within our means; introducing Producer Choice to bring our efficiency into line with the market; improving our commercial revenues; and increasing our licence income by reducing evasion and collection costs.

Most of the monies that we invested in additional programmes and services in the 1990s came from efficiency gains – but, as first Bob Phillis and later Rupert Gavin got to grips with BBC Worldwide, our commercial revenues grew substantially and added to the programme pot. And our licence income grew when we took over responsibility for collecting it from the Home Office in 1990, and John Smith transformed the efficacy of what had previously been a weakly managed entity. We introduced a welter of schemes to make the licence fee easier to pay, improving the database to identify evading and new households, making the detection equipment more portable and powerful, moving from prosecuting evaders to encouraging them to sign up on the doorstep – via mobiles – on direct debit. These actions drove evasion rates down to their lowest level ever and improved our revenue by the end of the decade by over £100 million a year.

As the 1990s progressed, politicians of all parties began to believe that we were serious about reform, that if they increased the licence fee the money would not disappear into a black hole, but would result in more programmes and services.

As early as 1993 the introduction of Producer Choice resulted in a thawing of relations with Conservative politicians, and a first modest reward. Secretary of State Peter Brooke was charged with setting the licence fee for the next three years. He was under pressure from within the government to pocket the BBC's efficiency gains by further reducing the licence fee, as had happened in 1991. Hussey argued forcefully with the sage and moderate Brooke that he (Brooke) would fatally undermine our reforms – and me personally –

if the BBC couldn't invest the painfully won efficiency gains in pro-grammes, and Brooke agreed. He wouldn't *increase* the licence fee, he said, but he would hold it static.

Brooke helped us in another way: he ruled that we must sell off the BBC's transmitters, something to which we had no objection – for transmission was not a core BBC activity. There was a snag, however. When we were close to making a sale I met a senior official in the Department of National Heritage who informed me that Hussey had agreed – at a private and unheralded lunch with Brooke's successor Stephen Dorrell – to split the proceeds fifty–fifty between the BBC and the Treasury. I was shocked and responded quite spontaneously that I knew nothing of this and that such a deal was 'unthinkable'. The transmitter network had been created over decades through licence funding rather than taxation, so the pro-ceeds should be returned not to the Treasury but to the licence-payer through investment in programmes. Hussey was shamefaced when I confronted him and denied bluntly ever agree-ing the deal with Dorrell. I put it down to a misunderstanding, but I stuck to my guns with the Department: the theology of the BBC's argument was impeccable and it would eventually be accepted by the Treasury. When our transmitters were finally sold to Castle Transmission Services in February 1997 – in a process expertly man-aged by Bob Phillis and Rodney Baker-Bates – we kept all the money: a magnificent windfall of £244 million.

In 1996, as we began to appreciate the challenge of new tech-nology, we faced another licence-fee review. I resolved to make the case for more money, to ask for the first increase for over ten years, to help us fund new digital services. Patricia Hodgson and I agreed on most issues, but on this we were divided. Patricia felt we could not succeed, that an ailing Conservative government, a year away from a general election, would not, could not, increase the licence fee, and that the inevitable rejection of our claim would weaken the BBC. I felt, on the other hand, that we had a strong case: the digi-tal challenge was real and manifest; and we had proved our ability

to help ourselves with efficiency savings and revenue-raising measures. Moreover, with Virginia Bottomley as Secretary of State and
John Major as Prime Minister, we had two BBC loyalists in key
positions. We would at least receive a fair hearing: nothing ven-
tured, nothing gained. The risk was worth taking.

Virginia Bottomley – often ridiculed for her hockey-captain,
head-girl style – has in reality a driving, energetic determination to
understand the critical issues, and a burning curiosity about people
and what motivates them. She also has a passionate conviction
about public service, an appealing, level-headed idealism which
runs far ahead of party- and self-interest. Bottomley was amused by
my thoroughness, and by the charts I used in the weighty presenta-
tions laying out the BBC's case for more money, but was persuaded
by my advocacy. She accepted, in principle, that the BBC did need
higher funding for our first foray into digital. She had to have, however, a cast-iron case for the stern, beady denizens of the Treasury.
She prepared the ground by commissioning a team of independent
economists and accountants from a division of Deloitte and Touche
to audit our books and to confirm that we had made the savings
from Producer Choice we claimed. To our relief, the Deloitte and
Touche team gave us a glowing report:

> We believe the BBC has advanced considerably as an
> organisation . . . and has made major steps forward in
> delivering new services and improved output while also
> reducing borrowings. These achievements have been
> financed largely by efficiency savings . . . The BBC made
> substantial efficiency savings in three years . . . which amount
> to 18.9% (compound) of the costs incurred by the BBC's
> output directorates . . . The BBC has reduced repeats . . .
> from 21% to 11% in BBC1's peak-time schedule . . . We
> believe the BBC's organisational ability to manage change
> has increased over the past three years due to: more effective
> financial and cash management; clearer programme

strategies which now provide a basis for resource allocation;
improved operational systems; experience of large scale
restructuring and the introduction of change culture; a
stronger management team . . .

Thus armed, Virginia Bottomley resolved to take a proposal to
Chancellor Kenneth Clarke and the Prime Minister to give the
BBC a five-year deal which would bring us an additional £180 mil-
lion (at 1997 prices) across the period. To protect her political flank –
with an election pending – she asked me if I could get the Labour
Opposition to agree not to attack any increase in the licence fee.

I went to see Tony Blair, and we had our most fundamental discussion ever about the BBC. Tony regarded the Corporation as
crucial to British culture – at its best a bastion of high ideals and
enlightenment. He was excited by the reforms and saw the BBC as
being ahead of the game, a model for other public services. I argued
that the BBC was the only bulwark against Murdoch, whose interests would be ever more powerful over the next ten years, and whose
values and attitudes would dominate as never before. Sky, I argued,
was on the march. Blair offered to write me a letter which I was not
permitted to copy or to show to Virginia Bottomley, but which I
could use to back up an ironclad assurance that Labour would not
oppose an increase in the licence fee. Blair duly sent the letter; I
briefed the Department; Bottomley went in to bat. Clarke and
Major agreed her proposal. In Major's case, this was in spite of his
deep unhappiness, at that point, with the way the BBC was covering
his much resisted NHS reforms.

The rise in our income from the Bottomley settlement was
modest but welcome – above all for what it signified: it would be our
first increase for thirteen years. The BBC had turned the corner
with the politicians.

Nineteen-ninety-nine was to be my last full year in the BBC. From
January, two processes ran in parallel: the appointment of my

successor; and the last climactic licence-fee negotiation with the
new Blair government.

I was cheered when Chris Smith, the Secretary of State at the
Department of Culture, Media and Sport, appointed Gavyn Davies
to chair a panel of inquiry into BBC funding for the digital age, and
when Smith picked alongside Gavyn a group of sensible, modern
individuals, warm to public service, many of whom I knew and
trusted. Gavyn was in my circle, and I had known him for years. As
a precociously able economist, he had worked in Downing Street in
his twenties for Wilson and Callaghan before moving to Goldman
Sachs. He was another *Weekend World* alumnus – following Terry
Burns and Alan Budd as an economic adviser to the programme –
and a friend of both Terry and Peter Mandelson. From our long
acquaintance I knew Gavyn as a person of solid, sound judgement –
he was straight, public spirited and anything but self-seeking. I was
especially confident that he would give us a sympathetic hearing
because, seven years earlier, working with the distinguished academic economist Andrew Graham, Master of Balliol College,
Oxford, Gavyn had composed the most elegant and compelling
theoretical justification for the BBC that I had ever read.

In the event, Gavyn's review was far bumpier than we had anticipated. Throughout its history, the BBC has always raised powerful
emotions and they surface whenever a decision is to be taken about
its funding or constitutional status. Some of the panel, it turned out,
had an instinct that the BBC was plenty big enough already; some
that, however slimmed down we had become, there was still significant scope for further savings; some that public monoliths should be
contracting rather than growing and threatening the nascent digital
market. Winning the argument with the panel for a major increase
in the licence fee was not going to be a shoo-in. Moreover, there was
noisy barracking in the background from the commercial broadcast
sector – particularly ITV and BSkyB – which were more united and
vociferous than ever before in resisting a newly muscular BBC,
moving forward in every domain. The commercial broadcasters

were particularly opposed to the device that Gavyn most favoured
for giving the BBC more money – a higher licence fee levied on digital television homes.

The argument for a special digital licence fee (DLF) was that, in
the past, expensive new developments like radio, TV and the advent
of colour had each in turn been funded by a new form of licence
fee. With a DLF, the user would again pay directly for new services
from the BBC, and the organisation would again enjoy continuous
buoyancy in its income as digital penetration grew. ITV, BSkyB and
the cable industry, on the other hand, argued vigorously that a digital licence fee would deter consumers and slow digital take-up. We
countered that a progressively higher BBC licence fee had not inhibited the historic growth of radio, TV or the introduction of colour
in the past – rather the opposite: well-funded BBC services seemed
to have *encouraged* take-up, as they would again with digital.

We conducted a long public campaign to support our case. In July
I gave a lecture in the Banqueting Hall in Whitehall under the auspices of the *New Statesman*. I concluded:

> Unless and until the BBC's income grows as the nation's
> income grows, and as the broadcasting industry's income
> grows, the BBC will gradually, slowly, imperceptibly,
> incrementally *diminish* in relation to the rest of broadcasting,
> and will play a reducing part in this nation's life.

When Gavyn's panel first convened, we were in the final stages of
our pioneering Hever strategy work, which was identifying the true
long-term implications of the digital age for the BBC, and plotting
a detailed path to a future world of on-demand, interactive BBC
services focused on the passions and interests of our licence-payers.
The Hever work proved instrumental. We used it not only to excite
the panel, and the Department, about the innovative and creative
services the BBC could provide – such as new children's services, or
a digital curriculum giving every child the opportunity to learn any

school course online in engaging and involving ways – but also to illuminate just how much was at stake, just how much extra income the BBC would need if we were to extend choice in the digital age as we had done in the analogue.

The tensions within Gavyn's panel finally resolved themselves into a recognition that the BBC needed some extra funds for the digital age, and a recommendation – delivered to the government in August – to back a digital licence fee, but at a disappointingly modest level, giving the BBC only a fraction of the sums we had sought. The Davies Report was generous about the past. Observing memorably that 'The BBC has been on a strict financial diet for many years', the report concluded that the Corporation was 'a much leaner and fitter institution than existed a decade ago. Efficiency savings have been running at a remarkable annual rate of eight to ten per cent of the relevant cost base for several years.' Gavyn's report went on to make an eloquent case for what the BBC could do in the digital age. Regrettably, though, the report didn't follow through the logic of its own arguments to a generous conclusion and recommendation.

I understood Gavyn's difficulties with his panel, but felt foiled and frustrated. I flew back from a holiday in Provence to attend a press conference on the day the report was published. Whitehall officials and many of my colleagues advised that the BBC should make a cautious response – their line was: the BBC is lucky to be alive; put the begging bowl away; settle without a row; do a deal behind the scenes, bureaucrat to bureaucrat.

Subsequently many Governors – though not Christopher Bland – were irritated by my response. One observed: 'The BBC is on a losing wicket. These are not generous times. We need to exercise extreme care. Diplomacy is all. We need to be realistic. We won't improve on Davies.' So far as I was concerned, however, this was a once-in-a-generation opportunity to establish a solid foundation for the BBC's finances. The BBC couldn't afford to fall behind in the digital age, to become – in its second century – increasingly

marginalised. I was told I was being seen within Whitehall and the
BBC as dogmatic and unrealistic. I was certainly dogged and determined: this was my last year as Director-General, my final chance
to make the case. So I went out on a limb and ignored the counsels
of caution: I welcomed – sincerely – the quality of argument in the
Davies Report, but I criticised the key recommendation. I argued
that the level of funding proposed was not enough: 'The panel has
not willed the means to achieve the ends it so clearly defines.' We
were going to fight for more.

A terrible tragedy struck the BBC in the spring of 1999 while these
events were unfolding: presenter Jill Dando was murdered on her
doorstep by an obsessive. It was a most dreadful blow for her family,
colleagues and admirers, all of whom loved her for her commitment, professionalism and sweet, warm decency. I had come to
know Jill because she had always been among the first to volunteer
to help the BBC to make its case publicly, and, like the rest of the
organisation, I was devastated by her loss.

The preparation of Gavyn Davies's report coincided with the
appointment of my successor. Anointing a new Director-General of
the BBC had always inspired passionate and intense interest, for the
process invariably unleashed potent forces of both ambition and
conviction. Appointing my successor would be no exception.

   The field was wide open, for there was no obvious candidate
that everyone could rally round. Internally, my two rock-solid battlefield commanders, Will Wyatt and Ron Neil, would have been
credible director-generals – but they would be fifty-eight and fifty-
seven respectively at the point of my own intended departure in
2000, and both had long planned to retire before me. There were
some proven and capable BBC executives in their early fifties who
were potential candidates – like Tony Hall, Patricia Hodgson and
Alan Yentob; and a crop of bright, rapidly rising but relatively
untried dynamos in their early forties – Mark Byford, Matthew

Bannister and Mark Thompson. Externally, there were hundreds of hopefuls and half a dozen credible candidates, of whom Greg Dyke, my old colleague from LWT, was the best known.

On this occasion – unlike my own smoke-filled-room corona-tion – the process would be open, prolonged and exhaustive. Christopher Bland attended to every detail himself, supported by Margaret Salmon. The post was to be advertised internally and externally. There was a real determination to establish the strongest possible field, so head-hunters Heidrick and Struggles were appointed to turn over every possible stone, to identify potential candidates, inside and outside broadcasting, at home and abroad, who might not be minded to apply.

The Governors, like any twelve people anywhere, held different positions on many issues but were broadly agreed that the BBC needed to maintain its strong strategic momentum, which they had wholeheartedly supported. Not surprisingly, though, they also felt that it was time to try to cheer up the institution after nearly thirteen years of intensive and wearying reform. I had long been aware myself of the ready opportunity my retirement offered to any successor to present 'a kinder, gentler' prospectus, to push the pain of change back into the past, to offer the promise of an easier path forward.

A strong field of runners and riders was assembled, including some whose candidacy never became known. Greg Dyke emerged as the bookies' favourite, and was soon under assault. *The Times* exposed him as a significant Labour Party donor. Greg is beguilingly incapable of hiding his views on anything, so *The Times* also had no difficulty uncovering a string of vivid, quotable assertions – many hostile to the Conservative Party – that Greg had made publicly over the previous five years. (When I had lunch with Murdoch at Microsoft a few months later, he volunteered straight away that he had had nothing to do with the *Times*'s campaign, though he thought it was justified.) A number of newspapers and columnists also declared their opposition to Greg's appointment, suggesting he was too overtly parti-pris. Peter Ainsworth, the Tory frontbencher who held the Department of Culture, Media and Sport portfolio, wrote to oppose Greg's candidacy. Later William Hague entered the fray and made his own opposition public. Both received short shrift from Christopher, rightly sensitive to such blatant political interference.

Before the process of winnowing down the applicants began, some lead candidates and Governors were suspicious of Christopher, fearing he would manipulate the process to re-establish the successful working relationship he and Greg had enjoyed together at LWT, where they had been Chairman and Chief Executive respectively. I witnessed the recruitment process from close at hand and am sure Christopher didn't do this. Indeed, if he had, his fellow Governors would have risen up in protest. Christopher was certainly keen to rule out candidates he thought were not up to the job, but he never attempted to clear the field for Greg. Sixteen candidates were interviewed by a small panel of Governors and reduced to a shortlist – which, again, never became known, the reports at the time being inaccurate. I offered to discuss any BBC issue with any candidate, and several took up the offer. I was invited to appear before the board to give my own appraisal of the strengths and weaknesses of all the leading candidates, which I did – comprehensively – but I was not asked to make a recommendation, and did not do so.

Greg stumbled when interviewed in the second round, in separate sessions with two blocs of Governors, and was widely declared to be out of the running. One Governor, inclined to be sympathetic to Greg, told me: 'He's completely blown it.' By common consent, Greg had been unconvincing in the formality of an interview on the public service rationale of the BBC, uncomfortable with the BBC's higher purposes. He came back into the reckoning for a number of reasons. First, his references from his current employers at Pearson came in and were glowing. Second, the *Sunday Times* outed me as a one-time Labour Party member, using information – I learnt – which was available, through skulduggery, only to someone who could dig deep into confidential and securely held Labour records. I had declared my membership to Michael Checkland on my appointment as Deputy Director-General. I had not been a donor or active in any way for twenty years, or a member since I was Director-General – but the revelation was enough to muddy the waters and to mitigate Greg's potential difficulties in the eyes of some Governors.

A third reason was that, although to the best of my knowledge the government was determined to keep its distance from the process and did, friends of Greg, including some old LWT alumni, ran a successful lobbying campaign, particularly with the growing number of Labour sympathisers on the board. A significant minority of Governors were sufficiently persuaded to settle on Greg. Fourth, and critically, it became clear that although at one time or another more than half the board had another candidate as his or her first preference, no other single candidate emerged around whom a large number of Governors could coalesce enthusiastically. Once it became obvious that Greg was attracting more first preferences then anyone else, the board became deeply divided, and feelings ran high. A significant number of Governors, which on some days looked as if it could be a majority, were opposed to Greg, mainly on the ground that he would not be a standard bearer for public service. Greg's supporters, on the other hand, argued he was a 'big' person, with substantial institutional experience and, above all, that he was just the leader – with his cheerful, confident, cheeky manner – to lift the BBC's spirits after a long period of trying change.

As the time for decision drew near, the Governors obtained opinion from leading counsel about whether Greg was appointable given his political actions and their obligations under the Charter in respect of impartiality. They received the advice that they could appoint him provided they satisfied themselves formally on a series of counts. The stage was set for the final encounter between Greg and the Governors.

Christopher Bland talked to me about how in practice Greg should deal with the many issues raised, then asked if I would meet Greg to rehearse all the arguments, particularly on what actions he should take to underline his commitment to political fairness. I agreed, and so Greg and I met in secret at my home in Wandsworth the night before his final interview. I found him unusually sombre and uncharacteristically resentful about his experience. He had hated dangling on a wire for the many months the process had lasted, being attacked and vilified. But he and I got down to work as we had done many times before, and identified together what he should say.

The next evening I was working late in my office on my papers when Christopher walked in to tell me that Greg was to be the BBC's next – its thirteenth! – Director-General. No vote was taken at the final meeting of Governors, but in effect the decision was by the narrowest of majorities. There was a significant risk of some deeply disheartened Governors resigning over Greg's appointment, but I and others pressed the dissenters to stay: we felt strongly that it was not in the BBC's best interest to parade division. Christopher and I then set out to apply balm to the wounds of the unsuccessful internal candidates, talking to and reassuring each person separately, and asking them to rally round the next Director-General. Finally I wanted to make sure Greg had the welcome to the BBC that I never had. In the days following the announcement of his appointment on 24 June, he and I visited every part of the BBC to be greeted by the executive concerned and his or her top team.

Greg didn't join the BBC until November, when our formal handover was to begin. I devoted all my attention in the intervening months to winning the case for an increase in the licence fee.

The final decision about the BBC's future funding would be made by Tony Blair, Gordon Brown and Chris Smith. James Purnell, who had been one of my key aides at the BBC, marshalled the process at Number 10. James would, I knew, be punctilious in serving the

Prime Minister, as he had served me, but I'd worked with James long
enough to know that he understood and privately supported our
case, which was more than I could conclude about the Secretary of
State. Chris Smith and I had a cordial but not close relationship. He
seemed never to have overcome his initial suspicion of me. As a
result, the Chairman, Christopher Bland, had taken over many of
the day-to-day dealings with the Department, and Chris Smith
seemed happy with that. Smith's views on the licence-fee settlement
were opaque, even to his officials. Unlike many politicians, he was
not comfortable thinking out loud about difficult decisions. Rather,
he would mull and mull, generally alone.

As the politicians deliberated during the autumn, BSkyB and
their commercial allies pounded away at the Davies recommendations. On the balance of argument, the BBC favoured the digital
licence fee solution; but in public we remained careful not to rule
out as an alternative an increase in the existing licence fee. In
October Christopher Bland fired a warning shot across Smith's
bows, stating bluntly that Gavyn's recommended settlement 'will
not be sufficient'. Freed from the constraints of his committee,
Gavyn himself worked behind the scenes to support our case for
more money than his committee as a whole had been willing to recommend.

At the very height of the lengthy, intense, bad-tempered public
debate about the BBC's funding, I was surprised when Chris Smith
and his cheerful, outgoing partner Dorian Jabri suddenly took up a
long-standing invitation issued by Jane to stay with us one weekend at
our home in Wales. Our friend Howell James completed the party. I
leapt to the conclusion that Chris, with the decision imminent, at last
wanted a no-holds-barred, entirely candid, mutually off-the-record
discussion of the kind I had hitherto enjoyed with most Secretaries of
State over thirteen years at the BBC. We passed a pleasant and
entirely social Saturday. On the Sunday morning, Howell, Chris and
I set off early to walk out of the Edw valley and up into the wild,
unspoilt hills of Radnorshire. Howell, a deep political sophisticate,

understood what was afoot. As we finished our breathless climb out
of the valley – and were rewarded with a magnificent panorama of
the whole range of the Brecon Beacons and the Black Mountains to
the south, and Cader Idris in the distance to the north – Howell
slackened his pace and dropped back so that the Secretary of State
and I could walk on alone.

I had thought hard about my advocacy. I had discussed the
licence fee with every kind of politician for a decade or more. I knew
every twist and turn of the argument, which points played best to
which constituencies. I had immersed myself in the digital challenge. There was a pregnant pause. Chris must have known what
was coming. I played the opening gambit, as I had planned, briefly
setting out the essence of what I hoped we could discuss, the bull-
points of the BBC's case. Then I stopped to give Chris a chance to
respond. I waited. He said nothing whatsoever. The pause continued for a slow-motion eternity. I must have reddened with the
awkwardness. Then Chris changed the subject. We were to have no
discussion at all. When I returned to the BBC the following day, I
found it hard to explain to my colleagues – eagerly anticipating hot
intelligence about the minister's true state of mind – why I had
nothing whatever to tell them.

Chris Smith finally got off the fence and made his private recommendation to the Prime Minister for a digital licence fee, but –
distressingly – at an even lower level than Gavyn Davies had proposed. Gordon Brown supported a DLF too, but not a high
quantum. Tony Blair remained a steadfast BBC supporter, but did
not want to inflame the commercial lobby by imposing a digital
licence fee. Intensive discussion between the three continued into
the new year, well past the time set for decision, and a few weeks past
my last days at the BBC. I remained, however, close to the deliberations. A few days after my departure, I was asked to present the
essential arguments for higher funding for the BBC in one last letter
to the Prime Minister, which I did, now writing from my home
address. I concluded:

May I express my hope that you will settle on the higher
figure . . . shared in confidence with me. A bold move to the
higher end of the range would mean a BBC over the next
ten years which will remain a civilising force, a substantial
player in the UK media environment, and a continuing
influence on the lives of every citizen of the UK.

After the letter was sent, I was phoned by a Downing Street
official for my judgement: if the Prime Minister agreed a substantial settlement, did I believe the BBC would spend it on building a
strong foundation for the digital future and not squander it on
sports rights or over-investing in BBC1? I gave my assurance. I said
that Greg might be new and his views not yet settled, but
Christopher Bland wholly supported the BBC's publicly proclaimed strategic vision, and was as deeply prejudiced as I was
about the BBC paying ridiculous sums for sports rights. Bland, I
advised, would see no point in using scarce funds to steal sport
away from the commercial sector at the expense of other BBC
programmes.

The next call I received was to be told that the Prime Minister
had ditched the unpopular digital licence fee, but had decided on a
settlement more generous than either Gavyn or his Secretary of
State had recommended and one far closer to our original bid. It
was the most bountiful and far-reaching settlement the BBC had
ever achieved. For an unprecedented seven-year term, the Corporation
would receive a 1.5 per cent real increase each year in the licence
fee, increasing revenues by £340 million a year by 2006, and by £1.5
billion extra over the period. I was elated. Tony Blair had shown
remarkable vision and boldness. I could have had no better parting
gift. After fifteen years of depressed revenue, the BBC would once
again be financially strong and healthy.

I was given a splendid send-off. Christopher Bland, in particular,
took enormous care over the arrangements. The main event was a

high-quality production in a large studio in the Television Centre, produced by Cathie Mahoney from Radio 4. Stephen Fry presided with wit and warmth in front of an audience of my family, friends, colleagues and people from public life with whom I'd been closely involved. Steve Coogan – in the guise of Alan Partridge – gave me a cack-handed tribute. Christopher Bland, Alan Yentob, Terry Burns and Laurie Taylor made me blush with considered and gratifying speeches. My pathetic goal in front of the Wembley Cup Final crowd was cut alongside Dennis Bergkamp's and Michael Owen's finest. John Major, Bill Gates, Giorgio Armani and the saintly comic genius Richard Curtis sent tributes. Most pleasing of all was Tony Blair's:

> Your reforms at the BBC stand out as one of the success stories of public service reform of recent years, just as the BBC now stands out as the world's most successful public service broadcaster . . . Without your vision, courage and enthusiasm, the BBC would not be in as good health as it is today.

At my leaving party that night I experienced a profound sense of personal peace about my time at the BBC, surrounded by some of the most extraordinary talents in every sphere of British society, whom it had been a privilege to know. I also had a powerful desire to be released, to be set free, a deep feeling of relief that I was about to leave. I felt like an ancient, scarred warrior, who had battled away for years – glad of victory, but weary of fighting. The BBC I left behind could not stand still: the job was never done: the organisation needed to continue to move on, to adapt and change; but I was proud of what I'd achieved in my time there. The BBC remained the most important cultural institution in the world, clear about and dedicated to its public purposes, more creative and journalistically stronger than ever – but now a lean, skilled organisation in the vanguard of modernity, focused as never before on the interests of its licence-payers; moving with the times; strategic, aware, agile; better positioned for the challenges of the digital age than any other established broadcaster in the world. The BBC was once again enjoying the confidence of Britain's leading political parties, and was once more in strong financial health.

In the heat of battle I had experienced great love and friendship, fierce loyalty and stalwart support; I had seen bravery and grace under fire; I had worked with – and learnt from – people of enormous talent, skill and dedication. Our achievements together made the hard, back-breaking, intense slog; the grim, bitter, vicious battling; the rancour, the betrayals, the fallings-out; the intrusions on my privacy; the impact on my family; the loss of a properly balanced life; the demonising and the caricaturing; the wicked, unjust unfairness of public comment, all just about bearable. But only just. Thirteen years at the top of British public life was a long sentence: it exacted a horrible price from me as it has from so many others. I was luckier than most: I survived the course; and I felt at every moment that the cause I fought for was a great one, the prize worth winning. And the prize was won.

Leaving the BBC marked the end of the most arduous and exciting stage of my life's journey. I had been caught up in the swirling forces and movements of my times, a boy from Bootle who had benefited enormously from new opportunities in a postwar world. I had ridden the exhilarating social and cultural waves of the 1960s, been forged and fashioned finally in the harsh crucible of the 1970s. In the 1980s and 1990s I had been a close witness to, and a participant in, the reconstruction of modern Britain. I had taken the harder path and enjoyed a great twentieth-century adventure.

On my last evening at the BBC, I assembled with close colleagues and family in the Council Chamber to unveil my official portrait – painted by Tai-Shan Schierenberg – due to hang alongside other BBC Director-Generals. I showed off my new BBC pensioner pass, issued that afternoon. Christopher gave me a big goodbye hug. Katie Kay and I bade each other a dewy-eyed farewell after twenty-three years of working together. I walked out of Broadcasting House into the night – arm in arm with Jane, JJ and Fozia, Eliza and Adam – and into a new life.

Postscript

After years of cosseting, I suddenly had to look after myself. I had to learn how to use a cash machine, how to cope with the horrors of helplines, how to navigate London by bus and Tube. For months I awoke each day rejoicing afresh that I no longer had the burden of a major institution on my shoulders. In my last weeks at the BBC I had been offered a peerage and I duly took up my place in the House of Lords as Lord Birt, of Liverpool. My mother and father were there to see me swear the oath. In 2001, we celebrated my dad's eightieth birthday. He worked on the day – as Chairman of the large block of flats where he and my mother live – as he has done every day since he began his first job in Bootle aged thirteen. I became Chairman of a venture capital fund, and adviser to McKinsey's global media practice. Tony Blair invited me to take a root-and-branch look at the causes of crime and to recommend what might be done over the long term to reduce it. In 2001 I was appointed the Strategy Adviser to the

Prime Minister, with responsibility for the oversight of key strate-
gic work commissioned by him. I still see Katie Kay most days as
she now works at Number 10 as the Prime Minister's personal
assistant. Patricia Hodgson left the BBC to become Chief
Executive of the ITC, Tony Hall to run the Royal Opera House,
Christopher Bland to chair BT. Gavyn Davies succeeded
Christopher as Chairman of the BBC. JJ and Fozia presented
Jane and myself with our first grandchild – the happy, smiling
Sulayman. When Garter King of Arms designed my coat of arms
to mark my peerage, he agreed to incorporate a bunch of bluebells
into the granting of arms to commemorate the walk in the woods
in Bangor my sixteen-year-old grandmother took with my grand-
father on the day they first met nearly a century before.

Acknowledgements

Philippa Harrison of Time Warner commissioned this book, and was my first editor before passing the baton to Alan Samson; Jonathan Lloyd of Curtis Brown became my literary agent. All offered a new and inexperienced author constructive advice and criticism, warm encouragement and support. Lauren, Jackie, David and Lucy translated my nearly illegible manuscript into type. Fozia copy-edited the typescript. Colette, Eduardo and St Catherine's loaned me quiet and peaceful places to write in Cassis, Acapulco and Oxford. A host of old school mates, good friends and former colleagues generously shared and stimulated memories, and helped bring shape to my life's journey. My father's and mother's painstaking research into our early family history was a key source for the early chapters. The BBC Written Archive Centre, Peter Heinze at Granada and Trevor Popple at LWT generously helped to document the past. The ITC library proved a valuable historical resource. Howell, Terry and Jane read the text, challenged my views, and made me think again. Professor Paddy Scannell, of the University of Westminster, did me a wonderful favour in introducing me to the young academic Emily Seymour. Emily helped me from the very beginning to research the political, social and broadcasting context in each phase of my life. She read and synthesised all my papers, putting them into coherent order; and she offered me insight and advice with a wisdom her years belied. To all these people: my thanks and gratitude.

Note

Where I have used dialogue in the text, it is based in most instances on the contemporaneous notes I made during or immediately following key events. On a small number of occasions, it is based on my or another participant's clear recollection.

Chronology

10 DECEMBER 1944	John Birt born, Walton Hospital, Liverpool
1944–7	Birt family live in University Road, Bootle
JULY 1947	Move to Lonsdale Road, Formby
1949–52	John attends Our Lady's School, Formby
1952–63	Attends St Mary's College, Crosby (excepting 1958–60 at St Mary's College, Middlesbrough)
SPRING 1963	Learns Spanish in Barcelona
OCTOBER 1963–JUNE 1966	Takes a degree in engineering at St Catherine's College, Oxford
SPRING 1964	Directs and produces *The Little Donkey*
14 SEPTEMBER 1965	Marries Jane Lake, Washington DC
OCTOBER 1966	Production trainee at Granada Television, Manchester

31 JULY 1967	*World in Action* with Mick Jagger
AUGUST 1967	Promoted to Director
SPRING 1968	Produces *Nice Time*, with Kenny Everett, Germaine Greer and Jonathan Routh
19 JUNE 1968	JJ born
AUGUST 1969	First Isle of Wight concert
SEPTEMBER 1969	Joint Editor, *World in Action*, with Gus Macdonald
NOVEMBER 1969	Washington Peace March (*World in Action: Five Days in Washington*)
FEBRUARY 1970	Chicago Eight trial
AUGUST 1970	Second Isle of Wight concert
28 JULY 1971	Eliza born
JULY–AUGUST 1971	The *Oz* trial
AUGUST 1971	Edward Heath profile *The Man from No. 10*
OCTOBER 1971	Lincoln Labour Party *World in Action*: *Labour in the Raw*
DECEMBER 1971	Leaves Granada Television for LWT
JANUARY–MARCH 1972	Works with David Frost
16 JANUARY 1972	*The Frost Programme*: Sheikh Mujib
30 JANUARY 1972	*The Frost Programme*: The Miners' Strike
6 FEBRUARY 1972	*The Frost Programme*: Bloody Sunday
13 FEBRUARY 1972	*The Frost Programme*: Ian Smith
I OCTOBER 1972	First *Weekend World*
JUNE 1973	Joint proposal (with David Elstein) for the fourth channel
17 JUNE 1973	*Weekend World* on Watergate
24 JUNE 1973	End of *Weekend World* series I, Peter Jay review
AUTUMN 1974	Head of Current Affairs, LWT
FEBRUARY 1975	*The Times*: 'Can Television News Break the Understanding Barrier?'
MARCH 1975	*The London Programme* begins

JUNE 1975   *The London Weekend Show* begins

JULY–OCTOBER 1975   Bias against Understanding debate

NOVEMBER 1976   Selsdon Park Conference; Cyril Bennett
                            dies

FEBRUARY 1977   Controller, Features and Current
                            Affairs, LWT

MARCH–MAY 1977   Produces the Frost–Nixon interviews on
                            leave from LWT

JANUARY 1978   *The South Bank Show* begins

OCTOBER 1979   Works on the Frost–Kissinger interview

JANUARY 1980   Works on the Frost interview with the
                            Shah of Iran, Panama

SEPTEMBER 1980   Interviewed for Chief Executive,
                            Channel 4

SEPTEMBER 1981   Director of Programmes, LWT

JULY 1985   *Real Lives* crisis (BBC)

NOVEMBER 1985   *Blind Date* begins

JULY 1986   Publication of the Peacock Report

OCTOBER 1986   Conservative MPs' libel case against the
                            BBC over *Panorama: Maggie's Militant
                            Tendency* is settled out of court
                            Marmaduke Hussey becomes
                            Chairman of the BBC

NOVEMBER 1986   Douglas Hurd announces a 25 per cent
                            independent production quota

JANUARY 1987   BBC Director-General Alasdair Milne
                            is sacked
                            In a raid on BBC Scotland offices,
                            Special Branch seize tapes of the *Secret
                            Society* episode on the Zircon satellite

FEBRUARY 1987   Michael Checkland becomes eleventh
                            Director-General, BBC

MARCH 1987   Approached to become Deputy
                            Director-General, BBC

11 MAY 1987	Arrives at BBC
JULY 1987	Leatherhead News and Current Affairs directorate conference
SEPTEMBER 1987	Policy and Planning Unit established Mrs Thatcher's Downing Street seminar on broadcasting
OCTOBER 1987	Michael Checkland launches his five-year plan
NOVEMBER 1987	BBC1 and BBC2 Controllers interview boards Michael Grade resigns
DECEMBER 1987	*Newsnight*'s 10.30 p.m. starting time promulgated Indexation of licence fee announced by Douglas Hurd
JULY 1988	*Panorama*: Peter Wright
OCTOBER 1988	The Government imposes a broadcasting ban on Sinn Fein
FEBRUARY 1989	Rupert Murdoch launches Sky Television
MARCH 1989	*Producers' Guidelines* launched
JULY 1989	*Panorama*: Lady Porter
DECEMBER 1990	Publication of the Broadcasting Bill
JANUARY 1990	*Funding the Future* brings new building projects at White City into question
FEBRUARY 1990	*Panorama*: Ulster Defence Regiment
OCTOBER 1990	Television Resources study steering group established
JANUARY 1991	*Panorama*: Supergun
MARCH 1991	Trip to the Gulf and Kuwait with Tom King
APRIL 1991	Duke Hussey is reappointed for five years
JUNE 1991	Presentation of the Television Resources study to the board; Producer Choice policy agreed

2 JULY 1991	Appointed Director-General-designate, to take over in March 1993
JANUARY 1992	Goes trekking in the Himalayas
AUGUST 1992	Michael Grade criticises BBC reforms in his McTaggart Lecture at the Edinburgh International Television Festival
10 NOVEMBER 1992	Michael Checkland announces he will stand down at the end of the year
24 NOVEMBER 1992	The Government publishes its Green Paper on the BBC
26 NOVEMBER 1992	Publication of *Extending Choice*
19 DECEMBER 1992	Becomes twelfth Director-General
28 FEBRUARY 1993	The *Independent on Sunday* breaks tax-status story
1 APRIL 1993	Producer Choice launched Formation of BBC Resources directorate
JULY 1993	Radio Academy Conference, Birmingham Mark Tully criticises BBC reforms
AUGUST 1993	Michael Cocks becomes Vice-Chairman Dennis Potter attacks the modernisation of the BBC in his McTaggart Lecture, Edinburgh
MARCH 1994	Radio 5 Live launched
APRIL 1994	Star Television ends the transmission of BBC World into China
MAY 1994	BBC Worldwide launched
JULY 1994	Publication of the White Paper: *The Future of the BBC*
MARCH 1995	BBC Steering Group for digital broadcasting project is established

APRIL 1995	Scottish interim interdict on *Panorama* interview with John Major
30 AUGUST 1995	Board of Governors approve 'Stage 6' co-siting of television and radio news and current affairs
20 NOVEMBER 1995	*Panorama* interview with Princess Diana
NOVEMBER 1995	Awarded International Emmy, New York
9 JANUARY 1996	Christopher Bland appointed Chairman of the BBC (to begin in April)
MAY 1996	Publication of *Extending Choice in the Digital Age*
	The BBC's Royal Charter renewed for ten years
JUNE 1996	Extended as Director-General for four years
	Restructuring announced: creation of BBC Broadcast and Production; World Service reforms announced
MARCH 1997	BBC signs deal with Flextech to launch new UK channels
JULY 1997	Visits new digital companies in California and Microsoft in Seattle
NOVEMBER 1997	BBC News 24 launched on cable
DECEMBER 1997	BBC Online launched
MARCH 1998	BBC America launched
JUNE 1998	BBC and BSkyB sign digital satellite deal
	Knighthood announced
SEPTEMBER 1998	Digital strategy convention, Hever Castle
	BBC Choice launched on digital
OCTOBER 1998	Secretary of State Chris Smith announces plans for a licence-fee review in 1999 (Gavyn Davies is appointed in November)

DECEMBER 1998   The Governors decide against a
                       devolved *Six O'Clock News* for Scotland
JANUARY 1999   Chris Smith announces the membership
                       of the BBC funding review panel
MARCH 1999   Applications are invited for the next
                       Director-General of the BBC
JUNE 1999   Greg Dyke is appointed the thirteenth
                       Director-General
JULY 1999   *New Statesman* lecture: 'The Prize and
                       the Price', calling for a rise in the
                       licence fee to fund new digital services
AUGUST 1999   Publication of the Davies Report, *The
                       Future Funding of the BBC*, recommending
                       a digital licence fee
31 DECEMBER 1999   Awarded a life peerage in New Years
                       Honours list
28 JANUARY 2000   Last day at the BBC
21 FEBRUARY 2000   The government approves an above-
                       inflation rise in the licence fee over a
                       seven-year term

Index

JB refers to John Birt
People, television and radio programmes are indexed selectively.